Organizational Communication

Organizational Communication

Challenges of Change, Diversity, and Continuity

William W. Neher

Butler University

Allyn and Bacon

Boston   London   Toronto   Sydney   Tokyo   Singapore

Series Editor: Carla F. Daves
Editorial Assistant: Andrea Geanacopoulos
Marketing Manager: Karon Bowers
Editorial-Production Administrator: Deborah Brown
Editorial-Production Service: SAXON HOUSE PRODUCTIONS
Text Designer and Page Layout: Glenna Collett
Composition Buyer: Linda Cox
Manufacturing Buyer: Suzanne Lareau
Cover Administrator: Linda Knowles
Photo Researcher: Laurie Frankenthaler

Library of Congress Cataloging-in-Publication Data

Neher, William W.
    Organizational communication : challenges of change, diversity,
and continuity / by William W. Neher.
        p.   cm.
    Includes bibliographical references and index.
    ISBN 0-205-15006-3 (casebound)
    1. Communication in organizations.   2. Organizational change.
3. Intercultural communication.
    HD30.3.N44   1996
    302.3'5—dc20   96-27061
                                                                CIP

Photo Credits: p. 13, Courtesy of NASA; p. 16, Gale Zucker/Stock, Boston; p. 37, Courtesy of NASA;
p. 54, UPI/Corbis-Bettmann; p. 65, Rabeuf/The Image Works; p. 70, UPI/Corbis-Bettmann; p. 82,
Archive Photos; p. 96, Will Hart; p. 104, Spencer Grant/Stock, Boston; p. 118, Will & Demi McIntyre/
Photo Researchers; p. 128, Claudia Dhimitri/The Picture Cube; p. 135, AP/Wide World Photos; p.
143, Barth Falkenberg/Stock, Boston; p. 163, Roy Bishop/Stock, Boston; p. 173, North Wind Picture
Archives; p. 185, Robert Harbison; p. 198, Robert W. Ginn/The Picture Cube; p. 216, Library of
Congress; p. 229, Reuters/Corbis-Bettmann; p. 248, Courtesy of Boeing Commercial Airplane Group;
p. 276, Sarah Putnam/The Picture Cube; p. 287, Jack Spratt/The Image Works; p. 314, Archive Pho-
tos; p. 326, Jeff Greenberg/Photo Researchers; p. 335, John Coletti/The Picture Cube; p. 350, Will
Faller; p. 357, Spencer Grant/Stock, Boston.

Printed in the United States of America

10 9 8 7 6 5 4 3 2 1   01 00 99 98 97 96

Contents

PART THREE   **Contexts and Applications for Organizational Communication**   *151*

CHAPTER **8**   **Channels, Media, and Communication Systems in Organizations**   *153*

CHAPTER **14**   Confronting Issues in Organizational Communication   345

Preface

This text is intended to provide a comprehensive introduction to the field of organizational communication for college juniors and seniors who may be majors in communication or a communication-related discipline or in business administration. Schools of business administration are increasingly adding requirements in communication for their majors and MBA students. The book is sufficiently comprehensive to be useful for these students as well as communication majors; however, the book would not be appropriate for a performance-oriented business or professional communication course.

The book, which is divided into four parts, provides coverage of the major theoretical approaches to the study of organizational communication. Students who wish to continue further study will be well prepared with an understanding of the nature of the field as will students who make this their only course.

The first chapter of the book sets a tone and context for understanding the forces that are impacting and transforming the nature of modern, complex organizations—primarily, the developing technologies of communication and the increasing global network that makes up modern communication.

Part One introduces the theoretical background for the field beginning with an overview of organizational communication. Chapter 2, the first chapter in Part One, through a review of the research, creates the framework of relationships between five principal topics of communication: (1) Context—the setting or environment or culture in which an organization exists; (2) Shape and Structure—the organization itself; (3) Message Behavior—verbal and nonverbal codes; (4) Method and Modalities of Communication—the channels or media; and (5) Communication Activities—problem solving or negotiation.

It is clear that society is entering a period of rapidly changing definitions and concepts regarding institutional and organizational life. The globalization of work and organizations means that we are living, more and more, in a multicultural and transnational world. Secondly, the daily changes in interactive technologies of communication mean that organizations and the people who constitute them are knit together by new kinds of links and networks that are not yet well understood. This book's approach points to the need of people in organizations to learn how to balance change and diversity while at the same time maintain some form of organization or order.

The propositions concerning organizational communication in Chapter 2 also make clear my belief that communication is fundamentally related to issues of leadership, problem solving, and multicultural diversity in organizations.

I believe that students beginning to study organizational communication should be aware of the differing perspectives held by researchers and scholars: functionalism, interpretivism, and critical studies. The framework in Chapter 2 includes approaches to research within these main perspectives. I do not argue for the superiority of one perspective over another but for understanding the point of view and usefulness of each one in approaching different problems.

Part Two focuses on different kinds of organizational theories and their implication for actual communication. The topics from Chapter 2 serve as a basis for summaries of various organizational theories.

Part Three covers the contexts and applications of organizational communication, particularly media or channels for carrying such communication: face-to-face or interpersonal communication (superior–subordinate communication, leader–member communication, and mentoring). There are separate chapters on leadership communication; group communication, emphasizing teams and problem solving (including quality circle and mediating groups); and public communication including risk and crisis communication.

Part Four ties together the preceding issues. Chapter 13 deals with methods for analyzing, evaluating, and assessing organizational communication, considering functional approaches, such as communication audits, and interpretative approaches, such as cultural analysis. Chapter 14 considers significant public and ethical issues confronting organizational communicators and those people who study the field. This chapter reemphasizes in a systematic framework many of the issues suggested in the ethics and diversity boxes throughout the first three parts of the book.

The boxes deal with communication ethics and diversity in organizations and highlight the major themes of the book. The boxes can be utilized in class discussions as case studies. I am careful to make students aware of the management bias of much of the organizational theory and communication literature, and the boxes challenge students' thinking to break through the orientation of many of these points of view. The last two chapters of the book call out the current trends toward the expanding global and technological advancements in communication and the need to address diversity as a focus of communication.

At the end of each chapter are exercises and questions for discussion to assist students in integrating the major theoretical points of each chapter. There are end-of-chapter bibliographies and background reading recommendations as well as a general bibliography at the end of the book.

ACKNOWLEDGMENTS

I wish to thank my family for their patience and support in this project, especially my wife, Linda. I am also grateful to Stephen P. Hull of Allyn and Bacon for encouraging me to begin this book and Carla Daves of Allyn and Bacon for her assistance. I also wish to thank Sydney Baily-Gould of Saxon House Productions for her editorial assistance in bringing the work to completion.

The reviewers of early versions of the manuscript were very helpful: James A. Benson, University of Wisconsin; Patt Brett, Emory University; Ann Cunningham, Bergen Community College; Judith Dallinger, Western Illinois University; Stanley Deetz, Rutgers University; Timothy M. Downs, California State University; Karen Fontenot, South Eastern Louisiana University; Lawrence H. Hugenberg, Youngstown State University; Steven K. May, University of North Carolina; Calvin Morrill, University of Arizona; Dennis K. Mumby, Purdue University; John Parrish-Sprowl, Indiana University, Purdue University; Lee Polk, Baylor University; Steven M. Ralston, East Tennessee State University; and Gary M. Shulman, Miami University.

CHAPTER 1

Transforming Organizational Life

CHANGING PERSPECTIVES ON THE NATURE OF MODERN ORGANIZATIONS

Organizations are the primary way in which people bring cooperative efforts to bear for solving problems and meeting basic needs. We are born into a world of organizations, and most of us can survive only in and through reliance on humanly created organizations. The social patterns and networks that we call organizations are possible only through human communication; thus human organizations and communication are inextricably linked. This link is the focus of the academic field of organizational communication.

The contemporary world challenges many traditional notions regarding the nature of human organizations. Many large-scale, complex organizations today are examples of "ordered chaos" or "chaotic order," rather than the rational systems of cooperation envisioned by earlier organizational theories. Is the Sony Corporation one or many organizations? Is it a Japanese organization or an international organization? The answers to these questions depend on how one looks at these issues. Sony manufactures electronic equipment and computer components, but it also runs American cinema chains, which can show movies that Sony has produced at Columbia Pictures, and it publishes books and recordings through CBS Records. There are Sony manufacturing plants in Alabama, California, Great Britain, and Singapore and Malaysia. The name is derived from the Latin word for sound, *sonus*, rather than a Japanese word. The founder of Sony, Akio Morita, carefully designed the corporation along American, rather than Japanese, lines.

What holds together all the strands of such complex organizations of the modern world? New developments in the technologies of communication are an important part of the answer, as this book will show. Without instantaneous, computerized communication, such complex organizations could not begin to operate on their usual global scale. Organizations, in addition, must meet the continual challenges of changing conditions and the demands of global markets. And they rely upon communication and cooperation among increasingly diverse participants within the same organization. These factors of change and diversity are major themes of this text. Organizations represent efforts to bring about and maintain order in the process of responding to change and diversity. As the title of this book implies, modern organizations must constantly balance the need to adapt to change and accommodate internal diversity with the need to simultaneously maintain some stable order, without which they would not remain what we call organizations. As two organizational researchers put it, "While it remains crucial for the organization to maintain a high degree of stability, it must simultaneously foster an acceptance of, if not a bias for, change to be successful in today's economic environment."[1]

The dynamic nature of what is meant by organization at the end of the twentieth century can be briefly illustrated by considering two issues: globalization and developments in cyberspace.

The New Order of Global Organizations

The Sony example demonstrates the incredible scale and complexity of some modern organizations. Many such organizations are larger and potentially more powerful than many members of the United Nations. Their mobility and range, enhanced through modern communication networks, may be "undermining the effectiveness of national governments to carry out essential policies on behalf of their people," the authors of the influential book *Global Dreams* maintain.[2]

These corporate organizations operate outside the usual structure of national economies and policies. No wonder it is increasingly difficult to determine whether a product is really "made in the USA" or made in some other country. A Toyota automobile, for example, may be entirely manufactured by American workers in Ohio. A friend who decided to buy a car that was distinctly from the United States later discovered that her new Buick was built in Ontario, Canada. In the *maquiladora* zone in Mexico, just south of the American border, international companies can set up manufacturing operations, paying lower prevailing Mexican wages, and import products into the United States on the favorable terms established by the North American Free Trade Arrangement, or NAFTA. Along with American firms, many Japanese corporations, including Sony, have taken advantage of the *maquiladora* opportunity.

Do such international, global organizations have much in common with smaller organizations, such as a local church congregation or parent–teacher organization? This is a basic question for the discipline that is known as organizational communication. Organizational communication began as a subfield of the discipline of speech communication, primarily concerned with business speech. As interest in the field grew, scholars of organizational communication began to look at the field not just in terms of business presentations, but in terms of wider issues of the dissemination of messages through complex organizational channels and networks. Organizational communication then occupied a niche between the study of small-group communication and that of mass communication.

This study assumed that scholars could make generalizations that could be applied to most organizations, regardless of size or complexity. Today, given the global reach and communication technologies of some huge corporations, people are less certain about the applicability of generalizations across the wide range of organizations from complex to small-scale, from global to local.

The approach taken in this book is to recognize the potential problems of assuming that generalizations and research apply at all levels of organizational size and complexity. Most research in the field has been based on the assumption that the corporation is the typical organization of concern. A corporation need not necessarily be a for-profit business, although it often is. Whether global or local, the organizations most often studied by scholars of organizational communication tend to exhibit a structure called the *corporate form*,[3] which characterizes governments, schools, religious organizations, and nonprofit charitable organizations as well as business firms.

At the top of a corporate-form organization (see Figure 1.1) is an upper-management group with central decision-making power. This group is often separate from the actual owners (such as stockholders) or constitutional authorities (such as the board of trustees of a university). A group of professionals and experts necessary for the organization's technical functions make up a second distinct group. Although these technical professionals report to the upper managers, they also exhibit allegiance to professional or technical associations. The third group in the corporate-form organization is usually the line or service workers, who perform the day-to-day tasks and activities of the organization. In sum, the corporate form is characterized by a management that is separate from ownership and reliance on technical experts, with both of these groups separate from the people who perform the basic work of the organization.

The globalization of this corporate form alters our view of the nature of complex organizations today.

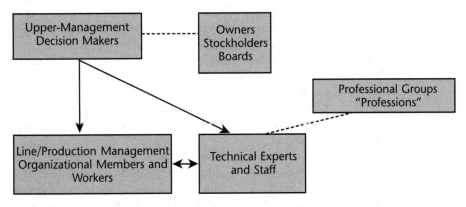

FIGURE 1.1 The corporate form.

The Emergence of "Virtual" Organizations

Perhaps we should begin with a discussion of when is an "organization" not an organization. The so-called information superhighway has been a continuing concern of governments and business corporations alike. This concern focuses on managing and controlling the Internet, or more specifically the World Wide Web, which appears to be the major forms this highway is taking. The Internet is basically a loose collection of various kinds of computer networks and individual users that from time to time are interconnected.

The corporate model of the information superhighway assumed that giant telephone or cable TV companies would construct and maintain lines connecting homes and institutions to wide arrays of information, entertainment, and communication services. While large corporations and governments were contemplating ways to build a super network, individual users began patching together a real live superhighway, the Internet, relying on the use of existing telephone lines.

The Internet is not run by any kind of central authority or organization. There is no center or even central network that receives requests, routes them to proper hosts, and sends messages on. The Internet is akin to an organic creature, almost like a parasite riding along the long-distance lines.[4] Messages are sent blindly through a series of interconnected computer systems, seldom if ever following the same route. Each system does nothing more than pass on a message to the next network; no one has a map for getting through the maze from start to finish. In other words, the Internet appears to provide order without organization (which may be much the way the human brain works). That is, there is the appearance of organization in the results, without the structure normally associated with our idea of organization.

As the British *Economist* magazine points out, in 1993 new features began to appear: "A combination of special software and a way of connecting documents allowed users to travel the network with pictures, sound and video, simply by pointing and clicking a mouse."[5] The Internet became something more than a way to exchange information: It became a forum for interaction and for mutual collaboration. While sitting in Indiana, with a couple of clicks of my mouse, as far as cyberspace is concerned I am suddenly in Cape Town, South Africa, conversing with colleagues there, exploring news accounts, and looking through libraries as if I were physically present.

The results of the organic growth of this communication medium for our concept of an organization have been far-reaching. One may think of an orchestra or other musical ensemble as something that should obviously be labeled an organization. The musicians work together, under the guidance of the central authority of the conductor, to blend their parts into a pleasing musical sound. It has been possible in the past to create ensemble music without the actual presence of all the musicians in the same place at the same time, of course, by laying down different recording "tracks" and re-recording over them. Now two students at Northwestern University have developed a system allowing musicians to perform together through cyberspace. The system, known as Distributed Real-Time Groove Network, or DRAGON, uses the telnet function of the Internet, connecting output to synthesizers and headphones so that participants can hear what is being performed. One of DRAGON's creators reports, "The feeling of jamming is maintained quite well. . . . Even across the ocean, we often end up simultaneously coming up with musical ideas that work really well together."[6]

This musical case is a good example of the effects of new communication technologies on the creation of "virtual" organizations, a concept borrowed from the idea of virtual reality. In the past, organizations were often defined in terms of a physical presence: People were brought together (implicitly in one place) to cooperate in order to meet some common goal. Organizations were often identified with a place or building; thus the "Pentagon" referred to the central command for the U.S. armed forces, and the "Kremlin" referred to the former government of the Soviet Union. Organizations that exist only in the interconnections among computer networks lack this sort of presence and the face-to-face nature of organizational communication.

Of course, there have always been decentralized and geographically dispersed organizations. The Roman Catholic Church throughout history and the Jesuits from the mid-sixteenth century on are good examples of dispersed organizations that existed primarily through long-distance communication between far-flung outposts and centralized authorities. Time and distance, however, were important limitations on the functioning of these institutions. Instantaneous communication makes time and distance irrelevant factors. Thus musicians on different continents can perform together. Publishing companies formerly housed editors, printing presses, and executives all in one building. Now books are created by authors working together in different states or countries; presses are located in Maryland, editors in New York work on text sent through the Internet, and the publisher's management is housed in Massachusetts.

These virtual organizations are more prone to "adhocracy" than are earlier organizations.[7] It is possible to bring parts of the organizations together for only the brief time needed to complete a particular project. Upon completion of that project, that organization is disbanded and a new one is quickly created in its place to work on the next project, and so on.

Some of the same technology that permits the impermanence of new organizations may also be used to re-create the sense of interpersonal interaction that is potentially lost. Two large companies, IBM and TelePort Corporation, have been building approximately six hundred "virtual dining rooms" to allow organization members to "do virtual lunch."[8] The rooms will consist of large, apparently round dining tables, with a video screen at the end of a semicircular table providing the "telepresence" of the other half of the table and its diners from some remote location. In addition to being located in corporate offices or field stations, such dining rooms may be set up by hotels and conference centers for rent to organizations.

THEMES OF COMMUNICATION ETHICS AND DIVERSITY

The changing nature of organizations brings to the fore many issues related to the human consequences of new organizational and communication practices. At the same time, organizations are growing more diverse in terms of racial, gender, and cultural composition. In Europe and North America, organizations in the past may have been expected to be run primarily by and for white males. New interactive technologies coupled with changing mores and expectations, however, bring together many different kinds of people under the same organizational umbrella.

For example, the new communication technologies such as cellular phones and pagers mean that separation between private time and work time is more difficult to manage. Personal communication devices mean that people are always within range of the workplace and problems that may arise there. Can organizations intrude on members' so-called free time or private space? Under what conditions may individuals set limits to their accessibility? These technologies and the nature of computer communications through E-mail have consequences for rights of personal privacy as well. How confidential are matters discussed in cyberspace? How confidential should they be? Related to these issues are questions about ownership of or copyright to intellectual property produced on or disseminated through new communication channels.

The diversity of the workforce similarly raises questions concerning interpersonal relationships within the organization. Sexual harassment, for instance, is an obvious abuse of interpersonal communication in an organizational setting. Increasing diversity within organizations leads to questions involving discrimination on the basis of race, religion, sexual orientation, cultural or national origin, and presumed physical disabilities. These are all potential problems of organizational communication.

Organizations can become powerful sources of internal and external messages, shaping the way people respond to the world around them. The seemingly impersonal nature of complex organizations can lead to lack of accountability for their messages and the effects of those messages. Operations of an organization may expose members to potentially harmful substances or situations. How is this risk communicated, if at all, to these organizational members? Similarly, operations may expose surrounding communities or the environment to health or safety risks. The organization may need to communicate with both its own members and the larger community regarding these hazards. These communications often raise important ethical questions.

For these reasons, the twin themes of communication ethics and human diversity run throughout this text. In each chapter, there are boxed sections discussing issues regarding that chapter's material that have been or could be raised. The diversity theme appears in boxes titled "Diversity Matters," allowing intentional ambiguity about whether *matters* is considered to be a verb or a noun (or both). The ethics theme appears in boxes labeled "An Issue of Communication Ethics." These themes reflect the growing concern of scholars and practitioners in organizational communication.

OVERVIEW OF THE PARTS AND CHAPTERS OF THE TEXT

The book is divided into four parts of varying length. Part One presents an overview of the developing field of organizational communication. Chapter 2 summarizes the state of scholarship and practice in this developing field, recognizing the concerns of both the scholar or researcher, on the one hand, and the practitioner or the person who wants to operate effectively in organizations, on the other. Chapter 3 presents an overview of the kinds of communication theories that are particularly relevant to the field of organizational communication.

Part Two places the major organizational theories within a context of communication study. The four chapters of this part consider the implications of classical management theories, human relations and human resource theories, systems theories, and the perspective of organizational culture for the nature of communication within organizations. The type of organizational theory or approach that is dominant within a particular organization will have important effects on the way in which communication is carried out in that organization.

Part Three looks more closely at communication within various organizational settings. First, the possible effects of media and technologies for organizational communication are discussed. Two chapters deal with face-to-face, interpersonal communication settings in organizations. Chapter 9 covers general issues of vertical and horizontal communication; thus, the superior-subordinate link is analyzed in some detail in this chapter. Chapter 10 focuses on the communication dynamics of leadership within organizations. Chapter 11 takes up issues of organizational team and group problem solving and decision making. Chapter 12 deals with the public messages of organizations, intended for both internal and external use.

Part Four of the text is labeled a "capstone" for students beginning the study of organizational communication. Chapter 13 is concerned with ways to research and assess the nature and effectiveness of communication within organizations. The concluding chapter, Chapter 14, brings together many of the developing issues facing contemporary organizations, focusing on the communication aspects of these issues. This chapter pulls together many of the questions developed in the ethics and diversity themes carried through the other chapters, control of information and access to communication, individual rights in the organization, the public interest and good in relationship to the organizational good, and issues related to possibly deceptive or abusive communication practices.

NOTES

1. L. A. Howard and P. Geist (1995), Ideological positioning in organizational change: The dialectic of control in a merging organization, *Communication Monographs 62*, 110–31.

2. R. J. Barnet and J. Cavanagh (1994), *Global dreams: Imperial corporations and the new world order,* New York: Simon & Schuster, p. 19.

3. J. McDermott (1991), *Corporate society: Class, property,* *and contemporary capitalism,* Boulder, Colo.: Westerview Press.

4. *The Economist,* July 5, 1995, p. 6.

5. *The Economist,* July 5, 1995, p. 3.

6. *The Chronicle of Higher Education,* July 7, 1995, p. A16.

7. R. H. Waterman, Jr. (1990), *Adhocracy: The power to change,* New York: W. W. Norton.

8. *Wall Street Journal,* June 28, 1995, p. B1.

Overview of the Field of Organizational Communication

Part One sets out the basic principles underlying the study of organizational communication. Chapter 2 stresses the importance of the modern organization in our lives and takes note of several phenomena that should transform our understanding of organizations and communication in the coming century. The typical, complex organization, dominant in the contemporary world, is fundamentally a corporate-form organization, as described in the first chapter of Part One. New technologies of communication will continue to change and extend the scope of these organizations. Telecommunication advances and the application of computer-mediated communication are examples of such transforming technologies. Our very concept of the term *organization* may be modified by the development of entities such as "virtual organizations."

Chapter 3 lays out the groundwork for the rest of this text, covering the meaning of the basic terms *organization* and *communication*. Five propositions are presented to indicate a point of view regarding the nature of organizational communication. The chapter delineates a framework to represent the various theories and research programs associated with the development of the field of organizational communication.

Chapter 4 provides an orientation to the study of and for theorizing about communication in the context of organizations. Communication is conceived as a special type of sense-making activity relying upon symbolic systems embedded in language and nonverbal communication. Communication is such a broad concept that it is helpful to think of the different perspectives that are brought to clarify different aspects of the act of communication. The perspectives summarized in this section include the rhetorical, transmissional, psychological, interactional, and transactional.

CHAPTER **2**

The Scope of Organizational Communication

CHAPTER OBJECTIVES

After studying this chapter, you should be able to:

- Appreciate the importance of modern organizations and organizational communication in our lives.
- Define the term *organization*.
- Explain the defining characteristics of *communication*.
- State five propositions regarding the field of organizational communication.
- Describe the relationship of organizational communication to other areas of communication study.
- Indicate the basic differences among the functionalist, interpretivist, and critical perspectives.

CHAPTER OUTLINE

The Importance of Communication in Modern, Complex Organizations

Definitions: Organization and Communication

    Organization

    ■ AN ISSUE OF COMMUNICATION ETHICS: Whistle-Blowing

    Communication

Propositions Regarding Organizational Communication

    ■ DIVERSITY MATTERS: Cultural Sensitivity

The Nature of the Field of Organizational Communication

    Relationship to Communication Studies

    Levels of Communication Study

THE IMPORTANCE OF COMMUNICATION IN MODERN, COMPLEX ORGANIZATIONS

On January 28, 1986, the space shuttle *Challenger* exploded 53 seconds after liftoff, killing all the astronauts on board, including Christa McAuliffe, who had been specially selected as the first teacher in space. The tragedy was witnessed by millions of people watching the live telecast of the launch. The president's State of the Union speech, scheduled for that evening, was postponed for two days because of the widespread shock.

The case of the launch of the *Challenger* illustrates in many ways the importance of organizational communication. The *Challenger* was originally scheduled to go up on January 27, but dangerous crosswinds caused cancellation of the launch. In planning for a launch the next day, managers became concerned about the very low temperatures predicted for January 28. The engineers at Morton Thiokol, the corporation that had produced the huge booster rockets, became worried about the possible effects of extremely cold weather on crucial parts of the shuttle's booster rocket engines. This concern led to a teleconference involving people at the Kennedy Space Center in Florida, the Marshall Space Flight Center in Alabama, and the Morton Thiokol people in Utah.

Relying on charts telecast through the teleconference net, the engineers at Morton Thiokol tried to show that the O-rings, designed to confine the blast of the rocket engines, might not operate properly at such low temperatures, creating a risk of the booster's exploding during launch. Because of the delays they had already experienced, project managers were displeased with the engineers' recommendation not to launch. As a result of a caucus and further teleconferencing, the Morton Thiokol people agreed to withdraw their recommendation against launch.

In the NASA system then in use, there were four levels in the chain of communication that led to the final decision to launch a shuttle. As a contractor, Morton Thiokol

*Breakdowns in organizational communication can
have life-or-death consequences.*

was at the bottom of the chain, at level 4. The engineers had communicated their concern about a possible explosion as a result of O-ring failure to the level just above them, level 3, the readiness review groups at Marshall Space Flight Center and the Kennedy Space Center. Their serious concern about the O-rings was not passed up the chain to level 2, the preflight readiness review group, nor to the highest level, level 1, where the final decision to launch was made.

The special presidential commission appointed to study the *Challenger* disaster, noting the failure to pass along crucial information about the engineers' concern, reported "failures in communication that resulted in a decision to launch 51-L [the *Challenger*] based on incomplete and sometimes misleading information."[1] The commission also faulted the management and communication structure for allowing certain critical problems to be overlooked or not reported through the channels.

The life-or-death implications of the *Challenger* case can be compared to events in the more recent Persian Gulf War, in which communication rules and channels dictated that a particular Iraqi plane not be shot down; it is feared that this warplane later accounted for the one American plane lost to enemy fire in the war. Allied fighter planes were placed under strict constraints concerning firing on enemy targets because of the large number of different nationalities and air forces involved in the attack on Iraq. Commanders feared that it would be easy to mistake a friendly aircraft for an enemy. For that reason, high-altitude reconnaissance planes (AWACs) had to authorize any shooting, regardless of what the fighter pilots saw with their own eyes. In the confusion over the skies of Iraq during the days of the air war, this policy probably prevented many shoot-downs resulting from so-called friendly fire, but in this one instance, the policy may have led to the loss of an American pilot with his aircraft.

These cases touch on issues that involve important aspects of the study of organizational communication. First, an organization usually has established channels and networks for communication, rules determining the use of those channels, and meanings attached to messages flowing through them. Different communication channels and technologies within the organization are intended to facilitate the flow of information and bring people together for interaction. Interpersonal relations and the roles people play in organizations can become significant factors in determining how messages are interpreted. At a pivotal point in the debate about the decision to launch the *Challenger*, the manager of the engineers was asked "to take off his engineering hat and put on his management hat,"[2] indicating recognition of the importance of the roles people play in an interaction.

The issues in these dramatic cases involving communication in organizations are the focus of this book. While not having life-or-death consequences for most of us, organizational communication is very important for our careers and lives, which are experienced largely through and within organizations. A major premise of this book is that *communication is fundamental to the creation and maintenance of organizations*. The insights being developed in the field of organizational communication are therefore crucial to an understanding of this part of our lives and our future.

Organizations will no doubt become increasingly, rather than less, important to our lives in the future, and so will the roles that people must understand and master in order to be successful in these organizations. There is a growing awareness of the need to adapt and change many of our organizations in response to new challenges. One example may help to explain this need. In the 1970s and 1980s, many corporations, borrowing from the successful examples of Japanese companies, began to develop and use quality circles. Quality circles are corporate-sponsored groups that bring together people at all levels of production, from workers on the line up through supervisors and executives, to discuss and formulate methods to improve quality in their operations. By the end of the last decade, many quality circles had fallen by the wayside, their failure due to a lack of adequate communication training for participants. The concept may have been sound, but the culture and training to support the kind of communication skills needed were not present.

Over the years, "quality circles" has been replaced as a buzzword (or buzzconcept) as new fashions have come on-line in efforts to adapt to the acceleration of change and innovation. Total Quality Management (TQM) and Continuous Quality Improvement (CQI) were new acronyms adopted by corporations to indicate their commitment to virtually constant change and improvement. "Reengineering" the firm followed these concepts, stressing the need to remake or restructure an organization and questioning the very processes that were the target of TQM or CQI or the earlier quality circles.[3]

The balance of this first chapter begins to present an overview of the meaning of the two basic terms of this field: *organizations* and *communication* (I say *begin* because the purpose of the entire book is to explore the meanings of and interrelationships between these two terms). Five propositions concerning the nature of organizational communication are then presented to preview the assumptions that underlie this text. In the final section, I review the nature of this relatively new field and the major perspectives that have been adopted by researchers engaged in its study.

DEFINITIONS: ORGANIZATION AND COMMUNICATION

We need to begin with a notion of what is meant by *organization* and *communication,* the two components of the term *organizational communication.* These ideas are developed further in Chapters 3 and 4; the definitions here are preliminary to these later discussions.

Organization

We all have a sense of what it means to be organized. One might say, "This semester I am going to be really organized and get a notebook to keep a schedule for all activities." Or, we say that to achieve a particular goal, such as bringing together people who are interested in chess on campus, we will have to organize a club or student organization. We organize homework by setting out a plan for proceeding through various assignments and readings. In other words, organizing carries the notions of planning, arranging things in a sequence, and following some kind of systematic approach. Individuals can be organized, groups of people can be organized, and tasks can be organized. When the result of such organizing brings people together to achieve some joint outcome, we say that there is now an organization.

By organization, I refer to an *ongoing, observable pattern of interactions among people;* usually these interactions are planned, sequential, and systematic. This pattern is stable over time and is sufficiently obvious to the members and to outsiders that there is usually a name or title placed on it, such as AT&T, NASA, or the University of Wyoming. People are members of organizations. There are stated goals for the organization, which are the desired outcomes of these patterns of interaction.

Occasionally people think of an organization as a building or a physical reality, such as a campus, a plant, or a group of buildings. We point to an area partially enclosed by a fence and say, "That is Harvard University." When we think this way, it becomes easy to separate the organizations from the people who constitute them. We tend to think of organizations as independently acting structures that do things that in reality are done by people within an organization. For example, someone reports that GM will raise prices on new automobiles. Actually, some people, probably high-ranking executives, have made this decision, not the seemingly impersonal organization.

An interesting characteristic of modern organizations is the development of their separate identities, the notion that they are entities that exist and act in the world almost like people but apart from people. People generally understand that the decisions behind these actions were actually taken by flesh-and-blood people, perhaps as a result of compromise or conflict between competing individuals and groups. Still, the idea that organizations are responsible individuals different from the people who

Many people identify an organization with a specific place or building.

constitute them is a handy and pervasive habit. William G. Scott and David K. Hart, in a book intended to raise concerns about the power of large corporate organizations in America, fear that one result of this *reification* ("thing-ification") of organizations is to absolve people in organizations of responsibility for decisions and actions they take in the names of organizations.[4]

American legal jurisprudence even recognizes this reification of the corporate-form organization. In 1886, the Supreme Court held that corporations could be considered "persons" for purposes of administering the due process clause of the Fourteenth Amendment of the United States Constitution. In a series of decisions in the late 1970s and early 1980s, the Supreme Court further extended rights of individuals to these special kinds of organizations. A case involving political communications by a large commercial bank led to the extension of the First Amendment right of free speech to corporations. The case, *First National Bank of Boston v. Bellotti* (known simply as *Bellotti*), held that corporations could make contributions and otherwise spend money in order to influence state political issues, such as referenda, regardless of whether these issues had anything to do with the operations of that corporation. Later cases in 1980 further expanded the notion of the corporate organization's right of free speech. Some writers have expressed concern over this legal reification of corporate organizations, given the massive resources of large corporations in comparison with those of the average, human individual.[5]

Organizations are typically larger and more institutionalized—that is, more formalized—than small groups. Organizations themselves often comprise several identi-

AN ISSUE OF COMMUNICATION ETHICS

Whistle-Blowing

Ethics in communication has been a central concern ever since Plato and Aristotle first wrote about the field of rhetoric, or oratory. In his famous work on rhetoric, Aristotle may have wished to demonstrate that a true art of public discourse was possible when based on the character, the *ethos,* of the speaker.

The reification of organizations referred to in this chapter has raised the danger that the people in an organization may not feel themselves personally accountable for decisions and actions of the organization. If a product is unsafe or causes illness, if the company is polluting the environment, employees can separate their personal selves from those actions—"it's just business." The organization's ethos is perceived to be completely separate from that of any individual.

Occasionally, individuals within a large organization do speak up and dissent from organizational decisions, as engineer Roger Boisjoly fought against the decision to lauch the *Challenger.* When such people feel ignored or suppressed within the organization, they may "go public," or go to outside agencies that can do something about unsafe, immoral, or illegitimate organizational behavior. The ethical dilemma faced by would-be *whistle-blowers* (the term for those people who go outside to report organizational wrongdoing) comes when deciding whether they are betraying their organizations or being disloyal. Will they be seen as noble souls placing the public good ahead of organizational goals, or will they be seen as snitches, unnecessarily "airing the organization's dirty linen in public"? A further dilemma results from the dangers that a whistle-blower may face: dangers of being demoted or fired and of hurting friends in the organization.

Health care workers may be under special constraints regarding an obligation to become whistle-blowers. Some states have passed laws requiring health care workers, such as nurses, to report incidences of incompetent or unsafe treatments that they observe. The definitions of such behavior are not always clear, however. A nursing journal reports that nurses who disclose damaging information may be victims of retaliatory actions, "such as dismissal, blacklisting, threats of violence, and general harassment."* Auditors working for organizations may find themselves in a similar situation, and many auditors have different views on the rightness or wrongness of whistle-blowing.

Some organizations have developed internal policies intended to allow employees to report unsafe or illegal activities to higher-ups without fear of reprisal. NASA, for example, has devised such an in-house dissent system since the failed launch of the *Challenger*. In addition, some states have enacted legislation making "public policy exceptions" to the general rule that companies can fire workers without cause.**

Still, there is considerable risk to becoming a whistle-blower, and one ought to be certain that there is sufficient evidence of wrongdoing and that all internal avenues of remedy have been exhausted before one goes outside an organization.

*J. Fiesta (1990), Whistleblowers: Heroes or stool pigeons, *Nursing Management 21,* 16–17.

**R. Chalk (1988), Making the world safe for whistleblowers, *Technology Review 91,* 48–57.

fiable small and large groups. While the members hold some organizational goals in common, they also have competing individual and group goals. And, the common goals of the organization may change over time.

In sum, organizations are created by people in order to achieve some human purpose. They are created by social processes. Attempts at organizing usually result from a feeling that individuals cannot satisfy certain goals without cooperating with others. Organizations may seem to have a life of their own and continue regardless of changing membership. Organizations persist over time, but what really persists are the cooperative efforts of people, who maintain an ongoing pattern of relationships that can be labeled as "the organization."

Communication

When we communicate with one another, we are usually trying to share something. This something may be a fact, a feeling, an intention, or a suggestion to take some action. Communication therefore involves some connection established between at least two people. We label the behaviors that establish these connections as signs or signals that constitute messages. Given the singularity of our own consciousness, we can never really get inside another person and observe directly the messages that person would like to share. Consequently, all human communication is indirect: We must use various gestures and symbols that we have agreed will have certain common interpretations. These gestures and symbols are observed as a result of some physical medium that permits us to see and hear the actions of the other person. Communication begins with mutual awareness and with the perception that another person wishes to share a message with us.

A key element in our understanding of communication is the use of signs observable through some medium—in other words, message behavior. Almost any behavior could be interpreted by another person as carrying some meaning or indicating some intention; that is, if we are not careful, "communication" can be defined as any human behavior that another person might happen to observe. One influential book concerning communication claims that when two people are in each other's presence, it is impossible for them not to communicate. Anything that either person does (or does not do) can be said to carry some message.[6] These authors intend to remind people that others *can* interpret any behavior as communication. But note that the claim is not that all behavior is communication, but only that any behavior, even if not intended to be so, can be interpreted as constituting communicative behavior.

Communicative behavior is therefore distinguishable from other kinds of human behavior. The distinction lies, first, in the use of signs. Recall that human communication is indirect; we cannot directly observe the thoughts or intentions within the minds of other persons. We can share a thought or intention only through the use of intermediaries, signs that stand for or signify that thought or intention. These signs can be put into physical form so that they can be observed by other people. Signs, then, are accepted within a certain community of people as pointing toward some interpretation.

Signs can be of three different kinds. There are signs that directly represent or picture what is intended—as when we draw a picture or diagram of something, or indicate the size or shape of something with gestures. Some signs are symptoms or clues that indicate or stand for a particular state of affairs. A cough is therefore taken as a sign of a cold; a white laboratory coat may be taken as a sign of a profession. Symbols, a third kind of sign, are of special interest in human communication. Symbols are created from whole cloth to stand for something, even though there is no direct relationship between the symbol and the thing represented. Hence, people speaking English have "agreed" that the opening in a room for usual entrance or exit is a "door"; people speaking other languages have "agreed" on a different combination of sounds or letters to be the symbol for that opening.

The second distinguishing characteristic of communication is the use of some physical medium by which the signs constituting a message are observable. That medium provides the means by which the sign behavior of one person can be brought to the attention of another person. The medium can be sound waves propagated through air, as when we hear another person speak. Or the medium can be based on visual observation, as when we see another person present in the same room or presented as an image on a television screen.

The signs of an original message can be carried by different media. For example, some people may be present as an audience when someone gives a speech, while other people may observe the same message later as the result of a videotaped rebroadcast. Similarly, the original message can be translated into different signs, as when the speech is translated from English into French. There may be philosophical reasons for objecting that the French message is not the same as the English message, and that is of course true to a certain extent. Still, we do hold that translations are possible, suggesting that some essential element of the meaning of the message in one language can be communicated in another.

Notice that I am *not* saying that the signs and the medium used for a particular act of communication *are the most important elements* in that act or that they should be the sole objects of study. I am saying that when these elements are present, we are safe in describing the behavior as communication. Obviously, communication also involves people, their intentions, their perceptions, their relationships with other people, and so on, as do other kinds of human behavior.

Because communication is a complex process, we are free to focus on different elements of that process depending upon the purpose of our inquiry. At times, people wish to focus on the communicators, the people involved in the process, and their goals, intentions, or perceptions. At other times, we may wish to focus on the pattern of communication interactions or the relationship between communicators resulting from the process of communication. Or, we may wish to study the content or structure of the messages used in the process. For these reasons, in Chapter 3 we will present different perspectives for analyzing communication.

Communication is therefore *the process of two or more people engaging in mutual awareness and sharing of facts, feelings, or intentions through the use of verbal and nonverbal signs observable in some medium.*

PROPOSITIONS REGARDING ORGANIZATIONAL COMMUNICATION

1. *Communicating is the fundamental process of organizing.*

Organizing requires getting people together to accomplish some purpose. An organization itself is made up of a pattern of interactions among people. Bringing people together and establishing interactions among them clearly involves these people in communication. More than that, however, this first proposition argues that the act of organizing is essentially communicating.

Nearly all the activities that we associate with the existence of human organizations are communicative activities. For example, the typical work of organizations requires the coordination of sequential and interlocked behaviors of several people. Such coordination can be achieved only by people communicating with one another. People are recruited to become members of organizations through various messages, such as announcements, advertisements, or broadcast appeals, and often face-to-face interviews. People within organizations find that they need to direct and control the behavior of other people, usually through communicating with these people. In many organizations, conflicts over methods, goals, or allocation of resources is normal; such human conflicts can be dealt with only through the processes of communication. Henry Mintzberg conducted one of the first studies based on the direct observation of exactly what executives do during a typical work day. He concluded that verbal and written exchanges constitute the manager's daily work; most of these exchanges are carried on through written documents (mail) and through verbal interactions, informal and formal meetings, and tours or observations. Mintzberg further concluded, "The manager clearly favors the three verbal media, spending most of his [sic] time in verbal contact."[7]

Focusing on organizations as ongoing communication reminds us that organizations do not have reality apart from human actions (acts of communication).

2. *Understanding organizational communication provides insights for understanding the working of organizations in our lives.*

This second proposition maintains that the study of organizational communication can allow us to become more effective in participating in and dealing with organizations. We cannot escape the pervasive effects that organizations have on our lives. We are surrounded by them, and we are often quite dependent on many organizations. By thinking about organizing and organizations as communication, we can envision the ways in which organizing works and what makes organizations the way they are.

When asked to list all the organizations to which they belong, some people produce long lists; others, short lists. This may be partly the result of individual differences: Some people may be "joiners," whereas others are "loners." Or, the differences may be due to different interpretations of what is an organization or what it means to be a member of an organization. For example, some people would include their immediate families as organizations, whereas others would not. Some people are not sure whether they are members of the university they attend or clients of that organization. When asked to list the organizations that have some effect on them, not just those to which they belong, people often come up with longer and more consistent lists. Various governmental agencies, such as the auto license branch, the school board, or the IRS, come immediately to mind. Businesses that one relies on, such as groceries and other stores, insurance companies, and the like, also spring to mind. Schools including colleges and universities, churches or other religious organizations, social organizations, and local and national media producers and distributors that bring us news and entertainment are other kinds of organizations that affect us daily.

The processes studied and the concepts developed in the field of organizational communication have helped to clarify the workings of organizations. As we shall see, scholars have taken different approaches in studying these processes. Some scholars emphasize that organizations have their own cultures, like small societies, and describe organizations using terms borrowed from anthropology that relate to the study of human cultures. Other scholars emphasize the functions that communicative activities fulfill within organizations. For example, the networks developed within an organization for handling internal messages can be studied with an eye to improving the speed or accuracy of these messages. We can take the insights provided by approaches of these sorts and enhance our own understanding in dealing with the organizations in our lives.

3. *Communication skills are the basis for effective leadership in organizations.*

This proposition highlights the importance that leadership skills have in the effective functioning of organizations. First, notice a distinction between leadership and leaders. A leader is an individual, usually designated to carry out some specific role within an organization that requires directing and controlling the behavior of others. Leadership refers to behaviors that move people toward desired goals or ends. Many people, whether they are designated leaders or not, can enact leadership behaviors within an organization. For example, when a coworker comes up with a way to summarize and organize a committee's ideas about solving a problem, that coworker is exhibiting leadership. When another committee member recognizes that the group is dividing into hostile camps and provides some relief of tension by telling a light-hearted story or joke, that member facilitates resolution of the conflict and moves the committee toward achieving its goals. In this case, even telling a joke could be considered exercising leadership.

Leadership encompasses activities that induce desired behaviors in other people. Such activities occur only as they are acted out in a communication. We can observe a person giving directions, persuading others to undertake some action, coordinating the messages and actions of others, and so on. Leadership, in other words, is embodied in the communicative behaviors of people. The skills that make up leadership are essentially skills of communication. By developing a better understanding of the concept of leadership in organizational settings, individuals can also conceptualize the skills necessary for becoming effective leaders.

4. *Communication is the key to sound decision making within organizations.*

Effective organizations are marked by both excellent leadership and sound decision making. Within organizations, decision making is often a cooperative or joint activity. Of course, there are individual roles within an organization that are designated as "decision makers." One may be reminded of the oft-quoted statement attributed to President Truman, "The buck stops here." Nonetheless, when the president of the United States makes a decision, that decision is often the end product of a long and complex process, involving several groups' gathering and analyzing data, developing alternatives, and discussing the ramifications of options. The president rarely (probably never) makes a significant decision in isolation, without thorough consultation and discussion with advisers and other leaders. When the president reports a decision, he or she is most likely reporting the consensus of some group.

Decision making and the previous point concerning leadership can be confused with or simplified to issues of power and authority. As Robert L. Dilenschneider points out in his popular book on executive power and influence, effective managers rely more on influence than on authority to get things done.[8] Decision making, then, highlights abilities to work with other people in developing understanding of some problem that needs to be resolved, a problem that requires a decision. Decision making involves the ability to formulate the issues involved in the problem and the possible outcomes of the decision. In other words, making and implementing good decisions require skills of communication.

5. *Diversity characterizes contemporary organizations.*

This proposition recognizes the increasingly multicultural nature of contemporary complex organizations. At an earlier time, the organizations of business, govern-

DIVERSITY MATTERS

Cultural Sensitivity

The increasing internationalization of business means that sensitivity to diversity and cultural differences must often work both ways. The largest corporation in Korea, Samsung, has embarked on a program intended to create more cultural awareness among its Korean managers and employees. Besides learning words and phrases in English or Japanese and taking lessons in table manners and dancing, about four hundred new executives are sent overseas by the firm for up to a year to "goof off" and get the feel of life in the United States or other countries that are important markets for Samsung's products.* The executives are supposed to hang out at malls, fast food restaurants, and other public places to get the feel of American life.

Similarly, Japanese executives coming to the United States as managers for Canon, NEC, and other Japanese firms find that they need special training to avoid cultural and legal missteps. Mitsui & Company USA provides videotapes and "acculturation seminars" for Japanese managers, and several other firms have developed long-range policies intended to bring their executives up to speed on antidiscrimination laws in the United States in an effort to avoid costly lawsuits.** The biggest problem has been learning to avoid personal questions when interviewing, such as asking female applicants if they intend to marry or have children, or asking about religion and age.

It is not only American firms that need to develop cultural sensitivity; international companies doing business in the United States find that they also must learn to understand the needs and requirements of embracing diversity.

*Wall Street Journal, December 30, 1992, p. A1.

**New York Times, September 9, 1990, p. E25.

ment, education, and so forth, were dominated by males. Today and in the future, we should expect much more balance in the gender of members and leaders of organizations. Women play increasingly prominent roles in contemporary organizations. At the same time, organizations are becoming more ethnically and culturally diverse, reflecting changes within our own society and the increasingly international nature of modern business and corporate society. In the United States, legislation such as the Americans with Disabilities Act of 1990 means that organizations must accommodate people with differences that in the past might have excluded them from roles in these organizations.

The growing diversity of organizations means that all the communication processes that make up their activities can involve cultural differences. For example, communication in decision making for German or Japanese organizations may be subject to rules and interpretations different from the rules and interpretations that American managers take for granted. The phrase "take for granted" should be emphasized, because one of the reasons intercultural communication is difficult is precisely because cultural matters are so often out of awareness, that is, taken for granted. Much organizational communication today is also intercultural communication. A study of organizational communication should therefore take account of the relationships between communication and culture.

THE NATURE OF THE FIELD OF ORGANIZATIONAL COMMUNICATION

Relationship to Communication Studies

Organizational communication is a relatively new field of academic study and inquiry. This field grew out of business speech or business communication in the early 1950s. Organizational communication began with a definite business orientation, with emphasis on improving one's skills in performing specific business communication activities. Early degree programs were developed at Purdue University, the University of Southern California, Northwestern University, and a few other institutions. The location of these programs within speech departments was probably due to recognition of the importance of speech and interpersonal communication in the day-to-day functioning of business organizations. Over time, theoretical interests have gradually taken on added importance as the field has expanded beyond the original practical concerns.[9]

While the field appears to have originated in courses with titles such as Business Speech and Managerial Communication, the adjective *organizational* signals a recognition that there are many modern organizations outside of the business world: universities, governmental agencies, nonprofit agencies, professional societies, and so on. Researchers have consequently tried to develop generalizations about communication that are applicable for many kinds of organizations.

The relationship of this subdiscipline to other fields of study within the broader discipline of human communication may help to clarify its development. The communication act is the object of study at several levels of analysis, determined in part by the number of participants and the setting in which it occurs. The first level, interpersonal communication, involves two people in face-to-face interaction. The study of intercultural communication often involves the same kind of face-to-face setting. Public speaking or public communication considers the situation of a speaker before a group of listeners constituting an audience. Group communication, or small group communication, studies the interactions of several people within some group. Mass communication refers to situations in which a message is disseminated widely beyond an immediately present audience. Such dissemination is usually through some mass medium, such as the press, radio, or television.

Levels of Communication Study

- Interpersonal communication
- Intercultural communication
- Public speaking, public communication
- Small-group communication
- Organizational communication
- Mass communication
- International communication

While organizational communication can be envisioned as located at a point in this scheme between small-group communication and mass communication, specific concerns of organizational communication touch upon principles or research concerning the other levels. For example, researchers in organizational communication are quite interested in the superior-subordinate relationship in organizations, and interpersonal communication research clearly bears directly upon this relationship. When organizational communication scholars consider communication between an organization and audiences in its external environment, they are concerned with factors studied in the field of mass communication. Organizational decision making often involves reliance on research about communication within small groups. Hence organizational communication scholars rely on the application of research in and principles resulting from the study of different levels of human interaction in organizational contexts.

At other times, organizational communication scholars are concerned with communication specifically on an organization-wide level, for example when studying the flow of messages through networks linking groups within an organization. Another type of organization-wide communication concerns organizational climate or culture, in which the whole pattern of relationships in an organization as a whole is analyzed.

In summary, the organizational context differentiates the focus of organizational communication from other related communication subdisciplines. Organizational communication, as a field, is concerned with communication activities relevant to the functioning of the organization. The interpersonal communication between superior and subordinate, for instance, is felt to have organizational ramifications, because the communication in this dyad can influence the overall effectiveness of an organization.

PERSPECTIVES FOR UNDERSTANDING ORGANIZATIONAL COMMUNICATION

The approach to a particular field of study that scholars and researchers take depends in large part upon certain assumptions that they make regarding the nature of the phenomenon to be studied and the nature of reality. It is not really possible for people to begin serious academic study in a field without some assumptions that shape the way they think about what they are studying. These basic assumptions lead to a perspective, a point of view. This perspective is important in determining the kind of observations they make and the kind of conclusions that they come to. Our beliefs about reality lead to decisions concerning what to look for and what to count as evidence.

The perspective that scholars choose for studying a process depends partly on the purposes of the study. It makes sense for physicists at times to take the view that light functions as tiny particles and at other times to think of light as consisting of continuous waves. The perspective provided by thinking of light as particles is useful for explaining some phenomena, while the wave theory is useful for making other observations. Similarly, we may find it useful to think of communication activities in organizations from different perspectives. When the purpose is to improve the handling of information within an organization, the perspective termed *functionalism* may be particularly useful. When we are trying to understand the feelings that organization members have regarding the organizations, we may find a different perspective more appropriate.

Of course, the different perspectives that people select when dealing with a subject such as organizational communication can reflect their definite philosophical differences about the nature of reality and society.[10] People holding such positions may reject strongly the suggestion that one can pick and choose among perspectives depending upon one's immediate needs or purposes.

Someone beginning the study of organizational communication, however, needs to be aware of the distinctions among these perspectives and the reasons for choosing one over others. As we begin to read in the literature of organizational communication, we need to be alert to these differences, as the perspective may shape the conduct and results of research.

Functional Perspective

Functionalism has been the dominant perspective for the study of communication within organizations over the years.[11] This approach studies communication activities as they bring about or cause intended and unintended outcomes. The organization is seen as an entity, and different communication acts are variables that shape and determine the operations of that entity.

Functionalists therefore focus on the "functions" of different kinds of messages and communication behaviors. Selection interviews, for example, are intended to fulfill the function of recruiting new members for the organization. These interviews may serve other functions as well, such as creating good will for the organization and portraying a desired public image. Notice that some of these functions may not be explicitly intended or may even be unintended.

Functionalists categorize messages or behaviors in terms of the functions they fulfill, such as task or maintenance functions. Task functions serve to carry on the basic work of the organization. Maintenance functions help to maintain the existing structures and procedures of an organization. Following this approach, messages that direct work processes are said to fulfill a task function, whereas messages that clarify or reinforce the organizational structure are said to fulfill maintenance functions. Functionalists occasionally include other functions for communication, such as human functions, which help to maintain harmonious relationships, and innovative functions, which provide for adaptation and change within an organization.

In the social sciences, functionalism developed first in the disciplines of anthropology and psychology. Functional anthropologists are interested in the purpose, or function, that various cultural activities fulfill for human groups. They believe that functions help to determine cultural structures. Functional psychologists conceptualize mental activities as ongoing processes rather than fixed states or mental structures. They study the activities of the mind in terms of the uses they have, or the functions they perform.

In the discipline of communication, functionalism typically follows a model that explains communication in terms of laws that can predict behavior and the effects of messages. Features of a communication event, such as the presence or absence of documentary evidence presented in a speech, are treated as variables. These variables can be manipulated to determine the effects that they have on the outcome. Generalizations are then drawn from these results to predict future effects from changes in the variables. The variables studied are therefore said to be the causes for certain effects.

Those who take the functionalist perspective in organizational communication are concerned with determining ways to enhance or improve communication systems and behaviors in an organization. Usually the hoped-for outcome is improved efficiency and effectiveness of the organization. One text explicitly based on the functionalist perspective uses the term *function* "to refer to the use of communication in different settings to achieve various goals and objectives."[12] Communication operates to fulfill some specific function. Studies of organizational communication dealing with the flow of messages through network channels and technological media, for example, often follow a functionalist perspective. Networks are described as structures that impede or facilitate the flow of messages, leading some to refer to this approach as structural functionalism, because of its focus on the functions performed by communication structures.

Given the emphasis in organizational communication studies over the years on improving the performance of organizations, it is understandable that the functional perspective has been so influential. The point of this approach is to isolate and control events in order to achieve a desired outcome. Functionalism is often associated with an administrative or management orientation for this reason.

Interpretivist Perspective

The interpretivist perspective is, at least in part, a reaction against the functionalist orientation. This reaction derives from the belief that human beings do not behave as predictably as objects in the physical sciences, from which functionalism takes its direction. Although the reactions of molecules of oxygen and hydrogen at a given temperature and pressure are very predictable, as when they combine to form water, people are able to choose different reactions even under seemingly identical circumstances. Therefore, we may be able to predict that most people or some people will react to a certain message in a certain way, but we cannot make the prediction for all people. Some people will do one thing and some another when presented with identical incentives.

Interpretivists argue that because people exhibit choice in responding to stimuli and are so complex in their behaviors, functionalist explanations and laws of behavior are inapplicable. However, although we may not be able to predict and control human behavior, we can understand and interpret it. The concern of this perspective is not to improve managerial control or to make the organization more productive, effective, or whatever, but to grasp the human experience of people within the organization.[13] The turn of some scholars toward an interpretive perspective represents a moving away from the strictly administrative concerns that directed early business-oriented studies in organizational communication. The emphasis shifts to understanding human communication within the organization rather than managing the organization. Linda Putnam draws the distinction between the first two perspectives: "Functionalists view social reality as objective and orderly; interpretivists reflect a concern for social order, but they treat society as constructed through the subjective experiences of its members."[14]

Researchers following an interpretivist perspective use a wide variety of methods for studying communication in organizations. Some of these research tools are derived from rhetorical criticism, intended to analyze the content and meaning of messages as rhetorical acts. Other researchers have used stories, dramas, fantasies, group myths, and organizational metaphors to arrive at an understanding of what communication means to people in an organization. Studies associated with the concept of "organizational culture" or "corporate culture" often, though not always, take an interpretivist approach.

Critical Perspective

The critical perspective derives from a school of thought often referred to as critical theory. This school developed in philosophy in Germany in the 1930s under the leadership of Theodore Adorno and Max Horkheimer at the Institute for Social Research in Frankfurt, Germany (hence, the term *Frankfurt school*). Probably the best-known contemporary theorist representing this school of thought is Jürgen Habermas. This view is also referred to, at times, as neo-Marxist, because of its inheritance of an analysis of modern society based on economic production and control of the rewards of that production. Critical theorists are consequently largely concerned with issues of power and control in modern organizations.

While the functionalist perspective is concerned with making the organization run efficiently and productively, the critical theorist is more concerned with the questions of efficiency and productivity *for what ends* and *for whose benefit*. Organizational communication is therefore studied in terms of hidden or implicit exercises of power and domination. Habermas, for example, has emphasized in his work "distorted communication," as opposed to ideal (or "pure") communication. In distorted communication, some of the people participating in communication are not aware that their premises or the context within which they communicate has been manipulated or distorted in ways that prevent a full and open discussion of important issues.[15] The critical perspective usually results in analyses of organizational communication that are more explicitly political and ideological than the analyses usually produced following the other perspectives.[16]

Some theorists subdivide critical theorists depending upon whether they take a structuralist position, which holds that outcomes are the results of material and structural factors, or a humanist position, which focuses more on human than on structural factors.[17] The distinction is probably not as important, at this point, as the emphasis on power and ideology, which serves to set critical theorists of all types apart from the functionalists or the interpretivists. For that reason, and in order to avoid too much complexity in our categories, critical theory will be considered as a single perspective in this text. One should be aware, of course, that there is a range of methods, approaches, and specific applications within each of the three broad perspectives identified here: functionalism, interpretivism, and critical theory.

Other Perspectives

In addition to these standard approaches to organizational communication, scholars have also distinguished among different perspectives for viewing the process of communication itself.[18] As Chapter 3 discusses, communication is not a single or easily defined concept; communication is more a family of concepts, each of which may emphasize a different element or aspect of the widely conceived process of communication. For example, one who emphasizes the transmission nature of communication can focus upon the channel or medium used in such transmission, and develop theories about noise or interference in such channels. Another scholar may focus upon the people involved and their psychological states while processing information used in communication. Others studying communication have emphasized the system created by a series of communications over time, looking for transactional effects. As a result, some writers, taking the transmissional perspective, consider communication as a series of back-and-forth events, like a Ping-Pong game. Others, taking the more transactional approach, see communication as simultaneous and coordinated behavior rather than a sequence of messages moving between individuals.

Also, different writers take different perspectives as they conceptualize the nature of organizations. As Chapter 3 develops, you will observe several different ways of viewing the nature of organizations and their management. These different management and organizational theories have shaped the conclusions that people draw regarding people's behavior in organizations. As will be seen, the classical management theories of organizations emphasize the importance of central managerial control, including control over the flow of messages and communication within an organization. The human relations theories emphasize more diffuse control and more openness in communication throughout an organization. Other perspectives on organizations result in other inferences concerning communication in organizations.

These other perspectives affecting theorizing about organizations and communication are discussed more fully in the following chapters dealing with communication theory and organizational theory.

FRAMEWORK FOR THE STUDY OF ORGANIZATIONAL COMMUNICATION

The following framework is intended to help you envision the various topics and levels of analysis developed in the field of organizational communication (see Table 2.1 for schematic). This framework is neither a model of an organization nor a model

TABLE 2.1 Framework of Organizational Communication

Context

Organizations exist in a context provided by:
- Environment—History (Time)—Ecology
- Culture
- Technology
- Material and economic conditions
- Purposes and goals
- People or members

Shape and Form

These factors largely influence:
- Organizational culture
- Patterns of interaction
- Relationships within the organization
- Networks for organizational communication

Communication within organizations is studied in terms of:

Messages
- Content
- Symbols
- Codes (verbal and nonverbal)

Methods and Modalities of Communication
- Channels
- Media and technologies of communication

Communication Activities
- Organizing, coordinating, or controlling
- Leading or motivating
- Problem solving and decision making
- Conflict managing, negotiating and bargaining
- Influencing organizational change and development

of the process of organizational communication. It is, rather, an attempt to indicate the factors that have been studied as part of this rapidly expanding field. This framework provides an overview of the topics that are presented and discussed in the text.

First, organizations and the communication within those organizations exist in and are partly shaped by a larger *context*. Various aspects of this context may be emphasized in order to elucidate the nature of organizational communication: the business or economic environment, the larger culture, history and prevailing technologies, relationships to other organizations, people available for membership, or purposes and goals determined by the dictates or demands of the context.

Second, organizational communication is also affected by the *shape and form* of the *patterns and relationships* of the organization itself. Some theorists, typically of the functionalist perspective, tend to emphasize structure as aspects of shape and form. Interpretive scholars usually prefer to look at the less formal patterns of organizational culture. Much work in organizational communication has focused on both formal and informal networks of communication flow within organizations. Some researchers focus on the shape or patterns of relationships at different levels within the organization: the group level (problem-solving groups, team building, quality circles) and the interpersonal level (superior-subordinate relationships, for example).

The final three headings of the framework concern aspects of the act of communication, as further explained in Chapter 4. First, organizational communication analysts can study *messages:* what is said, how it is organized, what symbols or meanings are brought into play. Messages can be coded in various ways, both verbal and nonverbal. The messages of communicators within the organization can be shared with others through various *methods* or *modalities*. Often communicators can choose the medium they will use for communicating with others, and this choice can make a difference. The relationships or networks of the organization can become channels of communication as well. Third, there are various *communication activities* that can be and have been the subject of organizational communication research. The basic organizational functions of coordinating and directing, motivating and leading are intrinsically communication activities. Solving problems, making decisions, dealing with conflict, negotiating, trying to effect innovation and organizational development are also primarily communication activities.

The perspective that one takes often determines which of the terms shown in the table are emphasized or deemphasized. Interpretivists, for example, emphasize organizational culture under shape and form, whereas functionalists more often emphasize structure and networks. Under communication activities, functionalists often focus on coordinating and directing in order to meet the goals of the administrators of the organization. Critical theorists may be more concerned with how conflict is controlled or managed.

SUMMARY

Organizational communication has enjoyed growing popularity in colleges and universities over the last several years. This increased interest no doubt results from recognition that organizations play an extremely important part in our lives. Communication has often been recognized as a crucial element in the effectiveness of organizations and of people within organizations. Organizational communication can even have life-or-death import, as it did in the cases of the space shuttle *Challenger* and the Persian Gulf War.

Modern organizations represent a relatively new phenomenon in the proliferation of forms similar to the corporate form, in which different elements within large organizations—professional managers, technical experts, and production workers—have interests and needs different from those of the owners or legal trustees of those organizations. These new forms place emphasis upon the understanding and communication flowing among and between these elements.

Organizations are defined as ongoing patterns of interactions among people; these patterns are usually planned, sequential, and systematic. Organizations are typically larger and more institutionalized than small groups, which are often parts of an organization.

Communication involves a sharing or connection created among people as a result of the use of signs in some medium that can be interpreted by the people involved. The emphasis in communication is therefore upon mutual awareness of the use of verbal and nonverbal signs.

Five propositions regarding organizational communication were presented:

1. Communicating is the fundamental process of organizing.
2. Understanding organizational communication provides insights for understanding the working of organizations in our lives.
3. Communication skills are the basis for effective leadership in organizations.
4. Communication is the key to sound decision making within organizations.
5. Diversity characterizes contemporary organizations.

The field of organizational communication developed out of pragmatic interests concerning business speech. The importance of the organizational context differentiates organizational communication from other subfields in the communication discipline.

Scholars in the field of organizational communication may view the object of study through different conceptual lenses. The functional perspective, historically the most widely used, focuses on the goals and outcomes of intentional communication acts. Interpretivists are more concerned with understanding the experiences of people engaged in organizational communication than in predicting and controlling outcomes. Scholars taking a critical perspective are more concerned with questions of dominance and political control in organizations. Scholars may also differ in terms of the perspectives they take regarding their views of communication and the nature of the organization.

EXERCISES AND QUESTIONS FOR DISCUSSION

1. Make a list of all the organizations that you belong to or have belonged to. Compare your list with those of other people in your group or class. What different kinds of collectives are included? Discuss the different kinds of groups or organizations that people have included. From your lists and on the basis of your discussion, develop a set of features defining *organizations*.

2. What organizations are currently the most important ones in your life? Do you expect this to change in the future? Are some people more subject to the

control of organizations than others? Discuss whether you believe that organizations have significant control over people's lives.

3. Write a preliminary definition of what you mean by *communication*. Compare your definition with those of others. Discuss the different aspects of the definitions developed. What are the most important elements or factors that you believe define communication?

4. Write down or discuss situations in which decision making or problem solving was enhanced or hindered by a group or organization.

5. Do you agree that leadership is expressed mainly through communication? Develop reasons to support your position. Can you think of examples of leaders who have been especially skillful or effective as communicators?

6. Why do you think that organizational communication has been a growing field over the past few decades? Why do you believe that the study of organizational communication may be particularly relevant or important to you?

SOURCES FOR FURTHER STUDY

Allen, M. W., Gotcher, J. M., and Seibert, J. H. (1993). A decade of organizational communication research: Journal articles 1981–1991. In S. Deetz (Ed.), *Communication yearbook 16.* Newbury Park, Calif.: Sage, pp. 252–330.

Alvesson, M. (1987). *Organization theory and technocratic consciousness.* Berlin: Walter de Gruyter.

Alvesson, M. (1993). Cultural-ideological modes of management control: A theory and a case study of a professional service company. In S. Deetz (Ed.), *Communication yearbook 16.* Newbury Park, Calif.: Sage, pp. 3–42.

Burrell, G., and Morgan, G. (1979). *Sociological paradigms and organizational analysis.* Ridgewood, N.J.: Forkner.

Clegg, S. (1990). *Modern organizations.* London: Sage.

Clegg, S., and Dunkerley, D. (1980). *Organization, class and control.* London: Routledge & Kegan Paul.

Deetz, S. (1982). Critical interpretive research in organizational communication. *Western Journal of Speech Communication, 46,* 131–49.

Deetz, S. (1992). *Democracy in an age of corporate colonization.* Albany, N.Y.: State Universtiy of New York Press.

Deetz, S., and Mumby, D. K. (1990). Power, discourse, and the workplace: Reclaiming the criti-

cal tradition. In J. A. Anderson (Ed.), *Communication yearbook 13.* Newbury Park, Calif.: Sage, pp. 18–47.

Dilenschneider, R. L. (1990). *Power and influence: Mastering the art of persuasion.* New York: Prentice-Hall.

Goldhaber, G. M., Yates, M. P., Porter, D. T., and Lesniak, R. (1978). State of the art: Organizational communication: 1978. *Human Communication Research, 5,* 76–96.

Habermas, J. (1979). *Communication and the evolution of society.* Trans. T. McCarthy. Boston: Beacon Press.

Held, D. (1980). *Introduction to critical theory: Horkheimer to Habermas.* Berkeley, Calif.: University of California Press.

Hutchinson, K. L. (Ed.). (1992). *Readings in organizational communication.* Dubuque, Iowa: Wm. C. Brown.

Krone, K. J., Jablin, F. M., and Putnam, L. L. (1987). Communication theory and organizational communication: Multiple perspectives. In F. M. Jablin, L. L. Putnam, K.H. Roberts, and L. W. Porter (Eds.), *Handbook of organizational communication: An interdisciplinary perspective.* Newbury Park, Calif.: Sage. pp. 18–40.

Larkin, T. J. (1986). Humanistic principles for organizational management. *Central States Speech Journal, 37,* 36–44.

McDermott, J. (1991). *Corporate society: Class, property, and contemporary capitalism*. Boulder, Colo.: Westview Press.

Meyers, R. A., Brashers, D., Center, C., Beck, C., and Wert-Gray, S. (1992). A citation analysis of organizational communication research. *Southern Communication Journal, 57*.

Mintzberg, H. (1973). *The nature of managerial work*. New York: HarperCollins.

Morgan, G. (1986). *Images of organization*. Newbury Park, Calif.: Sage.

Mumby, D. K. (1987). The political function of narrative in organizations. *Communication Monographs, 54*, 113–27.

Pacanowsky, M. E., and O'Donnell-Trujillo, N. (1984). Organizational communication as cultural performance. *Communication Monographs, 50*, 126–47.

Putnam, L. L. (1982). Paradigms for organizational communication research: An overview and synthesis. *Western Journal of Speech Communication, 46*, 192–206.

Putnam, L. L., and Pacanowsky, M. E. (Eds.). (1983). *Communication and organizations: An interpretative approach*. Newbury Park, Calif.: Sage.

Scott, W. G., and Hart, D. K. (1979). *Organizational America*. Boston: Houghton Mifflin.

Sypher, B. D., Applegate, J. L., and Sypher, H. E. (1985). Culture and communication in organizational contexts. In W. B. Gudykunst, L. P. Stewart, and S. Ting-Toomey, (Eds.), *Communication, culture, and organizational processes*. Beverly Hills, Calif.: Sage, pp. 13–29.

Vance, V., Monge, P. R., and Russell, H. R. (1977). *Communicating and organizing*. Reading, Mass.: Addison-Wesley.

Wert-Gray, S., Center, C., Brashers, D. E., and Meyers, R. A. (1991). Research topics and methodological orientation in organizational communication: A decade in review. *Communication Studies, 42*, 141–54.

NOTES

1. *Report to the President of the Presidential Commission on the Space Shuttle Challenger Accident* (June 6, 1986). Washington, D.C., p. 83.

2. *Report on the Space Shuttle Challenger,* p. 94.

3. M. Hammer and S. A. Stanton (1995), *The reengineering revolution: A handbook,* New York: HarperCollins, pp. 97ff.

4. W. G. Scott and D. K. Hart (1979), *Organizational America,* Boston: Houghton Mifflin.

5. H. I. Schiller (1989), *Culture, Inc.: The corporate takeover of public expression,* New York: Oxford, pp. 51–65.

6. P. Watzlawick, J. Beavin, and D. Jackson (1967), *The pragmatics of human communication,* New York: W. W. Norton.

7. H. Mintzberg (1973), *The nature of managerial work,* New York: HarperCollins, p. 52.

8. R. L. Dilenschneider (1990), *Power and influence: Mastering the art of persuasion,* New York: Prentice Hall.

9. The early development of the field is summarized by W. C. Redding (1992), Stumbling toward identity: The emergence of organizational communication as a field of study, in K. L. Hutchinson (Ed.), *Readings in organizational communication,* Dubuque, Iowa: Wm. C. Brown, pp. 11–44.

10. See L. L. Putnam (1982), Paradigms for organizational communication research: An overview and synthesis, *Western Journal of Speech Communication, 46*, 192–206.

11. B. D. Sypher, J. L. Applegate, and H. E. Sypher (1985), Culture and communication in organizational contexts, in W. G. Gudykunst, L. P. Stewart, and S. Ting-Toomey (Eds.), *Communication, culture, and organizational processes,* Beverly Hills, Calif.: Sage, p. 15.

12. R. V. Vance, P. R. Monge, and H. R. Russell (1977), *Communicating and organizing,* Reading, Mass.: Addison-Wesley, p. 55.

13. See L. L. Putnam and M. E. Pacanowsky (Eds.) (1983), *Communication and organizations: An interpretative approach,* Newbury Park, Calif.: Sage.

14. Putnam, p. 33.

15. J. Habermas (1979), *Communication and the evolution of society,* Trans. T. McCarthy, Boston: Beacon Press, pp. 1–68; J. Habermas (1984), *The theory of communicative action, Vol. 1,* Trans. T. McCarthy, Boston: Beacon Press; and D. Held (1980), *Introduction to critical theory: Horkheimer to Habermas.* Berkeley, Calif.: University of California Press, pp. 260–95.

16. See D. K. Mumby (1987), The political function of narrative in organizations, *Communication Monographs, 54,*

113–27; D. K. Mumby (1988), *Communication and power in organizations: Discourse, ideology, and domination,* Norwood, N.J.: Ablex Publishing; S. A. Deetz (1982), Critical interpretive research in organizational communication, *Western Journal of Speech Communication, 46,* 131–49; and S. Deetz and D. K. Mumby (1990), Power, discourse and the workplace: Reclaiming the critical tradition, in J. A. Anderson (Ed.), *Communication yearbook 13,* Newbury Park, Calif.: Sage, pp. 18–47.

17. Putnam; and G. Burrell and G. Morgan (1979), *Sociological paradigms and organizational analysis,* Ridgewood, N.J.: Forkner.

18. K. J. Krone, F. M. Jablin, and L. L. Putnam (1987), Communication theory and organizational communication: Multiple perspectives, in F. M. Jablin, L. L. Putnam, K. H.. Roberts, and L. W. Porter (Eds.), *Handbook of organizational communication: An interdisciplinary perspective,* Newbury Park, Calif.: Sage.

CHAPTER 3

Communication Theory for Organizational Communication

CHAPTER OBJECTIVES

After studying this chapter, you should be able to:

- Explain communication as a type of "sense making."
- Define the different conventionalized systems people use for communicating.
- Explain the effect of the theoretical perspective on approaches to understanding human communication.
- Associate each of the five perspectives with a central focus or concern.

CHAPTER OUTLINE

The Study of Communication in Organizations

Nature of Communication Theory
  Communication as Sense Making
  Human Communication Systems

Perspectives of Communication Theory
  Nature of Theory
  Rhetorical Perspective
  Transmissional Perspective
  Psychological Perspective
  Interactional Perspective

  ■ DIVERSITY MATTERS: Stereotyping

  Transactional Perspective

  ■ AN ISSUE OF COMMUNICATION ETHICS: Romance in the Workplace

Summary

THE STUDY OF COMMUNICATION IN ORGANIZATIONS

A headline in the *Wall Street Journal* announces, "Waste Management seeks an over-haul of corporate name."[1] The company's founder does not want people to think of the company as simply a trash hauler or dump operator. He intends to change the name of the company to EMX Technologies Inc. to indicate that his company does something more than just hauling trash. The founder fears that the company does not receive sufficient respect because of the old name's association with trash.

In his novel *The Moon and Sixpence,* W. Somerset Maugham, takes a somewhat pessimistic view of our ability to communicate with one another:

> Each one of us is alone in the world. He is shut in a tower of brass, and can communicate with his fellows only by signs, and the signs have no common value, so that their sense is vague and uncertain. . . . We are like people living in a country whose language they know so little that, with all manner of beautiful and profound things to say, they are condemned to the banalities of the conversational manual. Their brain is seething with ideas, and they can only tell you that the umbrella of the gardener's aunt is in the house.[2]

These examples point to some of the difficulties of human communication. The first case suggests that first impressions and symbolic meanings can seem more important than substance. People respond to the names of persons, objects, and organizations, and therefore naming assumes special significance. In the second case, the novelist is pointing out that human communication is never quite direct; we must use intermediate codes, signs, and symbols in an attempt to get other people to understand something the same way that we do.

On April 14, 1994, two helicopters carrying American officers and United Nations personnel from other countries were shot down by American fighter jets over a portion of northern Iraq designated a no-fly zone. The two F-15 fighters received no signals to indicate that the helicopters were friendly craft, and so they assumed that these were intruding aircraft and launched their missles at them. It turned out that the jet pilots were using frequency 52 for signaling, whereas the helicopters had switched to a new frequency, 42, per air force directives. The army pilots of the fighter planes were not informed of the changed frequencies until a week after the incident.[3] In this situation, being on the wrong frequency, or having signals crossed, led to a tragic accident. Communication is often a matter of being on the same frequency as other people, whereas miscommunication results when people are unaware that they are tuned to different signals.

This is a text about communication, specifically organizational communication. Although organizational theories are extremely important, so much so that the following chapters review important milestones in the development of these theories, the central topic is communication. We must begin, therefore, with some understanding of the process of communication and the important theories concerning the nature of that process.

Chapter 2 introduced some defining characteristics basic to the concept of communication. The two illustrations above, for example, point to the nature of communication as a process using signs and symbols for sharing messages among two or more people. This chapter builds upon this introduction while reviewing the problems inherent in providing a single, all-inclusive definition of the term. I will show that there are different ways of understanding the meaning of this concept by explaining different perspectives for analyzing communication.

On the other hand, occasionally communication works even better than expected. The tiny Pioneer space craft, launched during the 1970s as a probe of Jupiter and other planets lying beyond the earth in the solar system, is still sending its tiny signal over light-years of space as it prepares to leave the known boundaries of our solar

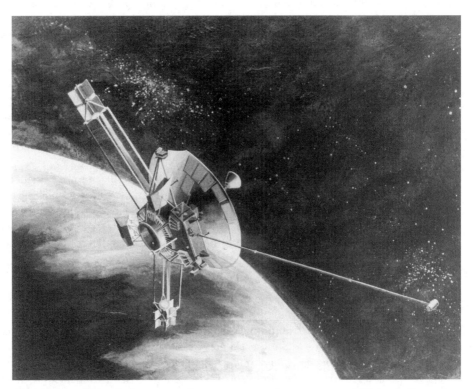

The Pioneer spacecraft demonstrated communication that was successful beyond all expectations.

system. The Pioneer is a symbol of one of the seeming paradoxes of communication: At times the most careful systems can fail, as shown in the case of the helicopters in the no-fly zone, and at other times, it works much better than could be expected.

NATURE OF COMMUNICATION THEORY

"Communication" shares a root with "communal," "community," and "common." The idea behind this root is the idea of people sharing something or holding something in common. In other words, communication is not a solitary activity. Even when the shipwrecked sailor, stranded alone on a Pacific island, puts a note in a bottle and casts it into the waves, the action has meaning only in terms of another person who may find and read the note. Communication is grounded in the notion of the possibility of human contact. In that human contact, something like the "note" in the bottle plays a key role.

When dealing with a phenomenon as basic and encompassing as human communication, it is extremely difficult to provide a simple or even a single definition of the term. For example, imagine how hard it is to define the term *life,* or *living.* Each attempt at a definition leaves something out or looks at the term from only one point of view (say a biological viewpoint or an experiential viewpoint). Similarly, definitions of communication are often acceptable only in terms of a certain point of view or interest. Like *life, communication* is a very rich concept, which means that it can be understood in different ways and approached from different angles. Often the definition of communication that one chooses depends on the purpose of one's analysis.

For this reason, communication is often said to be a family of closely related concepts or definitions.[4] At its broadest, communication can be viewed as any response by an organism to any stimulus. One could think of that response as the meaning of that stimulus for that specific organism. This view of communication is so broad that it can scarcely be used in any meaningful way.

Also tricky is the issue of intent: Do messages have to be intentional to count as communication? As noted in the first chapter, Watzlawick and colleagues maintain that communication is unavoidable when at least two people are together. Communication has occurred, in other words, if one person interprets any behavior of another as being a message, whether or not the person intended to send that message.

Communication as Sense Making

Scholars tend to prefer a more restrictive definition of communication, one that emphasizes some sort of *transferral* or sharing of *meaning,* usually intentional on the part of both parties. Communication, from this point of view, involves someone *interpreting* the actions of another. When we engage in communication, we are engaging in *sense-making behavior.* I interpret your behavior as indicating some kind of message, and I need to make some sense out of it. The sense that I make of it, the interpretation that I place on your behavior, becomes the meaning that is shared or transferred in communication.

This sense making is facilitated by the fact that over many centuries, human beings have developed conventions for interpreting one another's behaviors. Language obviously represents one of these conventional systems. Many animals have evolved systems of signals and calls to use among themselves for communicating—calls that mean "danger," "food here," and the like. Language is a much more complex system of signals and calls. It is not the only conventional system that people use, as we will see momentarily; however, the workings of language as a system illustrate how a system for interpreting meaning in the behavior of others operates.

Language is a symbolic system, depending upon conventionalized signs, as noted, but its actual functioning is more complicated than this picture might suggest. The individual elements of language, such as words, are not really signs or symbols in themselves. The word *pen* has no single referent or thing for which it stands, for example. This three-letter word could be a noun intended to make us think of a writing instrument or of an enclosure for livestock, or it could be a verb, used figuratively in place of "to write" or used to refer to the act of enclosing something. More abstract parts of speech—prepositions, such as *through,* and adverbs, such as *consequently*— are much more difficult to pin down. As a general rule, *words are not signs or symbols in themselves.*

Let's back up and think about the constituent elements of the word itself to get a better perspective on how words work. Linguists describe the word *pen* as consisting of a combination of three phonemes: /p/, /e/, and /n/. (The / marks are used by linguists to indicate phonemes.) Phonemes are the significant speech sounds that are used to construct the words of a language; no two languages in the world have exactly the same phonemic systems. (Letters in an alphabet are roughly similar to these individual sounds, but are not as exact.) The /p/ phoneme in English is actually a set of several similar sounds, all of which English speakers accept as standing for the same phoneme.

For example, when we say the word *pen,* in which the /p/ is in the initial position, we emit a puff of air with it; when we say *spin,* there is no puff of air emitted with the / p/. Phonemes, then, are abstractions: classes of related sounds that people who speak a particular language use to distinguish one word from another. By themselves, of course, they have absolutely no meaning—we do not know what /p/ by itself is for until we hear or see it in combination with /e/ and /n/. Then we recognize the word *pen.*

In the same way, we do not know what the word *pen* means until it is used in combination with other words. "Put the cattle in the pen" allows us to interpret the word in one way, whereas "I am writing this note with a pen" gives us another meaning of the word. The interpretation of the combination of words relies on our recognizing and choosing among several possible definitions for individual words (see Figure 3.1 on p. 40).

If we believed that the only possible meaning for *pen* was a writing instrument, we would have trouble understanding the first sentence. We must go back and forth between the possible meanings of individual words and their possible meanings in combination in order to arrive at the best interpretation. For that reason, some combinations are inherently ambiguous; no single interpretation seems better than another, as in the combination, "They are flying airplanes."

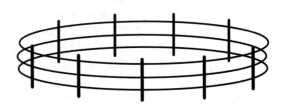

FIGURE 3.1 *Pen* versus *pen*.

To say that this system is conventional is to say that it follows a set of conventions, habitual ways of acting or sets of rules that are accepted by a group of people. As children grow, they acquire the linguistic habits of the people around them. They learn the conventions for forming the phonemes, the sounds of words; they learn the typical definitions for many words such formed; they internalize the rules for combining and interpreting patterns of words; and so on.

Human Communication Systems

Language represents one conventional system developed by people to allow them to interpret the communicative behavior of others, but, as already suggested, it is not the only system. We also interpret the facial expressions of others (smiles, frowns, and so forth), their gestures and other movements, their use of clothing and other objects, and their use of space and time. Some of these other conventionalized systems have been categorized as follows:

- Paralinguistics, or vocalics: the use of pitch, rate, nasality, tone, or other vocal qualifiers
- Kinesics: the use of facial expressions and gestures or movement in general
- Proxemics: the use of space; such as, how close we stand to other people during interaction and how we arrange the space around us
- Chronemics: the use of time, including the time of day for doing certain things; the amount of time we give to an activity; the amount of time we make others wait for us; and so on
- Oculesics: the use of the eyes, eye contact or gaze
- Haptics: the use of touch
- Objectics: the use of objects, such as uniforms or modes of dress; furnishings, to indicate the nature of an office or work; or so-called status symbols

People interpret elements from these various systems as signs intended to direct them to a certain interpretation, or meaning. Notice that I am using "sign" not in the sense of "something that stands for something else," but in the sense of "something that points to something." A sign points us in the "right" direction. A smile does not "stand for" happiness, but points the interpreter toward a particular interpretation of that facial expression. You may interpret a smile as meaning that the person is happy about something, but, like phonemes and words, smiles can be interpreted in different ways, depending on the combination of other signs from all the other systems. Standing closer than is normal for conversation in our culture could indicate warmth or pushiness, depending on the combination of other signs present in the situation.

This discussion reveals the complexity of communicative behavior. In order to understand completely the meaning of some piece of communication, one must consider together the movements and gestures, the facial expressions, the tone of voice, the distance between the people, and so on. We all know that *how* something is said changes the "meaning"—that is, the interpretation. "Smile when you say that" is a cliché reminding us of this fact.

Communication is thus one important type of sense making that people employ. We cannot read someone else's mind, and so human communication is always indirect. Conventionalized systems, such as language, have evolved over the years to provide groups of people with ready-made tools for interpreting the communicative behavior of others in the group. As these groups have evolved in some isolation from one another, the languages and other systems have become relatively unique for each community. Not only do Americans speak a different language from the French, but they also rely on different systems of gestures, facial expressions, proxemics, eye contact, and so on.

When people put together patterns of language and signs relying on conventions of nonverbal communication, we say that they are using messages. The use of messages dependent upon conventionalized interpretation systems is therefore fundamental to communication.

PERSPECTIVES OF COMMUNICATION THEORY

Nature of Theory

A theory of communication is intended to explain how communication works. People construct theories in order to give themselves a systematic way of describing some phenomenon or process. Developing a theory requires careful observation of the phenomenon and organizing those observations into some patterns that seem to make sense. We then look for these patterns in other manifestations of the phenomenon to see if the patterns hold true in new observations. These patterns suggest ways in which important factors, or variables, are interrelated in producing effects. A description of these patterns is usually referred to as a model of the process. A good theory is hence one that directs our attention, tells us what things to watch for, and also interprets those observations for us. We test the adequacy of a theory by seeing how well it predicts future states of the object or process being studied.

Hundreds of theories of communication have been formulated over the years. As explained previously, communication is such a broad concept that it is difficult to develop a single, comprehensive definition. Similarly, theories about communication proliferate because of the breadth and many possible interpretations of the basic concept. The kinds of theories that have been developed tend to depend upon the overall perspective that a theorist takes regarding the nature of communication. The influence of theoretical perspective on the nature of theories was explained in Chapter 2, when the functionalist, interpretivist, and critical perspectives on organizational theories were discussed. The point to remember is that one's perspective, the particular point of view one takes when considering communication, determines what elements and variables of communication one picks out as especially important.

Rhetorical Perspective

Some of the earliest systematic theories about communication were formulated by early Greek teachers, who claimed to be able to teach public leaders through the art of "rhetoric." A *rhetor* was a person who could lead the public assembly by his ability in oratory, or persuasive speech. Aristotle, who provides the most complete theoretical treatment of this art of political communication, posits a simple model of the elements in the communication process:

Speaker (Source) — Message (Speech) — Audience (Receivers)

The art of rhetoric was further systematized under the Romans, especially in the period 100 B.C.E. to 100 C.E. The works of Cicero and Quintilian provide the full treatment of the canons of rhetoric, describing it as consisting of the specialized arts of invention, organization, style, memory, and delivery. In combination, the ideas of Greek rhetoric, especially those of Aristotle, and of Roman rhetoric came to be known as classical rhetoric. The rediscovery of many classical texts during the Renaissance led to a new interest in classical rhetoric, which became the basis for humanistic education and literary style.

Today, rhetorical critics are interested in the persuasive effects of texts on intended audiences. For the ancients, these texts were speeches delivered in a public assembly. As democratic assemblies came to play a decreasing role in the autocratic governments of the Roman emperors and then the feudal lords of Europe, rhetoric lost its exclusive emphasis on this type of speech. Attention in the study of rhetoric turned to ornamental style, especially in literature and in sermons. In modern times, an interest in public persuasion has been restored, but the objects of study are not necessarily speeches: Advertisements, corporate annual reports, cartoons, or films can be considered examples of rhetorical discourse.

In organizational communication, there is new interest in using a rhetorical approach for analyzing both the internal and external messages of organizations. Hence, today scholars speak of "organizational rhetoric," exemplified through "organizational persuasion."[5] The rhetorical perspective is especially concerned with the analysis and explanation of the effects of persuasive messages, most often messages directed to the public that are intended to advocate some single organizational position.[6] The tools of rhetorical criticism could also be applied to messages intended for internal consumption, such as directive memos, safety reminders, or total quality management (TQM) campaigns. The tools of rhetorical criticism are generally concerned with discovering the strategies used by a communicator (source, speaker) to achieve some desired persuasive effect on an audience.

A rhetorical analysis of organizational rhetoric often follows a "burkean" method. Kenneth Burke is a literary critic who developed a useful system for analyzing persuasive messages of all kinds. Burke discerned that public persuasion often results from the strategy of identification, the process by which the speaker identifies him- or herself with the audience ("Since our interests are identical, what is good for me is good for you"). Identification may also require contrasting oneself with an enemy or scapegoat, with some "other."

The threat of competition from Japanese automobile companies, in other words, could be presented as a threat to the nation as a whole, not just to American auto makers. If the "Big Three" car manufacturers succeed in identifying their interests with national and public interests, they may succeed in the rhetorical attempt to persuade the public to accept restrictions on the purchase of non-American cars. The strategy of identification can also be applied in internal messages. The organization (that is, those at the top of the organization) can try to inculcate a close identification between the interests of the individual and those of the organization. The beepers that many people now carry on weekends or to social events are reminders that their primary identification is with the corporation or organization (hospital, government agency, etc.).

One series of commercials recently suggested that a corporation's people were so dedicated to the organization that they would stop in the middle of a holiday outing to phone a colleague with a sudden brainstorm: "What if we tried this . . ." The message is probably intended as much for internal as for external consumption. In addition, the internal organizational structure can be justified in terms of Burke's strategies of accepting order (hierarchy) and identification with one's peers.[7]

The rhetorical perspective therefore directs attention to the following aspects of communication in and of organizations:

- *Messages* of organizations
- The *persuasive strategies* employed in these messages
- The *intended purposes* of communication: A source intends to persuade some audience through the use of message strategies.

Transmissional Perspective

In a popular text on communication theory, B. Aubrey Fisher organized the many theories about communication into four categories, or perspectives.[8] His first perspective, labeled the "mechanistic" perspective, emphasizes communication as the transmission of messages through channels. The channels for communication are imagined as conduits or "conveyor belts," along which messages flow. The foundation for this perspective is the model of communication developed by Claude Shannon, an engineer, and Warren Weaver, a mathemetician, immediately after World War II. This

Shannon-Weaver model of communication became one of the most influential models of the communication process ever developed.[9]

Shannon and Weaver were concerned with the problem of getting a message from a source through to a destination with the highest possible fidelity, given the probability of noise or interference in the channel used for transmitting the message. *Fidelity* refers to faithfulness of reproduction; a message received with high fidelity reproduces the original message nearly exactly. A high-fidelity sound system, for example, reproduces the sounds produced in a concert hall or recording studio almost exactly as they would have sounded to a person present at the concert or in the studio.

In this perspective, the process of communication is envisaged as happening in these stages:

1. A source has the need to send a message to a receiver.
2. The message is encoded into some symbolic form.
3. The coded message is transmitted by transforming the coded symbols into physical representations (sound waves, electronic impulses, or whatever).
4. The message is sent as a signal through some physical channel, which has a limited capacity (can handle only so much of the signal per unit of time).
5. The signal is distorted by "noise," random interference in the channel.
6. The signal is received physically and decoded by some receiver.
7. The decoded message reaches the destination.

Whether the message reaches the destination with high fidelity depends on factors at each stage of the process, which can be illustrated by applying the model to the situation of one person talking to another. The first person, the source, must encode the intended messages, meaning that the person must find the right words to express the message. If the message is not properly encoded, the *intended* message will not be sent. The encoded message must then be transformed into physical actions as the speaker uses the vocal mechanism to transmit the sounds of the words that constitute it. Poor enunciation of the sounds could detract from message fidelity at this point. Sound waves provide the physical channel for the message; competing sound wave disturbances, other sounds, provide noise that could interfere with the intended message. The other person receives the message from the channel by hearing; if hearing is impaired or attention is directed to other sound messages, the message loses fidelity. The sounds of the message are then decoded, meaning that the receiver provides the meanings for the words heard. If the receiver has a different "dictionary" for decoding the words of the sender's message, there will obviously be a loss in fidelity at this point.

At each stage of the process, therefore, some of the intended message is probably lost. The usefulness of the Shannon-Weaver model lies in the identification of specific factors that can be manipulated to increase fidelity. For example, encoding strategies can help to overcome the problem of noisy channels. The basic strategy is redundancy, which involves including more in the message than is minimally necessary. Telegrams, for example, include a number at the end of a written message; the number indicates how many words were in the original message. By counting the words in the message as received, one can determine if any of the message has been lost. The number therefore provides redundancy, information indicating the level of fidelity in the message's transmittal. In the English language, agreement in number of subject and verb represents redundancy ("he does," "they do"). The ending of the verb draws attention to the fact that the subject was singular or plural, in case one missed it.

This model also points up the importance of channel capacity (see Figure 3.2). The channel is viewed as a physical medium, such as bandwidth for radio frequencies or the carrying capacity of wire or cable. The channel can accommodate only so many messages in a given unit of time, which leads to the notions of "information load" and "overloaded channels." The amount of redundancy necessary to ensure high fidelity can take up channel capacity, reducing the amount of new information that a channel can carry. Therefore, there is a trade-off between message fidelity, or accuracy, and channel capacity. For important messages, one may choose slower transmission in order to ensure more accurate reception. Different channels may have different capacities. A written report may deliver more information in a given amount of time than an oral presentation, but the oral presentation may provide more redundancy (facial expression, tone of voice, visual cues) and thus ensure better understanding of the message.

Many of these ideas depend upon the possibility of quantifying and measuring information. For Shannon and Weaver, information was measurable in terms of how much uncertainty was reduced by the receipt of a message. If the receiver knows that the message can be either "yes" or "no," the receipt of the message (let us say, "yes") contains one *bit* (binary digit) of information, because it selected from two possibilities; Shannon and Weaver saw this as the smallest unit of information. By this reasoning, the more unexpected the contents of a message, the more information it contains. This concept is related to the physical notion of entropy, which is further explained in Chapter 6, in the discussion concerning systems theories. The point here is that information is conceived of as something that can be quantified.

A final important idea included in this model of communication is that of feedback. *Feedback* refers to messages sent back to the source, indicating how well the original message has gotten through the transmission process. The source can improve fidelity by monitoring feedback from the receiver. Additional information can be sent in response to this feedback to correct errors in transmission or to fill in information that was lost somewhere along the line.

The air traffic control system in the United States illustrates the nature of this kind of communication model. The system depends on high fidelity: The messages

FIGURE 3.2 Channel capacity is restricted by noise and the need for redundant information to enhance fidelity.

between controllers and pilots must be sent and received with great accuracy. Coding has become highly specialized, so that there will be a high degree of agreement concerning the meaning of various instructions and messages. Each message sent by a controller must be acknowledged (feedback), and monitoring of the radar screen indicates to controllers whether or not pilots have carried out required maneuvers. The inventory tracking systems of many retail operations also illustrate this model in their careful attention to tracking and coding systems. Scanning bar codes into computer cash registers at the point of sale provides continuous feedback concerning the stores' inventory needs, the demand for certain products, and the effects of marketing campaigns.

The transmissional perspective on communication (Fisher's "mechanistic" perspective) emphasizes *fidelity, information, encoding* and *decoding, channel capacity, noise, redundancy,* and *feedback.* This perspective is well suited to a functionalist analysis of organizational communication, which assumes that the organization can design a system or structure (channels of communication) to facilitate improved fidelity in its communication. Attention is directed toward improving the transmission of messages through channels, without regard, necessarily, for the content of these messages. One is primarily concerned with the process of getting a message from one point to another with as much accuracy as possible. This perspective underlies studies of networks, channels, and direction of flow of communication within organizations.[10]

For example, the concepts of capacity and noise cause one to look for overloaded channels, or choke points, in the organizational communication networks. Is one person being required to deal with too many incoming messages at one time? Does the organization have a system for prioritizing incoming messages and processing the information to avoid overload? These are the kinds of questions suggested by this perspective.

The emphasis on a message moving through a channel (a physical image) also highlights other physical images, such as *breakdowns* or *barriers* to communication. The message can be distorted by exposure to noise during transmission. As a message passes from one source-receiver link to another, through a chain of individuals in a hierarchy, distortion and loss of meaning will result. This perspective therefore lends itself well to studies of the causes of such breakdowns and the nature of communication barriers. It places a premium on careful or proper encoding of messages, on an awareness that information can be lost at the point of decoding as well as encoding, and on the importance of monitoring feedback to overcome losses in fidelity.

Psychological Perspective

While the transmissional perspective directs attention to the movement of a message through a channel, the psychological perspective emphasizes the *cognitive structures* of the people involved, the senders and receivers (or sender-receivers). A person holding this perspective believes that the important events in communication occur in the minds of the individuals participating. To understand how communication works, therefore, one must analyze communicators' beliefs, attitudes, values, psychological needs, or other such mental constructs. The focus is thus more on individuals than on channels or the process of transmission.

Specifically, the key factors in communication are the *conceptual filters* through which incoming messages are processed. Instead of the physical image of the conduit or conveyor belt, one has the image of screens with which people sift the stimuli received through sensory organs (such as ears). These filters or screens (see Figure 3.3) cannot be observed directly, of course, but their nature is inferred by analyzing the behaviors emitted following the input of some stimulus. As Fisher points out, conceptual filters are thus essentially "black-box" concepts.[11]

This model of communication is based on *stimulus (S)* and *response (R)*, or S–R. Every person, presumably, is continually emitting behaviors and receiving incoming stimuli, which become the cause for emitting still more behaviors, and so on. Some of the incoming stimuli are words and gestures of another person. These stimuli become raw data that the individual interprets in terms of certain internal mental constructs. Thus a third element is added to the simple S–R model: The mental activity of the organism (the human being) intervenes and processes the stimuli, shaping the response, modifying the model to *S–O–R* (where O stands for organism).

Theories of communication based on this point of view attempt to discover, describe, and explain the conceptual filters that are particularly significant for understanding the effects of communication. Typically, attitudes are important conceptual filters in these theories. An attitude is described as a mental readiness or predisposition leading one to respond in one way and not another in the presence of a specific stimulus. An attitude has virtually a causal role in the behavior of an individual, especially in a choice situation. If you choose steak over quiche, one could say that you have a more positive attitude toward the one than toward the other. An important function of communication, therefore, is try to shape or influence these attitudes in order to achieve some objective. Attitudes are believed to exist in complex interrelationships with one another; one must therefore deal with sets or systems of attitudes.

Attitudes are not the only kind of conceptual filters said to influence communication effects. Other possible internal constructs include values, beliefs, a need for consistency, cognitive dissonance, and ego involvement. Values, for example, are thought of as more all-encompassing guides for life than attitudes. We may have a positive attitude toward aerobic exercise because of a fundamental value placed on good health and a long life. Messages can aim at evoking a particular value in an effort to try to create a desired attitude. The value thus operates to predict a certain response to a

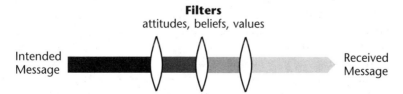

Filters
attitudes, beliefs, values

Intended
Message

Received
Message

FIGURE 3.3   Conceptual filters transform the original, intended messages.

message. The important theory of cognitive dissonance holds that there is a psychological need for people to perceive that their beliefs and behaviors are consistent (not dissonant). This need for consistency thus becomes a conceptual filter, as receivers tend to reject messages that seem to threaten their ability to maintain consistency. Bear in mind that these are all theoretical constructs, used to explain observations of people's responses to various incoming messages.

In summary, the psychological perspective is oriented toward mental processing on the part of individuals, especially individuals as receivers and interpreters of communication. In the quotation from *The Moon and Sixpence* at the beginning of this chapter, Maugham illustrates this point of view. Noise and breakdowns in communication are seen as generated internally, as the individual passes incoming messages through his or her conceptual filters.

For organizational communication, this approach focuses attention on the following aspects of communication in organizations:

- The focus is on *interpersonal communication,* such as that between superior and subordinate.
- The effectiveness of such communication (or lack thereof) is explained in terms of differing sets of *attitudes, values, psychological needs,* and so on.
- The *motivation* of individuals within the organization depends on appeals to these psychological needs.
- *Organizational climate* is described in terms of the perceptions individuals have of how well these psychological needs are met within the organization.

The human relations approach in management theory, described later, fits well with this kind of psychological understanding of communication.

Interactional Perspective

This perspective could also be labeled the "sociological" perspective, for many of the theorists providing its theoretical foundation are sociologists. From this perspective, communication occurs in the *social interactions* of several individuals; communication is part of how we behave as members of ongoing social groups. While the previous perspective emphasizes the individual, then, this perspective emphasizes the group, social network, society, or culture. Theoretical orientations of this perspective are usually derived from role theory and symbolic interactionism.

The basic tenets of role theory and symbolic interactionism go back to the seminal work of George Herbert Mead, a sociologist at the University of Chicago. Mead did not publish his ideas himself; they were disseminated through his students and through posthumous publication of his works.[12] The term *symbolic interactionism* was coined by one of his students, Herbert Blumer. In this view, the individual, and particularly the individual's concept of *self,* cannot be formed in isolation from other human beings. The self can emerge only from ongoing interactions with other people; the self, the individual, is therefore a product of such interaction. As individuals develop, they observe certain patterns of recurring behavior both in themselves and in others. Such

Stereotyping

Conceptual filters develop in order to allow people to operate in the world without constantly having to deal with overloaded mental circuits. People must quickly categorize situations and people in order to function in everyday settings. When dealing with a teller at a bank window, I have certain expectations about how that person will behave and how I should behave toward that person. When we place people into categories in order to determine how we should behave toward them, we are basically engaging in stereotyping—treating people as types instead of as individuals. The stereotype becomes a conceptual filter through which we process our perceptions of an individual.

In organizations, people tend to see some people as "normal," and therefore respond to them as individuals (in the United States, executives have been and continue to be "normally" white males; women, for example, hold only 5 percent of senior-level management jobs).* People who do not fit the "nor-mal" image are often responded to in terms of expectations about their type instead of in terms of their individuality. Women executives are asked, therefore, to explain the "feminine perspective" to a meeting of managers, African Americans may be expected to offer a "'black perspective," and so on. Expectations about child-rearing responsibilities in the United States have created stereotypical expectations regarding women in higher levels of management. One manager who has risen high in a Wall Street firm reports the trade-offs between her professional and public life, trade-offs that are usually not expected of male counterparts. She reports that she would probably not have had the opportunity to reach the position she now has were it not for an Equal Employment Opportunity Commission directive that opened the door for her in the 1970s.** The stereotypes of women executives still color expectations that superiors and subordinates may have regarding their behavior.

*Wall Street Journal, July 26, 1995, p. B1.

**Wall Street Journal, July 26, 1995, p. B1.

patterns associated with individuals lead to the notion of *roles* and *role playing*. One's self-concept includes notions concerning reactions that are consistent with these characterizations. One might say, "I would never react that way" in some situation. The idea is that this person sees certain reactions as not consistent with the way the person views his or her role.

The notion of roles and the ability to take on or play different roles are basic to the act of communicating. Let's say I want to communicate to you that I want you to undertake some action, such as passing the salt at dinner. I can imagine what someone who wanted me to pass the salt might say or do to get me to do this (I can visualize myself as an entity). I therefore put myself in your place—that is, take on your role—and try to envisage how I, in your place, would respond to such a message. The message that I choose to use is the one that I think I would respond to, if I were in your place. Communication consequently depends upon role-taking ability. Without this capacity for learned social interaction, there could be no communication.

The notion of symbols, as in *symbolic* interactionism, derives from this analysis. Some of the behavior that we have learned to interpret as a result of interaction is verbal and nonverbal behavior that represents objects or ideas. When a group of people learn to make the same (or very similar) responses to these representative actions, these actions (which can be words) have become symbols.[13] Symbols take on their meaning through interaction over time within a specific group.

Roles are defined in terms of the norms or expectations that become associated with enacting them. Similarly, the interpretation of symbols depends on the operation of rules, which may vary from situation to situation. Learning how to communicate in specific situations therefore depends upon learning the appropriate rules that apply in each. One function of interpersonal communication is thus to establish, and perhaps even to negotiate, the kinds of rules that will guide a given interaction. Such rules establish what a particular act or symbol means within a certain context. Insults, for example, can be interpreted as playful behavior in one context and as serious threats in another. Communicators need to adjust their orientation toward the applicable rules so that their messages and interpretations mesh in the hoped-for way (so that they are all playing by the same set of rules).

As people grow and become sophisticated through life experience, they develop more and more repertoire, one might say. They are able to imagine and perform a growing number of roles. Certain scripts and plots become more familiar over time. People develop certain habitual ways of enacting various performances, such as how they walk or talk in recurring circumstances. Of course, it is always possible, if sometimes difficult, to learn new scripts and new performances. This line of thinking about role theory has led to elaborations on drama as the metaphor or image explaining communicative interaction. The sociologist Erving Goffman is best known for developing such a dramatistic theory of human interaction.[14] By using terminology and concepts from the theater, he is able to analyze interaction in terms of performances taking place in scenes, with a cast, following a script. He posits on-stage and off-stage areas, the use of props, and so on in describing everyday behavior at home, at work, or wherever.

The interactional perspective of communication thus emphasizes the social nature of communication (*one* cannot, in fact, communicate, because there must be at least two people). Patterned behavior is learned over time through interacting with other people, leading to the construction of roles and symbolic communication. The ability to take on the role of another person is essential if communication is to occur. The meaning of roles and symbols is socially constructed, validated through social consensus. Through their interactions, groups put together, or construct, their own reality and the ways to interpret it. There is no one reality, from this point of view, that is "out there"; rather, there is one that makes sense for this or that group, society, or culture. The fidelity concept of the transmissional perspective suggests, on the other hand, that there is a single, definite reality to be communicated.

For organizational communication, this approach suggests the following emphases:

- *Cultural factors,* both at the national cultural level and at the level of "organizational" or "corporate cultures"

- Learning requisite *roles* and *rules* that fit with the organization's culture
- Organizations as the result of communicative behavior, the *social interaction*, of the members.

Whereas the transmissional and the psychological perspectives allow for the view that the organization is a container for the members or a source for communicating with its members, this view holds that the organization is the product of members' conversation, discussions, and other interactions.

Transactional Perspective

A transaction is an event that one can observe taking place between two (or more) people. While the last two perspectives focused on the people involved in communication (as individuals or in groups), this perspective looks at the event itself. Fisher labeled this point of view the "pragmatic" perspective and related it to systems theory.[15]

AN ISSUE OF COMMUNICATION ETHICS

Romance in the Workplace

Modern communication devices and technologies have made it increasingly possible for work time to intrude into what used to be considered private time. Pagers and cellular phones blur the line between personal and organizational life. On the other hand, when personal roles begin to intrude into organizational life, as when romantic roles are played out on company time, both managers and their employees may find themselves facing an ethical question. Many organizations feel that they need to protect themselves from sexual harassment allegations and by heading off budding office romances, but in doing so, they may seem to violate employees' rights to privacy.

Most companies no longer have rules forbidding dating among coworkers, but still regulate relationships between superiors and subordinates. An IBM manual, for example, states: "A manager may not date or have a romantic relationship with an employee who reports through his or her management chain, even when the relationship is voluntary and welcome."* If two people in this situation wish to develop a romantic relationship, they are required to report it to the company and seek a transfer to avoid the superior-subordinate dating prohibition. Obviously, the enforcement of this provision is rather difficult and has led to lawsuits claiming invasion of privacy. In 1994, IBM lost just such a lawsuit in California.**

For the individual, the ethical issue resides in the question of whether he or she could be fair and impartial in treatment of other subordinates while involved romantically with one of their number. Think of the implications for students if they knew that their professor was dating one of their classmates. How would you feel about such a situation? Are workplace romances something to be avoided? What kinds of restrictions should be placed on them? These are questions more and more organizations face as work time and private time become increasingly indistinguishable.

*Quoted in *New York Times*, February 14, 1995, p. B1.

**New York Times*, February 14, 1995, p. B1.

The relationship established between people through their communication is seen as a system that exists apart from the individuals themselves. This approach is linked with the research area known as relational communication.

The ideas underlying this perspective have been generated largely through the work of the anthropologist Gregory Bateson and a group of colleagues originally associated with Stanford University, the so-called Palo Alto Group. Bateson was influenced by the tenets of general systems theory, which was an attempt to develop an all-encompassing theory explaining all sorts of complex phenomena.[16] (Chapter 6 provides a more in-depth discussion of systems theory.) Bateson and his colleagues focus on the patterns of interchanges in an ongoing relationship; communication is understood in terms of this system of recurring patterns. This perspective is most applicable, therefore, for studying interpersonal communication in continuing two-person relationships, such as those between superior and subordinate, husband and wife, or friend and friend.

The fundamental work in relational communication is *Pragmatics of Human Communication* by Paul Watzlawick, Janet Beavin (Janet Beavin Bavelas), and Don Jackson.[17] Watzlawick and colleagues, as well as Bateson, began with an interest in therapeutic communication. They were interested in determining how ongoing systems of communication patterns could lead to behavioral pathologies and how to treat such pathologies. Families, for example, tend to develop habitual patterns of interacting; these patterns and resultant relationships establish a system. Change in one part of the system brings about changes in the other parts because of the interrelatedness of systems. Systems operate to maintain some kind of homeostasis, that is, steady state or balance. If the system is disturbed, jarred from its normal pattern of interaction, pressure is created to restore the homeostasis, or the preexisting balance in the system. If a person with a personality or social disorder is treated in isolation, then returned to the system that had accommodated (or even generated) the disorder, the chances are that the disorder will resurface.

Any ongoing human relationship can be analyzed in this systemic fashion. After the relationship is established, certain patterns tend to repeat themselves as the relationship becomes stable and achieves homeostasis. The participants then come to accept certain rules that operate to maintain the system. Someone researching communication using this perspective hence focuses not on the individuals, but on recurring patterns of transactions or interactions, cycles of interchanges between the participants.

The analysis of these communication patterns is guided by certain axioms of communication first advanced by Watzlawick, Beavin, and Jackson:

1. One cannot *not* communicate, which means that any behavior emitted by one person can be interpreted by another person as having communicative intent.

2. Every message contains both content and relationship aspects. Any act perceived of as communication not only provides some information but also indicates the communicator's understanding about the relationship between the two people involved. Hence, the other person can interpret your message as implying a certain kind of

relationship (superior-subordinate; teacher-student; minister-parishioner; counselor-client; friend-friend; enemy-enemy; and so on).

3. Sequences of communication events are subject to being punctuated differently by the parties involved. You think you are only responding to the other person, but the other person sees the sequence differently—he or she is merely responding to your prior utterance.

4. Communication relies on both digital and analogic coding. Digital coding is based on some arbitrary system of meaning, such as linguistic behavior; analogic coding is not based on discrete units, but is continuous and variable, a sort of acting out of intended meaning. Digital communication tends to carry discrete or definite meaning, the *content* in interactions; analogic messages tend to carry more of the *relationship* aspect (the tone of voice with which something is said, which is analogic, tends to indicate the nature of the relationship).

5. Each interaction indicates either a symmetrical or a complementary relationship between the two people. Symmetry indicates equal standing, a relationship between equals; complementarity indicates that one communicator is dominant. For example, the situation of a physician talking to a patient concerning medical treatment will typically show a complementary pattern of interaction.

These axioms provide a tool for analyzing breakdowns in communication as well as the difficulties in changing established patterns. For example, there could be disagreement between the two parties concerning the relationship implied in the pattern of communication. Or, there could be disagreement about whether the system calls for symmetrical or complementary interchanges. Competitive symmetry, in which both parties strive for control in the relationship, can mark such disagreement; it is also possible for both parties to try to avoid control.

For example, this type of breakdown in relational communication may have contributed to the accident at the Three Mile Island nuclear plant in 1979. An engineer had recognized that the potential existed for the kind of accident that actually occurred, and he tried to pass it on to the supervisor at Three Mile Island. The relationship part of the message, however, seemed to suggest criticism of the supervisor and an implied superiority on the part of the engineer. The supervisor responded that the engineer did not have the right to criticize nuclear operations at the plant (thus ignoring the content portion of the message).[18] The tools of relational communication are particularly applicable for understanding problems of this sort: similar problems in superior-subordinate communication or those between coworkers in an organization.

There is another way of looking at the nature of transactions in communication, and that is that the transaction, the outcome of communicating, transcends the intentions and behaviors of either partner. The relationship that develops is the "real message" resulting from communication. The communication is what the two people involved share between them.[19] As a result of such communication, both participants come to an understanding of affairs that is different from the understanding that each had prior to the interaction. Neither person "owns" the communication that they share.

Relational communication problems can lead to significant breakdowns.

The transaction of communication is something that cannot be reduced to the purposes and behaviors of individuals. The transmissional and psychological approaches are both reductionist, in the sense that the process of communicating can be reduced to a discrete set of factors or variables. The transactional view attempts to get away from this reductionism by viewing communication as resulting in a new state of affairs that is not entirely derivable from separate variables.

In this view, transactional communication can be seen as a positive goal to be sought by communicators, a state of understanding superior to the achievement of one's own instrumental goals. In the transmissional and functionalist tradition, the goal of communicating is seen as getting another person to accept the first person's understanding. But in this positive view of transactional communication, the individual's instrumental goal is less important than establishing a new consensus or understanding.

The organizational climate or culture may or may not be conducive to achieving these sorts of dialogic transactions. Critical studies of organizational communication can make particular use of this approach, as critical theorists are typically concerned about attaining situations of "authentic" or "ideal" communication (see the discussion of Jürgen Habermas's theories in Chapter 2).

SUMMARY

There are many possible interpretations of the concept *communication,* and no one definition is the best, or most accurate. We understand communication as a process by which people make sense of their world by sharing conventionalized systems of meaning with one another. Many such conventional systems have evolved, including language and various nonverbal systems.

What a particular theorist emphasizes in communication, however, depends on that theorist's perspective toward communication. Five potential orientations or perspectives include the rhetorical, the transmissional, the psychological, the interactional, and the transactional. Each emphasizes a different set of factors or elements in communication:

Theoretical Perspective	Emphasis
Rhetorical	Message; persuasive strategy
Transmissional	Channel; encoding and decoding
Psychological	Individuals' conceptual filters
Interactional	Group development of self, roles
Transactional	Pattern (system) of interchanges; the relationships.

Each perspective suits a particular approach to or purpose of studies in the field of organizational communication:

• The rhetorical perspective lends itself to studies concerning internal and external messages that advocate an organizational position (organizational rhetoric). This perspective may also be employed by critical theorists who are interested in uncovering rhetorical strategies of dominant groups.

• The transmissional perspective is used for many different kinds of organizational communication studies. It lends itself well to analysis of information processing, breakdowns or barriers in channels of communication, and formal and informal networks (structures) for disseminating internal communication. This perspective is generally allied with a functionalist orientation.

• The psychological perspective deals with individuals' processing of communication. The focus on individuals as the unit of analysis implies studies concerning interpersonal relationships and psychological barriers to communication. How receivers interpret messages (say from the organization) is a major concern. Organizational climate, from this point of view, is seen as the sum of individuals' perceptions of how well an organization meets their psychological needs.

• The interactional perspective looks to groups as the channel for working through and developing understanding of organizational processes, values, and reality. This view lends itself well to studies of organizational cultures, their development, value systems, and possible changes. The focus on groups also suggests studies of team building and group problem solving.

• The transactional perspective usually is concerned with dyads (two-person relationships that continue over time). This frame of reference is therefore useful for analysis of dyadic relationships throughout the organization. Patterns of communicative interchanges provide a way of describing and explaining problems or breakdowns in relational communication.

EXERCISES AND QUESTIONS FOR DISCUSSION

1. Reread the quotation from Somerset Maugham at the start of this chapter. Do you agree that people are "shut in a tower of brass," unable to communicate directly with one another? Is communication between people as difficult as the quotation seems to suggest? Why or why not?

2. Write a definition of communication; try to include every aspect of communicating that you think is important. Divide into small groups and

share definitions. Try to get group agreement on the three most important defining characteristics of communication. Was this agreement easily reached? Why or why not? Compare your group's list of the three most important characteristics with those of other groups.

3. Rewrite definitions of communication, this time one for each of the five perspectives described in this chapter (rhetorical, transmissional, psychological, interactional, and transactional).

4. Why is the sentence, "They are flying airplanes," ambiguous? If you were to hear someone say this sentence, what would indicate for you the appropriate (or intended) interpretation? As a group, try to come up with other sentences that are similarly ambiguous. How do people decide what the "real" or "correct" definition for a word will be? Can they?

5. If it is available in your library, look through the book *Kinesics and Context*, by R. L. Birdwhistell (1970, University of Pennsylvania Press). Consider the diagrams of units of gestural language in this book. Is it possible to develop a systematic grammar of gestures, similar to the system of phonemics or grammar for language? The distinction that Watzlawick, Beavin, and Jackson make between digital and analogic coding systems could be relevant to this discussion.

6. Describe examples from your own experience in which people's use of space (spatial relationships) and time communicated some message to you. For example, have you ever stood in a crowded elevator facing the the back of the compartment and the other people? What reaction would you get if you did this? Along the same line, how do people avoid the intimacy that would be suggested by standing as close as they must in a crowded elevator? What would happen if you sat down on the floor during the elevator ride?

7. Describe your culture's rules regarding eye contact in public and the use of touching. Discuss possible differences in these rules as one moves from one culture to another.

8. What do your possessions ("your things") communicate about you? Make a list of the most likely messages people can derive from your clothes, your means of transportation, and your favorite possessions.

9. Try to draw a picture or model that describes communication from each of the five perspectives discussed in this chapter. Compare your models with those of others. Can you agree on a single model for each perspective?

SOURCES FOR FURTHER STUDY

Berger, Charles R., and Bradac, James J. (1982). *Language and social knowledge: Uncertainty in interpersonal relations*. London: Edward Arnold Ltd.

Cheney, G., and McMillan, J. J. (1990). Organizational rhetoric and the practice of criticism. *Journal of Applied Communication Research, 18,* 93–114.

Dahnke, G. L., and Clatterbuck, G. W. (Eds.) (1990). *Human communication: Theory and research*. Belmont, Calif.: Wadsworth.

Fisher, B. A. (1978). *Perspectives on human communication*. New York: Macmillan.

Goffman, E. (1959). *The presentation of self in everyday life*. Garden City, N.Y.: Doubleday Anchor.

Goffman, E. (1967). *Interaction ritual: Essays on face-to-face behavior*. Garden City, N.Y.: Doubleday Anchor.

Goffman, E. (1974). *Frame analysis*. Cambridge, Mass.: Harvard University Press.

Hall, E. T. (1966). *The hidden dimension*. Garden City, N.Y.: Doubleday Anchor.

Hall, E. T. (1977). *Beyond culture*. Garden City, N.Y.: Doubleday Anchor.

Hall, E. T. (1983). *The dance of life: The other dimension of time*. Garden City, N.Y.: Doubleday Anchor.

Infante, D. A., Rancer, A. S., and Womack, D. F. (1990). *Building communication theory*. Prospect Heights, Ill.: Waveland Press.

Knapp, M. L., and Miller, G. R. (1985). *Handbook of interpersonal communication.* Newbury Park, Calif.: Sage.

Krone, K. J., Jablin, F. F., and Putnam, L. L. (1987). Communication theory and organizational communication: Multiple perspectives. In F. M. Jablin, L. L. Putnam, K. H. Roberts, and L. W. Porter (Eds.), *Handbook of organizational communication: An interdisciplinary perspective.* Newbury Park, Calif.: Sage.

Littlejohn, S. W. (1992). *Theories of human communication,* 4th ed. Belmont, Calif.: Wadsworth.

Luhmann, N. (1992). Autopoesis: What is communication? *Communication Theory, 2,* 251–59.

Mead, G. H. (1943). *Mind, self, and society.* C. W. Morris (Ed.). Chicago: University of Chicago Press.

Miller, F. E., and Rogers, L. E. (1976). A relational approach to interpersonal communication. In G. R. Miller (Ed.), *Explorations in interpersonal communication.* Beverly Hills, Calif.: Sage.

Mortensen, C. D. (1991). Communication, conflict, and culture. *Communication Theory, 1,* 273–93.

Motley, M. T. (1990). On whether one can(not) not communicate: An examination via traditional communication postulates. *Western Journal of Speech Communication, 54,* 1–20.

Parks, M. R. (1977). Relational communication: Theory and research. *Human Communication Research, 3,* 372–81.

Pearce, W. B., and Cronen, V. E. (1982). *Communication, action and meaning: The creation of social realities.* New York: Holt, Rinehart & Winston.

Ruesch, J., and Bateson, G. (1968). *Communication: The social matrix of psychiatry.* New York: Norton.

Shannon, C. E., and Weaver, W. (1949). *The mathematical theory of communication.* Urbana, Ill.: University of Illinois Press.

Shimanoff, S. B. (1980). *Communication rules: Theory and research.* Beverly Hills, Calif.: Sage.

Stamp, Glen H., and Knapp, Mark L. (1990). The construct of intent in interpersonal communication. *Quarterly Journal of Speech, 76,* 282–99.

Stewart, J. (1990). Interpersonal communication: Contact between persons. In J. B. Stewart (Ed.), *Bridges not walls,* 5th ed. New York: McGraw-Hill. pp. 22–24.

Stewart, J. (1991). A postmodern look at traditional communication postulates. *Western Journal of Speech Communication, 55,* 354–79.

Tompkins, P. K., Fisher, J. Y., Infante, D. A., and Tompkins, E. L. (1975). Kenneth Burke and the inherent characteristics of formal organizations: A field study. *Speech Monographs, 42,* 135–42.

Trenholm, S. (1991). *Human communication theory,* 2d ed. Englewood Cliffs, N.J.: Prentice-Hall.

Watzlawick, P., Beavin, J., and Jackson, D. (1967). *Pragmatics of human communication.* New York: Norton.

Whaley, S., and Cheney, G. (1991). Review essay: Contemporary social theory and its implications for rhetorical and communication theory. *Quarterly Journal of Speech, 77,* 467–508.

Wilder, C. (1979). The Palo Alto Group: Difficulties and directions of the interactional view for human communication research. *Human Communication Research, 5,* 170–86.

NOTES

1. *Wall Street Journal,* January 20, 1993, p. B5.
2. W. S. Maugham (1919), *The moon and sixpence,* Salem, N.H.: Ayer Co.
3. *New York Times,* June 16, 1995, p. A7.
4. F. E. X. Dance (1970), The "concept" of communication, *Journal of Communication, 20,* 201–10.
5. G. Cheney and J. J. McMillan (1990), Organizational rhetoric and the practice of criticism, *Journal of Applied Communication Research, 18,* 93–114.
6. Cheney and McMillan, p. 102.
7. P. K. Tompkins, J. Y. Fisher, D. A. Infante, and E. L. Tompkins (1975), Kenneth Burke and the inherent characteristics of formal organizations: A field study, *Speech Monographs, 42,* 135–42.

8. B. A. Fisher (1978), *Perspectives on human communication,* New York: Macmillan.

9. C. E. Shannon and W. Weaver (1948), *The mathematical theory of communicaiton,* Urbana, Ill.: University of Illinois Press.

10. K. J. Krone, F. F. Jablin, and L. L. Putnam (1987), Communication theory and organizational communication: Multiple perspectives, in F. M. Jablin, L. L. Putnam, K. H. Roberts, and L. W. Porter (Eds.), *Handbook of organizational communication: An interdisciplinary perspective.* Newbury Park, Calif.: Sage, p. 23.

11. Fisher, p. 145.

12. G. H. Mead (1943), *Mind, self, and society,* Ed. C. W. Morris, Chicago: University of Chicago Press.

13. See Fisher, p. 179.

14. E. Goffman (1959), *The presentation of self in everyday life.* Garden City, N.Y.: Doubleday Anchor; E. Goffman (1967). *Interaction ritual.* Garden City, N.Y.: Doubleday Anchor; E. Goffman (1974), *Frame analysis,* Cambridge, Mass.: Harvard University Press.

15. Fisher, pp. 195–96.

16. C. Wilder (1979), The Palo Alto Group: Difficulties and directions of the interactional view for human communication research, *Human Communication Research* 5, 170–86.

17. P. Watzlawick, J. Beavin, and D. Jackson (1967), *Pragmatics of human communication: A study of interactional patterns, pathologies, and paradoxes,* New York: Norton.

18. See *Report of the President's Commission on the Accident at Three Mile Island* (1979), Washington, D.C.: U.S. Government Printing Office, pp. 8–9; and C. G. Herndle, B. A. Fennel, and C. Miller (1991), Understanding failures in organizational discourse: The accident at Three-Mile Island and the Shuttle Challenger, in C. Bazerman and J. Paradis (Eds.), *Textual dynamics of the professions,* Madison, Wis.: University of Wisconsin Press, pp. 279–305.

19. See J. Stewart (1990), Interpersonal communication: Contact between persons, in J. Stewart (Ed.), *Bridges not walls,* 5th ed., New York: McGraw-Hill.

PART TWO

Implications of Organization Theories for Organizational Communication

As observed in Chapter 1, organizing is a central human activity. For example, organizing early hunting parties was probably crucial to the development of many human traits, such as the use of language. Without cooperative efforts, early human beings lacked the physical strength and size to hunt successfully while protecting themselves from competing predators. Reliance on cooperative activity became even more pronounced as people discovered agriculture and developed village communities and then cities. Some of these organizations had to be very complex in order to construct the great city walls, temples, and pyramids.

Two trends in history have led to types of organizations differing from earlier types. First, the period in the eighteenth century called the Enlightenment accelerated the secularization of people's thinking about their lives and societies. Max Weber, the German philosopher and one of the founders of sociology, maintains that prior to this secularizing trend, leadership and authority within human organizations was based upon traditional or religious justifications.[1] As people turned away from these rationales for the exercise of authority, the thinkers of the Enlightenment championed rational thought and the scientific method as the new foundations for rightful or legitimate authority.

Second, the Industrial Revolution of the nineteenth century led to new ways of organizing people for work and production. These new industrial organizations emphasized a systematic means of production, the division of labor, and specialized occupations. In the earlier guild or cottage industries, workers learned their trade at home from family members; the product was constructed from start to finish in the home or family shop. Industrialization brought many people together in a factory. New sources of mechanical power, such as water and steam from coal burning, and industrial machinery, such as huge power looms, meant that individual craft workers could not afford the most efficient means for producing their products. Individuals no longer made a product from start to finish, from the raw materials through to the item for sale.

The famous analyst of the economic meaning of this new industrialism, Adam Smith, describes the importance of specialization and division of labor using the example of pin making. Prior to the employment of the division of labor in assembly-line production, one pin maker could make only a few pins a day—certainly not as many as twenty a day. But in Smith's time (the book was published in 1776), "One man draws out the wire, another straights it, a third cuts it, a fourth points it, a fifth grinds it at the top for receiving the head; . . ." and so on.[2] Smith reports that he observed ten workers who could, in this way, produce as many as 48,000 pins a day, or 4,800 per person. This example dramatically illustrates the benefits of the factory assembly-line production system. In the larger factories, particularly the textile mills, the new industrial system placed a premium on organization and coordination of large numbers of people.

The trends of rationalism and industrialization came together in the modern corporate organization. Authority within these corporate organizations was based on rational criteria, such as education, credentials or certifications, and special training, rather than on inheritance or religious revelation. The Industrial Revolution created the need for large-scale organization of workers and these new rationally selected supervisors.

By the closing decades of the nineteenth century, people began to study this phenomenon—the new industrial organization—in an effort to understand and improve it. Attempts to develop theories about the management of such organizations have continued down to the present. We now turn to an overview of the organizational and management theories that have resulted from these studies, because one's theory about the nature of organizations and management significantly influences and, more importantly, constrains how one thinks about communication within organizations. The field of organizational communication itself represents the marriage between organizational theory and communication theory.

Before continuing, it is important to remember that organizations have continued to evolve in response to social and technological changes. Certainly, communication and, especially, the new technologies of communication are driving forces in this evolution. The instantaneous communication provided by these technologies has permitted far-flung and global relationships and complexities.

It is even difficult to delimit some of these new organizations. When AT&T, for example, acquires an important interest in a huge cellular communications corporation, such as McCaw Communications, do we think of these as separate organizations or as one new and larger organization? Multinational corporations and agencies offer the same kinds of perplexing issues regarding the boundaries or limits that we may use to describe contemporary complex organizations.

Organizational theory, as well as theories of organizational communication, must continue to evolve along with these changes. A review of organizational theories and communication theories must be seen as description of an evolving and ever-changing area of research and development.

OVERVIEW OF ORGANIZATIONAL THEORIES

Various schemes for categorizing the different kinds of organizational theories have been developed. Most such schemes tend to agree on the first two categories: *classical or scientific management* and the *human relations movement.*

Beyond these first two types, the taxonomy (classifying scheme) that one chooses is a little more arbitrary. Some writers refer to a "neoclassical" school deriving from the earlier form of the classical organizational theories, including the works of the "decision theorists" such as Herbert Simon, James March, and others. These decision theorists receive more attention in later chapters dealing with leadership and decision making, but are discussed in Chapter 4 in connection with classical management developments. Theories and principles concerned with human resource development appear to be largely derived from the human relations movement, and so I group those theories with the human relations theories in Chapter 5.

Systems theories, developed from the concepts of general systems theory, became very popular beginning in the 1970s for describing organizations as living, functioning systems. *Contingency theories* of management, which are in many ways closely related to systems theory, represent a fourth approach. The view of organizations as cultures, the organizational or *corporate culture* school, is a fifth category. Other approaches, such as group ecology theories and group life-cycle theories, could be reviewed as well, but these theories are further from the concerns of organizational communication.

The categories of organizational theories to be reviewed in Part Two are therefore as follows:

Classical and Scientific Management

Human Relations and Human Resource Development

Systems Theories

Contingency Theories

Organizational Cultures

The main concern, of course, is the consequences that these different theories have for the nature of communication within organizations. The foundations for contemporary thinking about management and organizational theories are found in the first two categories, classical management and the human relations movement, and these two approaches are explained in the next two chapters. The following chapters deal with the implications of systems and contingency theories (Chapter 6) and the newer organizational culture approach (Chapter 7).

NOTES

1. M. Weber (1947), *The theory of social and economic organization,* Trans. A. M. Henderson and T. Parsons, New York: The Free Press.

2. Adam Smith (1925), *An inquiry into the nature and causes of the wealth of nations, I,* London: Methuen & Co., p. 6.

CHAPTER **4**

Development of Organizational Theories: Classical and Scientific Management Theories

CHAPTER OBJECTIVES

After studying this chapter, you should be able to:

- Describe the characteristics of a modern bureaucratic organization.
- Explain the advantages and disadvantages of bureaucracies.
- Explain why Taylorism is also known as *scientific* management.
- Describe the influence of classical management theories on modern management.
- Discuss the implications of classical management theory for the nature of communication within organizations.

CHAPTER OUTLINE

A BRIEF HISTORY OF CLASSICAL AND SCIENTIFIC MANAGEMENT THEORIES

The theories designated as classical management theories or scientific management theories developed from efforts to apply scientific methods and principles to the management of modern organizations. Adam Smith's description of pin making in early industrial England illustrates a systematic management theory going back to the beginnings of modern economics. In 1832, the British mathematician Charles Babbage published *On the Economy of Machinery and Manufactures*, which represented an early management theory based on the new principles of industrial organizations.[1] Like Smith, Babbage emphasized the importance of sequencing activities and the division of labor.

Among the early economic theorists of the nineteenth century, Karl Marx analyzed the new organizational form in some detail.[2] Marx was especially concerned with the separation of the worker from the tools of production and from the right to dispose of the completed product (Marx referred to this separation as "alienation"). In the cottage or craft industries of an earlier time, a cobbler, for example, owned the tools for making shoes, produced the whole shoe or boot, and then sold the shoes for his immediate profit. In the new factories, the worker usually did not own the looms or power tools and did not own the product produced in the factory. Marx pointed up the growing differentiation between the role of "labor," the individual workers, on the one hand, and managerial and entrepreneurial roles, on the other. All these roles would have been filled by the individual craft worker in the days before the great mills of northern England.

Marx, of course, believed that this alienation would eventually lead the workers to revolt against their exploitation by the capitalist class. Even so, the industrial organization would not disappear but would be placed under the collective leadership of the representatives of the workers.

Later in the nineteenth century, Emile Durkheim developed even more elaborate theories regarding the effects of division of labor and specialization on society as a whole. Durkheim was a founder of the newly developing social science that is now called sociology, and one of the other early pioneers of sociology, Max Weber, turned his attention to the new rational structure at the heart of modern organizations: the bureaucracy.

WEBER AND THE MODERN BUREAUCRACY

Max Weber's description of modern bureaucracy seems very familiar to anyone today who works in a modern organization, such as a corporation, a university, a government agency, or a school district. Although one may imagine that classical management theory is old-fashioned, we would be very uncomfortable working for organizations that did not hold to bureaucratic principles such as requiring specific education or training for specialized positions, efficient record keeping, or predictable and fixed salaries, based on experience and level of expertise. In fact, organizations that do not adhere to such principles may find themselves in legal trouble, if they are not able to produce records to show that hiring and promotion practices are based on demonstrable and rational criteria.

Weber's lifelong project was to explain how the "modern" differed from earlier stages in the history of human societies and organizations. Clearly, the new economic and political organizations that developed after the Enlightenment and especially in the nineteenth century in the West were central features of this modernity.

Weber's purpose was to describe and understand rational bureaucracies, rather than to prescribe how they should be designed and managed. Weber's principles became part of management theory as other theorists took his analysis of the rational organization and made his principles into prescriptive guidelines. Weber's major works were not translated into English until 1947 and 1948, meaning that his discussion of

People encounter bureaucracies in carrying out all kinds of daily business.

bureaucracy was largely undiscovered by American theorists until that time. His insights were picked up quickly by writers such as Peter M. Blau and Amitai Etzioni, becoming a standard part of the classical theory of organizations.[3]

A delineation of the major characteristics of bureaucracy clarifies what is meant by the rational nature of modern organizations. In short, bureaucratic organizations are characterized by the following characteristics:

- Fixed, usually *written, rules* for administration
- A *stable hierarchy* of offices (higher offices supervise the lower, subordinate offices)
- Maintenance of *written records or files*
- The requirement of *specialized training* for the occupants of offices

From these principles flows the special nature of the position that a person occupies within such an organization:

1. The position represents a full-time occupation for the officeholder. In other words, holding a position is looked upon as part of a person's career, which may involve moving through other offices over a period of time. We thus speak of people moving up a ladder as they progress in their careers.

2. The individual is usually appointed to the position, which is to say that the person does not have a hereditary or other special right to the position (although superior positions may be elective). The appointment is based on credible, rational qualifications that are often published or written in a legal form. In the United States these credentials often take the form of academic diplomas or degrees. Some positions require a special license, such as that for a pharmacist or a physician. Accountants may be expected to have their CPA, and lawyers must have passed the required bar exam.

3. The position carries an expectation of stable tenure. Weber believed that in many bureaucracies, offices were held for life or good behavior; at least there are usually safeguards against arbitrary dismissals without good cause. This characteristic is related to the notions of stability and positions as lifelong careers. Note that this rule applies only to office holders in the administrative structure or bureaucracy. Line workers, everyday laborers, usually do not have such tenure, apart from labor union contractual agreements.

4. The officeholder receives a regular salary and other benefits, such as an expected pension. The individual is therefore not directly involved in the ownership of the bureaucracy's properties or funds. The relationship between the holder of a position and the organization is said to be professional rather than personal.

Weber maintains that this type of modern bureaucracy is different from the "bureaucracies" that administered earlier, even huge institutions, such as the Spanish or Turkish empires. In these earlier administrations, the officeholders were personal companions or servants of the ruler or inherited their positions. The authority and purposes of the various offices were not clearly described and depended upon the personal proclivities of individuals. These ancient and feudal organizations, in other words,

DIVERSITY MATTERS

The Debate over Affirmative Action

A fundamental tenet of bureaucratic organizations is a rational foundation for hiring and promoting. All personal feelings and connections are to be excluded from these decisions, as the organization seeks the best-qualified person to fill a particular position or office. Although "bureaucracy" usually carries negative connotations for most people, objective and fair standards for hiring and promoting seem positive to most people.

As noted above, these objective standards are usually operationalized in terms of degrees, certificates, diplomas, and similar credentials and, occasionally, so many years of certain kinds of experience. A problem arises, however, if certain categories or groups of people have been excluded from opportunities to obtain these credentials or kinds of experience. For example, if minorities have been discriminated against in a way that makes it more difficult for them to obtain the necessary degrees and certificates, the seemingly objective standards may actually operate in a way that restricts their access to positions.

The U.S. Congress and various state legislatures have enacted a series of laws intended to overcome such barriers that seemed to exclude minorities and women in a systematic way. These laws are usually lumped together and referred to as affirmative action requirements. Affirmative action goes beyond the earlier standard of equal employment opportunity, in that the former is active whereas the latter is a passive strategy. An affirmative action employer or school actively seeks out and recruits potential applicants from disadvantaged groups rather than merely waiting for them to apply.

Affirmative action policies of schools and other organizations have come under attack as being un-fair, allegedly giving an unfair advantage to some groups at the expense of the majority.

The existence of an affirmative action policy and the way in which it is carried out and administered are basically communication activities of an organization. Recruiting, hiring, training, and evaluating organization members involve communication. Some organizations see affirmative action programs as unnecessary, burdensome, or unfair, whereas others see them as good business. Eastman Kodak, for example, would maintain such a program with or without legislative mandates. A company spokesman is quoted as saying, "If affirmative action wasn't legislated, we'd still continue with our goal of building a diverse work force."* The reasoning is that the workforce and the American population is increasingly diverse, and so should be the business hierarchy. Still, even in corporations committed publicly to affirmative action, only about 5 percent of senior-level jobs are held by women, who constitute 50 percent of the workforce; only 3 percent of such jobs are held by African Americans and other minorities.**

The issue concerns the best ways to redress the imbalances in the gender and ethnic makeup of upper-level management positions while avoiding new kinds of discrimination and unfairness. Can the principle of objective and rational standards for appointment to positions in an organization be maintained?

*_Wall Street Journal_, March 20, 1995, p. B1.

**_New York Times_, May 5, 1991, p. F6; _Wall Street Journal_, March 20, 1995, p. B1.

were not based on rational, scientific principles of order, stability, and technical competence.

One foundation for modern theories of management was therefore the careful analysis of bureaucratic structures by Max Weber, who maintained that these new kinds of organizations were more rational and therefore more modern than earlier types. The next foundation was the application of modern scientific principles to the direct managing of work itself.

FREDERICK WINSLOW TAYLOR AND SCIENTIFIC MANAGEMENT

The American Frederick Winslow Taylor is often described as the "father of scientific management." Born in the middle of the last century, Taylor at first aimed for law school but instead turned to engineering work in a machine shop. He worked his way up to chief engineer for Midvale Steel Works in Philadelphia by 1890. Increasingly, he devoted himself to developing his theories of applying scientific and engineering principles to management until his death in 1915.

The concepts Taylor developed are still quite influential almost a century later. Edward Lawler, the director of the Center for Effective Organizations at the University of Southern California, writes, "Although the term *scientific management* is not widely used today, most of the concepts inherent in Taylor's early work dominate current thinking about how to organize and manage corporations."[4] These principles were based on the ideas of standardization and systematization. The work to be done was studied objectively and minutely in order to break it down into the simplest steps. Workers were then trained in the most efficient and least fatiguing way to carry out these steps. The function of managers was to plan how to carry out the work and to direct the workers in the execution of the plan.

An early example will indicate how these principles could be applied. Taylor noticed that the coal shovelers who were hired as day laborers at the steel yard all brought their own shovels from home—snow shovels, spades, whatever. He found that if the company provided each worker with a shovel of standard shape and size, the workers could handle three to four times as much coal per day as before. This increased productivity also resulted from training each worker in the most efficient technique for shoveling. Naturally, it would have been less productive to train a new set of workers each day, and so instead of day laborers, regular full-time laborers were hired as shovelers. Although fewer workers were needed as a result of the more efficient methods, those who were hired had more security and the benefit of regular wages.

"Taylorism" was thus based upon careful observation and measurement in order to determine the most efficient motions for carrying out a specific task. Taylor's principles have therefore given rise to so-called time and motion studies and efficiency experts. The consequence was the separation of the mental work of managers from the physical work of the laborers. The workers had no responsibility other than to do the work in exactly the manner prescribed by the managers. Taylor began his studies at a time when American industry was beginning to absorb a large number of immigrant workers, many of whom had only a limited grasp of English and were felt to be incapable of directing themselves. This situation is represented in the famous passage in Taylor's book on scientific management in which he portrays the pig-iron hauler, Schmidt, with a stereotyped and ungrammatical German accent, as in the following passage:

> "Schmidt, are you a high-priced man?"
> "Vell, I don't know vat you mean."[5]

Instead of the usual $1.15 per day, Schmidt is offered $1.85 per day to load a pile of pig iron onto a railroad car. When he understands that he is to get the higher pay every day that he loads that much, he agrees. The usual load a day was 12.5 tons; the new load would be 47 tons, nearly four times as much.

Schmidt is strictly directed to do exactly as he is told, with no back talk, if he is to be "a high-priced man." Pointing out a young supervisor, the manager orders Schmidt to do exactly what the young man says, "When he tells you to pick up a pig and walk, you pick it up and you walk, and when he tells you to sit it down and rest, you sit down. . . . And what's more, no back talk. Now a high-priced man does just what he's told to do, and no back talk."[6]

This separation in American industry between the functions of managers and workers was permanently set in labor law and union contracts beginning in the early part of this century. The division of employees into "exempt" and "nonexempt" or "bargaining unit" is now standard in many kinds of organizations.

Later, Taylorism was criticized for treating workers as living machines instead of as thinking human beings. But the division of the work into these two parts, mental and physical, Taylor believed, would lead to a genuine cooperation and feeling of teamwork on the part of workers and managers. He did not see this division of work as demeaning or dehumanizing to the laborer at that time. He further believed that the increased efficiency would lead to higher wages and increased happiness and security for the workers, resulting in an end to strikes and labor unrest. The principal object of scientific management, according to Taylor, "should be to secure the maximum prosperity for the employer, coupled with the maximum prosperity for each employee."[7]

For our purposes, the important element in Taylor's theories is the creation of the profession of management. The manager's skills were to be in managing per se, rather than in any particular manufacture or industry. The principles of management were the same, in Taylorism, whether one was involved in making pins, steel, or automobiles or in running a railroad. Professional managers therefore went to school to learn *managing* rather than a specific business. The management principles thus learned could be applied in other settings involving the coordination of the activities of large numbers of people.

These principles of scientific management were quickly adapted to other than industrial bureaucracies. A major example of such adaptation was the American public education system. The new industrial expansion of the early 1900s required a system of mass education that would indoctrinate large numbers of formerly rural people and immigrants in the habits and skills needed by employers. Consequently, there was

AN ISSUE OF COMMUNICATION ETHICS

Modern Times

The negative side of the impact of scientific management can be seen in fears of efficiency experts run wild. The overzealous application of scientific management methods was spoofed in Charlie Chaplin's famous film *Modern Times,* in which Chaplin's character is caught up in machinery, as a part of the machinery of a modern factory. The alienation of the workers in modern manufacturing plants has continued to be a theme of literature and film. The satirical film *Roger and Me* concerned an effort by a documentary filmmaker to get an appointment with Roger Smith, then head of General Motors, to get him to explain why he was closing plants in Flint, Michigan, leading to the economic decline of the filmmaker's home town.

The standardizing of work envisioned in Taylor's principles has become enshrined in many companies. The repetitive and unrewarding nature of such standardized jobs has made workers feel alienated and dehumanized—the complaint that people are treated as "units" rather than as human individuals. Health problems have also been traced to repetitive muscle actions, leading to conditions such as carpal tunnel syndrome.

In terms of communication ethics, the emphasis on the separation of "brain" work from the labor of people on the floor of manufacturing plants can lead to stereotyping of the line workers as somehow less valuable or worthy. As the American economy moves from an industrial to a ser-

Modern bureaucratic organizations can appear unfeeling to many people.

vice economy, there is a tendency to transfer similar attitudes to the service worker as well: the servers in restaurants, tellers in banks, clerks in stores, and so on.

The development of new technologies has permitted organizations to conduct sophisticated surveillance of their workers to monitor their behavior. The intent of such surveillance is to prevent employee theft as well as general goofing off or incompetence. Cameras have been placed in locker rooms, bathrooms, and changing rooms, allowing monitors to film employees changing clothes or engaged in presumably private behavior. Several workers have filed lawsuits in such cases, claiming invasion of privacy. Aside from the legal issues, there are questions involving feelings of trust and commitment to the organization. Some workers say that they feel betrayed when they learn that they have been filmed and spied on. One waiter secretly filmed in his underwear complained that after working hard for the company, he was spied upon: "This really soils it all," he concluded.*

The industry providing closed-circuit cameras and televisions for business surveillance is booming and will do an estimated $2.1 billion of business in the year 1995. Revenues of such companies are expected to increase 62 percent by the year 2000.** Technological improvements leading to smaller and smaller cameras that can be hidden in flowers, books, exit signs, and the like mean that workers can expect more secret monitoring in the future.

Should organizations communicate to workers that such surveillance devices are being used? Are the interests of preventing drug use and abuse on the job, theft, and slacking sufficient to justify these kinds of surveillance? How should organizations deal with the communication issues such activities involve?

Newsweek, July 17, 1995, p. 52.

**Newsweek*, July 17, 1995, p. 52.

a demand for a quick increase in the number of relatively inexpensive teachers. Taylor's principles seemed ready-made for this situation. Managers, nearly always male, became the directors and supervisors (principals) of a workforce of largely female, and therefore less powerful and less well paid, teachers. Instead of being generalists responsible for several different grades and subjects, teachers were now specialized by student grade and by subject, in the same way that manufacturing work had been compartmentalized and broken down into specialties. Teachers were given explicit instructions on what to cover, at what rate, often in lockstep fashion, as the pupils moved through a standardized curriculum, often subject to standardized tests. It is therefore not surprising that public teachers have become unionized like their laboring counterparts in American industry.[8]

The example of public education shows how Taylor's theories can be and were applied in nonindustrial settings. It also indicates the continuing influence of these theories. The notions of standardization and the separation of managing from performing the front-line work were seen as ways to create more efficient large-scale organizations. The third foundation of classical management theory involved elaboration of the notion of administration as a profession.

HENRI FAYOL AND ADMINISTRATION AS A PROFESSION

Like Taylor, Henri Fayol was extremely successful in applying his principles in a practical setting. Taking over a nearly bankrupt mining and manufacturing business in 1888, Fayol made this firm into one of the strongest in Europe by his retirement in 1918. Also like Taylor, he spent his retirement years advocating the application of his management theories in all kinds of fields. Fayol concentrated on the upper levels of administration, whereas Taylor had concentrated more on supervision at the work level.

Fayol emphasized that running a large organization required that some one person have a grasp of the overall picture and be responsible for general direction and planning. This overall responsibility was subdivided as specific functions were delegated to administrators, who reported directly to the top executive. The system hence depended upon departmentalization and a clear line of responsibility and command in a hierarchy, as represented in modern organization charts, such as that shown in Figure 4.1.

The work of the administrator is seen as something different from work carried out by other professionals. Henry Mintzberg began his famous study *The Nature of Managerial Work* by noting how difficult it sometimes is to specify exactly what it is that chief executives do.[9] Executives often respond that they are "in charge" or are "responsible for what goes on around here," but those responses do not describe actual activities. Fayol tried to answer this question. The five tasks that he saw for managers were the following:

1. Planning
2. Organizing, or bringing together the necessary elements for the organization to carry out its tasks
3. Commanding or directing
4. Coordinating the different functions and units of the organization
5. Controlling, or seeing that organization members complied with rules, procedures, and regulations

Carrying out these tasks requires that the executive's work be somewhat unstructured compared to that of middle-level supervisors and line workers. One day might be focused on planning; another, on overseeing compliance with procedures; another, with a combination of organizing and coordinating activities; and so on. Executives' work days are therefore varied and occasionally unpredictable.

In order to ensure the proper execution of these administrative tasks, the organization must follow certain basic principles in Fayol's system:

1. Division of work, or specialization and departmentalization.
2. Establishment of a clear line of authority, or chain of command. It must be clear who reports to whom concerning what tasks or functions.
3. Unity of command or authority. Each person should have only one superior to whom he or she is responsible, to prevent conflicting demands or loyalties.
4. Unity of direction, meaning that one department head is responsible for a similar group of activities directed toward the same objective (departmental responsibilities should not overlap).

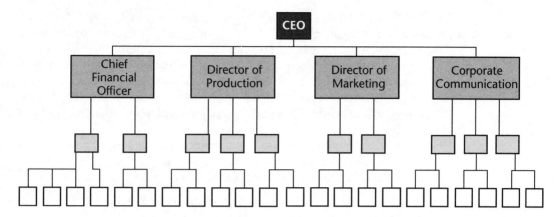

FIGURE 4.1   Hierarchical structure of a classically managed organization.

5. Authority accompanying areas of responsibility; in other words, a manager should have enough authority to ensure that his or her directions are carried out in meeting the responsibilities of that department or office.
6. Limited span of control. Each manager should be responsible for supervising a fairly limited number of subordinates to ensure that he or she can keep abreast of what each subordinate is doing.
7. Esprit de corps. Within the administrative ranks, there should be a loyalty and a spirit for promoting the general good of the organization. The administrators should think of themselves as a team working together.

Fayol also emphasized the importance of encouraging initiative as part of developing esprit de corps and improving efficiency. He believed that equitable and fair treatment of all in the organization also contributed to this more effective climate. Despite the appearance of strict adherence to departmentalization and chain of command, Fayol recognized that there were times when effective communication within the organization required some horizontal communication between people at the same level but in different departments ("Fayol's gangplank"). The limitation was that the immediate supervisors of the two members communicating across departments had to be informed and had to authorize the communication link. Fayol hence sought ways to make the bureaucratic organization, as described by Weber, more effective through these principles of esprit de corps, initiative, equity, and allowing limited horizontal communication.

CLASSICAL MANAGEMENT TRAINING

Fayol's principles should look familiar to some, because they became the initial basis for education in the field known as business administration in the United States. Today organizations are typically run by people whose training is in "administration," based upon the principles just described. The key point was the notion that the scientific method of careful observation and research should be applied to business management. In the mid-1920s, Mary Parker Follett emphasized that the use of arbitrary authority in the making of business decisions was diminishing, and that the self-taught leader operating on the basis of intuition and experience was no longer the norm.[10] While managers had by then accepted the idea that the use and control of the material and machines of production should follow scientific principles, they had not up to then accepted that scientific principles should be applied to the managing of people as well. But this application of science to the management of human resources was precisely the point of the new classical management.

In America, Fayol's principles were elaborated by writers such as Follett and Luther Gulick, who coined the acronym POSDCORB to describe the work of a chief executive. POSDCORB stands for the activities of administering:

Planning objectives and general methods for meeting those objectives

Organizing, which to Gulick implied establishing the formal structure for carrying out the organization's functions

Staffing by recruiting and training qualified administrators and staff

Directing, or making decisions and translating those decisions into orders or directives

Coordinating the various activities of the organization

Reporting by keeping appropriate administrators informed on progress, objectives, plans, and the like

Budgeting in terms of fiscal planning, record keeping, and control

Generations of business administration and MBA students have memorized this acronym. In his landmark study *The Nature of Managerial Work,* Henry Mintzberg reminds readers, "POSDCORB permeates the writings of popular theorists such as Peter Drucker," as well as industrial leaders who are asked to describe their functions.[11]

The notion that directing and controlling the work of human beings could be a true science was exciting to the founders of the field of business administration. The excitement led to a faith that research would reveal the best scientific and engineering principles for managing any kind of large organization. Many of the later directions in management theory are either responses to or efforts at refining the initial theories of Weber, Taylor, and Fayol.

COMMUNICATION IMPLICATIONS OF CLASSICAL MANAGEMENT THEORY

The very influential nature of classical management theory means that many organizations continue to be administered in accordance with these or very similar kinds of principles. By looking at the elements of the framework of organizational communication introduced in Chapter 2, the effects on organizational communication can be summarized.

Context

Classical management theory considered the internal management of organizations or businesses separate from their environment or relationships to other organizations. The emphasis was on developing methods that could be used for administering any kind of large organization, without regard to environment or competitors. As a result, in classical theories there is usually little concern over communication with other entities in the environment.

An important feature of the context at the time of the early development of these theories was confidence in the application of the scientific method to human behavior. In addition, the separation of thinking work (management) from physical work occurred in the context of a large influx of immigrant and rural labor in the new manufacturing firms of the later nineteenth and early twentieth centuries.

Organizational Shape and Structure

Weber and Fayol largely determined the structure within which communication ought to occur in bureaucratic organizations. They emphasized formal chains of command and lines of authority. The structure of the offices and their hierarchical relationships exist apart from the persons who work within them. The intent is to eliminate the effects of individual idiosyncrasies and personalities on the functioning of the organization. Individual motives, personal styles, and attitudes are therefore not to be factors in how the activities of the organization are carried out. Structure is more important than personal characteristics in classically managed firms.

A person's location in the hierarchy determines the nature of that person's work and the communication that that person has with others in the organization. Executives near the top of the organization chart have most interaction with other managers and their staffs. First-line supervisors are more likely to communicate directly with workers.

Message Behavior

Message behavior refers to the content, symbols, and codes that organization members use in their interactions. Fayol and Weber, as well as Gulick's POSDCORB, emphasize the importance of record keeping, which in turns places importance on written communication. Contemporary organizations are relying more and more on electronic record keeping as well. Taylor did allow for the importance of face-to-face verbal communication in giving directions and training for the workers. Clearly these are to be very specific instructions and procedures in a classically managed organization. There is little expectation of discussion with subordinates regarding the best way to perform their operations. The communication is nearly always envisioned as one-way, from managers down to workers. Recall that Schmidt was informed that "high-priced" workers did not question the directions they were given.

Methods and Modalities of Communication

Fayol's principles also emphasized the importance of vertical communication in maintaining the scalar chain and unity of command and action. Even when horizontal communication was allowed by his "gangplank," immediate superiors in the vertical line of communication had to be involved. The chain of command, in most cases, becomes a medium for transmitting messages from the top levels of the organization down to the bottom. As previously noted, permanent record keeping and filing are central concerns; memoranda tend to become the basis for the collective memory and precedents of the organization.

Until recently, IBM carried the concern with hierarchy and memos to something of an extreme. There were four kinds of memos, each with a corresponding type of envelope indicating the level of access and secrecy accorded to the message. The four levels, moving from the lowest level to the highest level of secrecy, were IBM Internal Use Only, IBM Confidential, IBM Confidential Restricted, and Registered IBM Confidential.[12] A set of written rules indicated exactly which level of the bureaucracy had access to which type of memo (and envelope). Now there is only one level of memo and one type of memo envelope. The rule book has been scrapped, replaced with the simpler idea that "confidential" relates only to information dealing with customer lists, technical data, and similar material that provides the company a competitive advantage. Now IBMers will have to exercise their own judgment concerning what should be classified confidential.

Communication Activities

Communication activities are clearly delineated according to one's place in the hierarchy. Managers have the specific functions of organizing, directing, and coordinating the activities of others. They provide the directions, and the subordinates carry them out. There is no real need for leading or motivating subordinates or organization members through communication; the motivation is provided by an understanding of the reward system of the organization. It is assumed that people will "soldier," to use Taylor's term, which means that they will generally do as little as necessary to get by unless they can be shown some immediate, tangible reward for increased effort. Like Marx, Taylor believed that economic rewards were the basis for motivation.

Problem solving and decision making are clearly functions of professional mangers, trained for their specific roles. The decisions are communicated to subordinates, who are not involved in the discussions regarding these decisions because it is assumed that they lack the education and special training necessary to participate meaningfully in such discussions.

Taylor assumed that the increased prosperity of workers and managers alike, following the application of scientific management principles, would lead to reduced industrial conflict. Organizations are seen as having a single goal and set of objectives determined by upper management, and so there is no need to resolve conflicts regarding such matters. Bargaining is thought of in terms of labor contracts concerning rates of pay, work conditions, and benefits.

Classical management approaches are compatible with a functionalist perspective on organizational communication, given the primacy assumed for management and administrative objectives. Attention is given to how best to further these objectives through effectively transmitting management's messages to organization members.

SUMMARY

Modern organizations developed in response to trends present in the Enlightenment and the Industrial Revolution, leading to increased rationalization in human affairs and corporate industrial structures. Various types of organizational theories have been developed to explain and analyze modern organizations. While there is no general agreement on ways to categorize all these theories, there is such agreement on the first two types: classical management theory and human relations theories.

Classical management theory rests on the foundational work of Max Weber (theories of modern bureaucracies), Frederick W. Taylor (scientific management), and Henri Fayol (administration as a profession applicable to any kind of organization). The principles of classical management, transmit-ted through systems like Gulick's POSDCORB, continue to exercise considerable influence.

The communication implications of classical theory include an emphasis on formal lines of top-down, one-way communication, relying on written records (files), memos, and directives. There is little expectation of or allowance for discussion at lower levels of the hierarchy. Organizations are seen as single-goal entities (the goals of upper management).

The human relations theories taken up in the next chapter share some basic concepts with classical management: Both emphasize the primacy of upper-management goals and reliance on social science methods.

EXERCISES AND QUESTIONS FOR DISCUSSION

1. Read and discuss the first chapter of Adam Smith's *Wealth of Nations*. Does his description of factory production sound up to date? Is "division of labor" a necessary feature of modern organizations? Give examples of increasing specialization in sports, entertainment, and education.

2. Why do the words *bureaucrat* and *bureaucratic* often carry negative connotations? Give examples of negative experiences that you have had with bureaucrats. Now try to develop a list of advantages of bureaucracies and bureaucrats. How have the rules of bureaucracy worked in favor of increasing opportunities for minorities, for example? What kind of organization would you find more agreeable than a bureaucratic one?

3. If available, read the complete section of Taylor's book involving the example of the pig-iron hauler, Schmidt. What are Taylor's views regarding immigrants? regarding laborers? How do you think these views influenced his principles?

4. Describe the job of an administrator. If possible, interview administrators at a school or university: How do they characterize the sort of work that they do? List the functions that administrators seem to have in common, regardless of the kind of organization involved. Is there a distinction between an administrator and an executive?

5. Discuss the issues involved in developing "objective standards" and credentials for hiring, firing, and promoting in bureaucratic organizations. When are such standards beneficial? Can they be detrimental? What are the implications for diversity in organizations? Is affirmative action usually beneficial or harmful?

6. Discuss the effects of standardization in the workplace. Are organizations justified in demanding conformity among employees? What about standardized clothing or dress codes? How do you feel about organizations secretly monitoring workers? Under what circumstances is this justified? How should organizations communicate about such policies?

SOURCES FOR FURTHER STUDY

Blau, P. M. (1956). *Bureaucracy in modern society.* New York: Random House.

Blau, P. M. (1974). *On the nature of organizations.* New York: Wiley.

Cherrington, D. J. (1989). *Organizational behavior: The management of individual and organizational performance.* Boston: Allyn & Bacon.

Clegg, S. R. (1990). *Modern organizations.* Newbury Park, Calif.: Sage.

Cyert, R. M., and Marsh, J. G. (1963). *A behavioral theory of the firm.* Englewood Cliffs, N.J.: Prentice-Hall.

Drucker, P. F. (1974). *Management: Tasks, responsibilities, practices.* New York: Harper & Row.

Etizioni, A. (1961). *A comparative analysis of complex organizations.* New York: The Free Press.

Fayol, H. (1937). The administrative theory in the state. Greer, S., Trans. In L. Gulick and L. Urwick (Eds.), *Papers on the science of administration.* New York: Institute of Public Administration.

Harrison, J. F. C. (1973). *The birth and growth of industrial England, 1714–1867.* New York: Harcourt Brace Jovanovich.

Herzberg, F. (1966). *Work and the nature of man.* Cleveland: World Publishing.

Koontz, H. (1961). The management theory jungle. *The Academy of Management Journal, 1,* 174–88.

Lawler, E. E. (1992). *The ultimate advantage: Creating the high-involvement organization.* San Francisco: Jossey-Bass.

Marshall, R., and Tucker, M. (1992). *Thinking for a living.* New York: Basic Books.

Matteson, M. T., and Ivancevich, J. M. (Eds.) (1986). *Management and organizational behavioral classics,* 4th ed. Homewood, Ill.: BPI-Irwin.

Mayo, E. (1933). *The human problems of an industrial organization.* New York: Macmillan.

Mintzberg, H. (1973). *The nature of managerial work.* New York: HarperCollins.

Parsons, T. A. (1956). Suggestions for a sociological approach to the theory of organization. *Administrative Science Quarterly, 1.*

Pfeffer, J. (1982). *Organizations and organization theory.* Boston: Pitman.

Presthus, R. (1962). *The organizational society.* New York: Vintage.

Pugh, D. S, and Hickson, D. J. (Eds.) (1989). *Writers on organizations,* 4th ed. Newbury Park, Calif.: Sage.

Scott, W. Richard. (1981). *Organizations: Rational, natural and open systems.* Englewood Cliffs, N.J.: Prentice-Hall.

Shafritz, J. M., and Ott, J. S. (Eds.) (1987). *Classics of organization theory,* 2d ed. Chicago: The Dorsey Press.

Simon, H. A. (1957). *Administrative behavior.* New York: The Free Press.

Smith, Adam (1925). *An inquiry into the nature and causes of the wealth of nations, I.* London: Metheun & Co.

Taylor, F. W. (1911). *The principles of scientific management.* New York: Harper & Brothers.

Weber, M. (1947). *The theory of social and economic organization.* Henderson, A. M., and Parsons, T., Trans. New York: The Free Press.

NOTES

1. C. Babbage (1989), *On the economy of machinery and manufactures,* New York: New York University Press.

2. Works by and about Marx are voluminous; the standard work setting forth his analysis of industrial society is Marx. K. (1936), *Capital, a critique of political economy [Das Kapital],* New York: The Modern Library; see J. Elster (1985), *Making sense of Marx,* Cambridge: Cambridge University Press.

3. S. R. Clegg (1990), *Modern organizations,* London: Sage, p. 27; P. M. Blau (1974), *On the nature of organizations,* New York: Wiley; P. M. Blau (1956), *Bureaucracy in modern society,* New York: Random House; A. Etizioni

(1961), *A comparative analysis of complex organizations,* New York: The Free Press.

4. E. E. Lawler (1992), *The ultimate advantage: Creating the high-involvement organization,* San Francisco: Jossey-Bass, p. 27.

5. F. W. Taylor, (1911), *The principles of scientific management,* New York: Harper & Brothers, p. 44.

6. Taylor, p. 46.

7. Taylor, p. 9.

8. R. Marshall and M. Tucker (1992), *Thinking for a living,* New York: Basic Books.

9. H. Mintzberg (1973), *The nature of managerial work,* New York: HarperCollins, pp. 1–2.

10. M. Follett (1986), Management as a profession, in M. T. Matteson and J. M. Ivancevich (Eds.), *Management and organizational behavioral classics,* 4th ed., Homewood, Ill.: BPI-Irwin, pp. 8–9.

11. Mintzberg, p. 10.

12. *Wall Street Journal,* April 4, 1995, p. B1.

CHAPTER **5**

Human Relations and Human Resource Development Theories

CHAPTER OBJECTIVES

After studying this chapter, you should be able to:

- Contrast the basic concepts of classical management theories and the human relations movement.
- Describe the development of theories from the early human relations movement to human resource development and participative management theories.
- Explain the importance of the concepts of organizational and communication climate.
- Explain the importance of organizational socialization and commitment in human relations theories of motivation.
- Compare and contrast the major implications for organizational communication of the different theories described.

CHAPTER OUTLINE

The Human Relations Movement
The Hawthorne Studies
Human Relations, Participative Management, and Human Resources

Developments in Human Relations and Human Resource Theories
Theory X and Theory Y
PDM (Participative Decision Making)
The Managerial Grid
Argyris and the Role of the Individual in the Organization
Highlights of the Human Relations Movement
■ AN ISSUE OF COMMUNICATION ETHICS: Participation or Manipulation

THE HUMAN RELATIONS MOVEMENT

The management theories associated with the human relations movement are often described as being in opposition to the scientific management theories. The seeds for the human relations theories of management, like those for scientific management, were sown in the early days of the English Industrial Revolution. At New Lanark, Robert Dale Owen demonstrated that treating the workers, the "hands," humanely and well could lead to increased productivity better than the workhouse methods so popular with other industrialists of the age.[1] Taylor himself approved of improving working conditions in many ways similar to the methods of the early human relations theorists. He cites favorably the example of shortening work hours (from 10½ hours per day to 8½ hours) and providing frequent rest stops for girls inspecting bicycle ball bearings.[2]

The Hawthorne Studies

The series of studies that became the basis for the human relations movement were begun in the spirit of scientific management in 1927. The empirical bent of scientific management suggested that physical conditions, such as fatigue, lighting, ventilation, and physical layout of the work space, were the main determiners of work output. The Committee on Work in Industry of the National Research Council therefore initiated a long series of studies at a Western Electric plant near Chicago in the hope of isolating these physical environmental conditions in more detail.[3] The research itself was

days and workweeks, and allowing refreshments at various times. In addition to varying these conditions, the experimenters occasionally returned to the original conditions with regard to rest periods, hours of work, and so on. No matter what changes were introduced—whether longer or shorter hours, whether more or fewer (or no) rest breaks—output rose steadily over the period of the experiments. There was no correlation between any of the changes and this continual rise in the workers' productivity. Finally, the researchers had to conclude that physical conditions alone could not account for the changes they had observed.

The researchers concluded that the key to the significant improvements in output over the period of the experiments lay in their interviews with the women who participated in the studies. The women were aware that they produced at a much faster rate in the experimental rooms than they had before and attributed this improvement to two factors: (1) working in the test rooms was more enjoyable, and (2) they felt more at ease with their new relationship with the experimental supervisors than they had with the older supervisory relationship in the original plant setting.[4]

The social conditions, including the relationships of the workers with one another and the relationship between the workers and supervisors, were determined to be the significant factors in improving productivity. First, the workers were allowed freer conversation among themselves; this had been severely restricted under the original work conditions. Second, the workers were aware they were participating in an important experiment; they therefore felt that they had more significance than when they were seen as simply operators or hands. Third, the women developed a strong liking for one another and their group, which seemed to result in their "carrying" one another and helping one another. Fourth, the group of workers exhibited internal, self-appointed leadership and goal setting that arose naturally from their own interaction. These factors all became important elements in the principles of human relations management and the developing field of industrial psychology.

In sum, the Hawthorne experiments, led by the Harvard researchers Elton Mayo and F. J. Roethlisberger, resulted in the conclusion that interpersonal and group relationships and communication were more important in determining worker effectiveness and efficiency than the external physical conditions emphasized in the scientific management approach.

Human Relations, Participative Management, and Human Resources

The original classical theorists believed that work output depended upon the structure of the organization (it should be rational and coordinated) and the physical conditions of the work. The human relations approach countered that people could be made more efficient, and could be better motivated to perform productively, when they were more personally involved and engaged in the work. Communication between managers and subordinates should be more open and involve sharing points of view (the favored term was *two-way communication*) rather than one-way, top-down directive communication *from* managers *to* subordinates.

DEVELOPMENTS IN HUMAN RELATIONS AND HUMAN RESOURCE THEORIES

Chester Barnard's 1938 book on management theory represented the new emphasis on interpersonal communication within the organization as a means to facilitate co-operation throughout the firm.[5] Barnard had had a very successful career as the head of New Jersey Bell and, like Fayol, believed that he had acquired insights from his experience that would be useful for others. He stressed communication as the central function of organizing.

A work of the 1950s, however, became especially influential in management and organizational theories, leading to many of the participative approaches popularized in the 1960s. This book, which became a standard for management seminars during this period, was Abraham Maslow's *Motivation and Personality,* and its most famous feature was Maslow's "hierarchy of needs."[6] Maslow theorizes that people are motivated to fulfill certain needs, which are arranged in order from lower, more basic survival needs to higher, more abstract personal needs. The lower, survival needs, such as food and shelter, must be met before a person is motivated to meet the higher-order needs, such as those for friendship, esteem, and, at the pinnacle of his hierarchy, "self-actualization."

Maslow's scheme thus shows these kinds of needs arranged from bottom (most basic) to top, the location of the "higher" needs:

Self-actualization

Esteem

Social needs, belongingness

Safety or security

Survival (food, water, etc.)

Refinements of this approach by later theorists, such as Clayton Alderfer and David McClelland, reorganized or renamed the kinds of motivational needs. The idea remained, however, that there were essentially needs related to existence and survival, those related to human and group relationships and affiliation, and those related to personal achievement and power. Obviously, classical or scientific management and human relations theories could be differentiated by showing how each appealed to different levels of needs on this hierarchy. The classical theorists believed in motivating people by appeals to basic survival needs (pay and secure employment), whereas the humanist approach appealed to needs for human relationships and affiliation and for personal growth and achievement.

Theory X and Theory Y

Douglas McGregor's distinction between two management philosophies regarding the nature of human motivation has become especially influential.[7] It is now standard to inquire whether an executive is a Theory X or a Theory Y manager. According to McGregor, those who held the first theory believed that people were motivated by material incentives, such as pay and bonuses, and by disincentives, such as threats and discipline. In other words, they looked to Maslow's lower-order physiological and safety needs. Those who held the second, Theory Y, believed instead that people were best motivated by having meaningful and enjoyable work to do, by being involved in decisions about the work, and by feeling that what they did was important (echoing the conclusions from the interviews with the women in the Hawthorne studies).

McGregor's theories are thus theories about human personality and motivation, rather than theories about management per se. The point is that the way managers behave in motivating their subordinates depends on which of the two theories they believe to be accurate. McGregor believes that the more productive organizations are those based on a Theory Y orientation rather than those that follow Theory X.

PDM (Participative Decision Making)

Rensis Likert was a professor of psychology and sociology at the University of Michigan when he presented his major work *The Human Organization* in 1967.[8] Noting that the physical assets, machinery, and equipment of an organization were unproductive without human effort, he maintains, "Every aspect of a firm's activities is determined by the competence, motivation, and general effectiveness of its human organization. Of all the tasks of management, managing the human component is the central and most important task, because all else depends upon how well it is done."[9] Likert, then, places emphasis on the human element in organizations. Likert's methodology for approaching the study of management practice was very much that of the functional, empirical school of behavioral science. He stresses at the beginning of his work, "The art of management can be based on verifiable information derived from rigorous, quantitative research."[10] His methodological approach is hence the same as that of Taylor, and of Mayo and Roethlisberger; both classical management and the human relations approach were grounded in a firm belief in the efficacy of the scientific method.

Likert's research method involved having managers fill out survey forms based on sets of continua, along which respondents indicated where they felt their firm fell, for a series of variables. Down the left side of the form were the organizational variables, such as leadership processes, motivation techniques used, and character of communication, that the respondents were to score.

Each continuum is divided into four sectors, labeled System 1, 2, 3, and 4 (see Figure 5.1). The left side, System 1, can be thought of as reflecting the management system enacted by someone who follows McGregor's Theory X philosophy, whereas

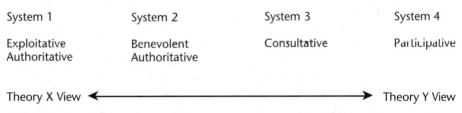

System 1	System 2	System 3	System 4
Exploitative Authoritative	Benevolent Authoritative	Consultative	Participative

Theory X View ⟵————————————————⟶ Theory Y View

FIGURE 5.1   Likert's systems of management, compared to McGregor's perspectives of Theory X and Theory Y.

the right side, System 4, is close to the system that would be used by a Theory Y manager. Likert describes System 1 as "exploitative authoritative," and System 2 as "benevolent authoritative." These two systems rely heavily on threats and rewards related to physical and economic security (the lower levels of Maslow's hierarchy). On the other hand, System 3 is labeled "consultative," and System 4, "participative." System 3 employs some involvement in decision making, as well as economic and some self-esteem motivators. System 4 provides for group goal setting and full participation in discussion of problems and solutions.

Likert's research and case studies convinced him that the most effective and productive firms were those that approached System 4. He found fewer unresolvable labor-management problems and lower costs associated with such organizations, for example. The disturbing tendency he discovered, however, was for companies to shift toward System 1, rather than System 4, when they felt the need to reduce costs and increase efficiency, as in downsizing or "reengineering." In other words, the actual tendency was counterproductive, in view of Likert's results.

Likert's System 4 management, the most productive and effective type, is characterized by three principles:[11]

1. Supportive relationships (between superior and subordinates, and within the work group)
2. Group decision making and supervision (the "linking pin")
3. High performance goals

First, supportive relationships are characterized by subordinates' feeling that superiors have confidence and trust in them, show interest and concern for them as individuals, provide them with help and training, and keep them well informed. This principle is compatible with the emphasis on the human resources as the most important factor in organizational success. It is also in line with a strong appreciation for "human resource development," which stresses continual education and training to upgrade the skills of organizational members.

Second, the concept of group decision making and supervision is a departure from what Likert saw as the one-to-one system of classical management (in which the CEO supervised a vice president, who supervised a director, who supervised a department head, and so on down the line). In System 4 management, there is instead an overlapping group structure. At each level, all subordinates and supervisors who may be involved in the results of a decision are involved in discussing it. Some persons who are members of the group at one level will also be members of the group at the next lower level of the hierarchy; these people are the *linking pins,* so famous in Likert's works. Likert maintains that in many cases the leader or superior is still responsible for the final decision, but it has been undertaken after full discussion with others affected.

Third, high goal aspirations were the product of the other two features, according to Likert. The participative and involving nature of supportive relationships and group participation in supervision and decision making often lead to higher levels of confidence and esprit de corps, which in turn lead to high aspirations. Likert found a direct correlation between the setting of high performance goals and highly supportive relationships between superiors and subordinates.[12]

Likert, in sum, placed new emphasis on human relationships and group processes in determining organizational effectiveness. His work brought to the fore the phrases linking pins and PDM (participative decision making).

The Managerial Grid

Likert's correlation between performance goals and supportive relationships foreshadows the Managerial Grid®, developed by Robert Blake and Jane Srygley Mouton, which later became an influential tool of organizational development (see Figure 5.2).[13] The managerial grid also correlates performance goals (emphasis on production outcomes)

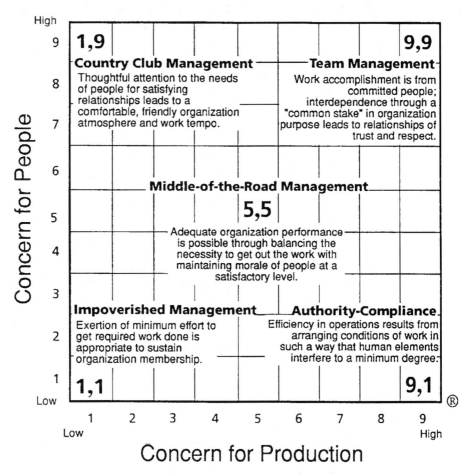

FIGURE 5.2 The Leadership Grid® Figure from *Leadership Dilemmas—Grid Solutions*, by Robert R. Blake and Anne Adams McCanse (formerly the Managerial Grid Figure by Robert R. Blake and Jane S. Mouton), Houston: Gulf Publishing Company, p. 29. Copyright © 1991, by Scientific Methods, Inc. Reproduced by permission of the owners.

and relationships (emphasis on human relations). The work of Blake and Mouton drew upon theories developed in the field of group dynamics, as well. Communication within an ongoing group can have one of two general purposes: to improve relationships among the people in the group or to move toward performing the task set for the group. Group dynamicists often speak of two kinds of group leadership: *Maintenance,* or socioemotional, leaders "maintain" good human relationships among members; *task* leaders help the group complete its work.

Blake and Mouton consider two dimensions that managers or leaders emphasize in exercising their leadership: concern for people and concern for production. They envision a manager's commitment to people or to production in terms of a nine-point scale or continuum, with 1 showing low commitment and 9, high commitment. These two scales can be laid out as the axes of a graph, creating their grid for describing types of leadership. For example, someone with high commitment to production but low commitment to people, similar to a Theory X manager or one practicing System 1 management in McGregor's and Likert's terminology would be at 9,1 on the grid.

Blake and Mouton hold that more effectively managed firms approach high concern for both human relationships and production. Their organization development model is designed to help move organizations from less productive leadership to more productive leadership.

Whereas McGregor suggests two management approaches, Theory X and Theory Y, and Likert allows for four management systems, Blake and Mouton theoretically envision up to eighty-one variations. In actuality, they feel that there are really seven major styles of leadership: the four corners of the grid plus the point in the middle (5,5) and two combination styles, the "paternalistic" and the "opportunistic."[14]

The paternalistic situation obtains when managers vary their treatment of subordinates in such a way that at times they come across as high on authority and compliance and other times as high on the rewarding style. When subordinates do as the manager desires, he or she assumes the highly approving style; but when subordinates do not perform as desired, the manager assumes the highly authoritarian approach. In the "opportunistic" mode, managers reciprocate the style evinced by subordinates, so that different organization members experience different leadership styles from the same manager. The grid system allows for more flexibility and variability in categorizing different approaches to management and leadership. Both Likert's systems and the Managerial Grid assume that there can be changes over time in an organization's management orientation.

Argyris and the Role of the Individual in the Organization

Another important figure in the development of the humanistic approach in the 1960s was Chris Argyris, a professor of industrial administration at Yale University. Like the previous theorists, he believes that organizations run strictly by the principles of classical and scientific management are not as effective as they could be. Argyris's work covered a span of several years and included several books (mainly in the 1960s, although a revised edition of *Integrating the Individual and the Organization* came out in 1990[15]). Also in common with the other authors in this chapter, he believes that the function of administrators and managers is to predict and to control the operations of the organization. He also maintains that the scientific method is best for developing principles for administration.

Argyris holds that there is a symbiotic relationship between human beings and organizations: Each requires the other. But he feels that there is typically a fundamental conflict between people and their organizations when these organizations are administered by the usual classical methods. To become a mature and fully "authentic" person, one must develop human relationships that enhance the self-worth of both oneself and others. Argyris is drawing on Maslow's self-actualization concept and on the works of Martin Buber, the Jewish theologian, and Carl Rogers, the psychotherapist, who emphasized the importance of open, authentic relationships as requisites to human maturity. The norms of modern organizations, on the other hand, seem designed to actively suppress the kinds of relationships and communication necessary for the full development of the human personality. These organizations do not allow for expressions of genuine feelings, for example.

This apparent difference between the needs of the individual and those of the organization is the heart of the conflict observed by Argyris.[16] This analysis leads him "to the conclusion that there is an inherent incongruency between the self-actualization of the two."[17] But, this need not be so. The solution proposed by Argyris includes *job enlargement,* which essentially means giving subordinates more responsibility and control. Coaching and training in new skills, for example, can provide job enlargement and lead to increased worker satisfaction. The second aspect of the solution is to move from authoritarian styles of leadership toward "a more *'democratic,' 'participative,' 'collaborative,' 'employee-centered'* one" (emphasis added).[18] He adds that democratic leadership is not to be confused with laissez-faire, do-nothing leadership; rather, it is leadership based on open discussion and participation by all those affected by decisions.

Argyris hence adds to the developing school of thought in favor of open communication and participative decision making represented by McGregor, Likert, and Blake and Mouton.

Highlights of the Human Relations Movement

The human relations movement is often presented as in opposition to the theories of classical and scientific management. In fact, they share significant points in common:

1. Both are concerned with making the organization, assumed to be a private company, more productive and effective. Both approaches, in other words, grant the primacy of the goals and objectives of the top leadership and administration of an organization. The purpose of the theories is to make managers more effective.

2. Both approaches share a commitment to and faith in the empirical methods of the behavioral sciences. Recall Likert's emphasis on the superiority of quantitative research methods for improving management effectiveness.

The precepts of the human relations movement, from which emerged the theories of human resource development and participative management, differ from those of

AN ISSUE OF COMMUNICATION ETHICS

Participation or Manipulation

The human relations approach is concerned with making the workplace more humane, allowing for open communication and discussion. Still, some have complained, the purpose is ultimately the same as in theories from classical and scientific management: to induce people to produce more for the organization. Is participation of lower-level people really genuine, or is it illusory? Human relations techniques can be a form of manipulation, in which organizational members are given the appearance of making decisions, while the real power still lies with the higher-ups.

The type of issue that is opened for discussion may indicate the extent to which an organization is committed to genuine participative decision making. Less critical issues may be brought before the whole group, with fundamental issues withheld from open discussion. In one case, for example, organizational members were invited to discuss methods and plans for discontinuing a particular line of products, a decision about downsizing made at the level of senior management. The critical question of whether or not to downsize or cut this particular production line was not open for general dis-

cussion. The result was that upper management was able to say that all organizational members participated in open discussions about downsizing and reorganization. The lower-level members of the organization were thus said to have bought into the downsizing exercise, even though they had not been involved in what was arguably the most important part of the decision-making process. An important element maintaining the power of upper levels of management is the ability to determine which decisions are open to discussion and which are not. One organizational theorist points out: "Power is effectively used when it is employed as unobtrusively as possible."* This is the case when the techniques of participative decision making *appear* to be in place.

To what extent are human relations methods, PDM, Theory Y, and so on sophisticated attempts at manipulating the organization's members? Are such techniques to be used only for less important matters and problems facing an organization?

*J. Pfeffer (1981), *Power in organizations*, Marshfield, Mass.: Pitman, p. 137.

classical management in the priority given to human relations and communication within the organization. The most effectively managed organizations, according to the human relations and participative management schools, were those that emphasized group involvement and supportive human relationships.

ORGANIZATIONAL CLIMATE

What does it mean to say that a group or an organization has a climate? The metaphor calls up images of weather. The weather can be a factor in determining how various activities come off or are perceived. It can spoil a picnic, a weekend, or a ball game. The climate of a region can be too hot for certain crops, such as rice, but just right for others, such as citrus. Climates determine, in part, the typical kinds of buildings, clothing, and occupations of people living in them.

People also use a meteorological metaphor when talking about human relationships or conditions. For example, people say that the "atmosphere" in a room was "chilly" or lacking in "warmth." They speak of certain feelings that were "in the air," or describe feelings in a meeting as "arid" or "sunny." The idea is that the climate or weather can be conducive to or appropriate for some actions but not others. On warm, sunny days we feel happier and more productive than on gloomy, cold days. This is the kind of imagery associated with the use of the term *climate* to describe an aspect of an organization. Note that the original meaning of the metaphor carries the idea that climate or weather is perceived as positive or negative, conducive or not conducive to certain activities.

The Concepts of Organizational Climate

The earliest social science description of social climate or atmosphere developed from the psychological field theory of Kurt Lewin and his associates. Field theory maintains that individuals' experiences occur against the background of a general, holistic impression of a setting, or field. This field provides the context for evaluating and interpreting perceptions. The term *climate* in a form similar to its current usage in "organizational climate" appeared in the famous study of leadership styles reported by Lewin, Lippitt, and White in 1939.[19] They found that the "social climate" characteristic of each separate boys' club was an important variable mediating the effects of the imposition of authoritarian, democratic, and laissez-faire leadership styles.

The Hawthorne studies and the development of the human relations theories highlighted the importance of group and social climates. Likert's four systems of management can be differentiated along lines that include the psychological atmosphere experienced within them. By the 1960s, organizational theorists began to give more sustained attention to the idea of climate. This attention reflected the belief that climate influences behavior, going back to the earlier ideas of field theory. Climate was seen as a characteristic (or the *sum* of a set of characteristics) associated with or possessed by a given organization. Climate then could be studied with a view toward predicting organizational members' behavior. In addition, climate was considered to be directly related to members' motivation.

A preliminary definition of "organizational climate," advanced by Renato Tagiuri, is often cited in the organizational literature:

> Organizational climate is a relatively enduring quality of the internal environment of an organization that (a) is experienced by its members, (b) influences their behavior, and (c) can be described in terms of values of a particular set of characteristics (or attributes) of the organization.[20]

Climate was thus an overarching construct that could bring together several individual variables that separately might contribute to how people felt about working in an organization. Tagiuri's definition first implies that an organization's climate is relatively stable, which means that although climate is something perceived by individuals, those perceptions are shaped by some enduring qualities of the organization. These perceptions are not just the idiosyncratic impressions of individuals but reflect actual and objective conditions.

Second, these conditions, perceived in combination as climate, influence individuals' behavior, which was of special interest. At the same time that the volume containing Tagiuri's analysis of the concept was published, the Harvard Business School published a companion volume concerning the relationship between organizational climate and motivation.[21] Like much early work on organizational climate, this work identified leadership style as an important determinant of climate.

The third implication of Tagiuri's definition of climate is that the attributes, as experienced, are described in terms of values.[22] So, for example, the atmosphere of a group or an organization could be described along a set of scales such as the following:

warm versus cold

friendly versus unfriendly

fun-loving versus serious

cooperative versus uncooperative

enthusiastic versus unenthusiastic

supportive versus unsupportive

and so on.

Often the climate varies from department to department or from unit to unit within large organizations. Climate appears to be immediately experienced through the communication activities of specific groups or units on a day-to-day basis. For example, the superior-subordinate relationship has been found to be an important element in determining an individual's views of climate.

To many theorists, an important question remained unanswered. If organizational climate was known only through the reports of individuals' perceptions, did the thing called "climate" reside only in individuals, or was it an actual characteristic of the organization? The problem here lay in the way in which climate was operationalized for the purpose of studying it. Usually, people researching the climate in an organization did so by distributing questionnaires to organizational members, asking them to indicate their feelings or attitudes regarding certain aspects of the organization. It was then assumed that one could average or aggregate all the individual responses to come to a general or organization-wide consensus deemed to be the climate. But remember that climate is intended to be an attribute of the organization rather than of its members as individuals.

This controversy raises the issue of reification of the organization as something apart from the people who constitute it. Concerning a related matter involving researching organizational cultures, Sue DeWine, who has conducted extensive research on organizational communication, questions whether it would be possible to study such aspects of an organization without starting with individuals.[23] Second, ambiguity frequently arises in these studies concerning how climate is differentiated, if at all, from such concepts as morale, job satisfaction, and work attitudes. In other words, it was not always clear that climate was operationally defined in a distinctive or consistent manner in the various research studies.

The concept of organizational climate originated from a functionalist perspective for studying organizations. The difficulties in defining the nature of climate and locating it at the individual or the organizational level may point to the problem of analyzing a "fuzzy" concept, such as climate, with the social scientific tools of functionalism. An interpretive approach, which allows for qualitative and descriptive analyses of how people develop, negotiate, and change perceptions of climate through communicative interaction, may be more appropriate for a concept of this sort.[24]

This approach maintains that it is the interaction patterns among people that persist over time, creating and then continually altering the organizational climate. In other words, climate is something that can cause certain perceptions and behaviors, and, in turn, people's perceptions and behaviors re-create and shape the organizational climate. The climate and individuals' responses continually influence one another.

Factors of Climate

Most early studies sought to identify variables that determine climate. These variables were seen as deriving from leadership styles. In their influential work, Litwin and Stringer identified the following typical variables for the literature on organizational climate:[25]

1. Structure and constraint. Is there a formal organizational chart and line of command, strictly followed?
2. Emphasis on individual responsibility. Do individuals simply follow directions and orders, or are they allowed to exercise initiative?
3. Warmth and support. Do people in the organization care for one another; are there expressions of support and acceptance?
4. Reward and punishment, approval and disapproval. Is there more emphasis on assessing blame or on motivating people with rewards?
5. Conflict and tolerance for conflict. Is conflict avoided or settled by waiting for higher-ups to make a judgment, or is conflict confronted and dealt with openly?
6. Performance standards and expectations. Are there clearly defined high standards for performance?
7. Organizational identity and group loyalty. Are there efforts to promote people's identifying with the group or organization?
8. Risk and risk taking. Do people avoid risks to protect themselves, or is risk taking encouraged?

Litwin and Stringer suggest that leaders in an organization largely determine how these variables are perceived by members. Structure, for example, refers to how much structure people see in a given organization, relationship, or task. An organization in which formal, hierarchical structure is emphasized by upper management would have a different climate from an organization in which more informal, open, and participative decision making is emphasized. Structural constraints, then, result from decisions made by organizational leaders, as aspects of their leadership style. The other variables are similarly thought to be the results of leadership behaviors and decisions. Climate studies were developed for the purpose of educating potential organizational managers and administrators, so naturally their emphasis would be on what administrators could do to influence the climate.

Interactionist theories concerning organizational climate emphasize the effects of interpersonal and group communication within specific teams, departments, or work groups. One department may be composed of friends, who thus experience a climate of more warmth and support than the rest of the organization. Regardless of attempts by upper management to shape a particular kind of organizational climate, people in their day-to-day conversations and dealings significantly determine their own experienced group climate, occasionally in intentional disregard of the efforts of management to inculcate a desired climate.

The variables influencing climate so far considered are largely internal, reflecting the values and styles of leaders and group members. Organizational theorist David Cherrington summarizes additional determinants of perceived climate:[26]

1. *Economic conditions.* Innovation and informal risk taking may be encouraged more during boom times than during periods of economic stagnation or decline.

2. *Member characteristics.* Given that climate is something perceived by individuals, individual personality characteristics or life experiences will naturally influence those perceptions. Demographic characteristics, such as age or level of education, may also partly determine how people feel about the organizational climate.

3. *Unionization.* This factor would obviously interact with the variables discussed earlier, such as individual responsibility and structure (more definitely spelled out and constrained in a unionized situation), the reward structure, and performance standards (probably more formalized and detailed in a unionized organization).

4. *Size.* Larger organizations tend to feel more impersonal and structured than smaller ones.

5. *Nature of the work.* The interlocking nature of different functions or the presence and urgency of deadlines may lead to feelings of stress or pressure, contributing to perceptions of the organizational climate.

These theories of organizational climate are clearly related to trends in both human relations theories and contingency theories. The human relations movement began with a recognition that the psychological atmosphere of a work group could affect productivity. McGregor's Theory Y and Likert's System 4 management both value a management approach that emphasizes a climate of warmth, support, and participative decision making. The contingency theories allowed for climatic variables as contingencies determining the kind of leadership or management styles called for. Theories concerning leadership took into account the quality of the relationship between leader and followers (which would be directly related to the climate of the work group).

The concept of organizational climate was developed in order to account for certain properties of organizations that determined people's feelings about their organization; these feelings, in turn, influenced members' motivation and behavior. The important elements of climate that emerged in these studies included warmth, consideration, and support experienced within the organization; the amount of individual autonomy and responsibility or control that people feel they have; and general attitudes toward risk taking, conflict, and rewards in the organization.

Communication Climate and Organizational Commitment

Communication climate concerns the perceptions that people have about the quality of the communication they experience within their organizations. Hence, it is similar to organizational climate, except that the focus is specifically on communication experiences. Redding believed that an ideal communication climate was characterized by the following factors:[27]

1. Supportiveness, especially as experienced in the superior-subordinate relationship
2. Participative decision making
3. Trust, confidence, and credibility given to messages within the organization
4. Openness and candor in ongoing relationships within the organization (with coworkers, between superiors and subordinates, and so on)
5. High performance goals

These factors imply that people are more productive when they are satisfied with these aspects of communication in their surroundings. The absence of supportiveness, trust, credibility, openness, and candor (items 1, 3, and 4 of Redding's list) would presumably lead to a defensive climate. In such a climate, people are so concerned with defending their positions and protecting themselves that they have less energy available for getting the work done. The belief that they have some say in decision making tends to give people a feeling of real participation and responsibility. The fifth factor, "high performance goals," may appear less obviously related to communication satisfaction than the others. Recall, however, that early research in organizational climate identified high standards of performance as conducive to a positive climate. Presumably, in communicating high standards, leaders in an organization also communicate that what people do there is important and worthwhile, leading in turn to enhanced morale and feelings of esteem.

The importance of communication climate lies in findings that *organizational commitment* is directly related to the member's satisfaction with the communication experienced in the organization. When one is committed to an organization, typically one identifies more closely with that organization and is more willing to exert extra effort for it. A recent study supported the notion that perceptions of the following factors were related to employees' feelings of organizational commitment:

1. The communication relationship between top management and employees
2. The quality of top management's communication
3. Superior-subordinate communication[28]

Especially influential was the perception of organizational support for members—that is, the extent to which the "organization" appears to value members' contributions and to care about them as individuals.

Communication from the top often sets the tone for organizational and communication climate.

Communication climate and organizational commitment are strongly affected by one's experience with different communication sources within the organization. First, the communication from top levels of administration ("top management") sets the tone and leads to judgments concerning the organization's overall supportiveness. Second, communication with one's immediate superior is important in terms of supportiveness, fairness of evaluation and treatment, openness to upward communication, and participation in decision making. Third, horizontal communication determines feelings of support and warmth within one's immediate environment.

One can delineate three different kinds of communication climate deriving from these different sources. Thus, in addition to an organizational communication climate, one could speak of a group communication climate and an interpersonal communication climate, respectively referring to perceptions of communication quality within a work group or department and within an ongoing dyadic relationship.[29] Certain conditions determine which factors take on significance. Under conditions of uncertainty or threat, messages from the top are especially important for reassuring people and providing them with needed information. If members are especially concerned with upward mobility in or long-term commitments to an organization, feelings of participative decision making become particularly important to them.

DIVERSITY MATTERS

Same Climates, Different Perceptions?

Climate is basically in the eye or ear of the beholder. The concept of organizational climate as a variable lies in collective perceptions of organizational members. As organizations become increasingly diverse, it becomes more likely that these perceptions will diverge more and more among members of the same organization. The notion of sexual harassment depends on some people perceiving a "hostile" work environment where others may not. Thus sexual joking and comments may be perceived by men one way and women another. The men engaged in the joking may perceive a fun, open climate, whereas women feel that it is closed and intimidating.

In the same way, members of minorities, such as African Americans, may experience an entirely different kind of organizational or communication climate from that experienced by others in the same organization. Graffiti on washroom walls or cartoons pasted on bulletin boards or walls may be seen as merely humorous by some and as demeaning or offensive by others. Complaints of racial harassment have been increasing in the workplace since 1990, according to the Equal Employment Opportunity Commission; they were up 17 percent in the period from 1990 to 1993.*

One young African American was driven to take a year's leave of absence because of stress caused by anonymous paging of his name, accompanied by a racial epithet. A class-action suit was filed against a large auto manufacturer because of claims of workplace racial harassment of this sort.** Clearly, these people perceived a more hostile climate than other workers probably did.

*New York Times, June 20, 1993, Sec. 3, p. 1.

**New York Times, June 20, 1993, Sec. 3, p. 1.

COMMUNICATION IMPLICATIONS OF THE HUMAN RELATIONS THEORIES

Context

The human relations theories were developed in order to improve the effectiveness of individual organizations. As with the scientific management theories, principles were intended to be transferrable from one organization to another. There was therefore little concern with the relationship of the organization to its environment or its communication with other organizations. Each organization was consequently seen as compartmentalized, with a recognized major purpose. Organizations were not thought of as having mixed goals or motives; the goals of upper management were essentially the only goals to be considered. The human relations theories were intended to allow for more effectively reaching those goals.

The educational and technological sophistication of the American workforce had improved since the latter part of the nineteenth century. There was consequently more faith in the ability of line workers to participate actively in their own management and goal setting. Another effect of the educational context was undoubtedly the development of schools of business administration, especially at the graduate level, and the disciplines of social psychology and industrial psychology.

Organizational Shape and Structure

The human relations theorists still envision a hierarchically organized structure, but one that is less rigid than that proposed by classical theorists. Likert particularly emphasizes the group nature of discussion and decision making at each level, with overlapping "linking pins" provided for communication among the levels.

A major distinction of the human relations approach is the stress placed on the human element regardless of the structure or form of the organization. The relationships are to be more democratic, involving considerably more "two-way" communication, than those in the bureaucratic structures. There is less emphasis on the sharp distinction between managers who *think* and workers who *do,* but do not think.

As a result, the human relations theory places greater emphasis on the concept of organizational climate than do classical theories. Climate takes account of the feelings or attitudes that members have regarding the organization's atmosphere. A supportive and open climate is seen as conducive to fostering members' commitment to the organization and its goal. Providing a supportive climate is therefore seen as an important element in enhancing worker productivity and effectiveness.

Message Behavior

The human relations approach allows for more variety and freedom in the types of messages shared at all levels within the organization. Subordinates are expected to provide suggestions and even criticisms in response to messages from superiors. There is more conversation, more allowing for developing what Likert calls "supportive relationships." Messages are not strictly "businesslike," as would be expected in a classically managed organization. There is more freedom for discussion of personal matters, aspirations, and the like.

The human relations approach therefore places more emphasis on face-to-face, interpersonal communication than does the classical management approach. There is more informality in messages and less emphasis on formal written records. The "communication climate" of a particular organization is seen in terms of positive messages that enhance members' feelings of support, warmth, and openness.

Methods and Modalities of Communication

Human relations theories emphasize informal, verbal, face-to-face communication. Group discussions become a central method of communication. Instead of emphasis on vertical, downward communication, there is more emphasis on upward as well as downward communication. There should also be more freedom for horizontal communication in the various group and informal meetings encouraged by these theories.

The emphasis on developing the human resources of the organization means that more communication will occur in settings of informal and formal training and education. In fact, training becomes an important means for communicating the values and goals of the organization to members. Argyris particularly emphasizes the need for job enlargement, which became the notion of job enrichment. Coaching and training therefore become important forms of administrative and managerial organizational communication.

Communication Activities

Compared to classically managed firms, there is less distinction between the communication activities of upper management and those of lower-level organizational members. Rather than assuming that managers give directions and instructions, there is more expectation of discussion and participative decision making. These expectations place a greater stress on interpersonal and discussion skills at all levels in the organization. Hence, there is more need for training to develop such skills.

Problem solving and decision making require wide discussion; there is more stress on team building at all levels in the organization. There may be conflict within the organization, but it should be dealt with openly and handled through discussion whenever possible. Likert, for example, believes that the more organizational members feel directly involved in making decisions in the organization, the easier it will be to resolve conflicts.

SUMMARY

The development of human relations management, beginning with the Hawthorne studies in the late 1920s, did not change the basic functionalist nature of organizational theories. These theories were still concerned with discovering and improving the performance of the functions that were perceived to be necessary in making an organization productive and efficient. These theories give priority to communication functions, especially interpersonal communication and superior-subordinate communication.

Human relations theories, however, go on to stress the importance of interpersonal communication and discussion at all levels of the organizational hierarchy. Effective organizations allow members (employees) to realize and fulfill individual psychological needs; productivity and proper motivation derive from feelings of supportiveness,

trust, and open communication. Later theorists such as McGregor, Likert, Blake and Mouton, and Herzberg stress the importance of participative decision making in allowing for full development of an organization's human resources. These theorists posit different orientations that managements often take, ranging from a highly directive sort (Theory X, System 1, High Task–Low Human Concerns) to a highly integrative, productive sort (Theory Y, System 4, and so on).

Communication in organizations based on the human relations approach should be vertical and horizontal *simultaneously*, with allowance for open discussion and even debate at all levels of the hierarchy. People should perceive that they can, to a certain extent, control the pace and nature of their work and participate in making important decisions relating to them.

EXERCISES AND QUESTIONS FOR DISCUSSION

1. What were the original expectations of the Harvard researchers conducting the Hawthorne studies? Discuss the actual results of changing the lighting and other work conditions. Would the same results be found if this study were con-

ducted in the 1990s rather than the 1920s? Why or why not?
2. Describe McGregor's different theories concerning human nature and motivation. Discuss experiences you may have had with a Theory X–

or a Theory Y–type manager. Compare Mc-Gregor's theories with the management systems of Likert and the orientations of Blake and Mouton. Describe the changes in expected communication patterns as one moves from the highly directive end of the scale toward the participative end of the scale. Do you agree that open discussion and participative decision making are always preferable for running an organization? Why or why not?

3. Prepare a ten-minute briefing to provide background on and to explain one of the theories or theorists discussed in this chapter. The briefing must draw out explicit implications for communication (see the list of sources for references). Possible topics:

Max Weber and bureaucratic structure
Henri Fayol's development of administrative theories
The career of Frederick W. Taylor
Elton Mayo and the Hawthorne studies
Chester Barnard's functions of the executive
McGregor's theories of human nature
The needs pyramid of Abraham Maslow

Likert's development of the four systems of management
The managerial grid of Blake and Mouton
The "motivator-hygiene" theory of Frederick Herzberg

These could be individual or group presentations.

4. Discuss the concept of organizational climate. Think of clubs and organizations to which you have belonged: Can you describe the climate of each of these organizations? What weather metaphor best describes the climate in your living unit? in one of your classrooms? in a student organization? Discuss methods that could be used for discovering and analyzing the organizational or communication climate of one such organization.

5. Do you believe that organizational commitment is an important motivator for members of a given organization? How can an organization foster commitment on the part of members? Describe examples of effective or ineffective attempts at fostering commitment from your own experience.

SOURCES FOR FURTHER STUDY

Allen, M. W. (1992). Communication and organizational commitment: Perceived organizational support as a mediating factor. *Communication Quarterly, 40,* 357–67.

Argyris, C. (1957). *Personality and organization.* New York: Harper & Brothers.

Argyris, C. (1962). *Interpersonal competence and organizational effectiveness.* Homewood, Ill.: Irwin.

Argyris, C. (1990). *Integrating the individual and the organization.* New Brunswick, N.J.: Transaction Publishers.

Barnard, C. (1938). *The functions of the executive.* Cambridge, Mass.: Harvard University Press.

Blake, R., and Mouton, J. S. (1964). *The managerial grid: Key orientations for achieving production through people.* Houston: Gulf Publishing.

Blake, R., and Mouton, J. S. (1968) *Corporate excellence through grid organizational development.* Houston: Gulf Publishing.

Cherrington, D. J. (1989). *Organizational behavior:*

The management of individual and organizational performance. Boston: Allyn & Bacon.

Falcione, R. L., Sussman, L., and Herden, R. P. (1987). Communication climate in organizations. In F. M. Jablin, L. L. Putnam, K. H. Roberts, and L. W. Porter (Eds.), *Handbook of organizational communication: An interdisciplinary perspective.* Newbury Park, Calif.: Sage.

Goodell, A. L. (1992). Organizational climate: Current thinking on an important issue. In K. L. Hutchinson (Ed.), *Readings in organizational communication.* Dubuque, Iowa: Wm. C. Brown.

Harrison, J. F. C. (1973). *The birth and growth of industrial England, 1714–1867.* New York: Harcourt Brace Jovanovich.

Herzberg, F. (1966). *Work and the nature of man.* Cleveland: World Publishing.

Litwin, G. H., and Stringer, R. A., Jr. (1968). *Motivation and organizational climate.* Boston: Harvard University Press.

Mayo, E. (1933). *The human problems of an industrial organization.* New York: Macmillan.

Pfeffer, J. (1982). *Organizations and organization theory.* Boston: Pitman.

Poole, M. S. (1985). Communication and organizational climates: Review, critique, and a new perspective. In R. D. McPhee and P. K. Tompkins (Eds.), *Organizational communication: Traditional themes and new directions.* Beverly Hills, Calif.: Sage.

Redding, C. (1972). *Communication within the organization: An interpretive review of theory and research.* New York: Industrial Communication Council.

Sass, J. S., and Canary, D. J. (1991). Organizational commitment and identification: An examination of conceptual and operational convergences. *Western Journal of Speech Communication, 55,* 275–93.

Tagiuri, R., and Litwin, G. H. (Eds.) (1968). *Organizational climate: Explorations of a concept.* Boston: Harvard University Press.

NOTES

1. J. F. C. Harrison (1973), *The birth and growth of industrial England, 1714–1867,* New York: Harcourt Brace Jovanovich, pp. 110–12.

2. F. W. Taylor (1911), *The principles of scientific management.* New York: Harper & Brothers, pp. 94–95.

3. G. C. Homans (1989), The Western Electric researches, in M. T. Matteson and J. M. Ivancevich (Eds.), *Management and organization behavior classics,* Homewood, Ill.: BPI-Irwin, pp. 193–202.

4. Homans, p. 200.

5. C. Barnard (1938), *The functions of the executive,* Cambridge, Mass.: Harvard University Press.

6. A. Maslow (1954), *Motivation and personality,* New York: Harper & Row.

7. D. McGregor (1960), *The human side of enterprise,* New York: McGraw-Hill; and D. McGregor (1967), *The professional manager,* C. McGregor and W. Bennis (Eds.), New York: McGraw-Hill.

8. R. Likert (1967), *The human organization: Its management and value.* New York: McGraw-Hill.

9. Likert, p. 1.

10. Likert, p. 1.

11. Likert, pp. 47–52.

12. Likert, p. 51–52.

13. R. R. Blake and J. S. Mouton (1964), *The managerial grid.* Houston: Gulf Publishing.

14. R. R. Blake and A. A. McCanse (1991), *Leadership dilemmas—grid solutions,* Houston: Gulf Publishing.

15. C. Argyris (1990), *Integrating the individual and the organization,* New Brunswick, N.J.: Transaction Publishers.

16. C. Argyris (1957), *Personality and organization,* New York: Harper & Brothers; C. Argyris (1962), *Interpersonal competence and organizational effectiveness,* Homewood, Ill.: Irwin.

17. Argyris (1957), p. 175.

18. Argyris (1957), p. 188.

19. K. Lewin, R. Lippitt, and R. K. White (1939), Patterns of aggressive behavior in experimentally created "social climates," *Journal of Social Psychology, 10,* 271–99.

20. R. Tagiuri (1968), The concept of organizational climate, in R. Tagiuri and G. H. Litwin (Eds.), *Organizational climate: Explorations of a concept,* Boston: Harvard University Press, p. 27.

21. G. H. Litwin and R. A. Stringer, Jr. (1968), *Motivation and organizational climate,* Boston: Harvard University Press.

22. Tagiuri, p. 27.

23. S. DeWine (1988), The cultural perspective: New wave, old problems, in J. A. Anderson (Ed.), *Communication yearbook 11,* p. 349.

24. See M. S. Poole and R. D. McPhee (1983), A structurational analysis of organizational climate, in L. L. Putnam and M. E. Pacanowsky (Eds.), *Communication and organizations: An interpretive approach,* Newbury Park, Calif.: Sage, pp. 195–220.

25. Litwin and Stringer, pp. 46–63.

26. David J. Cherrington (1989), *Organizational behavior,* Boston: Allyn & Bacon, pp. 494–95.

27. C. Redding (1972), *Communication within the organization: An interpretive review of theory and research,* New York: Industrial Communication Council.

28. M. W. Allen (1992), Communication and organizational commitment: Perceived organizational support as a mediating factor, *Communication Quarterly, 40,* 357–67.

29. R. L. Falcione, L. Sussman, and R. P. Herden (1987), Communication climate in organizations, in F. M. Jablin, L. L. Putnam, K. H. Roberts, and L. W. Porter (Eds.), *Handbook of organizational communication,* Newbury Park, Calif.: Sage, pp. 204–17.

CHAPTER **6**

System and Contingency Theories of Organizations

CHAPTER OBJECTIVES

After studying this chapter, you should be able to:

- Describe changing views of organizations that led to development of system theories.
- Explain the grounding of a systems approach in biological views of the organism and information theory.
- Distinguish the characteristics of an open system from a closed system.
- Describe the application of open systems theory to organizations, as in the work of Katz and Kahn and organizational ecologists.
- Explain the development of contingency theories from a systems approach.
- Identify the major factors that have been treated as contingencies.

CHAPTER OUTLINE

THE ORGANIZATION AS A SYSTEM

Hospitals are certainly one place where we hope that communication works flawlessly, but that is not always the case. Reports continue to show that Americans occasionally receive incorrect medications or the wrong amounts of such medicines in hospitals. There have been horror stories about surgeons removing the wrong limb or organ by mistake. Researchers trying to analyze the causes of such medical mishaps have determined that rather than with individual carelessness, the fault often lies with the *system* of health care in the hospital itself. Efforts to locate the individuals responsible for each error may therefore miss the point. Findings of recent exhaustive research have indicated that no single drug seems to be a problem (thus remedies aimed at specific training in dealing with a particular drug would not help), nor did it appear that any one doctor or nurse could be singled out as solely responsible for each error studied.[1]

The system problems found in the hospital research result from the sheer amount of information relating to drugs, their uses, and potential interactions with other drugs and the lack of computer tracking and monitoring of prescriptions and drugs as they flow through huge hospitals from pharmacy to patient. Often drug names sound alike, causing confusion when staff members are under stress and time pressure. Potassium chloride (fatal unless given in diluted form) may be mistaken for the harmless sodium chloride, used for flushing catheters; Levoxine, a thyroid drug, sounds like Lanoxine, a heart drug (Levoxine has since been renamed Levoxyl).[2]

Some hospitals found that mistakes were occasionally the result of their systems of communication.

Like organizational theorists, these health-care researchers have begun to think of large, complex organizations as systems. The implications of this view for organizational theory and organizational communication is the subject of this chapter.

Although the human relations approach was intended to counter the trends of scientific management, the two approaches shared many basic assumptions. Notably, they both characterized the organization as having a single goal or purpose, determined by the "owners" or management; they both emphasized the rational and scientific nature of management; they both accepted the idea that the purpose of organizational theories was to develop principles for more effective administration that could be generalized and applied to any kind of complex human organization. In short, both approaches hoped to develop a science of administration.

The theories reviewed in this chapter reveal some misgivings about the hopes and assumptions of the earlier management theorists. Changing ideas about organizations included a realization that most organizations exhibited mixed motives—not all members agreed on the main purpose or goal. As a result, conflict was accepted as a normal feature of complex organizations. Theorists also began to take the role of the environment in shaping the organization into account as well.

System and contingency theories assume that an organization is something like a living organism, in that it must rely on nourishment from and interaction with an environment. Contingency theories are considered along with systems theories because both rely on organizations' adapting to environmental and systemic factors.

SYSTEMS THEORY

The Canadian organizational theorist Gareth Morgan maintains that one's view of how organizations work depends on the image one adopts concerning them. For example, the classical management theory clearly envisages organizations as machines. The discovery, by Mayo and others, of the importance of the human needs of people in organizations led toward viewing organizations more as families, or perhaps living entities. The full-blown image of the organization as organism, however, came with the growing popularity of so-called *systems theory*.[3]

It would be a mistake to think of these differing approaches as existing in watertight compartments. Elements of the human relations approach are already present in the theories of Taylor and Fayol. Taylor believed in the importance of treating workers humanely in order to increase their productivity. Elements of a systems approach are present in earlier theories as well. Likert, for example, insists on the need for what he calls a "systems approach," and it is instructive that the labels he selects for his management categories are *System* 1, 2, 3, and 4.[4]

Despite these nods toward the importance of a systems approach, both classical, scientific management theories and the human relations and human resource theories tended to focus on the individual, or the micro level of the organization. They generally emphasized the individual manager or worker's behavior and the development or training of the individual.

In taking a systems view of an organization one considers the overall pattern of interrelationships and interlocking behaviors covering all members and units. The systems view emphasizes the relationship between the organization (or organism) and its *environment*.

Foundations of Systems Theory

In sum, then, systems theory stresses two aspects of any organization:

1. The *interrelatedness* of its parts, or subsystems
2. The interaction with its *environment*

The approach that is now called systems theory began with a biologist, Ludwig von Bertalanffy, whose intent was to develop a *general systems theory*.[5] He preferred the term *general theory* because he hoped that general principles concerning the nature of all kinds of systems could be discovered and then applied to the analysis of any system, from the molecule or the living cell up to the solar system and beyond.[6]

The model for identifying these general principles was the biological organism (microbe, plant, animal, and so on). Each organism, thought of as a system, comprises several constituent systems, referred to as subsystems. For example, our body (the system) is made up of a circulatory system (blood vessels, heart, lungs, etc.), the muscular system, the skeletal system, the endocrine system, the gastrointestinal system, the nervous system, and so on. Each of these subsystems, in turn, is made up of constituent parts, or its own subsystems. A change in one of these systems usually has an impact on all the other systems—the notion of interrelatedness, or *systemic* effects. The various subsystems do not exist in isolation but in continuous relationship and interaction with other subsystems, as shown in Figure 6.1.

A second important feature of plants and animals is that they must constantly exchange food and energy with the surrounding environment in order to to stay alive. Plants must take in carbon dioxide and give off oxygen and receive energy from sunlight in order to carry on photosynthesis. Animals, obviously, must breathe in air to get oxygen and give off carbon dioxide continuously in order to survive. In addition, animals need to take in energy in the form of food and eliminate waste products from the utilization of that food. Plants and animals, therefore, are *open systems,* meaning that they exchange material and energy with their surroundings.

The biological metaphor can be taken a step further by assuming that organizations, like biological organisms, are subject to environmental pressures to change, adapt, mutate, or die off. In other words, the analogy of biological evolution and natural selection can be applied to human organizations.

In addition to this biological foundation, the other major trend in systems theory derives from *information theory* or *cybernetics.* This theory emphasizes the importance of information and feedback. Biological organisms depend upon exchanging energy

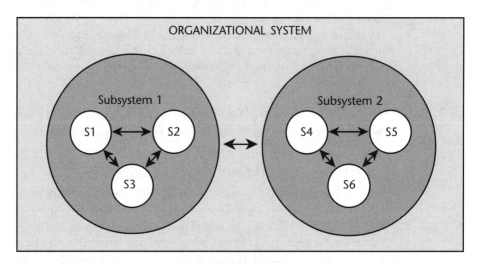

FIGURE 6.1 System consisting of subsystems, themselves made up of subsystems (S1, S2, etc.), in an environment, which contains other organizational systems.

(such as sunlight) and materials (such as food) with their environments. Organizations also depend upon the exchange of information. Information is processed differently from material inputs or energy: It depends upon symbols, and it is not consumable in the same sense as raw materials, food, or energy. (When I share my food with you, I give some of it away, and I no longer have it. When I share information with you, I still keep the same amount that I started with.) The main concepts from information theory that influence the systems approach are information, the related notion of entropy, feedback, and homeostasis.

We may think we have a fairly good idea of what we mean by *information,* but information theorists, beginning with Shannon and Weaver, endeavor to be precise in order to measure and quantify information. They begin with the notion that information is something that is news to someone; that is, it is something that provides some person with knowledge that he or she did not have before receiving the information. The quantitative value of information, therefore, is determined by how much uncertainty that piece of information removes for some person. For example, the uncertainty that I have about the coin just tossed under my cupped hand allows for just two possibilities: It is either heads or tails. By removing my hand, I receive the information that it is one or the other, removing one bit of uncertainty by reducing two possibilities to one actuality. By this reasoning, information theorists conceive of information as quantifiable.

Information is related to the physical concept of *entropy,* borrowed from physics and the second law of thermodynamics. This law holds that the elements in any closed system tend toward disorder or randomness. For example, hot water poured into a tub gradually exchanges its heat with the surrounding air, the tub itself, and other parts of the water. It becomes less "organized," less differentiated from its environment, as its energy, heat, becomes randomized throughout its environment. Information, as described here, reduces uncertainty. Therefore, by reducing uncertainty about some state of affairs or system, information can reduce entropy.

The physical law holds that closed systems inevitably run down and revert to a complete state of entropy. If no more heat is introduced into the tub of water, it will inevitably cool off until its temperature matches the surrounding temperature. Open systems, on the other hand, are able to bring in more energy or information to hold off, at least for a time, the inevitability of entropy.

To keep the water in the tub above room temperature, we need to monitor its temperature to determine when more heat is needed to maintain the desired temperature. This monitoring of the state of the system is *feedback*. By using such feedback, we are able to maintain a steady state, or what information theorists and systems theorists call *homeostasis* (which is simply Greek for "same state"). Our bodies maintain a homeostasis of 98.6° Fahrenheit when we are healthy, regardless of the temperature of the outdoors or room in which we find ourselves. We have built-in feedback monitors that keep track of internal body temperature and external temperature and trigger energy consumption or cooling mechanisms to hold this homeostasis. The steady state could also be one of growth or change, as when an organization determines that it will maintain a steady growth of profits at 5 percent per year.

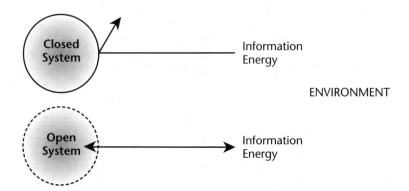

FIGURE 6.2   Open systems, unlike closed systems, constantly exchange information and energy with their environments.

Open systems thus import information from the environment and monitor feedback from the system and the environment (see Figure 6.2). The interchange of information, as well as energy and materials, with the environment allows the system to maintain some desired homeostasis.

The biological metaphor and concepts from information theory provide the basic elements of a systems analysis:

1. *Systemic interrelatedness.* A system is not made up of a conglomerate of parts, but rather of organized subsystems, which are in turn made up of constituent subsystems, and so on. A change in one subsystem ripples through all the others.

2. *Boundaries.* Systems (and subsystems) are defined by and set off from their environments by some kind of boundaries, so that one can differentiate the system from its environment. Systems differ in the permeability of their boundaries.

3. *Open versus closed systems.* Open systems have very permeable boundaries that allow information, energy, and materials to flow back and forth across them. Closed systems have impermeable boundaries that do not permit such flow. If the boundaries are too permeable, too open, the system disintegrates into the surrounding environment; if the boundaries are too closed, the system tends toward entropy and death.

4. *Specialization and coordination.* The subsystems of a larger system perform different functions. The subsystems need to be sufficiently differentiated to avoid too much overlapping, and they have to be sufficiently coordinated to work together. It is possible for subsystems to acquire new functions as conditions change. For example, the production of speech in human beings has been added on to the original function of the respiratory system.

5. *Input, output, and "throughput."* The systems approach stresses continual interaction with an environment. The organization's survival depends upon importing inputs into the system, performing some operation on these inputs internally (the so-called throughput), and then returning some output to the environment.

6. *Homeostasis*. By monitoring feedback from the system (subsystems) and from the environment, information is acquired to indicate the need for inputs and outputs to maintain a desired state of the system.

7. *Sequences of events and life cycles*. Like living organisms, systems go through stages, both as single systems and as populations of similar organizations. Each individual system repeats a regular cycle of events involving input–throughput–output. A university, for example, regularly recruits a freshman class, provides them with the tools and information of an education, and graduates the class four or so years later.

8. *Equifinality*. This term is derived from the Latin for "equal end state," meaning that there are many routes to the same final destination. Because open systems interact with the same environment as other open systems, those that perform a similar function come to resemble one another regardless of different beginning points. For example, most universities have a remarkably similar structure today (faculty, divided into standard disciplinary departments; administration, also divided into fairly standard functions, such as admissions, buildings and grounds, financial affairs, and so on). But individual universities began operations under widely differing conditions at many different times.

Application of Systems Theory for Organizational Analysis

The most influential application of systems theory to organizations is that of Daniel Katz and Robert L. Kahn,[7] who have been the champions of the open system approach to the study of organizations. Although the origin of their work lay in the human relations approach, especially the research led by Rensis Likert, Katz and Kahn shifted from that approach's emphasis on individual psychology to a wider emphasis on systems as whole constructs.[8]

Systems concepts, as described above, have obvious attractions for organizational analysis. An organization appears to be a system par excellence, and features such as open versus closed systems, interrelatedness, homeostasis, and feedback seem ready-made for applying to organizations. Consider the observation that organizations with restrictive memberships, with little opportunity for acquiring new members, show difficulty adapting to new conditions. We say that they need "fresh ideas" or "new blood." Such an organization is a closed system, tending toward entropy.

A major attraction of systems theory is that it concentrates on the dynamic process of patterned activities rather than on the static objects or supposedly unchanging attributes of individuals. Organizations are defined by the patterned activities of a fairly constant set of people. When a group of people complete a *cycle of events* and repeat that cycle in regular ways, we can say that we have an organization. Recurrent activities that are interdependent and interrelated distinguish an organization from a crowd, like that at a sports event or concert (whose activities may be patterned but are not recurrent or ongoing over long periods of time). The boundaries of a system-organization, then, are determined by the extent of these recurrent, patterned activities. Thus, a local church congregation is defined not by its membership, which it may share with many other local businesses and organizations, but by the patterned activities these members perform on a regular basis (typically on Sunday mornings).

The idea that organizations are *open* systems causes many aspects of organizational life to fall neatly into place for Katz and Kahn. The problem with earlier organizational theories, from their point of view, was that these theories considered organizations to be closed systems, in which all the elements necessary to predict and control organizational behavior were in place; hence, Taylorism holds that there is one best way to perform operations, and Fayol could insist on a best form of administrative structure. "It is true," Katz and Kahn point out, "that under fixed and known conditions there is one best way, but in human organizations the conditions of life are neither fixed nor fully known."[9] This point foreshadows contingency theories, which are discussed in the following section.

Organizations tend toward *dynamic homeostasis;* that is, the steady state is one of growth and increasing complexity. The tendency for mature organizations to exhibit increasingly complex structure and subsystems is thereby explained.

A system consists of differentiated or subsystems performing specialized functions. Katz and Kahn see five types of subsystems as "generic" for most organizations:[10]

1. Productive or technical subsystem, directly concerned with the throughput, getting the work done
2. Supportive subsystem, concerned with maintaining a favorable climate and relationships with the environment
3. Maintenance subsystem, focused on recruiting, socializing, and coordinating the human resources of the larger system
4. Adaptive subsystem, concerned with monitoring and forecasting changes in the environment, including technological changes that affect the operations of the system
5. Managerial subsystem, concerned with the overall direction and control of the activities of the other subsystems

Most prior organizational theories had concentrated only on the first and the fifth subsystems on this list, production and management. The systems approach highlights the importance of other functions: maintaining good relations with significant elements in the environment (the supportive subsystem); maintaining good internal relations and developing the human resources of the system (the maintenance subsystem); and acting to adapt to changes in the environment (the adaptive subsystem). Thus many organizations assign people to follow the news: actions of competitors, legislative bodies, courts, and other external groups. In addition, organizations have internal systems, such as personnel and training departments, to monitor special needs of organizational members. The supportive and adaptive subsystems highlight the importance of interaction with the environment, while the maintenance subsystem does the same for the internal systemic relationships of the organization.

System Darwinism: Organizational Ecology Theories

Systems theory emphasizes context considerably more than do classical or human relations theories of organizations. One consequence of this emphasis has been a move toward organizational theories that stress an ecology of organizations.[11] These theories maintain that the environment eventually determines the life span of organizations, just as the physical environment leads to the natural selection of plant and animal species. This line of thinking goes back to the nineteenth-century sociologist Herbert Spencer (1820–1903), who is credited with developing the main concepts of "social Darwinism." Spencer elaborated the analogy between social systems and biological organisms, linking social evolution to responses to competitive pressures in the environment.

Organizations tend to develop habitual responses to environmental feedback, which means that as they become more specialized and complex, they may become less adaptable to change. These responses are often routinized, meaning that inputs are processed in routine or "programmed" ways that were at one time adaptive for the system. To borrow another biological concept, organizations become "imprinted" with the environmental conditions that existed at the time of their founding.[12] A wet environment selects for organisms particularly suited to those conditions; when the ocean becomes a desert, those organisms can no longer survive.

The purpose of these theories is therefore to explain the *life cycle of organizations* and to emphasize their dependence upon the resources in their environments (resource-dependency theory). As a result, this approach is concerned with populations of organizations rather than with individual organizations. The focus is on explaining how types of organizations fare in relation to other types or populations, given changing conditions. For example, private colleges used to outnumber public colleges and universities in the United States. The environment since World War II, however, has placed selective pressure on these institutions, so that public institutions are now far more numerous than private ones.

Similarly, one could argue that the automobile manufacturing industry in the United States became imprinted with the market conditions of the 1950s and 1960s. They thus had a difficult time adapting to changes in their environment resulting from competition from new foreign imports, especially from Japan. The electronics industry in the United States suffered even more in this way. The introduction of cable TV and direct broadcast TV (home satellite dishes) is having a similar impact on the population of television networks in the United States.

These theories are pessimistic regarding the ability of individual organizations to adapt to their environments through better communication or other means. As one organizational ecologist puts it, these theories do not "subscribe to the adaptation model of organizational change," but rather follow a "selection model" of organizational change.[13] They are consequently subject to the criticism that they are overly deterministic. These theories are much concerned with identifying species and populations of organizations, which is becoming more difficult with the proliferation of multinational conglomerates with diverse operations and purposes.

COMMUNICATION IMPLICATIONS OF SYSTEMS THEORY

Systems theory has been especially popular among organizational communication scholars and theorists. The systems approach, as noted above, seems tailor-made for applications to many communication issues.[14] Communication is viewed as fulfilling a central function in human systems.

Context

The context or environment assumes special importance in systems theory, and thus more attention is given to communication between the organization and its environment than in earlier theories. The emphasis that Katz and Kahn give to maintenance subsystems in their analysis places stress on the internal communication systems as well.

A most significant aspect of the environment highlighted by this approach is the *information* it provides. One of the most important functions of the system, therefore, is the processing of this information (dealing with informational inputs and feedback). The major purpose of organizational communication, in the view of an important text based on the systems approach, is developing systems that are most effective in information processing.[15]

Information theory introduces the notion of uncertainty as a variable determining the amount of information potentially present in a situation (or environment). Systems theorists are therefore concerned with the level of environmental uncertainty, which may be characterized by *turbulence*,[16] which suggests an image of chaotic, swirling bits of information that must be sorted and interpreted by the organization. Turbulent information environments are associated with increased *information load,* which is the perceived number of decisions that one must make in processing incoming information. Organizations in such turbulent environments need to give special attention to subsystems for dealing with communication load.

Important concepts in this kind of systems analysis are therefore *communication load* (especially overload), *channels,* and the *capacity* of channels for handling and disseminating environmental information.[17] The case of hospitals in the research introduced at the beginning of this chapter represents a situation in which the system faces overloaded channels of communication, especially in regard to the range of drug therapies and dosages. The system needs to be constructed in such a way that drug information is monitored for patients, doctors, and nurses. This approach gives priority to organizational roles for people who monitor the environment and bring external information into the organization.

Organizational Shape and Structure

Katz and Kahn view organizations as consisting of recurring cycles and patterns of events. Systems make up these patterns of interdependent relationships. These patterns of relationships are established and maintained by communication, much of it face-to-face or, increasingly, carried on through electronic media. Special structures, or subsystems, are needed to maintain the flow of information throughout the elements of the entire system. Effective organizations have in place structures (*networks* and *channels*) for acquiring, processing, and disseminating the information that is the lifeblood of the system.

The structure of the organization is a social structure, rather than the physical structure of buildings and geography. The simplest social structure includes two persons in a continuing relationship (such as two coworkers, or a superior and subordinate). Increasingly complex social structures, each with its own systemic properties, result when more people and functions are added. It is possible to analyze a social structure as a subsystem or system at any level throughout the organization. For example, one could determine whether a particular work group is relatively closed or open as a system, whether it is taking in sufficient information; whether the channels of communication between it and other subsystems are overloaded, and so on.

Again, one of the systemic problems found by the recent research concerning hospitals was the relative isolation of decisions made between doctor and patient in a hospital room from other treatments, patients, and demands on nursing and pharmaceutical staff. In working with individual patients, doctors and nurses may have conceived the situation as a closed system, when in fact it was an open one.

Message Behavior

A systems theory approach to organizational communication places importance on how messages are handled, but less on the content of these messages. As in information theory, the concern is for the efficiency exhibited by some system in getting a message from one place to another with the fewest possible distortions (noise). There is concern, therefore, with the appropriate *coding* of messages. Katz and Kahn maintain that one of the common characteristics of open systems is "information input, negative feedback, and the coding process."[18] Informational inputs are distinguished from energy inputs in that the former provide signals indicating the nature of the environment and the functioning of the organization in that environment.

A system develops a method for selecting certain signals from the environment and translating them into forms understandable to and usable by the system (this is *coding*). One of the most important kinds of these signals for coding is *negative feedback*, which indicates how well the organization is succeeding in meeting its goals. Systems are viewed as especially sensitive to negative feedback messages that help to maintain the desired homeostasis.

Internal messages are concerned with providing the information necessary to maintain internal homeostasis. The maintenance and adaptive subsystems of organizations are especially concerned with messages of this type. Thus it is important for executives in an organization to be aware when morale problems are interfering with efficient performance of duties in parts of the organization.

Methods and Modalities of Communication

Systems theories tend not to specify media for internal organizational communication. The systems approach implies a functionalist perspective, meaning that the analysis is focused on functions rather than specific methods. Channels of communication are described as networks or patterns of relationships. Whether these networks carry their messages by face-to-face interpersonal communication, through electronic or computer-mediated systems, or by written notes, mail, or memos is not given as much theoretical attention. The important point is whether the channels exist and have the capacity to carry the necessary information.

As noted in discussing communication to and from the environment, a systems analysis emphasizes such features of channels as their capacity and load. Network analysis has become a primary method of communication study in the systems theory approach.

Communication Activities

A systems analysis of communication in an organization throws light on the coordination of subsystem activities for the maintenance and functioning of the organization, especially in terms of predictable cycles of input, throughput, and output. "Boundary spanners," individuals who maintain communication links across system and sub-

---

AN ISSUE OF COMMUNICATION ETHICS

College Marketing Strategies

One possible criticism of a systems approach to organizations is its emphasis on monitoring and responding to feedback from the environment. Not only can this emphasis lead to reactive rather than proactive organizations, it can also lead to organizations occasionally giving responses that are in line with what they think groups in the environment want to hear, regardless of their truth. One of the reasons given to justify the growing use of personal attacks in political campaigning is that the feedback politicians receive tends to be positive (attackers get elected).

Universities and other agencies that are held to generally high standards of ethics and conduct may also succumb to this type of reasoning. Studies conducted by the *Wall Street Journal* discovered that many colleges and universities falsified data they submitted to college rating services, such as *Barrons'* and *US News and World Report* magazine. College admissions officers noticed that there seemed to be a definite correlation between high ratings or rankings by one of these services and the following year's freshman enrollment. In other words, the

feedback from the publications' college ratings were noticeable and significant. One temptation in responding to this kind of environmental feedback is to fudge the data reported to these publications. One eastern university that enrolls a large proportion of international students, for example, reported the SAT mathematics scores for all students, including foreign students, who tended to have much higher math scores than American students, while reporting SAT verbal scores for American applicants only, thus removing students whose English was not as strong from the pool.* When an admissions official at another university was confronted with these kinds of false reporting of data, he preferred to term such practices "marketing strategies" rather than lying.

The emphasis on system survival and maintaining a steady state of growth or profit may lead to an overly instrumental use of communication, raising ethical questions of this sort.

*Wall Street Journal, February 15, 1995, p. 1.

system boundaries, are particularly important. Communication activities emphasized, therefore, include monitoring feedback and dealing with information load.

This implication of the systems approach is seen in Katz and Kahn's discussion of conflict.[19] Conflict between systems (whole organizations) is expected in view of the desire of each system to maximize its intake of materials and energy from the environment. Internal conflict is also likely, but it must be subordinated to the needs for overall coordination. Differentiation, in other words, should not take precedence over integration. Conflict is something that should be limited or reduced within the organization. The organizational ecology approach, on the other hand, accepts that organizational systems are inherently mixed-motive systems, which is one of the reasons that organizations are often unable to adapt to a changing ecological environment.[20]

The major communication activities assumed for systems are indicated by the five generic subsystems described by Katz and Kahn: communication activities are categorized by whether they fulfill functions of production, support, maintenance, adaptation (innovation), or management (coordination and direction).

The systems approach tends to view organizations as responding to environmental information, which may overemphasize a reactive view of organizations. The organization's overall goal is usually seen as being maintenance of homeostasis or stability. The organization's communication is therefore concerned with regulating information inputs and outputs and the flow of information through the subsystems. Organizations may thus be seen as relatively passive processors of external information.

CONTINGENCY THEORIES

Systems theory holds that an organization is in continual, dynamic interaction with its environment. The structure of the organization reflects the functions needed to deal with the inputs from that environment. A systems approach thus suggests no single best structure or method for managing an organization: It depends on the situation, and specifically on the *contingencies* of the situation. The concept of *equifinality*, which maintains that organizations with similar purposes in similar environments tend to resemble one another, indicates that different organizational strategies are appropriate depending upon the resources available, the nature of the task, the uncertainty in the environment, and the needs of the people available for carrying out the task.

As two early proponents of contingency theory put it, "The beginning of administrative wisdom is the awareness that there is no one type of management system."[21]

Identification of Contingencies

In the 1950s, research sponsored by the Tavistock Institute in Britain led to the elaboration of the idea of the "environment," so important in systems theory. The environment comprised not just the task demands and inputs, information concerning resources available, the technology available, and the like. There was also a "social environment." Early studies of changing technologies in coal mining in Great Britain led to the notion of a "socio-technical" system providing the contingencies that an organization must deal with. Technology and social factors, in other words, interact in determining the productiveness of an organization.

Technology was also an important contingency in the studies of Joan Woodward, also conducted in Britain mainly in the 1950s.[22] Woodward identifies three types of technologies: those involving small-scale operations, such as printing shops or tailors; large-scale, assembly-line-type operations, as in automobile manufacturing; and what she called "continuous process production," such as oil refineries or power plants (in which the product is in continuous flow). She concludes that assembly-line technologies are characterized by little communication, and what there is consists mainly of vertical, top-down, written directions. The other two forms of operation exhibit more open, face-to-face communication.

Mechanistic and Organic Systems. Two other English researchers focused more on the nature of uncertainty in the environment as a major determinant of organizational type. Tom Burns and G. M. Stalker are credited with coining the useful distinction between *mechanistic* and *organic* organizations. Like other contingency theorists, they did not believe that there was one ideal type of management system, but believed that the most appropriate type depends on, first, extrinsic factors: "These extrinsic factors are all, in our view, identifiable as different rates of technical or market change."[23] The point here is the *rate of change* occurring in the relevant environment. If the rate of change is rather slow, then there is a relatively stable environment; a faster rate of change is associated with a turbulent, uncertain environment.

Mechanistic systems (from the model of the machine) are most suited to a stable environment. Mechanistic systems exhibit many of the characteristics of the bureaucratic structure described by Weber: an emphasis on specialization and departmentalization by function; a rather strictly observed hierarchy of positions, with precise (written) rights and responsibilities for each position; priority given to vertical interaction (superior to subordinate); and responsibility for control and direction at the top of the hierarchy. In addition, mechanistic organizations give more attention and prestige to internal or local knowledge than to external or general expertise. Borrowing from the work of Herbert A. Simon, Burns and Stalker indicate that these organizations rely more on "programmed decision making," meaning that decision making results from plugging relevant information into a preexisting formula or program.[24]

Organic systems are better suited to changing conditions and turbulent, uncertain environments. Individual roles and tasks are subject to continual redefinition, rather than being given by rules or contract or place in a hierarchy. Everyone pitches in, contributing special knowledge or expertise as needed in response to the changing nature of the task at hand. As Burns and Stalker phrase it, there is "no longer omniscience imputed to the head of the concern"; special knowledge may be located anywhere in the firm.[25] There is more stress on all types of internal communication, and there is more horizontal or lateral communication than vertical communication. This communication is more like consulting than like commanding; its content consists of information, advice, and problem solving. Expertise and experience tend to count for more than bureaucratic position. There is hence more prestige associated with externally based, technical knowledge. The type of decision making in these organizations is more of a nonprogrammed type.

Contingency Theory of Lawrence and Lorsch. Contingencies so far identified include the socio-technical system, the technology of an enterprise or industry, and the turbulence of the relevant economic and technical environment. While many of these ideas had been developed by British researchers, two Harvard theorists, Paul R. Lawrence and Jay W. Lorsch, put systematic form to what they now called explicitly *contingency theory.*[26]

The main systemic features they concentrated on were *differentiation* and *integration.* In using an organismic model for describing organizations, systems (and likewise contingency) theorists maintain that the major purpose of an organization is survival. This purpose transcends the stated or assumed purpose of an organization, such as making steel, educating children, or selling insurance. Survival depends upon successful adaptation to relevant conditions in the environment.

For Lawrence and Lorsch, relevant conditions include the external demands of technological and market changes and the internal demands of needs of organizational members.[27] In addition, the complexity of the task leads to the creation of differentiated organizational structures appropriate for a given environment. In general, the more complex the environment, the more differentiated organizations operating in that environment tend to be. Increasing differentiation (specialization) leads to greater strains on the integration of the subsystems into the overall operations of the whole system. Methods for integrating differentiated subsystems, such as effective conflict resolution, therefore become central problems for managing complex organizations. Uncertainty in the environment relevant to each unit or subsystem determines the amount of formal structure appropriate for that unit, in line with the findings of Burns and Stalker. Environmental turbulence, therefore, may seem different for different parts or units of the whole organization; the different units may consequently be structured differently.

These notions lead to the concepts of *loose and tight coupling,* popular among later contingency theorists. If the units or subsystems of an organization are relatively independent of one another, so that each is allowed to adapt to its own perceived needs and environmental conditions, we say that the system as a whole exhibits loose coupling. The units are not highly interdependent. In tightly coupled systems, there is greater need for constant control and coordination of the operations of the various units, given that each one depends significantly on the operations of the others. This idea of coupling is similar to the features of differentiation and integration as viewed by Lawrence and Lorsch. Technologies that require interdependence, or tight coupling, show more need for systemic integration.

Leadership Contingency Models. Fred Fiedler has developed a contingency theory specific to selecting the appropriate leadership style.[28] Fiedler is concerned with determining when a leader should emphasize a task orientation (akin to a bureaucratic,

Theory X approach) and when he or she should emphasize more of a person orientation (similar to a human relations, System 4 approach). The appropriate leadership orientation depends on what Fiedler refers to as the "favorableness" of the situation (hence the label sometimes used for this approach, "situational leadership").

This favorableness depends upon three variables: the power of the leader, the clarity of the task, and the relationship between the leader and subordinates. A highly favorable situation is one in which the task is clearly structured (not highly uncer-

DIVERSITY MATTERS

Physical Diversity as a Contingency

The Americans with Disabilities Act (ADA), passed in 1990, has meant that many organizations have had to adapt to contingencies related to their members' health and physical conditions. Employers have found that they had to rewrite many job descriptions and employment announcements to communicate more precisely with potential employees and to avoid charges of discrimination.

Any requirement listed for filling a position must be one that can be defended as functionally essential to the job; that is, it must be a BFOQ (bona fide occupational qualification). Workers confined to wheelchairs, for example, cannot be excluded on the basis of lack of mobility for a warehouse job, say, unless it can be shown that it is not feasible for the company to provide wheelchair access to all parts of the warehouse to which the potential employee needs to go in the normal carrying out of his or her duties.

BFOQs must also be shown to be genuine in regard to hiring decisions that seem to favor one sex over the other. Women cannot be excluded from selling jobs involving lots of travel or evening work hours because they may have child care responsibilities. All candidates (male and female) can be screened for possible limitations on working late hours or traveling, but such restrictions must be equally applicable to all. Travel or late hours may be a BFOQ, but being male may not be (assuming

that a potential employer believes that males are more free to travel and work late hours).

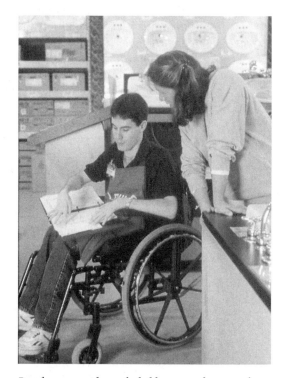

People may not be excluded because of supposed disability.

tain), the power position of the leader is strong, and the relationship with the followers is good. An unfavorable situation is one in which the task is poorly structured or uncertain, and the leader has little formal power and poor relationships with followers. In both highly favorable and unfavorable situations, Fiedler finds that directive, task-oriented leadership is most effective; in intermediate situations, a person-oriented leadership style is more appropriate. The rationale for the surprising idea that directive leadership is appropriate for favorable situations is that relationships are already good, and so the leader can concentrate on the task.

Like the other contingency theorists, Fiedler takes account of uncertainty in the task and the environment but also brings in the situational power of the leader and the interpersonal relationships between leader and follower. Paul Hersey and Ken Blanchard have popularized a *situational leadership model* similar to Fiedler's that takes into account what they refer to as the "maturity" of the followers as a contingent factor.[29] Their theory posits four "styles," designated as delegating, participating, selling, and telling. The first two represent highly nondirective, participative leadership styles, whereas the other two represent more directive styles.

The relationship between organizational communication and leadership is further developed in Chapter 10 of this text.

Karl Weick's Approach to Organizing. Finally, Karl Weick's influential work on organizational theory, although difficult to categorize simply, falls partly within the scope of contingency theory so far described.[30] Weick emphasizes that the term *organization* ought to be replaced by the action *organizing* in this kind of theorizing. Organizations depend upon informational inputs that are interpreted by actors who are involved in some particular organizing. Much of the relevant environment is therefore "enacted," through processes of organizational actors. The organizing is intended to reduce the "equivocality" (uncertainty) that organizational actors perceive in their environment. If the environment tends to present highly equivocal inputs, rules for dealing with the inputs should be kept simple and general; in environments in which inputs are not so equivocal, there can be more specific rules for dealing with them. The relevant contingent factor for Weick is thus informational equivocality.

Highlights of Contingency Theories

In sum, contingency theories have identified the following types of relevant factors, or contingencies, requiring appropriate organizational responses:

- Environmental uncertainty, turbulence, equivocality
- Technological systems
- Nature of the task; clarity of the task
- Nature of power of the leader
- Interpersonal relationships within the organization
- Equivocality of inputs

COMMUNICATION IMPLICATIONS OF CONTINGENCY THEORIES

Context

Contingency theories give top priority to considerations of organizational context. The major survival goal of the organization is to adapt to the relevant external environment (an attempt doomed to failure, according to organizational ecologists). Weick and others therefore stress the importance of dealing with the informational inputs from the environment to facilitate this adaptation. The organization operates as part of the larger system that is the environment. The air that it breathes is largely information.

Contingency theories therefore place a high priority on boundary-spanning communication activities. Attention must be directed toward keeping in place and valuing systems that bring in, evaluate, and disseminate information from the environment.

Organizational Shape and Structure

There is no one best way to shape all organizations, but there is a best way for each organization. Each organization must adapt to its environment. In general, the continuum of possible effective organizations ranges from highly structured, directive, hierarchical ones, at one end, to loosely structured, participative, open organizations, at the other. In well-understood, stable environments, the first type of organizational structure seems effective, whereas in turbulent, changing environments, exhibiting new or less well understood technologies, the less structured organizations seem more effective.

One popular response to the need to adapt organizational structure to environmental and task demands has been the development of the *matrix* form of organization. In a matrix organization, teams are formed to complete specific tasks. The teams are made up of representatives from different functional units or departments, with a team leader or manager. For the duration of the project, team members report to the team leader, while still reporting to a departmental or functional manager, as well (see Figure 6.3).

The communication implications of these two basic types of organizational structure are well summarized in the discussion of the theory of Burns and Stalker. The first type relies more on vertical, formal communication; the second type, on horizontal, informal communication. Weick emphasizes the need for communication rules of interpretation responding to different levels of equivocality in the organization's informational inputs. Perrow and others stress the appropriate amount of loose or tight coupling, which concerns the amount of interdependence versus independence of organizational subsystems. Lawrence and Lorsch speak of the balance between differentiation and integration.

Message Behavior

The characteristic types of messages within an organization differ according to the contingencies and the resultant organizational structure. Burns and Stalker point out that in tightly controlled organizations (stable environment), messages tend to be di-

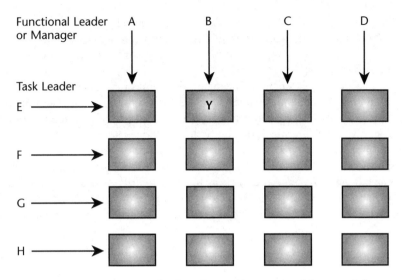

FIGURE 6.3   Matrix organization: Person Y reports to Manager B for functional purposes and to Team Leader E for a specific task or project.

rections, commands, or instructions. In less formal organizations (unstable or uncertain environment), messages take the form of questions, consultations, or giving and receiving advice. Situational leadership theories differentiate between task-oriented messages and relationship-oriented messages. The preponderance of one over the other depends on relevant contingencies.

Methods and Modalities of Communication

The adaptive ability of an organization depends on the system in place for disseminating important environmental information to the appropriate units of the organization. Lawrence and Lorsch emphasize the importance of each unit's interacting with its relevant environment to develop its own adaptive structure. Like systems theories in general, therefore, these theories highlight the capacities of channels and internal networks to handle the necessary flow of information and feedback throughout the entire organization.

Burns and Stalker believe that written channels predominate in more structured, mechanistic organizations, whereas "verbal" (presumably face-to-face) channels are preferred in organic systems.

Communication Activities

In responding to different environmental conditions, organizations enact different primary tasks, carried out partly through different communication activities. In sum, it appears that in turbulent environments, characterized by rapid change and high levels of uncertainty, the primary activities of the organization should facilitate the

Industrial plants were the site for early experiments that led to the human relations movement.

conducted by members of the Department of Industrial Research of Harvard's Graduate School of Business Administration.

The theory of human behavior behind these hypotheses was the same one that was behind scientific management: that external conditions can predict (or determine) human actions. These actions are thus responses to external stimuli. This theory posited that people choose certain behaviors in the expectation of an exchange: In return for performing certain actions they will receive some benefit or reward.

The first physical feature to be studied was the amount of illumination in the work area. Following the initial experiment, which did not produce any meaningful results (at least not meaningful in terms of the original expectations of the researchers), a small group of workers was isolated from the others in order to control more carefully all aspects of the work environment. Over the following years (up to 1933), meticulous records were kept concerning the workers' output and conditions. The experimenters tried varying times and lengths of rest periods, varying lengths of work-system's learning how to respond to change. Special priority should be given to innovation and problem solving. In more stable environments, the primary activity can be more operational, more concentrated on getting on with the normal work of the organization.[31]

As in systems theories in general, the point of view is wholly that of upper management. The goal of the organization is to communicate messages that further goals that are more or less taken for granted. The perspective is mainly functionalist, in other words. Communication activities are judged according to their effectiveness in fulfilling survival goals attributed to the system as a whole. Conflict management systems, for example, are in place to bring about the desired amount of integration, so that all the subsystems are working together to further the system's overall's purposes. Communication activities, it is assumed, can be designed for given conditions (contingencies) that allow for efficient control and direction of the system.[32]

SUMMARY

The organizational theories discussed in this chapter move away from the hope of discovering the "one best way," the magic formula for organizing. These theories also move away from the mechanistic images of earlier theories. The images of organizations are those of a living organism. They also give more attention to the environment and context within which the organization exists.

Systems theories stress the interdependence of the components that make up a system and the open system's constant interaction with its environment. An open system exchanges energy, materials, and information with its environment, through a process of inputs, throughputs, and outputs. In this way, the organization maintains a desired level of maintenance or growth (homeostasis). Systems theories place importance on communication in the system, especially in terms of processing information inputs from the environment and from one subsystem to the others. Feedback is particularly important for the functioning

of open systems. Population-ecology organization theories take the view that the environment selects for certain types of organizational species over others; while organizations function as systems, they are not really adaptive systems in the long run.

Contingency theories developed from systems theories. They stress that there is no one best form or structure for an organization: it depends upon environmental variables. Contingency theorists identify different relevant variables, or contingencies, but there is general agreement on the importance of uncertainty or turbulence in the environment, the nature of the technology of a given organization's operations, and relationships among organization members. Monitoring and interpreting information from the environment becomes especially relevant in contingency theory. The communication patterns of the organization are intended to deal with these inputs and to develop optimum strategies for adapting to the organization's environment.

EXERCISES AND QUESTIONS FOR DISCUSSION

1. Explain how an animal or plant can be said to consist of "systems." Choose an organization, such as a company or a university, and describe the different subsystems that make up the whole

system (for example, begin with the units and administrative structure of your college or university).

2. Explain the meaning of entropy and its relationship to a closed system. How does an open system avoid the law of increasing entropy? Have you observed organizations that are either too closed or too open? What happened in each kind of case?

3. Can you describe cases that illustrate the system feature of equifinality? Consider athletic teams, television productions, and magazines. How have environmental changes represented by the diffusion of cable systems affected the systems in the television industry?

4. Are there examples that back up the notion of the organizational ecologists that environmental conditions ultimately dictate survival for organizations? Give examples of types of organizations that have not survived such environmental changes.

5. Discuss the importance of organizational communication for systems theorists. Why is communication more central in these theories than in classical management theories?

6. Give examples of mechanistic and organic organizations. How would you categorize the organizations that are important in your life (where you work, your school, clubs or social organizations)? Are some structured as mecha-

nistic that should be organic organizations? Do they show loose or tight coupling? Why do you think these discrepancies occur?

7. Prepare a ten-minute briefing on one of the important topics or theorists discussed in this chapter (see the sources at the end of the chapter for references). Briefings must include a discussion of the implications for communication. Topics for briefings could include the following:

Ludwig von Bertalanffy and general systems theory

Entropy and open versus closed systems

The concepts of homeostasis and equifinality

Katz and Kahn's open system theory for organizations

Organizational population ecology theories

Joan Woodward's contingency theory of technologies

Burns and Stalker's mechanistic and organic systems

Lawrence and Lorsch's contingency theory

Loose and tight coupling (Perrow)

Fred Fiedler's model of leadership contingencies

Hersey and Blanchard's situational leadership

Karl Weick's theory of organizing and "equivocality"

These briefings can be individual or group presentations.

SOURCES FOR FURTHER STUDY

Bertalanffy. L. v. (1968). *General systems theory: Foundations, developments and applications.* New York: George Braziller.

Blau, P. M. (1974). *On the nature of organizations.* New York: Wiley.

Bullis, C., and Bach, B. W. (1989) Socialization turning points: An examination of change in organizational identification. *Western Journal of Speech Communication, 53,* 273–93.

Burns, T., and Stalker, G. M. (1961). *The management of innovation.* London: Tavistock Publications.

Burrell, G., and Morgan, G. (1979). *Sociological paradigms and organisational analysis.* London: Heinemann.

Carroll, G. R. (Ed.) (1988). *Ecological models of organizations.* Cambridge, Mass.: Ballinger.

Clampitt, P. (1991). *Communicating for organizational effectiveness.* Newbury Park, Calif.: Sage.

Clegg, S. R. (1990). *Modern organizations.* Newbury Park, Calif.: Sage.

Clegg, S. R., and Dunkerley, D. (1979). *Organization, class and control.* London: Routledge & Kegan Paul.

Deal, T., and Kennedy, A. A. (1982). *Corporate culture: The rites and rituals of corporate life.* Reading: Mass.: Addison-Wesley.

Farace, R. B., Monge, P. R., and Russell, H. M. (1977). *Communicating and organizing.* Madison, Wis.: WCB Brown & Benchmark.

Fiedler, F. (1967). *A theory of leadership effectiveness.* New York: McGraw-Hill.

Frost, P. J., Moore, L. F., Moore, M. R., Lundberg, C. C., and Martin, J. (Eds.) (1985). *Organizational context.* Beverly Hills, Calif.: Sage.

Hall, R. H. (1991). *Organizations: Structures, processes, and outcomes.* Englewood Cliffs, N.J.: Prentice-Hall.

Hannan, M. T., and Freeman, J. (1989). *Organizational ecology.* Cambridge, Mass.: Harvard University Press.

Hersey, P., and Blanchard, K. (1982). *Management and organizational behavior.* Englewood Cliffs, N.J.: Prentice-Hall.

Kanter, R. B. (1977). *Men and women of the corporation.* New York: Basic Books.

Katz, D., and Kahn, R. (1978). *The social psychology of organizations,* 2d ed. New York: Wiley.

Klimann, R. H., Saxton, M. J., and Serpa, R. (Eds.) (1985). *Gaining control of the corporate culture.* San Francisco: Jossey-Bass.

Lawrence, P. R., and Lorsch, J. W. (1967). *Organization and environment: Managing differentiation and integration.* Boston: Harvard University Press.

Likert, R. (1967). *The human organization.* New York: McGraw-Hill.

March, J. G., and Simon, H. A. (1958). *Organizations.* New York: Wiley.

Millman, M., and Kanter, R. M. (1975). *Another voice: Feminist perspectives on social life and social science.* Garden City, N.Y.: Anchor.

Morgan, G. (1986). *Images of organization.* Newbury Park, Calif.: Sage.

Pacanowsky, M. E., and O'Donnell-Trujillo, N. (1982). Communication and organizational culture. *Western Journal of Speech Communication, 46,* 115–30.

Perrow, C. (1972). *Complex organizations: A critical essay.* Glenview, Ill.:Scott, Foresman.

Perrow, C. (1984). *Normal accidents: Living with high-risk technologies.* New York: Basic Books.

Peters, T. J., and Austin, N. (1985). *A passion for excellence: The leadership difference.* New York: Random House.

Peters, T. J., and Waterman, R. H., Jr. (1982). *In search of excellence: Lessons from America's best-run companies.* New York: Harper & Row.

Pettigrew, A. M. (1979). On studying organizational cultures. *Administrative Science Quarterly, 24,* 570–81.

Presthus, R. (1962). *The organizational society.* New York: Vintage.

Putnam, L. L., and Pacanowsky, M. E. (Eds.) (1983). *Communication and organizations: An interpretive approach.* Newbury Park, Calif.: Sage.

Schall, M. (1983). A communication rules approach to organizational culture. *Administrative Science Quarterly, 28,* 557–81.

Schein, E. H. (1991). *Organizational culture and leadership.* San Francisco: Jossey-Bass.

Scott, W. R. (1981). *Organizations: Rational, natural, and open systems.* Englewood Cliffs, N.J.: Prentice-Hall.

Simon, H. A. (1957). *Administrative behavior.* New York: Macmillan.

Weick, K. E. (1976). Educational organizations as loosely coupled systems. *Administrative Science Quarterly, 21,* 1–16.

Weick, K. E. (1979). *The social psychology of organizing,* 2d ed. Reading: Mass.: Addison-Wesley.

Woodward, J. (1965). *Industrial organization: Theory and practice.* London: Oxford University Press.

NOTES

1. *Wall Street Journal,* July 5, 1995, p. B6.
2. *Newsweek,* July 17, 1995, p. 54.
3. G. Morgan (1986), *Images of organization,* Newbury Park, Calif.: Sage, pp. 40–45.
4. R. Likert (1967), *The human organization,* New York: McGraw-Hill, pp. 186–87.
5. L. v. Bertalanffy (1968), *General systems theory: Foundations, developments, applications,* New York: George Braziller.
6. G. Burrell and G. Morgan (1979), *Sociological paradigms and organisational analysis,* London: Heinemann, p. 58.
7. D. Katz and R. L. Kahn (1978), *The social psychology of organizations,* 2d ed., New York: Wiley.
8. Katz and Kahn, p. v.

9. Katz and Kahn, p. 32.

10. Katz and Kahn, pp. 51–67.

11. M. T. Hannan and J. Freeman (1989), *Organizational ecology,* Cambridge, Mass.: Harvard University Press.

12. Hannan and Freeman, p. xiii.

13. G. R. Carroll (1988), Organizational ecology in theoretical perspective, in G. R. Carroll (Ed.), *Ecological models of organizations,* Cambridge, Mass.: Ballinger, p. 2.

14. See R. B. Farace, P. R. Monge, and H. M. Russell (1977), *Communicating and organizing,* Reading, Mass.: Addison-Wesley; or G. M. Goldhaber (1993), *Organizational communication,* Madison, Wis.: WCB Brown & Benchmark.

15. Farace, Monge, and Russell.

16. G. P. Huber and R. L. Daft (1987), The information environments of organizations, in F. M. Jablin, L. L. Putnam, K. H. Roberts, and L. W. Porter (Eds.), *Handbook of organizational communication: An interdisciplinary perspective,* Newbury Park, Calif.: Sage, pp. 130–64.

17. Farace, Monge, and Russell, pp. 97–125.

18. Katz and Kahn, p. 26.

19. Katz and Kahn, pp. 615–18.

20. Hannan and Freeman, p. 5.

21. T. Burns and G. M. Stalker (1961), *The management of innovation,* London: Tavistock Publications, p. 125.

22. J. Woodward (1965), *Industrial organization: Theory and practice,* London: Oxford University Press.

23. Burns and Stalker, p. 96.

24. H. A. Simon (1957), *Administrative behavior,* New York: Macmillan; see Burns and Stalker. p. 115.

25. Burns and Stalker, p. 121.

26. P. R. Lawrence and J. W. Lorsch (1967), *Organization and environment: Managing differentiation and integration,* Boston: Harvard University Press; W. R. Scott (1981), *Organizations: Rational, natural and open systems,* Englewood Cliffs, N.J.: Prentice-Hall, p. 114, points out that Lawrence and Lorsch coined the term *contingency theory.*

27. Lawrence and Lorsch, p. 155.

28. F. Fiedler (1967), *A theory of leadership effectiveness,* New York: McGraw-Hill.

29. P. Hersey and K. Blanchard (1982), *Management of organizational behavior,* Englewood Cliffs, N.J.: Prentice-Hall.

30. Scott, pp. 117–19; K. E. Weick (1979), *The social psychology of organizing,* 2d ed., Reading, Mass.: Addison-Wesley.

31. Burrell and Morgan, p. 172.

32. S. Clegg and D. Dunkerley (1979), *Organization, class and control.* London: Routledge & Kegan Paul, pp. 256–57.

CHAPTER **7**

Organizational Culture

CHAPTER OBJECTIVES

After studying this chapter, you should be able to:

- Explain the widespread popularity of the concept of organizational culture, especially in business circles.
- Discuss the purposes that culture fulfills for human beings.
- Explain the metaphor implied when speaking about organizational cultures.
- Show how culture differs from the concept of organizational climate.
- Identify elements that constitute a given organizational culture.
- Describe the culture of an organization.
- Discuss the problems of intercultural communication as related to organizational cultures.
- Summarize the communication implications of taking a cultural approach to the study of organizations.

CHAPTER OUTLINE

POPULARITY OF THE CULTURAL METAPHOR

When Walt Disney Co. announced that it was taking over Capital Cities/ABC Inc., questions were raised concerning a potential *cultural* clash between the two partners. The *Wall Street Journal,* for example, expressed the fear that such differences in corporate culture could amount to an "enormous hurdle" for the new organization.[1] Disney was described as having a tough, battling kind of culture, despite its family-type image, whereas Capital Cities was seen as having a more courtly style with emphasis on consensus building. In the same way, when Westinghouse Corporation acquired the CBS television network, questions about cultural compatibility were raised. Again, the *Wall Street Journal* suggested that Westinghouse's corporate culture was the major "roadblock" in the way of a successful merger.[2] The culture was described as "numbers-driven" and "distant," with top executives carrying around so-called death cards in their wallets, cards with the dates of their intended retirement from the company.

Corporate cultures are important, it seems, not only when there are mergers, but also when organizations are looking for top executives. Recently business publications began to feature stories with headlines such as: "Exxon, Mobil Pick New Top Officers, Men Who Fit Their Corporate Culture."[3] Cultures are also important during times of significant corporate change, as when General Motors attempted to revise the culture of its Saturn division to make it more like other GM divisions, such as Chevrolet or Buick. The effort recognized that there had been a concerted effort to create a different kind of culture at Saturn.

This chapter deals with the concept of *organizational* or *corporate culture*. Communication takes place within an environment, which shapes and determines the communication experiences people have; but, on the other hand, communication also plays a role in structuring the context. In other words, there is an ongoing interrelationship between communication and the setting in which it occurs. Often we cannot know the meaning of a particular message or interchange between people without knowing the context, or the organization's culture.

The first part of the chapter discusses what is meant when we say that an organization has a culture. An organizational culture is differentiated from an organizational

Many wonder if the Disney culture will be changed by mergers.

climate. The elements that constitute an organizational culture are described next, with special attention to the role that communication plays in the expression of culture. Whether an organization's culture can be changed or managed is the next topic. The importance of culture also raises questions concerning intercultural communication within an organization and the relationship between an organization's culture and the broader national or ethnic culture in which the organization is situated.

THE CONCEPT OF ORGANIZATIONAL CULTURE

Some concepts from the systems or contingency schools of thought overlap with those of the cultural approach. A central notion of the contingency theorists, that successful organizations exhibit distinctive characteristics, was picked up and supported by studies that popularized the idea of organizational culture.[4] These studies were the bases for the "excellence" series of books, initiated in 1982 with *In Search of Excellence,* by Thomas Peters and Robert Waterman. These studies select successful companies and organizations and try to find what they have in common. What they seemed to have in common was something that the authors called a "strong culture."

The metaphor for describing organizations shifted from that of a biological organism to that of a small-scale, anthropological culture. An organization was likened to a small society with its own language, customs, forms of dress, imagery, heroes, myths, and rituals. As a cultural anthropologist might go into the field among the villages of a remote people, so the analyst approaches the organization.

The Meaning of Culture

To anthropologists, *culture* refers to a fundamental set of *persistent characteristics* associated with a particular group of people, typically ethnically based. Simply put, the purpose of culture is to make life predictable and understandable for members of that group; it has been referred to as "shared programming of the mind" of entire social groups "which is stable over time and leads to the same person showing more or less the same behavior in similar situations."[5]

Take one of the most fundamental markers of culture, language. Obviously, if you know each day that the people you must deal with will all be speaking the same language as you, generally defining words as you define them, an important element of uncertainty is removed from your life. In a similar way, other decisions about conducting your life can be reduced to predictable, taken-for-granted patterns: how to dress, how to meet people, how to stand and look at other people, and so on. Without the patterns of culture, we would have to meet each day and each person anew, working out very basic details concerning our interactions over and over. Little time would be left for dealing with other matters.

A shared culture also defines for a group the important issues and values in life. If the patterns of status in a culture have come to emphasize wealth, then a motivation to gain wealth is taken for granted; people can assume this motivation in others. They may also assume that others will accept this motivation as appropriate and even praiseworthy. A set of values and fundamental beliefs about the nature and purpose of life therefore underlies the concept of culture.

The most immediate difference people notice when going from one culture to another is that they can no longer understand the language. But that is not all that is different. Many other things that people take for granted in their own culture are handled differently. These differences forcefully make the point that culture is not given by nature or biology but created by human beings.

In summary, culture refers to stable patterns of behavior representative of a defined human group. Culture provides predictability in these persistent patterns. An important set of these patterns involves the values that give meaning to these people's activities. Culture is not given by nature but represents a series of human decisions made over years or centuries. Culture is the result of human beings making sense of their existence and experiences.

The Metaphor of Organizational Culture

The term *organizational culture* may have first been used in its current sense in 1979 in an article in the *Administrative Science Quarterly,* although Blake and Mouton used the term earlier in reference to organizational climate.[6] Even earlier, an anthropologist, W. Lloyd Warner, was the primary designer of one of the Hawthorne studies at the dawn of the human relations movement. This appears to have been the first use of an anthropologist to look for some sort of work or organizational culture.[7]

The widespread popularity of the term in management circles dates from the publication of works such as *In Search of Excellence* and *Corporate Culture: The Rites and Rituals of Corporate Life,* by Terence Deal and Arthur A. Kennedy (also published in 1982).[8] At about the same time, the challenge of "Japanese management" reinforced interest in culture, and William Ouchi's book on Theory Z became a best-seller.[9] The subtitle of Ouchi's book is instructive in this regard: *How American Businesses Can Meet the Japanese Challenge.*

Underlying the popularity of the concept is the sense that it takes account of the seeming irrationality or *non*rationality of real-life organizations. In the 1950s, Herbert Simon and his colleagues at Carnegie-Mellon began to discuss the "bounded rationality" and the tendency toward "satisficing" in actual (as opposed to theoretical) organizations. They meant that people in organizations did not behave as fully rational actors, seeking to maximize benefits. Rather, the rationality that people employ is *bounded,* or limited, in that only certain options or perspectives are considered. The idea was further developed by Irving Janis in his analysis of what he called "groupthink," group processes that actually interfere with groups' ability to discover optimal solutions.

The supposed nonrationality of human groups and organizations, of course, may simply indicate that they are following a different kind of rationality, one in tune with symbolic meanings and human relationships. These symbolic and human factors are understood and communicated in terms of traditions, stories, myths, and rituals—in other words, the cultural practices of an organization. Analytic studies of organizations following a cultural approach, therefore, tend to appear "soft" rather than "hard," qualitative rather than quantitative, and interpretive rather than functionalist. These generalizations do not apply across the board: There are efforts to quantify organizational cultural variables and to manipulate culture for administrative ends.

The national or ethnic culture, such as American culture, Japanese culture, or Kikuyu culture, represents the background culture within which organizations exist. Organizational cultures are thus microcultures, the patterns of making sense and experience characteristic of a specific organization.

The wider national, ethnic, or societal culture does affect an organizational culture. During the Industrial Revolution, the creation of the factory system required a cultural change within the population of Great Britain (and later France, Germany, the United States, and so on). Attitudes about clock time, for example, required radical alteration. People had to be imbued with a new respect for punctuality, as well as the other virtues now referred to under the popular heading of the *work ethic.* These virtues were not given by nature or by experiences of people up to that time (the late 1700s). One purpose of early public education in this country was to inculcate such virtues in a majority of the population.

Organizations consist of people who get together and talk, tell stories, and work out their personal needs and even frustrations as they work on some common goal. Many of the activities of the organization may not make sense if analyzed in terms of rational management theory or contingency theory, but these activities may make sense if they are seen as symbolic, fulfilling some "ritual" need. Studying a set of statistical projections, Gareth Morgan points out, may be no more "rational" or scientific than the studying of celestial omens or the entrails of sacrificed animals among ancient Romans or Etruscans.[10] Managers feel more comfortable about their decisions after consulting these tables, however, just as their Roman forebears felt more comfortable after hearing the omens or reading the entrails.

The elements that make up organizational culture were first identified by Deal and Kennedy as the business environment, shared values, heroes, rites and rituals, and the "cultural network."[11] One symposium refers to organizational culture in these terms: "Operationally, culture is defined as shared philosophies, ideologies, values, beliefs, assumptions, and norms. These are seldom written down or discussed, but they are learned by living in the organization and becoming a part of it."[12] The *values* are the bedrock, the basis for how things are typically done in a given organization. The *heroes* embody and illustrate these values in positive ways for members of the organization. The *rites* and *rituals* provide symbolic ways of enacting and reminding members of these values. The *cultural network* represents the way in which the values and the culture in general are transmitted and maintained throughout the entire organization.

Culture Distinguished from Climate

Both terms, *climate* and *culture,* have been subject to varying definitions and interpretations, and the two concepts may occasionally seem to overlap. As a result, some writers have suggested, "Organizational culture in many respects represents a reformulation of variables previously grouped under the heading 'climate' by traditional organizational literature."[13] And others suggest that organizational culture research is a continuation of climate research under a "new wave" title.[14] In other words, it may not be obvious how the two concepts differ.

It is helpful to hold on to the original meanings of climate and culture to understand their different uses. Climate suggests a feeling that people have about the atmosphere within an organization, particularly whether that atmosphere is positive or negative (chilly and cold, or warm and sunny). Culture is a more all-encompassing concept pointing to a historically developed set of shared values and beliefs of a defined group of people. Culture provides the unspoken guidelines for a group's procedures and actions as well as how those procedures and actions are to be interpreted and understood. These guidelines become so ingrained within a particular culture that they are taken for granted and therefore operate outside of everyday, or conscious, awareness.

Cultural factors determine how people experience and therefore evaluate an organizational climate. Picture a culture in which formality is stressed, and there is a high value placed on avoiding open conflict. Someone from a culture that values open and heated debate would probably describe the climate of this first culture as "cold" or "hostile." Those who are members of the culture, on the other hand, would find the climate reassuring and predictable, and therefore describe it in more positive terms.

This discussion implies some basic distinctions between these two concepts along these lines:

1. *Evaluation.* An organizational climate is usually described as either positive or negative, supportive or not supportive, whereas a given culture is value-neutral (neither good nor bad). However, the culture provides the basis for making value judgments concerning climate.[15]

2. *Awareness.* People within the organization are able to describe their perceptions of the atmosphere or climate. The way that climate is studied in organizations is to ask for just such descriptions. On the other hand, many aspects of an organization's culture are taken for granted and therefore are not noticed by members, or at least are not brought to mind quickly and easily. An organization member can probably tell an outsider immediately what the climate in the organization is like but would have more difficulty responding to the question, What is your organization's culture?

3. *Breadth.* It probably would not take long to describe one's feeling about an organization's climate, but presumably it would take much longer to describe the culture.

4. *Purpose.* Culture was developed by human beings in order to make their lives more predictable and thus more subject to their control.[16] Climate does not have this taken-for-granted predictive or control function for the individual experiencing it; rather, it is experienced as conducive or not conducive to certain behaviors.

5. *Norms.* The beliefs and values underlying a particular culture generate the guidelines and norms for behaviors, including communication. Climate may represent an expression of the culture's underlying values and assumptions, but it is not the basis for such norms.

In sum, the concepts of climate and culture are closely related and even interrelated. As used in this text, culture is the broader concept, suggesting the basis for determining and evaluating the climate experienced by individuals within an organization. H. M. Trice and J. M. Beyer, in their study of work cultures, summarize the differences when they point out, "As originally conceptualized, organizational climate referred to psychological environments in which the behavior of individuals occurred" and "[t]hus it focused on measuring the perceptions of individuals about their organizations, rather than beliefs, values, or norms shared by groups of people."[17]

Interpretivist and Functionalist Perspectives on Culture

Most of the organizational theories discussed in the earlier chapters take a functionalist perspective, concerned with administration and control of an organization. Functionalists seek variables that will explain how an organization works, in the hope that by manipulating those variables, they can make the organization work better. Interpretivists, on the other hand, seek to understand the lives of people as experienced in organizations. Understanding and interpretation are therefore the purposes of this second perspective.

The cultural metaphor is compatible with an interpretivist perspective. Cultural theorists are attuned to the stories that organizational members tell in order to make sense of their organizational experiences. Cultures are socially constructed and depend upon symbolic images and rituals. The social reality that people experience within an organization is therefore largely subjective. From this point of view, culture and communication are not variables that can be manipulated to produce desired ends; rather, they are "vehicles through which reality is constituted in organizational contexts."[18]

But not all organizational cultural approaches are interpretivist. In fact, the point of the early popularized books of Deal and Kennedy and Peters and Waterman was to use culture, to manipulate it to further organizational ends. This point of view is emphasized by Edgar Schein when he raises the possibility that "the *only thing of real importance that leaders do is to create and manage culture.*"[19] (Emphasis in original.) The difference comes down to this: whether organizations *have* culture, which is another variable that can be manipulated, or whether organizations *are* cultures.

Thus, two very different views concerning the nature of organizational culture have emerged. The question of whether culture is something to be managed and manipulated is discussed later in this chapter, following the discussion of the elements that make up or indicate an organization's culture.

ELEMENTS OF ORGANIZATIONAL CULTURE

What does one look for when trying to describe and then understand a particular organizational culture? One begins with the elements, the largely visible activities, symbols, and messages that characterize the culture. Deal and Kennedy identified five components of corporate culture:

1. The business environment, or the marketplace in which the organization operates
2. Values, which define success and lead toward success
3. Heroes, whose examples and lessons are presented in myths
4. Rites and rituals, including symbolic repetitive activities and ceremonies
5. The cultural network, processes and roles that transmit, maintain, and educate newcomers in the culture

Values are the bedrock of an organization's culture in this scheme. Heroes and especially narratives about the heroes communicate and inculcate these values. A lot of attention is given to founding heroes, such as Watson at IBM. Rites and rituals function to build solidarity and to reduce tension.

Many supposedly rational activities are carried out for symbolic and ritual purposes. Techniques such as MBO (management by objectives) and strategic planning, for example, are often symbolic. Everyday contingencies and habitual patterns of behavior overwhelm the MBO objectives and strategic plans, which typically remain quietly in files until they are brought to light to be revised at the next annual review or planning conference.

The cultural network, in Deal and Kennedy's model, includes roles for transmitting and maintaining the culture, such as *storytellers* to pass on the narratives and myths, *priests* to remember the correct rituals and precedents, *gossips* to maintain the informal grapevine, and even *spies, whisperers,* and *cabals.* These writers thus began an effort to identify important elements of organizational cultures that could be observed and used to analyze a given culture.

Geert Hofstede, who has been particularly active in cross-cultural analyses of organizations, and his colleagues have attempted to classify the elements of organizational culture in a more systematic way. The four manifestations of culture are

Symbols

Heroes

Rituals

Values

The first three elements are identified as *practices;* they are directly observable by someone studying the culture. The core of the culture, however, is represented by the values, which are defined as "broad, nonspecific feelings of good and evil, beautiful and ugly, normal and abnormal, rational and irrational—feelings that are often unconscious and rarely discussable."[20] The values, therefore, are not directly observable but can be inferred from choices made among alternative ways of behaving.

Symbols are defined as "words, gestures, pictures, or objects that carry a particular meaning within a culture."[21] Symbols, which take on unique meanings for a particular group, are carried in both verbal and nonverbal channels. Heroes are models for valued attitudes or behaviors and are hence also symbolic. Rituals are patterned activities that are not necessary for the ostensible or technical functioning of the organization. Note that saying that these activities are not technically necessary is not the same as saying that they are unnecessary. A meeting may not contribute to producing an organization's product but may be socially necessary to maintain confidence, morale, and people's sense of identification and motivation. It may serve to remind participants that the organization values good process and participative decision making. Hofstede and his associates thus try to show the relationships among the elements as one moves from outer, surface manifestations toward deeper levels of culture.

Similarly, Edgar H. Schein emphasizes the deep structure of culture, the "basic underlying assumptions," which he identifies as the ultimate source for both values and observable actions.[22] What he labels *artifacts* are all the visible symbols, messages, role models, and rituals.

Schein believes that it is relatively easy to observe and describe the artifacts (the visible elements of culture), but that such observations are subject to different, reasonable, and yet inaccurate interpretations. The essential or "real" meanings of these artifacts can be apprehended only through deeper involvement in the culture as a participant-observer in an effort to come to know the more basic underlying assumptions.[23]

In another recent work, H. M. Trice and J. M. Beyer provide a rather thorough framework focusing on specific communication behaviors that manifest organizational culture.[24] Trice and Beyer agree with the general tenor of the other approaches that values (or some underlying deep structure of values or assumptions) are basic to the formation and definition of particular cultures. The *cultural forms,* however, are the the media and the messages that embody the organizational culture.

These elements are organized in terms of increasing complexity as follows:

- *Symbols* (objects, settings, performers, roles); nonverbal communication
- *Language* (jargon, humor, metaphors, slogans, gestures); verbal communication
- *Narration* (stories, legends, sagas); verbal communication
- *Practices* (rituals, taboos, rites, ceremonials); both verbal and nonverbal communication

The first level for expressing organizational culture is mainly *nonverbal communication*. Proxemics, chronemics, and objectics (as discussed in Chapter 3) provide the symbolic cues and settings communicating a certain kind of culture.

Take the use of space. An organization that places people in an open, shared space communicates cultural values of collaboration, openness, and cooperation. On the other hand, one that separates people into cubicles or offices may emphasize hierarchy and specialization. The space creates an ambience that is intended to send a message; for example, fast-food restaurants that emphasize gleaming clean surfaces versus a more elegant restaurant with warm, red tones, comfortable seating, and dimmed lighting. Some management consultants maintain that messy washrooms can be a sign

Certain symbols, such as uniforms or distinct clothing, are obvious indicators of organizational culture.

of low morale or employee dissatisfaction. They say that for employees, trashing the bathroom can be a way of "acting out their frustration."[25] The treatment of such space can therefore send negative messages about the corporate culture. The time devoted to different activities may also serve to symbolize the importance or lack of importance placed on those activities.

Objects can be used for giving cultural messages. Uniforms indicate status, function, or special skill, for example. Judicial robes in the United States, as well as the additional wigs in British systems, symbolize that judges represent the law rather than themselves. Computers, cellular phones, and other such devices indicate technological sophistication. Objects used as symbols can be relatively overt, such as diplomas and certificates displayed on walls, flags, emblems, and signs prohibiting certain behaviors. Or, symbols can be more subtle, as when an official places family photographs on the desk or pictures of fly-fishing or other hobbies on the walls. Objects can become *logos,* used to represent the values of an organization, such as the solidity of the rock of Gibralter. People or characters are used in this way as well, as when the rugged cowboy represents an organization's independence and self-reliance.

The second level in Trice and Beyer's scheme emphasizes verbal communication, the verbal means of expressing the beliefs and values of a culture. Slogans and sayings summarize cultural ideas and values, as when a company claims that "Quality is Job One." The use of slang and jargon sets members of the organization apart from other people and emphasizes their roles in the culture. The military, the police, and space exploration are well known for their heavy reliance on initialisms for shorthand communication. The Navy especially relies on terms like ComSubPac, NELC, and NAVREGS, for example. Slang words also mark members of organizational cultures and subcultures, as when policeman refer to "perps" (perpetrators, people who commit crimes) and Disney "cast members" refer to "good Mickeys" (fortunate events or actions).

Humor and jokes are especially culture-bound forms of language use. Whether something is funny and why often depends on an insider's understanding and background experience. The extreme case, of course, is represented by the group who repeated so many inside jokes that they simply numbered them for easy reference. To tell a joke, all a member needed to do was to call out a number and the others would laugh uproariously (or so the story goes). In other words, humor can be used to distinguish insiders from outsiders, as when a musician refers to a nearly impossible task as the same as playing the piccolo part to "Stars and Stripes Forever" on a pair of hand-tuned tymps.

Humor may also be used to uphold or maintain certain values of the culture. An attorney friend reports an effort he made when arguing his first case before the U.S. Supreme Court. The opposing attorney, at the end of her presentation, had accidentally spilled her water glass on her papers. My friend began his presentation by hoping that the justices would see that her arguments were now all wet. No one cracked a smile: Humor was considered quite out of place in that culture.

Metaphors convey a complex idea or image of the organization in quick, shorthand form. A well-known example is the use of a theater metaphor for Disney World and Disneyland. Employees are "cast members" who are presenting a theatrical performance for "guests," rather than customers. Another popular metaphor for many organizations is that of the family—at least until economic times become tough and the "family" suddenly becomes a business again.

Trice and Beyer include gestures as language when these gestures have direct verbal translations, such as the index finger and thumb touching at the tips to mean "O.K." in American culture.[26] In distinctive organizational cultures, such gestures are usually understood only by members or participants. The hand signals used in the trading pits of the Chicago commodities market are good examples.

Narration (more elaborate forms of verbal communication) represents the next type of cultural form. Such narratives are classified as "stories," "sagas," and "myths." Stories are brief descriptions, usually of a single event that may or may not have happened. Often such organizational stories, like stories in the wider culture, show similarities across organizations. In everyday life, people from communities all over the United States tell stories about the "choking Doberman," or the "alligators in the sewer," or the "hook on the car door." Students, especially graduate students, regardless of university, tell the same "good student dream" story. In this story, there is a course that for some reason you have never attended, and you find yourself in an examination room being tested on the completely unfamiliar material.

The observation that similar stories are repeated in different cultures suggests that the purpose of the stories is to describe not what did happen but what *should* have or *could* have happened. Stories are thus creative expressions shared by word of mouth to help people understand and deal with their experiences in the organization.[27]

Sagas are stories that deal with heroes; typically they deal with the struggles and vision of founders. Sagas are usually longer narratives than stories, taking the heroes through several challenges and triumphs. The founding and development of Ben & Jerry's Ice Cream, in which the founders share a vision for a certain kind of organization that fulfills high ideals, is a good example of this type of saga.

Myths are even more complex narratives, intended to provide the basic rationale for both values and important organizational beliefs about the nature of the world. Myths are not necessarily either true or false, but they are intended to justify some basic belief in recounting a pivotal event or crisis. In Chapter 4, in the discussion of classical management theory, for example, there is a reference to Taylor's convincing an immigrant workman named "Schmidt" (his name actually was Henry Noll) to follow Taylor's methods of pig-iron handling. The description of persuading Schmidt/ Noll to follow precise, scientifically developed procedures seems to have been largely invented retroactively, more to illustrate techniques at a later stage than to recount what actually happened in the first stages of scientific management.[28] The Schmidt/ Noll story then became a myth among Taylorist managers to point out the purported precision of Taylor's methods from the very first. Ironically, in today's climate, the stereotyping of Schmidt in the story casts a negative pall over Taylor and his views of immigrant laborers.

Finally, the most complex cultural forms are extended performances and practices involving both verbal and symbolic nonverbal communication: rituals, taboos, rites, and ceremonials. In their effort to be systematic, Trice and Beyer divide these practices into two categories: rituals and taboos, and rites and ceremonials.

Rituals and taboos, the first category, are simple, brief, habitual behaviors that generally have no direct practical function. Rites and ceremonials, the second type, are more elaborate performances of longer duration; they require more extensive coordination and preparation. Rituals include setup routines that workers may follow, in which certain operations are always completed in the same order regardless of practical necessity. Taboos refer to actions, objects, or people habitually avoided for apparently superstitious reasons; an example would be not mentioning a no-hitter to a baseball pitcher while he is throwing one. Commencement ceremonies at colleges are a good example of what is meant by a rite. Other organizational rites might include training seminars, annual meetings, special events like Christmas parties, and so on.

In sum, the observable elements of organizational culture are mainly verbal and nonverbal communication signs and events. The systems for categorizing such elements provide a useful framework for carrying out systematic observations of an organizational culture.

Observers are thus directed toward a wide range of communication activities and message systems:

Objects (or persons) as symbols

Proxemics

Chronemics

Language forms:
    slang, jargon, initialisms
    humor and jokes
    gestures (emblems)
    slogans, proverbial sayings
    metaphors

Narratives
    stories
    sagas (featuring heroes)
    myths (crises or turning points)

Rituals and taboos

Rites and ceremonies

CAN ORGANIZATIONAL CULTURE BE MANAGED? THE CASE OF TQM

The idea that culture is not static but undergoes fairly continual if often imperceptible change leads to the controversy over whether or not an organizational culture can be intentionally manipulated. This controversy is foreshadowed in the earlier discussion concerning functionalist and interpretivist perspectives on organizational culture. The point of books such as those by Deal and Kennedy was to show top executives how to manipulate elements of culture. Popular management trends such as Total Quality Management (TQM) involve shaping and changing an organization's values to increase members' commitment to quality. Also, a fairly large consulting industry has grown up to engineer (and "reengineer") and produce packages to change corporate cultures.[29]

Those who believe in the possibility of changing a culture in a desired direction, therefore, see culture as a factor that affects the organization; other factors might include the standard technology in the field, competing organizations, the population being served, and so on. Culture is thus conceived to be an independent variable that can take on different values to influence some dependent variable, such as productivity or quality. Culture is described as an attribute of the organization; as such, it can be functional or dysfunctional. The job of managers or consultants, then, is to fix dysfunctional cultures.[30]

The competing view is that culture is not a variable distinguishable from the organization as a whole. One studies an organization's culture in order to understand that particular organization or organizations in general. Culture is not under the control of a small group of top managers, in this point of view, but is shaped and developed by continuous interactions at all levels of the organization. The first view represents a functionalist, administrative perspective, whereas the second represents the interpretivist view.

In the end, even those who believe in the possibility and desirability of changing organizational cultures admit some limitations, such as the following.

First, culture exists at different levels. The deepest levels of values or basic assumptions are difficult to make explicit and even more difficult to change. The practices and symbols, the observable cultural elements, are more subject to change. Thus, even proponents of the culture-change approach are led to explain, "although the deeper approaches initially seem to be more penetrating, in practice they seem to be impractical; and although the more superficial approaches at first appear to disregard the more fundamental bases of culture, in practice they appear to offer some specific handles for managing culture."[31] In other words, we may not be able to change the deep levels of culture, but changing surface elements and behavioral norms can be effective anyway.

Second is the problem of multiple cultures within the same organization: Does an organization have one or several cultures? Take the case of a university: The teaching faculty experience one culture, whereas administrators, custodial staff, and students, among others, probably experience different organizational cultures within the university. Technical people often feel themselves to be part of a wider occupation-specific culture more than part of a local organizational culture. When consultants or upper management decide to change "the" culture, which culture will be affected? Should they try to change all or only some of the distinct cultures or subcultures? Again, change proponents accept that implementing change is easier in cases in which the culture is uniform than when there are many smaller subcultures.

The works advocating managing culture that are popular among business leaders suggest methods for changing corporate cultures. The tenth chapter of Deal and

Kennedy's book deals with ways to reshape the culture, in order to develop a *strong culture*. But change attempts are difficult and time-consuming and are not to be undertaken lightly, they warn. *Symbolic managers* who would successfully manage culture must build carefully on consensus and trust. They give special importance to putting a recognized *hero* in charge of the change, developing new transition rituals and symbols, using outside *shamans* (consultants) to deflect resistance, and emphasizing security and training for current members.

In their book *In Search of Excellence,* Peters and Waterman are less directly prescriptive but do list attributes that they maintain are hallmarks of "excellent" organizations. James Lewis prescribes a specific program for implementing cultural change through the use of "Theory Z," the humanistic management style popularized by William Ouchi's book of the same name.[32] His prescriptions are similar to those of Deal and Kennedy, stressing emphasis on training, especially "people-oriented" and "people-building" approaches, using existing organizational structures, building on consensus decision making, and team building.

Several academic conferences were held in the 1980s for the purpose of developing programs for changing and managing organizational culture.[33] These conferences often stressed the difficulty of changing organizational culture, especially the deeper aspects involving fundamental values and assumptions, as noted above. There were case studies of what were deemed successfully implemented cultural changes, as at AT&T following the divestiture and breakup of the Bell monopoly in telecommunications. Still the emphasis was on caution: Certain very favorable conditions had to be present or change attempts were likely to be ineffective or even complete failures. Not only should the already existing culture be tolerant of change and innovation, but there must often be a startling, precipitating challenge or threat calling for the change.[34]

The introduction of TQM in the United States, largely in response to competitive pressures from Japanese and other international competitors, illustrates the continuing widespread and influential belief in the importance of changing organizational cultures.

TQM has emerged in American business circles as an effort aimed at changing corporate cultures to ensure higher quality of performance. The standard method of quality assurance had been the use of inspections to detect and eliminate faulty products and services. The inspection method is an after-the-fact or reactive approach to quality maintenance, since inspection occurs after production to remove defective products.

TQM, however, is intended to inculcate a commitment to quality at all stages of the operation rather than leaving quality control as a last step in the process. Making quality control a commitment of all people throughout an organization often represents a major effort at changing corporate culture.

Boeing, for example, has developed an extensive educational effort to implant a cultural value of commitment to total quality in its workers. Materials developed by this firm emphasize that CQI (Continuous Quality Improvement, Boeing's version of TQM) involves more than changing practices and techniques: "CQI represents a significant cultural change and a shift in the fundamental philosophy of doing business."[35] Boeing intends to change the mindset, that is, some of the basic beliefs and assumptions, of the people in the corporation. The company hopes that people experience a "breakthrough" in their thinking and arrive at the new cultural beliefs and values implied by a commitment to total quality.

Clearly TQM goes beyond earlier efforts at improving quality through procedural or technical changes. The movement is based on the notion that organizational cul-

AN ISSUE OF COMMUNICATION ETHICS

Managing Cultures

Even when begun with the best intentions, efforts at revamping corporate cultures can go awry. One serious problem can result from employees questioning the motives behind efforts to remake a culture. The perception of hidden motives or a hidden agenda can raise ethical questions in the minds of organizational members. They may come to believe that TQM or CQI has been seized on by upper management as a ploy, with downsizing or cost cutting as the real goal.

Many managers may in fact believe that TQM is a method for cutting costs, which it may or may not be. They hope that improved quality will lead to savings, as it did at Motorola, which reportedly saved $6.5 million in manufacturing costs through a TQM program.* The danger comes when TQM is used as a cover for eliminating jobs. So-called downsizing undercuts one of the principles of TQM and cultural change. People need to feel secure in order to embrace efforts at cultural changes, such as TQM, as noted above. Xerox, for example, has experienced what has been described as "11 years of wrenching change" since adoption of a TQM program in 1983, as a result of continual layoffs and downsizing.

Lands' End, the successful mail-order clothing supplier, has experienced the difficulties of instituting cultural changes, which may in fact fly in the face of an already existing, deeply embedded culture. Lands' End's home base is in Dodgeville, Wisconsin, a small community with only two stoplights. Everyone in town either works for Lands' End or knows someone who does. Four years ago, the CEO decided it was time to introduce new management techniques and remake the company's culture. New methods for evaluating employees' performance were introduced, and new executives were brought in from the outside to implement the changes. Some employees found that their workweek began to grow longer as more time was spent in meetings, leaving less time for getting their basic jobs done. Morale dropped as people felt that outsiders were telling them to do things they felt they had already been doing for years, such as making each customer a friend.** Efforts to introduce team building seemed contrived and had the unintended effect of leading to feelings of depersonalization rather than the opposite. The high-priced management consultants from outside may have been resented in the small community (and small-town corporate culture) as well.

What pitfalls should an organization be aware of when introducing culture-changing ideas or methods, such as TQM or team building, or embracing diversity programs? How can organizational communicators be made aware of the potential ethical questions that may be raised about such efforts?

*The Economist, January 14, 1995, p. 55.

**Wall Street Journal, April 3, 1995, pp. A1, A4.

tures can be understood and changed, and, furthermore, that such cultural change will be more effective than technical or procedural changes alone. Interestingly, many of the ideas built into this CQI program came from a study group sent to observe Japanese corporations' methods of quality control, reinforcing the importance of the Japanese "challenge" in leading to cultural interpretations in current organizational theory and practice in the United States.

Have these efforts at remaking organizational culture been successful? The answer may depend upon one's perspective or point of view. Boeing has been credited with major improvement in planning and production capabilities in regard to the rapid development and production of new wide-bodied jets, such as the Boeing 777 in Everett, Washington. Whether these improvements represent changes in the culture or a natural response to market demands is a matter of definition. Interpretivist theorists would probably maintain that the culture in place at Boeing allowed for these practical changes, rather than seeing the changes as cultural shifts in themselves.

INTERCULTURAL COMMUNICATION IN THE MULTICULTURAL ORGANIZATION

This book emphasizes the growing cultural diversity of modern organizations. A discussion of culture in organizations must take account of this diversity. What is the relationship between national or *background* culture and organizational or corporate culture? To what extent can individuals from different cultural backgrounds be integrated or assimilated into an organizational culture?

These questions are of growing importance for at least two reasons: (1) the cross-national and global nature of many large, complex organizations, and (2) the increasing diversity of even local organizations.

In regard to the first reason, we must be careful about the different meanings of the term *culture*. The larger, national culture refers to constructs such as Japanese, German, or American culture. Presumably, the cultural values and life patterns of these larger cultures provide the background and the environment for particular organizational cultures within their boundaries. Hence, some theorists suggest that so-called Japanese management techniques would not work in the United States because they rely upon the unusually homogeneous Japanese culture.

There are consultants to help Americans do business with the Japanese, or the Germans, or the Russians, or whomever. And efforts are made in the opposite direction as well. As noted in Chapter 2, the Samsung group, one of the largest firms in Korea, tries to educate young Korean executives in other cultures, especially the American culture, by sending them abroad for a year to stroll around malls, trying to absorb the pace and tastes of everyday life.[36]

These examples imply that there are American, German, Dutch, or Japanese ways of doing business. The organizational cultures of a Japanese and an American organization would therefore be somewhat different just because of their location within two different national cultures. Hofstede's in-depth study of Dutch and Danish firms' corporate cultures supports this presumption. The differences in the values underlying

International corporations endeavor to learn the cultures of the nations in which they do business.

the corporate cultures seemed more dependent upon the national culture and demographic features such as age, education, and seniority than on the organization.[37] In other words, the values of Dutch firms tended to be more like those of other Dutch firms than like those of Danish firms regardless of the business in which the firms were engaged. Differences in regard to symbols, heroes, and rituals were not as dependent upon national culture or demographics.

The situation is made even more complex in transnational firms, which transcend national boundaries and identifications. So far, most transnational organizations recall a base in some nation, as Royal Dutch Shell recalls its Dutch roots and IBM, its American ones. Even international organizations such as the United Nations or bodies governing international athletics still exhibit their cultural foundations in Western Europe or the United States in the way they do business. As corporations and international organizations become more genuinely transnational or *non*national, it will be interesting to observe the kinds of organizational cultures that they develop.

The second reason focuses on problems of socializing people from diverse cultural backgrounds into a single organizational culture. Deal and Kennedy saw efforts to enculturate women and minorities into some strong organizational cultures as "rituals that fail."[38] By strong cultures, they meant cultures that were fairly homogeneous, that showed a good deal of consensus throughout the entire organization. These strong cultures seemed to maintain this homogeneity more easily when the

DIVERSITY MATTERS

Diversity Training

One approach that organizations have taken to deal with the issue of diversity has been to *embrace the diversity* and try to remake the culture into one that celebrates its multicultural nature. Several organizations have consequently launched "diversity training" programs. Trainers see their function as specifically that of changing an organizational culture in an effort to overcome prejudices against or negative stereotypes of women or minority groups. Part of the obvious tension is that between the belief that a strong culture (showing wide consensus) is desirable and the belief that cultural diversity is a positive value as well. Such programs have at times backfired, as when a group of women successfully sued a corporation, using as evidence remarks intended to bring to the surface potential prejudice made by male managers in a diversity training workshop.*

In this case, a California-based grocery chain was sued as a result of exercises that took place during a workshop intended to make store managers more sensitive to ethnic and gender diversity. During one of the sessions, trainers asked supervisors to articulate various stereotypes that they had heard expressed concerning women or minority group members as managers. The intention was to bring such stereotypes out in the open in order to neutralize them. Notes that some of the women took during these sessions were later used in a lawsuit against the company to show its systematic bias; the stores lost the suit and found themselves facing a $90 million judgment against them.**

Before embarking on programs of diversity training, therefore, organizations should be careful to determine exactly what their goals are and what training techniques will be used. It would seem best to avoid confrontational tactics that pit one group against another or that seem to suggest that current employees are or have been bigoted.

The question becomes, then, how can one communicate the message that diversity in an organization is positive without at the same time communicating negatives about current members or the culture of the organization? Such negatives could lead to resentment, resistance, or even, in some cases, lawsuits.

*New York Times, August 1, 1993, p. F5.

**New York Times, August 1, 1993, p. F5.

members were drawn from similar (formerly middle-class, male, white) backgrounds. Strong cultures, in other words, tended to exhibit demographic, ethnic, and gender uniformity.

COMMUNICATION IMPLICATIONS OF ORGANIZATIONAL CULTURE

Communication is the means for transmitting and maintaining an organizational culture. Communication and culture have a reciprocal relationship in that what we mean by culture comes into being as people communicate with one another. Culture is formed in the act of communicating. On the other hand, culture shapes and directs the kinds of communication conducted within it.

The kinds of questions that are asked or the kinds of problems that are noticed in an organization depend, to some significant degree, on the local culture. Thus, sales- and marketing-oriented cultures are likely to be aware of problems related to selling and marketing and to formulate solutions that involve stepped-up efforts in marketing. Technologically based firms show a cultural proclivity to see problems and solutions in technological terms. And so on. The culture, in other words, encourages certain topics for communication and discounts others. In addition, the culture often determines who talks with whom, on what occasions, and concerning what matters.

The content, preferred channels of communication, and nature of communication activities such as decision making are therefore dependent upon aspects of the organizational culture. The purpose of culture is to provide background assumptions that people can take for granted, enhancing predictability. Because these assumptions are rarely brought to the surface and questioned, internal communication continues along the courses laid out by these cultural assumptions. But communication is not entirely determined by culture, because communication also shapes and alters the cultural assumptions over time, especially in times of crisis and organizational change.

Context

The context in which communication occurs is the culture of the organization as well as the wider culture or background culture. Cultural values and practices evolve through some organizational history, which becomes an important element in context. Messages and actions are interpreted in terms of whether they fit with this cultural context or not.

Functionalists and interpretivists differ concerning whether the organizational culture is a variable element of the context or whether it is not subject to being managed.

The cultural context provides the framework for making sense of what goes on in the organization. A basic element in this framework is a pattern of related shared values. In strong cultures, there is widespread agreement on and commitment to these shared values. In fractured or weak cultures, there are diverse and often competing sets of values in different parts of the organization. The communication of organization members can be analyzed in terms of the values upheld explicitly or implicitly.

Organizational Shape and Structure

Different cultures exhibit different patterns of interactions in an organization. Deal and Kennedy suggest four typical "tribes," or organizational cultures. (Terms such as *tribe* or *tribal societies* are today considered not only perjorative but of uncertain meaning: Why are Bosnians and Serbs ethnic peoples, while Zulu and Dakota are tribes?) The environment largely determines the type of culture adopted by an organization. Endeavors marked by high risk and competitiveness select for what Deal and Kennedy call "tough guy—macho" cultures. The hero in this culture is the tough, self-sufficient battler. The "work hard–play hard" culture, on the other hand, favors teamwork and collaboration, emphasizing building solidarity through shared experiences. The "bet your company" culture exists in an industry in which the risks are high but very long-run; the hero is the technical expert who can manage long-run planning. Their fourth category, "process" cultures, emphasize following correct procedures and due process. The hero is often the "priest" who knows all the precedents and correct rituals.

Each of these types represents a different structure and pattern for carrying on organizational communication. There is no one best form (contingency theorists would agree); rather, the culture should match the relevant environment conditions.

Message Behavior

The organizational culture approach places special emphasis on the role of symbols and images in organizational messages. "Symbolic managers" who can work with and through the "cultural network" are to be emulated. Those following the functionalist perspective believe that managers and leaders should give attention to ritual and symbolic meanings in their messages. The purpose of these messages is to create and maintain a set of cultural values desired by the organization's leadership.

Interpretivists study the messages of organization members for insights concerning how these members use interactions to interpret and give meaning to their experiences. Significant messages for analysis would include stories (such as stories about the founders of the corporation or stories that show the heroes enacting a value). One approach, called convergence theory, studies such stories as "fantasy themes," which are narratives that dramatize the important beliefs and values of an organization.[39] Other messages that could provide these kinds of insights include internal memos, corporate slogans, organizational publications, and internal training manuals.[40] These methods are discussed in more detail in Chapter 13, which deals with the assessment of organizational communication.

Methods and Modalities of Communication

Organizational culture is especially revealed in the informal patterns of talk and interaction within an organization. But, formal events can be interpreted as ceremonies, carrying important symbolic value, as well. The media preferred for communication within an organization could reveal its cultural values. For example, high-tech cultures may favor the use of electronic and computer-based media over written and even face-to-face channels. Meetings may be especially important in organizations that emphasize careful attention to process and building consensus.

Communication Activities

The sort of communication activity that one focuses on depends partly on whether one takes a functionalist or an interpretivist perspective on organizational culture. A functionalist perspective is concerned with activities intended to create or manipulate the variables associated with culture. One therefore gives attention to motivating rituals and messages based upon a desired set of cultural values. There is an attempt to foster the development of rituals and heroes that further the goal of managing the culture. Organizational change (seen in terms of changing the organizational culture) becomes a fundamental purpose of manipulating cultural values and symbols.

Interpretivists are concerned with those communication activities that reveal how people make sense of their surroundings. Planning, especially long-range planning, often takes on a symbolic function in many organizations, for example. Decision making follows certain predictable and ritualized paths. Conflict is dealt with in acceptable patterns, revealing the cultural assumptions regarding the nature and value of conflict.

SUMMARY

Organizational cultures have become especially popular with management theorists. The organization is viewed as a microculture, existing within a larger background culture. Organizations exhibit characteristic sets of values, maintained through certain myths and stories, often dealing with heroes. There are symbolic rituals and ceremonies that serve to maintain the cultural values. Symbols and images become important in understanding the organizational communication of these microcultures. Interpretivists view cultures as socially constructed processes through which organization members make sense of organization life. Functionalists view culture as a variable to be manipulated to bring about desired organizational changes.

Whether one believes that cultures can be manipulated, managed, or changed depends on one's perspective concerning culture. Theorists who support the notion that cultures can be changed, say by putting TQM programs in place, still note that it is quite difficult to change the basic elements or deep structures of an organizational culture.

Organizational cultures are probably influenced by the wider background culture in which the organization operates. The cultural, ethnic, and gender diversity of most large, complex organizations may exacerbate the problems of developing a unified or strong organizational culture. Some organizational cultures may come to include values that welcome or embrace such diversity.

EXERCISES AND QUESTIONS FOR DISCUSSION

1. Describe the organizational culture of your living unit, your university, or a club or other organization to which you belong. Review the elements of organizational culture to look for. Can you identify heroes, narratives, such as sagas and myths, the symbols of the culture (as in the scheme of Trice and Beyer)? What are the bedrock values of this organization? Describe methods for revealing these deep values. Try to verify by interviews with members the values you have identified.

2. Explain what it means to say that the purpose of culture is to make life more predictable. Try to list the communication behaviors of others that you take for granted every day. Would life be more difficult without these expectations?

3. Can an organization change its culture? Is it possible for a nation to change its culture? Does it seem easier in one case than in the other? What does it mean to say that one can manage culture?

SOURCES FOR FURTHER STUDY

Allen, M. W. (1992). Communication and organizational commitment: Perceived organizational support as a mediating factor. *Communication Quarterly, 40,* 357–67.

Bormann, E. G. (1983). Symbolic convergence: Organizational communication and culture. In L. L. Putnam and M. E. Pacanowsky(Eds.), *Communication and organizations: An interpretive approach.* Newbury Park, Calif.: Sage.

Cherrington, D. J. (1989). *Organizational behavior.* Boston: Allyn & Bacon.

Deetz, S. (1988). Cultural studies: Studying meaning and action in organizations. In J. A. Anderson (Ed.), *Communication yearbook 11.* Newbury Park, Calif.: Sage, pp. 335–45.

DeWine, S. (1988). The cultural perspective: New wave, old problems. In J. A. Anderson (Ed.), *Communication yearbook 11.* Newbury Park, Calif.: Sage, pp. 346–55.

Faules, D. F., and Drecksel, G. L. (1991). Organizational cultures reflected in a comparison of work justifications. *Communication Reports, 40,* 90–102.

Feldman, S. P. (1990). Stories as cultural creativity: On the relation between symbolism and politics in organizational change. *Human Relations, 43,* 809–28.

Frost, P. J., Moore, L. F., Louis, M. R., Lundberg, C. C., and Martin, J. (Eds.) (1985). *Organizational context.* Beverly Hills, Calif.: Sage.

Frost, P. J., Moore, L. F., Louis, M. R., Lundberg, C. C., and Martin, J. (Eds.) (1991). *Reframing organizational culture.* Newbury Park, Calif.: Sage.

Gudykunst, W. B., Stewart, L. P., and Ting-Toomey, S. (Eds.) (1985). *Communication, culture, and organizational process.* Beverly Hills, Calif.: Sage.

Kanter, R. M. (1975). Women and the structure of organizations: Explorations in theory and behavior. In M. Millman and R. M. Kanter (Eds.), *Another voice: Feminist perspectives on social life and social science.* Garden City, N.Y.: Anchor Books.

Kanter, R. M. (1977). *Men and women of the corporation.* New York: Basic Books.

Klimann, R. H., Saxton, M. J., Serpa, R., and Associates (Eds.) (1990). *Gaining control of the corporate culture.* San Francisco: Jossey-Bass.

Knuf, J. (1993). "Ritual" in organizational culture theory: Some theoretical reflections and a plea for greater terminological rigor. In S. A. Deetz (Ed.), *Communication yearbook 16.* Newbury Park, Calif.: Sage, pp. 61–103.

Lewis, J., Jr. (1985). *Excellent organizations: How to develop & manage them using Theory Z.* New York: J. L .Wilkerson.

Lincoln, J. R., and Kalleberg, A. L. (1990). *Culture, control and commitment.* London: Cambridge University Press.

Mumby, D. K. (1987). The political function of narrative in organizations. *Communication Monographs, 54,* 113–27.

Pacanowsky, M. E., and O'Donnell-Trujillo, N. (1982). Communication and organizational culture. *Western Journal of Speech Communication, 46,* 115–30.

Pacanowsky, M. E., and O'Donnell-Trujillo, N. (1984). Organizational communication as cultural performance. *Communication Monographs, 50,* 126–47.

Pettigrew, A. M. (1979). On studying organizational culture. *Administrative Science Quarterly, 24,* 570–81.

Pilotta, J. J., Widman, T., and Jasko, S. A. (1988). Meaning and action in the organizational setting: An interpretive approach. In J. A. Anderson (Ed.), *Communication yearbook 11.* Newbury Park, Calif.: Sage, pp. 310–34.

Poole, M. S., and McPhee, R. D. (1983). A structurational analysis of organizational climates. In L. L. Putnam and M. E. Pacanowsky (Eds.), *Communication and organizations: An interpretive approach.* Newbury Park, Calif.: Sage.

Sass, J. S., and Canary, D. J. (1991). Organizational commitment and identification: An examination of conceptual and operational convergences. *Western Journal of Speech Communication, 55,* 275–93.

Saville-Troike, M. (1989). *The ethnography of communication: An introduction,* 2d ed. New York: Basil Blackwell.

Schall, M. (1983). A communication-rules approach to organizational culture. *Administrative Science Quarterly, 28,* 557–81.

Schein, E. H. (1992). *Organizational culture and leadership,* 2d ed. San Francisco: Jossey-Bass.

Schneider, S. C., and Shrivastava, P. (1988). Basic assumptions themes in organizations. *Human Relations, 41,* 493–515.

Smircich, L., and Calás, M. B. (1987). Organizational culture: A critical assessment. In F. M. Jablin, L. L. Putnam, K. H. Roberts, and L. W. Porter (Eds.), *Handbook of organizational communication: An interdisciplinary perspective.* Newbury Park, Calif.: Sage.

Sypher, B. D., Applegate, J. L., and Sypher, H. E. (1985). Culture and communication in organizational contexts. In W. B. Gudykunst, L. P. Stewart, and S. Ting-Toomey (Eds.), *Communication, culture, and organizational process.* Beverly Hills, Calif.: Sage.

Trice, H. M., and Beyer, J. M. (1993). *The cultures of work organizations.* Englewood Cliffs, N.J.: Prentice-Hall.

NOTES

1. *Wall Street Journal,* August 2, 1995, p. A1.
2. *Wall Street Journal,* July 21, 1995, p. A6.
3. *Wall Street Journal,* February 4, 1993, p. B5.
4. Morgan (1986), *Images of organization,* Newbury Park, Calif.: Sage, p. 59.
5. G. Hofstede (1984), *Culture's consequences,* Beverly Hills, Calif.: Sage, pp. 13–14.
6. G. Hofstede, B. Neuijen, D. D. Ohayv, and G. Sanders (1990), Measuring organizational cultures: A qualitative and quantitative study across twenty cases, *Administrative Science Quarterly, 35,* 286; A. E. Reichers and B. Schneider (1990), Climate and culture: An evolution of constructs, in B. Schneider (Ed), *Organizational climate and culture,* San Francisco: Jossey-Bass, p. 15.
7. H. M. Trice and J. M. Beyer (1993), *The cultures of work organizations,* Englewood Cliffs, N.J.: Prentice-Hall, p. 24.
8. T. J. Peters and R. H. Waterman (1982), *In search of excellence,* New York: Harper & Row; T. E. Deal and A. A. Kennedy (1982), *Corporate cultures: The rites and rituals of corporate life,* Reading, Mass.: Addison-Wesley.
9. W. Ouchi (1981), *Theory Z: How American businesses can meet the Japanese challenge,* Reading, Mass.: Addison-Wesley.
10. Morgan, pp. 134–35.
11. Deal and Kennedy.
12. R. H. Klimann, M. J. Saxton, R. Serpa, and Associates (Eds.) (1985), *Gaining control of the corporate culture,* San Francisco: Jossey-Bass, p. ix.
13. J. J. Pilotta, T. Widman, and S. Jasko (1988), Meaning and action in the organizational setting: An interpretive approach, in J. A. Anderson (Ed.), *Communication yearbook 11,* Newbury Park, Calif.: Sage, p. 316.
14. S. DeWine (1988), The cultural perspective: New wave, old problems, in J. A. Anderson (Ed.), *Communication yearbook 11,* Newbury Park, Calif.: Sage, p. 350.
15. G. H. Litwin and R. A. Stringer, Jr. (1968), *Motivation and organizational climate,* Boston: Harvard University Press, p. 1.
16. See G. Burrell and G. Morgan (1979), *Sociological paradigms and organizational analysis,* London: Heinemann, pp. 79–80.
17. H. M. Trice and J. M. Beyer (1993), *The cultures of work organizations.* Englewood Cliffs, N.J.: Prentice-Hall, p. 19.
18. B. D. Sypher, J. L. Applegate, and H. E. Sypher (1985), Culture and communication in organizational contexts, in W. B. Gudykunst, L. P. Stewart, and S. Ting-Toomey (Eds.) (1985), *Communication, culture, and organizational process,* Beverly Hills, Calif.: Sage, p. 17.
19. E. H. Schein (1991), *Organizational culture and leadership,* San Francisco: Jossey-Bass, p. 2.
20. Hofstede, Neuijen, Ohayv, and Sanders, 291.
21. Hofstede, Neuijen, Ohayv, and Sanders, 291.
22. E. H. Schein (1992), *Organizational culture and leadership,* 2d ed., San Francisco: Jossey-Bass. p. 17.
23. This viewpoint is echoed in other works: "Operationally, culture is defined as shared philosophies, ideologies, values, beliefs, assumptions, and norms. These are seldom written down or discussed, but they are learned by living in the organization and becoming a part of it." Klimann, Saxton, and Serpa, p. ix.
24. Trice and Beyer.
25. *Indianapolis Star,* July 2, 1995, p. E3.
26. Trice and Beyer, p. 91.
27. See S. P. Feldman (1990), Stories as cultural creativity:

On the relation between symbolism and politics in organizational change, *Human Relations, 43,* 814.

28. Trice and Beyer, pp. 106–7.

29. A. M. Pettigrew (1990), Organizational climate and culture: Two constructs in search of a role, in B. Schneider (Ed.) *Organizational climate and culture,* San Francisco: Jossey-Bass, p. 415.

30. Schein (1992), p. 15.

31. R. H. Klimann, M. J. Saxton, and R. Serpa (1985), Introduction: Five key issues in understanding and changing culture, in R. H. Klimann, M. J. Saxton, R. Serpa, and Associates (Eds.) *Gaining control of corporate culture,* San Francisco: Jossey-Bass, p. 9.

32. J. Lewis, Jr. (1985), *Excellent organizations: How to develop and manage them using Theory Z,* New York: J. L. Wilkerson.

33. Klimann, Saxton, Serpa, and Associates (Eds.); P. J. Frost, L. F. Moore, M. R. Louis, C. C. Lundberg, and J. Martin (Eds.) (1985), *Organizational context,* Beverly Hills, Calif.: Sage; P. J. Frost, L. F. Moore, M. R. Louis, C. C. Lundberg, and J. Martin (Eds.) (1991), *Reframing organizational culture,* Newbury Park, Calif.: Sage.

34. C. C. Lundberg (1985), On the feasibility of cultural intervention in organizations, in P. J. Frost, L. F. Moore, M. R. Louis, C. C. Lundberg, and J. Martin (Eds.), *Organizational context,* Beverly Hills, Calif.: Sage, p. 183.

35. "Managing for World-Class Competitiveness," internal document, Boeing Company, August 10, 1992, pp. 3–5.

36. *Wall Street Journal,* December 30, 1992, p. A1.

37. Hofstede, Neuijen, Ohayv, and Sanders, p. 306.

38. See Deal and Kennedy, Chapter 4.

39. E. G. Bormann (1983), Symbolic convergence: Organizational communication and culture, in L. L. Putnam and M. E. Pacanowsky (Eds.), *Communication and organizations: An interpretive approach,* Newbury Park, Calif.: Sage, pp. 99–122.

40. C. R. Bantz (1983), Naturalist research traditions, in L. L. Putnam and M. E. Pacanowsky (Eds.), *Communication and organizations, An interpretive approach,* Newbury Park, Calif.: Sage, pp. 55–72.

THREE

Contexts and Applications for Organizational Communication

Part Three deals with organizational communication as it occurs in various organizational settings. First, Chapter 8 begins with an overview of the organization as a communication system. The structure of the organization, consisting of the patterns of interaction that make up an organization, provides the channels through which organizational communication flows. Of special interest in Chapter 8 are the effects of newly developing communication technologies, especially computer-mediated communication systems.

Chapter 9 is concerned with the nature of interpersonal, face-to-face communication in the organization. Interpersonal communication focuses on the dyad, two people who are in a stable, continuing relationship. The most important such dyad for organizational communication is that between superior and subordinate. Other dyads that can be important are those between a mentor and his or her protégé and those between coworkers. Dealing with interpersonal conflict is an important issue in these relationships.

Chapter 10 considers the interpersonal dynamics of the exercise of organizational leadership, recalling one of the basic propositions of this text: Leadership is expressed through communication in the organization. The roles of power, leadership, and politics are discussed in connection with the bases for communicating leadership in organizations.

Chapter 11 turns to the setting of the small group, which includes the work team and department. Team building is of growing concern in many organizations today. Ad hoc teams or groups are brought together to perform a variety of tasks, placing more emphasis on the functioning and dynamics of small-group communication.

Chapter 12 focuses on the public communication of organizations: one source communicating to many, either in meetings or through various forms of mass media. Both internal and external communication are considered.

The themes of communication ethics and organizational diversity continue through these chapters, with boxed cases discussing issues relevant to the material covered in each chapter.

CHAPTER 8

Channels, Media, and Communication Systems in Organizations

CHAPTER OBJECTIVES

After studying this chapter, you should be able to:

- Distinguish formal and informal organizational structure.
- Differentiate communication problems of tall and flat organizations.
- Explain the limitations of channel capacity and communication load.
- Describe methods for dealing with communication overload.
- List and describe typical channels for downward, upward, and horizontal communication.
- Describe the nature of communication networks.
- Discuss the effects of different network characteristics and structures on organizational communication.
- Explain the concept of "media richness" and its relationship to the selection of various media for organizational communication.
- Discuss typical effects of computer-mediated communication systems on internal organizational communication.

CHAPTER OUTLINE

ORGANIZATIONS AS PATTERNS OF COMMUNICATION

Recurring patterns of interaction provide organization members with predictability and stability. These patterns emerge from and are maintained by ongoing communication. In their communication activities, members affirm or deny or modify the links that form the organizational structure. These patterns of interaction, together with the means that facilitate such interaction, are the subject of this chapter.

The patterns of interaction, the formal and informal structures of an organization, set up channels and networks for upward, downward, and horizontal communication. These channels can be analyzed in terms of their capacity for various kinds of messages. Internal networks, patterns of linkages among various groups or departments, are also channels for organizational communication.

The development of computer technologies has had a significant impact on these organizational channels. The final section of this chapter discusses the effects and impact of computer-mediated communication in organizations.

ORGANIZATIONAL STRUCTURE AS A COMMUNICATION SYSTEM

The formal organizational structure represents links or relationships prescribed by the organization, through rules, lines of reporting, chains of command, and the like. The formal structure is also partly determined by physical layout as determined by the organization: who is located near whom.[1] Functionally, the structure reflects the organization's needs to gather, process, and disseminate information that is important for its operations and survival.[2] An informal structure exists alongside the formal structure.

The informal and social links that people develop undergo continuous change as new friendships are made and as new people enter and leave the organization. The geographical layout of the organization encourages the development of these informal links, as well as facilitating formal or prescribed relationships. Former acquaintance-ship or shared memberships in other organizations obviously account for other infor-mal links. For example, organizational members who attend the same church or participate in the same service club have a basis for an informal network. These link-ages are said to be *emergent,* because they are continually emerging from ongoing interactions. In other words, structure is not static.

Organizations can be described as either *tall* or *flat* (see Figure 8.1). A tall organi-zation has a large number of steps between the top and the bottom of the hierarchy:

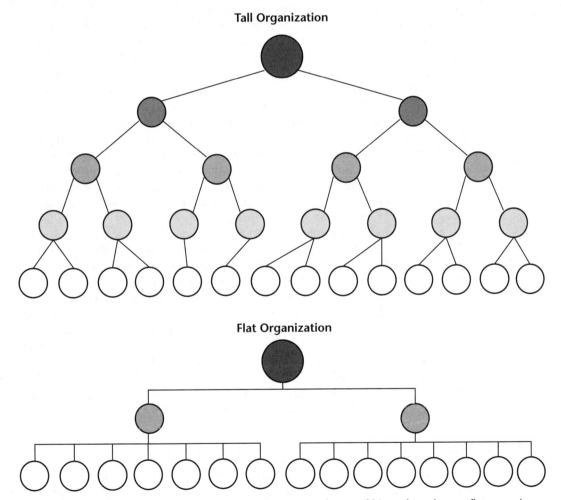

FIGURE 8.1   Tall organizations have many layers of hierarchy, whereas flat organiza-tions have few.

president, vice president, associate vice president, divisional manager, area manager, district supervisor, local manager, assistant local manager, and so on down to the person who does the work. A flat organization, in contrast, has relatively few steps from top to bottom. Typically, one's *span of control* (the number of individuals reporting directly to a supervisor) is wider in a flat organization, because there are fewer levels in the hierarchy.

In a tall organization, messages moving up or down the chain of command must pass through more intermediaries than in a flatter organization. The vice president reformulates the message he or she received from the president when passing it on to the associate vice president, who in turn passes it on to the next level, and so on. As Weick puts it, "In general, the flatter the organization, the less likely it is that communication will become distorted, since there are fewer decision points through which it passes before it reaches the unit that must take action."[3]

The disaster of the shuttle *Challenger,* which blew up just after launch in 1986, illustrates the potentially serious distortions that can occur at these decision points. (See Chapter 2.) NASA established four levels of hierarchy for deciding whether or not to go through with a launch. At the lowest level, level 4, engineers warned that there might be an explosion if the shuttle were launched in the expected low temperatures. Their concerns never really got above level 3, except that people at level 2 were told that while there had been some discussion about the weather, the concerns had been allayed; the seriousness of the engineers' worries was downplayed. Virtually none of the concerns reached the top level, where final decision-making authority resided.

Flat organizations also have some communication disadvantages. Because one person may be responsible for communicating with a large number of others who report to him or her, that person may become overloaded and unable to process all the messages moving up or down the ladder.

Current trends in organizational structure and information technology suggest that by the end of the decade companies will, on the average, be flatter as well as leaner than they are today.[4] Some of this flattening will be due to downsizing, as corporations strive for greater efficiency, but advances already taking place in processing and disseminating information will be responsible, too. The report *Workplace 2000* maintains, "the flow of information will change drastically. The sharing of information will be of critical importance . . . , and new technology will make the sharing possible."[5] New technologies of communication can provide nearly instant feedback at all levels of the organization. The middle levels of hierarchies, those that have provided a filtering and gatekeeping function in the past, may become redundant. The tall hierarchies of the typical organization chart can be replaced by teams and task forces designed to deal with immediate and shifting problems.

COMMUNICATION CHANNELS IN ORGANIZATIONS

The mechanistic or transmissional perspective of communication emphasizes that communication takes place in a channel.[6] This view is well suited for analyzing problems of communication flow within an organization when the major concern is message fidelity. *Fidelity* refers to the faithfulness of reproduction of messages: The message that enters the channel at one end is faithfully or accurately reproduced at the other end. Communication theorists do not believe that any channel is capable of 100 percent fidelity, meaning that there is always some meaning lost in the transfer of a message from one point to another. Furthermore, some channels are "noisier" than others, and some channels have greater capacity for carrying lots of messages.

Channel Capacity and Noise

The transmissional perspective views communication channels as conduits, like pipes. The greater the diameter of a conduit, the more material it can carry per unit of time, just as a larger pipe can carry more water than a smaller pipe. Channels that can carry lots of information have a greater capacity than restricted, narrow channels.

Some channels are better suited than others for certain kinds of information. Mintzberg, in his famous study of how executives actually spend their working time, discovered that they preferred face-to-face and other instant channels of communication over written forms; he writes, "A most interesting phenomenon was that of 'instant communication'—the very current, 'hot' information that flowed frequently and informally, by telephone or unscheduled meeting."[7] The processing of incoming mail was seen as largely routine and often of little interest. Many written reports from company units were also given little attention by the chief executives because of this thirst for the latest information. In fact, Mintzberg discovered that the executives often accepted a high degree of uncertainty in their information and seemed willing to accept word-of-mouth speculations, rumor, and even gossip and hearsay as long as it was fresh.[8]

Statistical data, drawings, and diagrams, on the other hand, may be more efficiently conveyed in visual form. Some speed may be sacrificed in waiting for data to be put into tabular or graph form, printed, and distributed, but it takes an individual less time to read or visually scan information in this form than to listen to the same kind of information presented orally. The widespread use of computer-mediated systems for analyzing and communicating data can reduce the time required for preparation, printing, and distribution. In sum, certain channels have more capacity for conveying certain kinds of information than do other channels.

Channels also differ in terms of their relative noisiness. *Noise* is any sort of random interference that distorts the communicated signal as it passes through a channel. On the floor of a manufacturing plant, the noise is obviously the physical sound itself: Spoken messages have to be shouted and repeated in order to be heard. Electrical fluctuations, perhaps from storms, can interfere with signals sent through wires or cable. Turgid or unclear language creates noise in written channels. Most channels of communication are subject to some kind of noise or interference.

The noisiness of a channel is directly related to its capacity. The noise takes up some of the room in the conduit, displacing the desired message. But noise also affects the capacity of the channel in another way. In order to overcome the distortions of noise, communicators increase the redundancy of their messages. *Redundancy* refers to anything added to the message above and beyond what is minimally necessary to state it. Repetition, as when senders simply repeat the important parts of a message—"Please do not, repeat, DO NOT, send any more widgets"—is an obvious form of communication redundancy, but it is not the only form. Such repetition or any other form of redundancy uses up channel capacity that could have otherwise carried additional new messages.

Another aspect of communication systems intended to overcome noise is *feedback*. Feedback refers to the sender's monitoring of a message to check its fidelity at the other end of the channel. Leaving room in the channel for a feedback signal further reduces the amount of channel capacity available for transmitting the original message.

Channel capacity is thus reduced both by noise and by the need for redundancy and feedback in noisy channels. In order to achieve higher levels of fidelity, communicators sacrifice channel capacity.

Information Load

Someone in the organization deals with incoming messages, deciding which ones to act on or to retransmit. Some channels bring in information from the external environment, such as information about the availability and costs of raw materials, pricing strategies of competitors, and the like. Other channels are mainly internal, monitoring operations, receiving sales orders, communicating evaluations, and so on. Arthur Stinchcombe, in his study of information processing in organizations, observes that it is crucial for an organization to be "where the news breaks," to get information about external and internal uncertainties related to the organization's needs as quickly as possible.[9]

Information load refers to the quantity and rate of incoming information to be processed through a single channel. The load for a given channel thus depends, first of all, on the sheer number of inputs per unit of time. Mintzberg's study of executives' use of time revealed the extreme fragmentation and variability in their communication activities. Unscheduled meetings with subordinates were interrupted by telephone calls requiring immediate attention, while yet other subordinates waited for the manager's attention. Air traffic controllers are usually subject to high information loads, for another example.

Furthermore, one's location in an organizational structure can determine how many incoming messages one receives. Compared to members in other roles, "boundary spanners" or "cosmopolites," who bring information from the outside into the organization, are exposed to more inputs of various sorts. Managers and supervisors also receive large numbers of message inputs. All these people serve as "gatekeepers," determining which messages are to be passed up or down a hierarchical chain.

The sheer number of information inputs may be a consequence of the nature of an organization's environment. For example, changes in the field of communication technologies, with developments in cellular phones, fiber optics, and interactive systems, create a highly unpredictable, uncertain environment for many organizations. For another example, organizations that wish to do business in areas of Eastern Europe and the former Soviet Union operate in a highly turbulent information environment. The rules for doing business and even the identities of governing officials and agencies are subject to daily change. *Turbulence* means that one is faced with constant changes that are mostly unpredictable. Organizations in environments of this kind require much more information in order to deal with all the uncertainties.

Information overload is a subjective matter that depends on factors beyond the sheer number of incoming messages. Someone who receives many routine or unimportant messages probably does not feel swamped or overloaded. An airline pilot in the cockpit of a jet has a large number of gauges and lights before him at any one time, but as long as they appear to be providing routine information, they are not overwhelming. When you receive a lot of so-called junk mail, unsolicited advertisements and flyers, you probably do not feel that you are suffering information overload.

Computer networking software, however, as it becomes more powerful and more sophisticated, can lead to feelings of information overload. Software makers are now coming up with "agents" that can be built into programs to seek out information that may be of special interest to the user, reducing the amount of time that would otherwise be devoted to scanning all kinds of material to find the few items of interest. Such programs can also provide "Bozo filters," which can be used to screen out unwanted messages.[10]

An important insight developed by Richard Farace, Peter Monge, and Hamish Russell in their structural-functional analysis of organizational communication is that the perception of overload depends not so much on the number of inputs as on the requirements for processing them—that is, what a person has to do with or in response to the incoming information.[11]

One of the major purposes of analyzing the flow of communication through channels and networks in an organization is to locate and deal with bottlenecks or people suffering information overload. The concept of information load allows us to identify such potential problems. Information load is the result of the combination of the following factors:

1. The *number* of incoming messages, or inputs, to any one point in the organization
2. The *uncertainty* or *turbulence* in the organization's environment
3. The *unpredictability in the messages* (routine messages contribute less to load than unexpected ones)
4. The *unpredictability of the channels* carrying the incoming messages (messages received from unexpected channels may receive increased attention, as when we receive a telegram)
5. The *quality* of decisions that one has to make concerning the incoming messages (if only slapdash decisions need be made, the information load does not seem as great as when we have to be very careful in responding to the information)

Although channels and individuals can suffer from information underload, as well as overload, resulting in lack of stimulation and, possibly, lowered achievement,[12] overloaded channels are the more typical cause for concern. There are various strategies for dealing with overload, depending on the effort and expense that can be allocated to the problem.[13]

In response to information overload, people in many organizations just keep working at the same pace in processing messages and let a backlog build up. Eventually, the problem may go away, or others may step in to help deal with the messages. A better minimal effort strategy is to prioritize messages, dealing with only selected inputs and ignoring others. Professionals, such as physicians and pharmacists, often find that they are inundated by journals reporting the latest research in their field. The only way to keep up with this knowledge explosion is to seek out those articles that are specifically related to one's specialty or area of interest and set the others aside. This strategy requires *scanning* in order to choose the high-priority messages.

At some organizations, voice-mail answering services represent an effort to delegate the sorting of incoming messages to the callers themselves. Instead of a human gatekeeper dealing with and routing each input, the computerized system allows the inputs, in a sense, to direct themselves.

Other strategies for dealing with information overload involve study and analysis of how the organization handles information inputs, training members for improved information processing, or expanding the number of people that deal with information, either through temporary subcontracting, perhaps using outside services, or through expanding the staff. Many organizations invest in major computerized management-information systems, as noted in the *Workplace 2000* report referred to earlier, in order to eliminate midlevel steps in information processing.

VERTICAL AND HORIZONTAL COMMUNICATION CHANNELS

Communication flows up, down, and across the chain of command of a typical organization. *Vertical communication,* especially downward communication, or sending orders and instructions down the chain of command, was emphasized in classical management theories. Upward and horizontal communication received more attention in the human relations and human resource development approaches. *Horizontal communication* is that which flows between individuals or groups and departments at the same level in the hierarchy. The term *lateral communication* is occasionally used to refer to communication from one part of the organization to another that does not precisely fit these definitions, such as communication from one individual to a peer's supervisor in a different part of the organization.

Downward Communication Channels

Bureaucracies depend on downward communication. Taylor, the father of scientific management, stressed that the manager's job was to instruct and direct the workers. Fayol's five functions of upper management also emphasize downward communication. Because of the felt need for control, especially financial or budgetary control, many executives continue to rely heavily on downward channels.

Mintzberg found that upper-level managers spent 48 percent of their time in contact with subordinates and that 55 percent of their mail was sent to subordinates.[14] At the same time, there is ample evidence that people continue to be dissatisfied with their organizations' downward communication. The National Study of the Changing Workforce conducted by the Families and Work Institute, which covered a national sample of 2,958 wage and salary workers, discovered loyalty to employers and their organizations markedly declining.[15] When employees are asked what attracts them to a particular job, the top-ranked reason considered "very important" was "open communication," and improved communication would improve feelings of commitment and loyalty, according to the survey. Another study found that upper managements do an especially poor job of communicating plans for changes and restructurings, damaging morale and worker trust.[16]

More recently, a survey of over 90,000 employees of the IRS (Internal Revenue Service) reveals similar problems with internal downward communication. Only about one-third of the respondents felt that they received sufficient information about what was going on in the agency. Worse yet, only one-fourth felt that upper-level management communicated honestly with them, and almost half felt that serious problems were usually ignored or downplayed.[17]

Typically, downward communication is intended to meet the following purposes:

- Instructions and training
- Information giving (company policy, trends, plans, and so on)
- Providing rationale for directions and policies
- Evaluating work performance

Some authorities add that another function is to inculcate an ideology, justifying management control, market mechanisms, the need for hard work (the work ethic), and similar values.[18]

The channels frequently used for downward communication reflect its general informative and persuasive purposes:

1. *Written or print channels,* such as
   handbooks
   instruction manuals
   job descriptions
   work rules
   internal newsletters
   memoranda
   pay inserts
   letters (to members' homes)
   print advertising (aimed partly at organization members)
   bulletin boards, posted notices, posters
   information racks, pamphlets, and handouts
   annual reports
2. *Interviews, face-to-face meetings,* such as
   employment interviews
   performance evaluations
   disciplinary interviews
   on-the-job training, giving instructions
   conferences

chain of command (serial transmission of message through steps in the hierarchy)

mentoring

3. *Group meetings,* such as

orientation and training groups

department meetings

committee meetings

quality circles

mass meetings, speeches

4. *Media channels,* such as

video presentations, films

telephone "hot lines"

computer bulletin board messages

E-mail

fax messages

voice mail

videoconferences

advertising, as on radio and television

Upper management tends to rely heavily on print or mediated channels for downward messages. This reliance on formal, especially written channels is probably one of the main reasons for the reported dissatisfaction. Many organization members would prefer to receive information about company policies, plans, or prospects through face-to-face channels. A survey of 32,000 employees in 26 organizations, and other similar studies, reports that employees prefer personal, direct communications from (1) immediate supervisors, (2) senior executives, and (3) small-group meetings, in that order.[19] This preference for live contacts leads to reliance on informal channels, such as the grapevine and rumors; surveys indicate that the grapevine is the second most often cited source of organizational information, considerably ahead of company media messages (immediate supervisors are the first source).[20]

Face-to-face contacts vary in formality and structure. In some organizations, performance appraisal processes are quite formalized, for example. On the other hand, contacts with mentors can be quite informal and spontaneous. Many corporations have initiated *mentor* programs in order to socialize new members in the corporate culture as well as to provide training and development. At the same time, the relationship between mentor and protégé is obviously more two-way than much downward communication, and consequently can keep upper management in touch with what is going on or being thought at lower levels.

Passing a message down through intermediate face-to-face contacts leads to filtering and distortion as the message passes through several persons before reaching the intended recipient; recall that fidelity is lost at each step. Filtering results from a person's deciding what is the "real" or main message to be passed on. Details may be omitted, or the message may be softened in order to shield a subordinate from hurt feelings, for example.

AN ISSUE OF COMMUNICATION ETHICS

Blurred Lines

The increasing use of new kinds of communication technologies has meant that it is more difficult to draw the line between organizational time and private time. Even on vacation, many executives find that they are in constant communication with their offices. One Chicago executive suffered from ulcers, leading his physician to prescribe rest at a vacation cottage. Still, the fax, modem, and telephone kept him touch with work continually, even at the cottage. The ulcers subsided only when he found a location in Mexico remote from all electronic communication devices.* He was probably lucky to be high enough in the organization to have control over his time in this way. What does a more junior employee do or say when a boss orders her to carry a pager seven days a week, twenty-four hours a day?

Many people have welcomed the freedom of being able to work at home in "virtual offices,"** communicating through fax, modem, and personal computer. Still, problems can arise in such arrangements, stemming from the difficulty of separating work life from personal and home life. Tele-commuters report feelings of isolation, and some experience more work pressure at home than in the office. The social setting of a regular office allows many people to let off steam and relax by sharing

Telecommuters use communication technologies to link them directly to their company and office.

the pressure with coworkers. Many telecommuters find that they work longer hours with fewer breaks than they otherwise would.†

The intrusive nature of computer and personal communication technologies raises the ethical issue of how far an organization can go in communicating that a member is on call at just about any time of day or night. Organizations must also confront the issue of providing social and other support for the growing numbers of telecommuters and home workers.

---

*Wall Street Journal, July 3, 1995, p. B1.

**Virtual office is typically the term for people tele-commuting from home, hotels, or other off-site locations. Virtual organization usually refers to an organization consisting of an administrative core that contracts out most of its ac-

tual work. I am indebted to Phil Salem of Southwest Texas University for this information, OrgComm Hotline of Comserve @Rpitsvm, February 28, 1994.

†Wall Street Journal, December 14, 1993, p. B1.

Internal organizational communication systems are experiencing rapid change because of mediated message systems, particularly computerized or cellular communication. While one-way formats, such as videotaped or film presentations from the president, do not usually allow two-way interaction, computer chat-lines, voice mail, and E-mail can be quite interactive. Telephone hot lines are occasionally set up to deal with rumors quickly, often during times of crisis related to restructuring, corporate takeovers, or industrial accidents.

E-mail can provide direct contacts across hierarchies, as a lower-echelon person may communicate directly with a chief executive, or vice versa. E-mail messages, as is discussed in a later section of this chapter, tend to be more informal and can allow for immediate response and feedback. And pagers and cellular phones can mean that organization members are rarely out of range of downward communication, even on weekends or vacations.

Upward Communication Channels

In classical management theory, upward communication provided management with reports and other information that they needed in order to monitor subordinates' production rate and performance. Human resource development theories encouraged other uses for upward communication, including messages concerning morale, commitment, and even personal problems. Upward communication can thus provide feedback for upper management regarding policies and practices, allowing for wider participation in decision making and providing an outlet for members' concerns, worries, or complaints.

Channels used for upward communication include the following:

1. *Written or print channels,* such as

   suggestion or complaint systems (such as the old-fashioned suggestion box)
   formal evaluation systems
   opinion surveys
   memoranda
   written reports

2. *Interviews, face-to-face meetings,* such as

   appraisal interviews
   grievance interviews or hearings
   conferences
   exit interviews
   mentoring

3. *Group meetings,* such as

   department meetings
   quality circles, TQM meetings
   training groups
   question-and-answer sessions
   training sessions

4. *Media channels,* such as

   telephone hot lines
   video- and teleconferences
   E-mail, computer messages

Clearly, some channels used for downward communication can also be used for upward communication: mentoring, interviews and conferences, quality circles, hot lines, and computer-mediated message systems. Suggestion systems have recently received renewed interest with the TQM emphasis. Often bonuses and other rewards go to employees whose suggestions result in improved quality and significant financial savings. Quality circles are intended to encourage this same kind of upward communication.

Some of the new computerized communication systems have had some unexpected effects by allowing more open upward communication, as noted already. E-mail allows subordinates to communicate directly with higher-ups more easily and directly than traditional paper and face-to-face channels. Also, many executives read their E-mail without having secretaries or subordinates screen the messages, as they typically would with phone and written communications. One executive at Chemical Bank in New York reported that use of an electronic bulletin board brought out into the open false rumors that would otherwise have been spread in whispers around the watercooler.[21]

The key link in upward communication is the superior–subordinate relationship, which is discussed in more detail in Chapter 9. There is a general belief, supported by surveys and anecdotal evidence, that upward communication in many organizations is inadequate. The survey results in the prior section bear out this belief. The implication is that those at the upper levels of organizations are not well informed regarding activities and problems at lower levels, although specific research regarding this situation has been somewhat limited.[22]

Most superiors tend to be overly optimistic about their own openness to upward communication: "My door is always open," they say. Subordinates, however, are less likely to initiate communication with superiors than the other way around. The boss can stay behind the "open door" and be fairly secure from unwanted or unexpected messages or intrusions. A recent episode in the cartoon series *Dilbert*, makes this point. Dilbert and another engineer wander into the new vice president's office to check out his announced "open-door policy." The two lounge around on the office furniture making small talk, when the VP icily asks whether there is something he can do for them. Dilbert and his friend, intentionally or otherwise, misunderstood the nature of this open door.

Superiors usually need to seek out and initiate contact rather than waiting for others to come to them—hence the popularity a few years ago of the MBWA (management by walking around) idea. The effectiveness of an open-door policy is related to the consistent finding that trust is one of the most important factors leading to open and frequent upward communication. The supposed openness of the boss's door is less likely to be a factor.

In addition to trust, other factors determine the effects of upward communication. First, messages that reinforce policy and meet existing expectations are more likely to be received and acted on. The principle of cognitive dissonance, of course, supports this reinforcing function of most upward communication. Second, subordinates are often reluctant to send negative messages up the chain of command. The desire for upward mobility may contribute to the filtering of potentially negative messages ("Just give them good news if you want to be promoted"). These factors suggest that upward communication is often distorted or incomplete.

Upward communication can do more than simply provide needed feedback or information for management levels in an organization. Substitute locomotion theory, for example, holds that some people who do not expect to be promoted to higher levels use communication with superiors as a substitute for higher rank. Upward communication thus satisfies a need for association with influential or powerful members of the organization.

Horizontal Communication Channels

Upward and downward communication have received more attention over the years, possibly because horizontal communication can become a sort of miscellaneous category for communication not obviously classified as upward or downward. *Interdepartmental communication* is a more specific term for the flow of messages from one part of the organization to another. *Peer communication* can refer to communication between individuals who are at precisely the same rank or level in the hierarchy.

Fayol coined the term *bridge* or *gangplank* to refer to communication from one person to another at the same level without sending the message up or down through the hierarchy. In order to save time, person A can send a message directly to person B so long as their superiors in the hierarchy have already approved this link for certain types of messages. The provision for prior approval maintains the control characteristic of classical management theory.

Horizontal communication may become a substitute for preferred upward or downward communication. In other words, lacking the opportunity for vertical communication, people turn to talking with their peers to seek out information they need or desire.

Channels for horizontal communication can include the following:

1. *Written or print channels,* such as

    memoranda
    reports

2. *Interpersonal or face-to-face channels,* such as

    informal conversations (as at lunch)
    grapevine contacts
    conferences

3. *Group settings,* such as

    committees
    interdepartmental task forces
    orientation and training groups
    quality circles

4. *Media channels,* such as

    E-mail
    voice-mail
    telephone
    teleconferences
    videoconferences

Organizations typically have fewer channels for horizontal and upward communication than for downward communication. This situation results from upper management's access to so many print and other media channels, such as newsletters, manuals, handbooks, pay inserts, public addresses, and the like. The relatively small number of channels for horizontal communication, however, may also reveal its lower priority in many organizations.

Several reasons account for limitations on interdepartmental horizontal communication. First, different departments often represent different specialties or areas of technical expertise. Engineering may feel that it has little in common with sales or accounting, for example. Technical specialties rely on different technical languages, which can also restrict interdepartmental communication. Second, a perceived need for turf protection may hinder free and open communication. Third, in many organizations, there is no real history or tradition of such interchanges, possibly for the first two reasons.

TQM and quality circle groups represent an effort to encourage horizontal interchange in order to improve quality and productivity. These efforts, together with increased reliance on computer-mediated communication, may lead to more horizontal communication in the future. These trends grow from the need for improved coordination as organizations become more complex and diversified. One recent study indicates that as organization members become more individually specialized, the need for such coordination increases.[23] This result is even more likely when power is dispersed or decentralized in the organization rather than concentrated in a formal hierarchy. Horizontal communication, especially of an unscheduled or informal type, is therefore more probable in a complex organization existing in a fairly uncertain or unstable environment.

COMMUNICATION NETWORKS AS CHANNELS OF COMMUNICATION

Networking, referring to making contacts with others, who in turn had contacts with someone else who might have useful information, was a buzzword of the 1980s and 1990s. Networks in organizations are the *stable patterns of relationships* by which communication flows through several contacts linking one point to others. These links tend to be clustered in groups, which are connected to one another by individuals. Hence, a network can be envisioned as clusters of groups connected in patterns of links, which are usually dyadic, or one-to-one, relationships.

Early network studies looked at whether the structure of problem-solving groups aided or hindered their effectiveness.[24] Centralized groups, in which members could communicate with one another only through one member located at the center (the "wheel"), tended to be faster and more accurate in solving clearly structured, fairly simple tasks. Openly structured groups, in which any member could directly communicate with any other member at any time, took longer on such tasks, and the emergence of leadership was delayed. On the other hand, the decentralized groups were superior in dealing with novel and very complex problems. Some groups, such as the "line," in which each member could communicate only with the person on either side, tended to be slow and caused frustration because of the difficulty in moving messages from one part of the line to another. Even given the artificiality of the setting for these studies, they still pointed to the effects of the flow of communication through various kinds of networks.

Network Roles

Communication within organizational networks can be further analyzed in terms of the different functional roles individuals play within these networks. As with network properties, several different schemes have been developed for categorizing network roles.

Members. They serve as senders and receivers or participants in network communication. The other roles, except for isolates, are special kinds of members. Members usually participate in "cliques," which are groups whose members tend to communicate more often with other group members than with other units in the larger network.

Isolates. They are usually outside the interactions carried on in networks. A scientist working alone in a laboratory (perhaps an inventor) or, often, a traveling salesperson may operate much of the time as an isolate. There may also be isolated dyads or small groups, who seldom have communication with other parts of an organization.

Liaisons. They provide a link between one group or clique and others. Communication flows from one region of a network to others through these linking individuals. Liaisons may be staff or administrative persons who keep various departments of the organization informed on policy or collect information from these areas. They may come to their role informally as a result of social or friendship links with members of different cliques.

Bridges. They are individuals who connect two groups in a network by being members of both. Likert, for example, describes such persons are *linking pins*. An example of a bridge or linking pin is a department head, who is, of course, a member of his or her department and also a member of a management team of department heads who may meet as a regular group. A member of a quality circle would be a bridge between that group and his or her regular department. Members of committees serve the same function.

Cosmopolites or Boundary Spanners. They are network members who communicate with people or organizations outside the organization. Interestingly, boundary spanners can be of either high or relatively low status within the organization. For example, sales associates, bank tellers, and repair and service workers, typically of low organizational status, deal directly with consumers and can provide instant feedback from the environment. On the other hand, executives and other high-status individuals often travel and communicate outside the organization, attending meetings, conferences, board meetings, and the like.

Gatekeepers. They determine which messages pass through a particular link in a network. Like boundary spanners, they can be of high or low organizational status. Secretaries and receptionists often make gatekeeping decisions, for example. High-status decision makers, such as vice presidents or managers, may also decide which information to pass on to others; in fact, part of their organizational power derives from this gatekeeping function.

Opinion Leaders. They influence other members in a network more than do other participants. The concept of opinion leaders results from the two-step flow-of-communication models developed from studies of the effects of mass communication. The idea is that the effect of a message, say from top management, is reinterpreted by an influential opinion leader. Ordinary members rely on these opinion leaders, who appear to be more "plugged in" to wider sources of information than others. These opinion leaders explain incoming messages or place them in an understandable context for others. People can become opinion leaders either through the formal position they hold in the organization or as a result of informal esteem or influence that they have acquired. Some studies refer to a person with this kind of influence as a *star,* although others use this term for a person who is most often mentioned by others as a member of a network.[25]

Persons who hold linking positions (liaisons or bridges) and opinion leaders usually have higher status, formal or informal, in the organization. They have more communication contacts, feel they have access to more information, and see themselves as having more influence than other organization members. Liaisons, who are usually of high organizational status, are more likely to feel that they have higher influence than bridges have. Bridges may feel that they are only conduits, passing information back and forth. Given their access to wider sources of information, liaisons tend to see the organization as more open than do other members.

Gatekeepers, liaisons, bridges, and boundary spanners are prone to communication overload. How they deal with this may be related to their status or power in the organization. Gatekeepers who are lower in the hierarchy are more likely to use minimal-effort strategies for dealing with overload, because they feel they have little power to do otherwise. They may insist on "going through channels" or "working to specs," even though that leads to a backlog or bottleneck. Higher-status gatekeepers may perceive that they have more authority to cut through such restrictions and deal with overload by setting new priorities, delegating responsibility, or initiating reorganization of the structure.

As the representation of a typical network in an organization, Figure 8.2 (on p. 170) allows us to identify network roles and links within this hypothetical organization. Dark lines represent regular and fairly constant communication between the people represented as letters in circles. On the left-hand side of the diagram, there are two

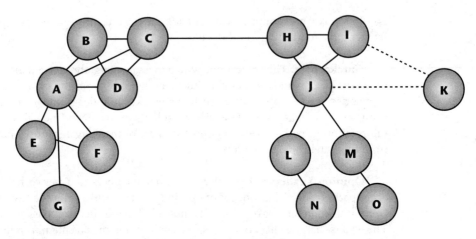

FIGURE 8.2   Communication networks in a typical organization.

groups, A-B-C-D and A-E-F-G. Person A is therefore a linking pin or bridge between the two groups. Through communication between C and H, there is a link between group A-B-C-D and Group H-I-J. C and H are therefore potential gatekeepers as well. J is the link for passing communication on to L and M and thence to N and O, who are less connected to the network than other, more centrally located members. Person K appears to be relatively isolated from the flow of communication, with occasional contacts, indicated by dashed lines, with persons J and I. We would expect persons J and A, given their positions in the network, to be more powerful and influential than other members.

Communication Characteristics of Networks

Communication networks in organizations exhibit different kinds of characteristics that can affect communication through them. General properties of networks include the following.

Size. Whole-system networks are those that cover the entire organization; they represent the channels used for getting messages to all members of an organization. Networks smaller than the whole system are clique networks that link specific groups within the organization. Personal networks, the personal relationships and contacts that one person has based on work function or friendships, are usually but not always still smaller.

Network size is occasionally described in terms of *reachability,* which refers to the number of links required to get a message from one point to another. Presumably, larger networks will have longer such paths. In Figure 8.2, more links are required to get information to persons N and O.

Content or Function. There are often different networks for different purposes. For example, safety officers may be appointed from each department in a manufacturing corporation. These individuals attend special meetings with other safety officers and receive messages through a network that is set up for disseminating safety-related information. Each year, a corporation may set up a special network for encouraging charitable donations to a United Way campaign or for a blood-donor drive.

Functional analyses of organizations usually list three or four standard functions: production, organization maintenance, social connection, and, some would add, innovation. Production refers to performing the major task, or throughput, of the organization. Maintenance is concerned with keeping the organizational structure operating; this includes recruiting and orienting new members. Messages dealing with morale, providing a pleasant and warm organizational climate, supporting members' efforts, and allowing for social relationships flow through the social network.

An innovation network suggests that innovativeness or creativity requires its own communication network. Organizations often have long-range planning committees or special task forces for reviewing and revising their operations. Recent research indicates that elite members of networks, those members who are seen as particularly influential, are especially important in communicating new ideas to other network members.[26]

When links in a network serve to carry communication concerning more than one function, the link is said to be *multiplex*. The notion of multiplexity in networks is discussed subsequently.

Formality. In any organization, there will probably be both formal and informal networks. Someone's personal network, for example, is most likely informal. The bureaucratic hierarchy, or chain of command, is the best example of a formal network. Some organizations have replaced the vertically oriented chain of command with other kinds of networks, such as a matrix organization, in which individuals report through two channels, one representing a specific task or assignment and the other a specific function.

Informal networks develop through friendships, contacts outside the organization, and proximity within the organization, such as sharing the same lunchroom or other facilities. The most studied informal network is the *grapevine,* which in many organizations allows for the rapid dissemination of rumors and gossip as well as hard and accurate information.

Centralization or Dominance. Early studies of networks concentrated on this property, setting up physical barriers to communication except through certain links or individuals. In highly centralized networks, all messages from one part of the network to another must go through one individual, who could be a chairperson or gatekeeper. Similarly, dominated networks are those in which one individual or clique tends to control, or dominate, the flow of messages. Dominance can be the result of informal or social influence rather than formal, position power. In other words highly influential persons can dominate a network regardless of their formal position or authority. Hence, person J in Figure 8.2 is dominant, especially on the right side of the diagram.

Centralized networks, such as formal bureaucracies, maintain more control over communication. In general, highly centralized networks are effective in dealing with straightforward problems and simple or well-understood technologies. Centralization is common in organizations engaged in tightly coupled operations or technologies. As noted in Chapter 6, coupling refers to the dependence of one step in a process on another and the amount of slack allowed for variations in how operations are performed.[27]

The person or clique at the center of a dominated network, such as person J in Figure 8.2, is of course prone to information overload, especially in volatile and complex situations. On the other hand, those near the center are more likely to achieve leadership, higher status, and influence. Centralized networks tend to result in fewer innovations and lower satisfaction for members who are not at the center.

A network feature that is complementary to centralization is network *connectedness,* which refers to the number of active links or relationships compared to the total number possible. In a network in which every member continually communicates with every other member, there is complete connectedness, and consequently less centralization or dominance.

Multiplexity. This feature of networks relates to the extent to which different networks within the organization overlap, as when the same channels or links are used for more than one or kind of content. Multiplex links are those used for more than one kind of message.[28] For example, two people who are part of a network coordinating production may also be linked for messages concerning organizational innovation. These links and networks are sometimes referred to as multivariate rather than multiplex.[29]

Multiplex links tend to be stronger, showing much more communication activity, than those that are uniplex. People in such networks are connected to a diverse range of organizational communications and often feel more involved and more committed to the organization as a result.[30]

Network Openness. Some networks are more open (or closed) than others. For example, some networks, such as those dealing with marketing research, are specifically designed for bringing information from the outside into the organization. Open networks are characterized by *boundary spanners,* individuals who cross over the boundaries of a designated system or network for the purpose of importing and exporting communication. Networks that are closed are more internally oriented.

Informal Networks: The Grapevine

During the American Civil War, the telegraph came into its own as a means for quick communication from one part of a battlefield or theater of operations to another. As they moved forward with advancing troops, communication officers quickly strung wires over bushes along the way. The wires thus strung resembled grapevines: hence, the source of the term. A grapevine later came to mean any kind of jury-rigged, temporary, or informal network for communication.

The term grapevine *was coined during the American Civil War.*

The grapevine is one of the most often used channels of communication about organizational policies and problems. The grapevine is not the preferred channel—face-to-face communication with superiors is preferred—but it is fast and often accurate.[31] Communication on the grapevine is usually oral, through personal and informal contacts. It is not yet clear what effect the availability of E-mail and other electronic media may have on the transmission of rumors and other grapevine messages.

Messages on grapevines tend to be the sort that would be perceived as inappropriate for formal channels. Gossip, for example, is usually personal information that is considered confidential or unrelated to organizational functions. Gossip might deal with office romances, personal problems, and the like. Rumors, on the other hand, tend to have some relevance for the organization itself: unconfirmed reports of impending layoffs, reorganizations, and takeovers, for example. Rumors tend to flourish in situations of high uncertainty or when there is a lack of hard information about important matters.

In general, the more important the issue and the more ambiguous or uncertain the information concerning it, the more likely it is that rumors will travel up and down the grapevine. It is not surprising, therefore, that corporate takeovers and reorganizations (especially cutbacks) lead to increases in the number and frequency of rumors, especially when managers try to control or withhold information.

COMMUNICATION TECHNOLOGIES AND MEDIA

At this time, about one out of every seven American companies offers employees the option of telecommuting, and the trend points to continuing growth of this practice in the future.[32] Telecommuting allows a person to live in Vermont, for example, while working every day for a company in New Jersey, linked to the office by a modem, personal computer, and fax machine.

People can be plugged into a network through cable and telecommunications systems. The advent of E-mail, voice mail, teleconferencing, and videoconferencing, augmented with satellite communications, allows for communication links and networks unconstrained by time and space. The new technologies mean that individuals have a wide choice in selecting the medium that is most appropriate for their intraorganizational communication.

Previous sections of this chapter have described the patterns that make up internal communication; this section concerns factors in choosing a particular medium and the effects that medium may have on the interpretation of messages.

A *medium* is the physical means by which a signal is transmitted from one point to another. Mintzberg discovered that executives preferred face-to-face interaction for most of their communication. This preference is related to managers' desire for "hot" news, the latest information, which tends to travel more quickly through oral channels. Since Mintzberg's studies, many computer-mediated systems have developed that might provide similar kinds of up-to-date information.

Media Choice

Which medium is selected usually depends on the following factors:

- Media richness
- Situational factors
- Symbolic meaning of media

The notion of media *richness* is that some media provide richer, or more complete, information than others. In terms of the transmissional view of communication, richer media have more capacity than leaner ones. Media richness has four components:[33]

1. Timing and amount of feedback; a rich medium provides for instantaneous feedback.
2. Presence of multiple cues, such as nonverbal communication, facial expressions, tone of voice, and so on
3. Natural language use versus mathematical symbols or other nonlinguistic codes
4. The personal material allowed or encouraged in the message; this factor is also referred to as *social presence.*

Face-to-face conversation represents the richest medium for communication according to these criteria: Feedback is simultaneous with message production and clearly visible; the full range of nonverbal messages accompanies the verbal; speech is the most natural form of language; and emotional cues and personal feelings are immediately evident. A written, statistical report would have much lower richness (be leaner): Feedback is delayed, if a response to the report is sent at all; only the written symbols are available for interpretation; the language is partly represented in numerical codes; and personal feelings are absent. The telephone lies between these two media in terms of richness, closer to face-to-face than to written forms: Feedback is immediate through audible signals but not visual cues, for example. E-mail typically uses a natural form of language, but nonverbal elements and immediate feedback are lacking (although some systems now allow for an immediate reply, making more immediate feedback possible). Voice mail usually lacks immediate feedback (unless someone "picks up" during transmission of a voice-mail message).

Downward communication in many firms is criticized for the use of what are perceived as inappropriate media. Management relies on written or other impersonal (less rich) media, whereas people would prefer the richer face-to-face channels. Richer media are more effective in communicating messages in situations of high uncertainty, anxiety, or complexity. Routine messages that are seen as nonthreatening can be carried effectively by leaner media. One study suggests that rich media are preferable for equivocal messages, those that are potentially subject to different or ambiguous interpretations.[34] High-level management decisions often involve uncertain situations and incomplete information, which may account for these executives' preference for the richer face-to-face or telephone media.

It is possible to employ a medium that is richer than necessary for the message. Delivering routine or trivial messages through a very rich medium may lead to their overemphasis or to people's searching for some hidden meaning.

In addition to media richness, there are situational factors in selecting a particular medium. Time, distance, and financial constraints may dictate the choice of certain media over others for particular messages. Telephone and fax are more likely to be used when time is short and a quick response is needed. Ready access to another person, say right in the adjoining office, may lead to quick face-to-face conferences on all sorts of matters (or even calling over a partition). The accessibility of a medium may determine or limit its use as well. Perhaps not all intended receivers are hooked up to the E-mail system, or perhaps they are on incompatible systems. E-mail messages can be sent to several receivers simultaneously over phone lines, whereas it would take much longer to call each person one at a time on the telephone.

Marshall McLuhan reminded everyone that the medium can be the message: Media choice may be guided by the symbolic meaning attached to the use of certain media. Something in writing, such as a memorandum or report, looks more concrete and seems to commit the writer more fully than an oral message. The felt need to "put it in writing" may differ with the organizational culture of particular organizations: Some cultures may emphasize such formality more than others.

Lengthy reports, loaded with evidence and statistical information, may be intended to symbolize the competence or importance of an individual. In a recent movie, one character carried a phony cellular phone in his car so that he would appear to be "with it" by talking into the unconnected instrument while whizzing along the interstate.

Some people have been known to wear dummy pagers on their belts in order to enhance their perceived importance or status.

The selection, then, of a particular medium may be intended to send a *symbolic message*. Sending a fax may indicate that this message is critical or that the sender values speed and high technology. One may hope to attract more attention to a message or to heighten a particular interpretation of the content by the selection of certain media.

Computer-Mediated Communication Systems (CMCS)

The integration of computers into electronic communication systems has dramatically increased potential communication channels in organizations. The growth of telecommuting mentioned at the start of the section is a good example. The ability to plug laptops and PowerBooks directly into a telephone and the development of portable and cellular phone technologies, fax machines, and satellite links for video interactions are further developments of new media. Advanced groupware programs can connect hundreds of users in an organization, allowing them access to a wide range of information. Data that formerly were known only to higher-ups become disseminated through all levels of an organization, diminishing hierarchical power based on control of information.[35]

A historical case shows the relationship among organizational complexity and size, and available technology. Prior to the middle of the nineteenth century, business correspondence used the format of the formal letter, with polite salutations, close, and so on. The complexity, large size, and geographic dispersal of industrial firms led to the need for internal written communications, which at first followed the letter form. The typewriter, however, with capital and underlining features and tab stops, made possible the new memo form; the uniformly sharped and formatted pieces of paper could be readily stored in file cabinets, maintained by a new army of secretaries, clerks, and typists.[36] The memo form, which developed in this way, is now the model for the new electronic mail systems. E-mail messages tend to look like memos on a screen. CMCS should lead to the development of new forms and uses of internal communication in the same way that the typewriter and later the telephone shaped earlier organizational communication.

Other types of CMCS coming into widespread use in organizations include computer conferencing, which is considered as well in Chapter 11, dealing with group communication. On the other hand, computer bulletin boards are a more passive, less interactive mode of computerized communication.

Computer messaging systems appear to have special kinds of effects on internal communication. In a book devoted to computer-mediated communication, communication scholars James Chesebro and Donald G. Bonsall summarize some of these positive and negative effects.[37] Psychologists have also begun to study the effects of CMCS.[38] Some of the findings are in conflict, and as computerized communication becomes more widespread and accepted as normal, some of the novelty effects may wear off. Some generalizations regarding the effects on communication of CMCS include the following.

Asynchronicity. Messages can be sent or received at any time. This can mean a delay in receiving messages, especially if one participant does not remember to check his or her E-mail. The advantage is that people do not have to coordinate their schedules or appointments. People can be included who might otherwise have been excluded because of time constraints. Obviously, space or geographic distance are not limitations. However, the order of messages and their timing can be lost, since a participant can read messages in any order and may not read a message until the issue it discusses no longer seems as important as it did at first.

These technologies can be used to create entirely new working relationships, in which time and space are not constraints. The advantages and disadvantages of telecommuting and virtual offices were discussed in the box, "An Issue of Communication Ethics," earlier in this chapter. IBM, Tandem Computers, Eastman Kodak, Ernst & Young, and Aetna Insurance, among many other corporations, have begun to replace standard offices with work pods, available on a first-come, first-served basis when the worker happens to be at one of the firm's permanent buildings. Otherwise, the employee works from customers' or clients' premises, a hotel, or his or her home, connected to a local area network (LAN) through modems and phone lines.[39]

Tendency Toward Lean Communication Media. The lack of regulating feedback can make interpretation of messages more difficult, or lead to different interpretations among the various participants. People lose nonverbal and vocal cues in reading messages on a screen; one's sense of urgency or sincerity may be distorted. This feature can be an advantage, according to Chesebro and Bonsall, in that "computerized communication possesses the advantage of focusing attention upon the written word, inviting extraction of as much as possible from this source of communication. The mode also allows or forces users to employ words concretely, vividly, and meaningfully."[40]

Allowance for Network Creation and Proliferation. The removal of time and space limits means that people who might otherwise never have the opportunity to meet or converse can be electronically brought together for interaction. The growth of the Internet, for example, allows for instantaneous global communication. Of course, such new contacts may also facilitate the flow of rumors and gossip. Such messages can reach a large number of people very quickly, making it more difficult to track down and correct misinformation.

Elimination of Nonverbal Cues of Status and Authority. An Air Force officer at Wright-Patterson Base in Ohio reports, "Rank doesn't really matter when you're online."[41] Enlisted men and women can communicate directly with higher officers through the E-mail system. The asynchronous sharing of messages may make it more difficult for someone to be in the center and to assert leadership. It is not clear how one would "chair" a computer-conference committee. High-status individuals may have less power than in face-to-face meetings. Low-status people may become more assertive or even aggressive. The lack of social identification and hence lower inhibition may lead to *flaming,* the computer term for unusually strong or vituperative language by computer users.

Restriction of Problem Solving. Studies of three-person groups interacting through computers indicate that they take longer to solve problems than face-to-face groups,[42] although Chesebro and Bonsall report that, with experience, computerized groups tend to be more efficient and use less time.[43] The lack of leadership cues may account for the observations that computerized groups take longer; also, the lack of nonverbal cues may delay the realization that others are agreeing or disagreeing with what is being proposed. Finally, people take longer to express and explain their ideas when typing on the keyboard than in face-to-face situations.

Tendency to Show More "Choice Shift." Findings suggest that people in computer conferences feel less attached to a particular position or opinion and are more likely to change either in the course of the conference than are people in face-to-face groups.

DIVERSITY MATTERS

Responses to and Uses of CMCS

The increasing use of computer-mediated communication technologies in organizations and in society in general leads to questions concerning differing attitudes toward or responses to these technologies among different populations. Some people have wondered whether reliance on computer communication may tend to favor one ethnic group or gender over another. Research in this area is just developing.

With regard to attitudes toward use of computers, there appears to be a gender difference. A review of published research in this area found that studies indicate that males' more positive attitudes toward computer use persist into adulthood and hence onto the job.* In general, women seem to exhibit less positive attitudes toward computers and technology than men do, although this situation may change with time and work experience.

Regarding ethnic cultures, some research suggests that there are cultural differences regarding attitudes toward and responses to computer communication systems. The low context of text-only E-mail or computer conferencing may handicap people from what Hall described as "high-context" cultures, in which indirect or nonverbal communication is essential for interpreting verbal messages.** Another well-defined cultural difference is that of individualist cultures versus collectivist cultures. In a global corporation, when an American manager asks a Greek subordinate to indicate how much time he will need to finish a report, the Greek is bewildered, expecting the superior to give a definite deadline. Without the face-to-face opportunity to work out the full meaning of typewritten text, the American manager and Greek worker experience a communication breakdown.†

Multicultural diversity in complex organizations may complicate the use of CMCS, at least in the short run.

*S. L. Lindsley (1992), *Through a cultural looking-glass: Ethnic and gender related perspectives of new computer technology,* Paper presented at the Speech Communication Association Convention, Chicago, Ill.

**Hall, E. T. (1976), *Beyond culture,* New York: Doubleday.

†B. A. Olaniran (1992), *Computer-mediated communication (CMC): A look at intercultural implications,* Paper delivered at Speech Communication Association Convention, Chicago, Ill.; W. B. Gudykunst and Y. Y. Kim (1992), *Communicating with strangers: An approach to intercultural communication,* 2d ed., New York: McGraw-Hill.

Appearance of Less Effectiveness. Conflicts tend to require richer communication media for resolution than do those in face-to-face communication. Issues are more complex, often having emotional overtones as well as involving substantive matters. Media that allow for more social presence, such as telephone or face-to-face meetings, are preferred for dealing with these matters.

Tendency to Blur the Lines Between Private and Organizational Lives. With modems, telecommuters can plug into their offices at any time of day or night. Similarly, pagers and cellular phones place all organizational members within continual range of job-related communication. Coupled with satellite technologies, instant global connections are possible, making day and night irrelevant considerations. Such systems also make monitoring of employees on a round-the-clock basis more possible, raising questions about privacy and confidentiality. These matters were discussed in the "Issue of Communication Ethics" box earlier in this chapter.

Highlights of the Effects of New Media

Computer technologies are constantly changing and being updated. The generalizations summarized here may be made obsolete by the appearance of new technologies. Already, the upgrading of cellular technology, fiber optics, and the growing availability of virtual reality technologies may render many of these findings concerning computer communication obsolete.

For example, cellular systems may be replaced by *PCS*, personal communication services, which are essentially wireless telephones that one can take anywhere. PCS may lead to individuals being assigned a permanent telephone number regardless of location. Voice-mail systems are becoming increasingly sophisticated. Banking and similar transactions, for example, can be made via voice mail, or *interactive telephony,* or *automated voice response.*

Finally, the techniques of *virtual reality* may restore face-to-face richness to forms of electronic communication. Certainly, we will see many innovations in communication media available for organizational channels and networks in the coming decade.

SUMMARY

According to the Framework for Organizational Communication, communication is influenced by the shape, form, or structure of the organization in which it occurs. Structure refers to the fairly stable patterns of interaction and communication flow in an organization. Structures differ in being formal or informal and tall or flat. Informal structures are often described as *emergent,* developing from on-going interaction. Tall structures tend to be char-acterized by more distortion of serially transmitted messages than flat ones; flat organizations can experience more overloaded channels, however.

Channel capacity represents the amount of information a channel can convey per unit of time. *Noise* decreases capacity, and noisy channels therefore require more *redundancy,* further reducing capacity. *Communication overload* is a subjective judgment that depends on the perception of complexity, unpredictability, and effort required to process messages, as well as the sheer number of incoming messages.

Communication flows can be envisioned as *vertical* (upward and downward) and *horizontal* or *lateral*. Downward communication tends to rely on formal and print media, although these are not the media most desired by receivers. There are fewer upward than downward communication channels. The superior–subordinate link is key for upward communication. The introduction of mentors and quality circles may provide for additional interpersonal upward links. Horizontal communication is often neglected in organizations, because of differences in technical areas, lack of interest, and protection of turf.

Communication *networks* are the recurrent patterns for the flow of messages through the organization. Networks are characterized by their size, function or content (the kinds of messages usually carried), formality, amount of centralization, multiplexity (same network links being used for more than one function), and openness to outside messages. Roles typically found in network communication include:

Members

Isolates

Liaisons

Bridges

Cosmopolites and Boundary Spanners

Gatekeepers

Opinion Leaders (or Stars)

The *grapevine* represents an informal network, usually for transmission of personal messages, gossip, or rumors. Rumors are most likely to occur in highly uncertain situations in which adequate information about crises, emergencies, changes, and the like is unavailable.

The media for communicating in channels and networks have been augmented by new electronic and computerized technologies. The media selected for various messages can alter the meaning or interpretation of the messages. Media differ in terms of their *richness,* situational factors, and symbolic meaning. *CMCS* (computer-mediated communication systems) are of growing significance for organizational communication. They tend to be neither time-bound nor space-bound and they establish new networks, but they are usually lean media, and hence tend to be ineffective for conflict resolution and some complex problem solving.

EXERCISES AND QUESTIONS FOR DISCUSSION

1. Think of the organizations to which you belong. Can they be considered tall or flat organizations? Discuss the effects on communication of such tallness or flatness. What kinds of problems have you observed or experienced?

2. Have you ever felt overloaded by too many messages or too much communication? Can you describe the features of the situation that contributed to your feeling of being overloaded? Can you relate each of the potential factors in overload discussed in the chapter to your own experiences? Could you have used any of the techniques discussed for dealing with overload? Which would have been effective?

3. Explain why members of many organizations tend to be dissatisfied with vertical communication in their organizations. What can be done to enhance the effectiveness of downward communication? of upward communication? Describe the typical limitations people experience with upward communication. What can organizations do to improve the upward flow of communication?

4. Explain why there is often little horizontal communication in complex organizations. Have you experienced problems of this sort in the organizations in which you participate? Discuss some measures that could be taken to improve horizontal communication.

5. Consider an organization that you belong to or one that you can observe. Try to chart the major networks for the flow of communication in

this organization. Are you able to discover different networks for production, maintenance, social relations, and innovations in this organization?

6. Describe the network role that you fulfill in some of the organizations to which you belong. Are you satisfied or dissatisfied with this role. Why?

7. Why are grapevines often effective means for communication? What are the situations that seem conducive to the sprouting of grapevines? Should organizational leaders try to control or eliminate grapevines? Why?

8. Discuss the effects of various forms of media on the flow of communication through the channels discussed in this chapter. What are the potential effects of electronic or computerized systems on rumors, grapevines, and informal communication in general?

SOURCES FOR FURTHER STUDY

Albrecht, T. L., and Hall, B. (1991). Relational and content differences between elite and outsiders in innovation networks. *Human Communication Research, 17,* 535–61.

Alvesson, M. (1993). Cultural-ideological modes of management control: A theory and a case study of a professional service company. In M. Deetz (Ed.), *Communication yearbook 16,* Newbury Park, Calif.: Sage, pp. 3–42.

Boyett, J. H., and Conn, H. P. (1991). *Workplace 2000: The revolution reshaping American business.* New York: Penguin.

Bullis, C., and Bach, B. W. (1991). An explication and test of communication network content and multiplexity as predictors of organizational identification. *Western Journal of Speech Communication, 55,* 180–97.

Chesebro, J. W., and Bonsall, D. G. (1989). *Computer-mediated communication: Human relationships in a computerized world.* Tuscaloosa, Ala.: University of Alabama Press.

Corman, S. R. (1990). A model of perceived communication in collective networks. *Human Communication Research, 16,* 582–602.

Farace, R. V., Monge, P. R., and Russell, H. M. (1977). *Communication and organizing.* Reading, Mass.: Addison-Wesley.

Fisher, B. A. (1978). *Perspectives on human communication.* New York: Macmillan.

Fulk, J., and Steinfeld, C. (Eds.). *Organizations and communication technology.* Newbury Park, Calif.: Sage.

Jablin, F. M. (1987). Formal organization structure. In F. M. Jablin, L. L. Putnam, K. H. Roberts, and L. W. Porter (Eds.), *Handbook of organizational communication: An interdisciplinary perspective.* Newbury Park, Calif.: Sage.

Kiesler, S, Siegel, J., and McGuire, T. W. (1984). Social psychological aspects of computer-mediated communication. *American Psychologist, 39,* 1123–34.

Leavitt, H. J. (1951). Some effects of certain communication patterns on group performance. *Journal of Abnormal and Social Psychology, 46,* 38–50.

Mintzberg, H. (1973). *The nature of managerial work.* New York: HarperCollins.

Monge, P. R., and Eisenberg, E. M. (1987). Emergent communication networks. In F. M. Jablin, L. L. Putnam, K. H. Roberts, and L. W. Porter (Eds.), *Handbook of organizational communication: An interdisciplinary perspective.* Newbury Park, Calif.: Sage.

Perrow, C. (1984). *Normal accidents: Living with high-risk technologies.* New York: Basic Books.

Stinchcombe, A. L. (1990). *Information and organizations.* Berkeley, Calif.: University of California Press.

Tichy, N. M., Tushman, M. L., and Fombrun, C. (1979). Social network analysis for organizations. *Academy of Management Review, 4,* 507–19.

Trevino, L. K., Daft, R. L., and Lengel, R. H. (1990). Understanding managers' media choices: A symbolic interactionist perspective. In J. Fulk and C. Steinfield (Eds.), *Organizations and communication technology.* Newbury Park, Calif.: Sage.

NOTES

1. S. R. Corman (1990), A model of perceived communication in collective networks, *Human Communication Research, 16,* p. 584.
2. A. L. Stinchcombe (1990), *Information and organizations,* Berkeley, Calif.: University of California Press, p. 3.
3. K. Weick (1979), *The social psychology of organizing,* 2d ed. Reading, Mass.: Addison-Wesley, p. 17.
4. J. H. Boyett and H. P. Conn (1991), *Workplace 2000: The revolution reshaping American business,* New York: Penguin, p. 2.
5. Boyett and Conn, pp. 4–5.
6. B. A. Fisher (1978), *Perspectives on human communication,* New York: Macmillan, pp. 107–24.
7. H. Mintzberg (1973), *The nature of managerial work,* New York: HarperCollins, p. 36.
8. Mintzberg, p. 36.
9. Stinchcombe, p. 3.
10. *Wall Street Journal,* December 9, 1993, p. A1.
11. R. V. Farace, P. R. Monge, and H. M. Russell (1977), *Communicating and organizing,* Reading, Mass.: Addison-Wesley, pp. 101–15.
12. Farace, Monge, and Russell, p. 110.
13. See Farace, Monge, and Russell, pp. 117–24.
14. Mintzberg, p. 45.
15. *Wall Street Journal,* September 3, 1993, p. B1.
16. *Wall Street Journal,* November 2, 1992, p. B1.
17. *Wall Street Journal,* August 17, 1994, p. A1.
18. See M. Alvesson (1993), Cultural-ideological modes of management control: A theory and a case study of a professional service company, in M. Deetz (Ed.), *Communication yearbook 16,* Newbury Park, Calif.: Sage, pp. 3–42.
19. E. Z. McCathrin (1989), Beyond employee publications: Making the personal connection, *Public Relations Journal, 45,* pp. 15–16.
20. McCathrin, p. 16.
21. *Wall Street Journal,* December 9, 1993, p. A1.
22. F. M. Jablin (1987), Formal organization structure, in F. M. Jablin, L. L. Putnam, K. H. Roberts, and L. W. Porter (Eds.), *Handbook of organizational communication: An interdisciplinary perspective,* Newbury Park, Calif.: Sage, p. 401.
23. J. R. Barker, C. W. Melville, and M. E. Pacanowsky (1993), Self-directed teams at Xel: Changes in communication practices during a program of cultural transformation, *Journal of Applied Communication Research, 21,* 299–301.
24. A. Bavelas (1948), A mathematical model for group structures, *Applied Anthropology, 7,* 16–30; H. J. Leavitt (1951), Some effects of certain communication patterns on group performance, *Journal of Abnormal and Social Psychology, 46,* 38–50.
25. N. M. Tichy, M. L. Tushman, and C. Fombrun (1979), Social network analysis for organizations, *Academy of Management Review, 4,* 507–19.
26. T. L. Albrecht and B. Hall (1991), Relational and content differences between elite and outsiders in innovation networks, *Human Communication Research, 17,* 535–61.
27. C. Perrow (1984), *Normal accidents: Living with high-risk technologies,* New York: Basic Books, pp. 89–93.
28. P. R. Monge and E. M. Eisenberg (1987), Emergent communication networks, in F. M. Jablin, L. L. Putnam, K. H. Roberts, and L. W. Porter (Eds.), *Handbook of organizational communication: An interdisciplinary perspective,* Newbury Park, Calif.: Sage, pp. 314–16; C. Bullis and B. W. Bach (1991), An explication and test of communication network content and multiplexity as predictors of organizational identification, *Western Journal of Speech Communication, 55,* 180–97.
29. J. D. Johnson (1987), Multivariate communication networks, *Central States Speech Journal, 38,* 210–22.
30. Bullis and Bach, p. 192; R. L. Hartman and J. D. Johnson (1989), Social contagion and multiplexity: Communication networks as predictors of commitment and role ambiguity, *Human Communication Research, 15,* 523–48.
31. C. Stohl and W. C. Redding (1987), Messages and message exchange processes, in F. M. Jablin, L. L. Putnam, K. H. Roberts, and L. W. Porter (Eds.), *Handbook of organizational communication: An interdisciplinary perspective,* Newbury Park, Calif.: Sage, pp. 480–81.
32. *The Christian Science Monitor,* February 25, 1993, p. 7.
33. L. K. Trevino, R. L. Daft, and R. H. Langel (1990), Understanding managers' media choices: A symbolic interactionist perspective, in J. Fulk and C. Steinfield (Eds.), *Organizaitons and communication technology,* Newbury Park, Calif.: Sage, p. 75.
34. Trevino, Daft, and Lengel, pp. 74–83.
35. *Wall Street Journal,* December 9, 1993, p. A1.
36. J. Yates and W. J. Orlikowsli (1992), Genres of organizational communication: A structurational approach to studying communication and media, *Academy of Management Review, 17,* 311–16.
37. J. W. Chesebro and D. G. Bonsall (1989), *Computer-mediated communication: Human relationships in a computerized world,* Tuscaloosa, Ala.: University of Alabama Press.
38. S. Kiesler, J. Siegel, and T. W. McGuire (1984), Social psychological aspects of computer-mediated communication, *American Psychologist, 39,* 1123–34.
39. *Indianapolis Star,* July 2, 1995, p. E1.
40. Chesebro and Bonsall, p. 118.
41. Quoted in *Wall Street Journal,* December 9, 1993, p. A7.
42. Kiesler, Siegel, and McGuire, p. 1128–29.
43. Chesebro and Bonsall, p. 123.

CHAPTER 9

Interpersonal Communication in Organizations

CHAPTER OBJECTIVES

After studying this chapter, you should be able to:

- Explain the defining characteristics of interpersonal and dyadic communication.
- Explain the developmental perspective of the study of interpersonal communication.
- Discuss how people form impressions of interpersonal communication partners.
- Explain the effects of attribution theory and uncertainty reduction on the development of interpersonal relationships.
- Discuss relational communication in the development and maintenance of ongoing interpersonal relationships.
- Draw implications from theories of interpersonal communication for leader–member communication.
- Discuss the advantages and challenges of communication in mentoring relationships.
- Discuss effects that gender and cultural differences can have in the development of interpersonal communication in organizations.

CHAPTER OUTLINE

Defining Interpersonal Communication

Development of Interpersonal Communication in Relationships
Developmental Perspective
Relationship Development and Impression Formation
Organizational Socialization
Review of Relationship Development

DEFINING INTERPERSONAL COMMUNICATION

In spite of the growing enthusiasm for interactive, computer-mediated communication and information superhighways, much important organizational communication is and will continue to be face-to-face. Most people in organizations continue to prefer face-to-face channels, especially for information regarding organizational policies, plans, and prospects. Personal channels represent the richest medium because so many verbal and nonverbal cues are instantly available to the participants.

For most people, the interpersonal contacts that they experience in their organizational life provide important social as well as professional relationships. The direct experience that we have of an organization is based on talk with other individuals. Outside the family, relationships with others in organizations, whether at church, in social organizations, or at work, constitute most people's major source of involvement with others. It is hard to "get a life" outside of an organization. The quality of the interpersonal communication people experience in an organization goes a long way toward determining their success and satisfaction in that organization.

This chapter focuses on the communication setting that scholars refer to as *interpersonal communication*. In the domain of communication studies, interpersonal communication usually refers to communication that exhibits the following characteristics:

1. It involves just two people.
2. These two people are in a persisting relationship.
3. The mode of their communication is face-to-face spoken and nonverbal communication.

A couple of clarifications are in order. The restriction of the definition to just two people is not always scrupulously observed, as occasionally interpersonal communication is used to refer to general face-to-face interaction, which might involve more than two people. The growing use of interactive communication technologies may allow us at times to talk about interpersonal communication even when two people are communicating through computer-mediated and video systems (and are thus not face-to-face). One thinks of the virtual lunchrooms set up to allow executives to appear to "do lunch" even though they are actually in separate cities. The three characteristics listed here, however, represent the conditions of most of the academic research done in the area called interpersonal communication.

Several situational factors tend to distinguish the different levels of communication study, including the number of participants, the proximity among the participants, the number of channels available for use, and the immediacy of feedback.[1] In mass communication, for example, there are many participants (a large audience), who are at some distance from one another, using only one channel (say the sounds of a radio), with little opportunity for immediate feedback because audience and speaker(s) are not physically sharing the same space. In interpersonal communication, there are only two participants, in close proximity (physically or possibly through video), making use of verbal and many nonverbal channels, and having the possibility for exchanging immediate feedback.

Interpersonal communication is undoubtedly very important on the job.

Interpersonal communication emphasizes communication in a *dyad,* which is the special term used to describe an ongoing, two-person relationship. A dyad is thus more than just a pair of people, who may be together for a one-time or casual encounter, such as the relationship between a sales associate and a customer making a one-time purchase in a store. The difference lies in the continuing, patterned nature of the relationship over time.

Studies of interpersonal communication focus on various kinds of settings and relationships, not all of which are necessarily relevant to organizational communication. For example, interpersonal communication includes such forms of communication as health communication (patient and physician), marital communication (husband and wife), and social relationships (friend and friend). In organizational communication, the relationship is often *more positional and formal,* such as that between supervisor and supervisee, superior and subordinate, mentor and protégé, or two coworkers. In many cases, the two participants have not sought each other out for the relationship, but are thrown together by the requirements of the job or the organizational structure. The interpersonal link that has most often been the focus of organizational studies is that of superior–subordinate, or leader–member, although there has lately been growing interest in the mentoring dyad.

A vast and growing literature concerning interpersonal communication exists, and whole textbooks and courses concentrate on this subject. This chapter is intended to provide a brief overview of this field as it relates to contexts relevant to organizational communication. The first part of this chapter therefore considers factors in the development of interpersonal relationships and the maintenance of such relationships. The second part takes up more specific issues, including the areas of superior–subordinate or leader–member communication, mentoring, and cultural and gender diversity.

DEVELOPMENT OF INTERPERSONAL COMMUNICATION IN RELATIONSHIPS

Developmental Perspective

An interpersonal relationship develops over time, and the communication patterns characterizing that relationship depend on the course of this development. Gerald Miller and other theorists, who take a developmental perspective, point out that some relationships become increasingly interpersonal with continued interaction and growing familiarity.[2] As a relationship becomes more interpersonal, the participants rely sequentially on different forms of information concerning the other party to the relationship. A specific formulation of this view is the theory of *social penetration,* which posits increased interpersonal communication as the relationship develops, moving from exchanges of superficial information to exchanges of more intimate kinds of information, typically through the process of reciprocal self-disclosure.[3]

On first acquaintance, people tend to rely upon *cultural information,* which is readily available and known because of broad cultural understandings. For example, in meeting others like ourselves in an American organization, we can assume that we will use English, that certain greetings are expected, and so on. At this point, then, we make assumptions about how to carry on our communication with the other person depending on a stock of culturally based information.

As we gain more data about the other person, we begin to use *sociological information* as the basis for predicting his or her actions and responses in continued communication. Sociological information refers to general knowledge about social groups. After some conversation with the other person, we may discover that he or she can be categorized based on certain membership groups and reference groups. For example, when we determine that the other person is an accountant or an engineer, we begin to make predictions about how that person might respond to different topics or questions for discussion. One's educational or socioeconomic status provides a basis for similar inferences.

Reference groups are those that set certain norms or expectations of behavior for that person, whether or not he or she actually belongs to them. A person's stated goals, such as occupational objective, may indicate significant reference groups. While in pharmacy college, an undergraduate may pattern certain behaviors on those of practicing professional pharmacists, a reference group to which the student does not yet belong. This knowledge of social categories allows us to make more specific generalizations about the other person than we can with simply cultural information.

More specific kinds of information are available at the *psychological information* level, at which we can make predictions based on the personal characteristics, proclivities, or idiosyncrasies of the other person. At this level, the other person stands out as an individual, differentiated from cultural or social groups. He or she does not always react or behave in line with cultural or sociological expectations. The cultural and sociological levels of knowing other people are more superficial or impersonal, whereas psychological information provides for more personal or interpersonal modes of communicating. Although Smith may be an accountant, he may not fit one's image of a typical accountant. It may turn out that Smith likes to take "adventure vacations," and has actually tracked wild ibix in Mongolia and grizzly bear in the Rockies (as is the case with a head of an accounting firm whom the author once met).

At the deepest level of knowing, one person can not only predict the other's actions but offer reasonable explanations for them. Imagine that someone has become interested in Smith because she has discovered that she is going to have to work closely with him on a long-term project or as a result of a permanent reorganization, because Smith will become her manager or superior. In this case, she will be interested in a far larger range of Smith's behaviors and attitudes than just those concerning the one-time project. Because this relationship has become more significant, she now needs to develop information that will explain Smith's behaviors in a large number of circumstances and settings.

Relationships become more interpersonal, then, as we move from the *cultural* to the *sociological* to the *psychological* levels of information (see Figure 9.1, on p. 188). In relationships that do not become highly interpersonal, the need for psychological and explanatory information remains at a minimum, perhaps just enough to conduct some

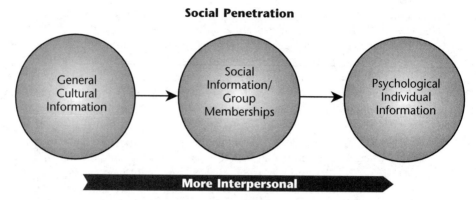

FIGURE 9.1   Stages of social penetration, as the relationship becomes more interpersonal.

transitory business. If we need only one piece of predictive or explanatory information about another person, we would not speak of that relationship as being interpersonal. Perhaps George can predict how a waiter will always greet him at a customary lunch site, and even explain the greeting in terms of the waiter's hoping for a tip; still, the relationship does not share a wide range of psychological and explanatory information beyond this one facet.

Relationship Development and Impression Formation

When it is clear that we will be communicating with another person in a continuing relationship on the job, we first try to determine what makes him or her tick. In order to be able to understand the person's communication behaviors, we need to decide what motivates or causes these behaviors. In the early stages of the relationship, therefore, we gather information in order to achieve this kind of explanatory power. Two kinds of interpersonal theories have been particularly powerful in describing this stage of impression formation: *attribution theory* and *uncertainty-reduction theory.*

Attribution Theory. Attribution theory, developed by Fritz Heider, Harold Kelley, and others, is a form of naive psychology that holds that we all behave as amateur psychologists when trying to figure out the causes of other people's behaviors.[4] When we observe a piece of behavior by another person, such as volunteering to donate blood, we can assume that this action is caused by (*attributed* to) either internal or external factors. Internal motivators could be altruism or humanitarian feelings; external causes could include peer pressure from friends planning to give blood at the same time. The question is whether this kind of action springs from relatively constant personality factors or from changeable external factors.

To take a more negative example, suppose we observe a coworker cheating on an expense account report. We could attribute this behavior to internal causation, such as a general tendency toward dishonesty embedded in his or her personality. Or, we could attribute the cheating to unusual and extreme pressures on this person, such as personal or financial pressures, that almost force a behavior that would otherwise be uncharacteristic. Obviously, our judgment or evaluation of that person's character depends to a large extent on whether we attribute the behavior to internal or external causes.

We attribute causes to our own behavior when we feel a need to explain our own behavior to ourselves. In explaining our own behavior, we feel privy to more knowledge about our own motivations than about those of other people. This fact can lead to a *fundamental attribution error,* or a *self-serving bias.* In choosing whether to rely on internal or external causes of behavior, we depend on a private perspective. When we ourselves commit some act that may be seen as negative, such as inflating an expense account or misreporting income to the Internal Revenue Service, we tend to attribute it to external forces, because we "know" that we ourselves are basically honest and upright. Only powerful external forces could cause us to behave against this basic orientation. Others who cheat, however, are probably just acting from their own selfish motives.

In an organizational relationship, such as that of a superior and a subordinate, attribution theory can provide both parties with information they feel they need about each other. It makes a difference whether positive or negative actions are attributed to stable personality factors, which can be expected to stay the same regardless of circumstances, or to changing environmental factors. Let us say that we have decided that a particular supervisor is a brilliant administrator, with only the best interests of the organization at heart. If we observe this administrator behaving in a way that degrades or takes advantage of a subordinate, we can interpret that information in terms of our "already knowing" that the administrator is a good person. The cause of this apparently negative behavior, therefore, must be found in the behavior of the other person or other external circumstances.

In other words, new information is not always taken at face value, but is placed within the context of already determined expectations. New information, then, does not necessarily change those expectations, but instead is interpreted in a way that allows for the least amount of change in prior beliefs. In this way, we can maintain fairly stable constructs concerning ourselves and others. The manner in which attributions are formulated when developing an impression of another person can thus have long-lasting consequences for continuing interaction.

A second way in which attribution theory has significant consequences for the superior–subordinate relationship involves evaluation and attribution of internal or external causes. If a supervisor tends to believe that his or her subordinates' actions result from internal rather than external causes (that is, that they are *high internals*), he or she may judge these subordinates' work and potential for development differently from another supervisor who usually credits external causes. The supervisor may not feel that training or changing work conditions would be effective if the behavior is seen as the result of stable personality factors. Similarly, when trying to motivate others, a person may rely on internal motivators, as in human relations type theories, or on external motivators, as in the classical management theories. Internal motivators could include appealing to self-esteem, pride in accomplishment, or increased participation in decision making. External motivators include salary, bonuses, or other tangible benefits.

Uncertainty-Reduction Theory. Uncertainty-reduction theory (URT) concerns communication in early stages of relationship formation.[5] This theory, developed by Charles R. Berger and colleagues at Northwestern University, holds that an important motive for interpersonal communication is to reduce levels of uncertainty about oneself and the other person in the interaction. According to the theory, this motivation is stronger when people will have to work with or have a lasting, significant relationship with another person, as would be the case when assigned to work with a particular person or superior in an organization.

Uncertainty makes interpersonal communication more difficult, because people are unsure about how the other person will respond to various messages. Consequently, Berger maintains, "Coping with uncertainty is a central issue in any face-to-face encounter, whether interactants are conscious of this fact or not."[6] Attribution theory provides the original underpinnings for uncertainty reduction theory, in that by reducing uncertainty, people enhance their ability to make seemingly accurate attributions.

Uncertainty-reduction theory maintains that two kinds of uncertainty are significant: *cognitive* uncertainty and *behavioral* uncertainty. Behavioral uncertainty is about the meaning of the actual behaviors observed. Cognitive uncertainty is about the attitudes or motives behind those behaviors, the reasons for a person's behaving in a particular way. Obviously, reducing cognitive uncertainty provides explanations for a person's behavior. While very early stages of interaction aim to reduce *behavioral* uncertainty, people quickly move toward discovering the underlying reasons for the behavior by reducing *cognitive* uncertainty.

The strength of the need to reduce uncertainty varies from relationship to relationship. In short-term or casual relationships, there is no great need for such an effort. Under certain circumstances, however, there is a higher-than-normal motivation for reducing initial uncertainty:

1. When the interaction promises to provide one with significant benefits or losses
2. When the other person in the interaction behaves in erratic or deviant ways
3. When there is a perceived probability of continued interaction with the other person

Presumably, the third condition applies most often in organizational settings. When the interaction is communication with one's superior, the first condition also applies. One hopes that the second condition rarely applies in work settings, although there is a growing self-help literature concerned with how to deal with "difficult people." The second condition may also apply in unfortunate situations such as those involving discrimination or sexual harassment. At any rate, significant or lasting work relationships in organizations are characterized by the conditions that motivate toward communication behavior to reduce uncertainty, according to URT.

As an interpersonal relationship develops, the participants use various communication strategies to reduce uncertainty. Berger and his colleagues divide these strategies into three types:

1. Passive (observation of reactions, disinhibition searching)
2. Active (interrogating third parties, setting up situations)
3. Interactive (direct interrogations, self-disclosure)

Passive strategies, perhaps the simplest, involve observing the target person, perhaps in situations of special problem solving or crisis. A second type of observation is called *disinhibition searching* because it involves trying to observe the person in situations in which he or she is presumed to be relatively uninhibited and unaware of being observed, such as during lunch with friends in the company cafeteria.

Active strategies require actively seeking out information about the target person, perhaps by asking colleagues or coworkers what it is like to work with or for Smith or Jones. Alternatively, one could try to arrange special situations, perhaps by arranging to work on a committee with the other person before the beginning of the anticipated work relationship.

Interactive strategies involve communicating directly with the target person. *Direct interrogation* is probably the most obvious interactive strategy. For example, one may ask the other about his or her pet peeves to get insight into motivations. A second strategy is that of *self-disclosure,* in which the first person offers certain self-descriptions in the expectation that the other person will reciprocate with similar kinds of revelations.

Uncertainty-reduction theory thus provides theoretical support for the finding from research that members report higher satisfaction with organizational climates that allow open communication (as discussed in Chapter 5). On the other hand, openness in communication may have some limits. Occasionally, ambiguity in communications allows people to maintain working relationships, particularly when colleagues or leaders and members differ on some attitudes or goals.

Theorists of interpersonal communication have suggested modifications and changes in the basic principles of URT. Social exchange theory and the predicted outcome values theory of Michael Sunnafrank, for example, are especially concerned with interpersonal relationships formed *voluntarily,* unlike many of the dyads in organizational settings.[7] These theories emphasize that the expected outcomes each participant may receive from the interaction are major determinants of uncertainty-reducing communication. Expected outcomes determine whether or not the relationship will continue. For the purposes of organizational communication, however, Berger's point remains of special interest. Obviously, one does not always have a choice regarding superior–subordinate relationships, one's coworker, or even a mentor–protégé relationship in organizations in which mentors are assigned.

Finally, the growing cultural diversity of contemporary organizations leads to special problems of uncertainty reduction communication in *cross-cultural dyads* or settings. William Gudykunst has extensively researched this issue.[8] When people from significantly different cultures constitute a dyad, one can assume that initial uncertainty will be especially high. The differences in cultural expectations, values, and behavior patterns all significantly increase the amount of uncertainty the partners experience.

Conceptualizations of the major dimensions of cultural differences are derived mainly from the work of Edward T. Hall and Geert Hofstede, as we have already seen. Hall provides the concept of high-context and low-context cultures,[9] whereas Hofstede's research highlights four dimensions of cultural differences: uncertainty avoidance, individualism versus collectivism, masculinity, and power distance.[10] Although all four of Hofstede's dimensions can affect the ongoing stages of social penetration in interpersonal relations, Gudykunst finds that Hall's high-low context dimension and Hofstede's individualism dimension are most closely related to the process of uncertainty reduction.[11]

In high-context cultures, people pay special attention to the often nonverbal or unstated context surrounding verbal messages to derive significant levels of information. In low-context cultures, the verbal messages rather than the context are given more weight. In practice, these tendencies suggest that for uncertainty reduction, persons from high-context cultures can be expected to focus on information concerning the other person's social groups, background, education, and the like. Those from low-context cultures can be expected to rely on verbal information gathered from oral and written messages.[12] When exchanging business cards, Japanese businesspeople study the cards carefully for indications of the person's role and status within his or her organization. Such information is also expected to indicate one's likely background and training, thus providing even more context for understanding the other person. Americans, on the other hand, frequently place business cards in their pocket or folder without a great deal of study. Presumably, what the other person says is of more importance in reducing uncertainty than background information.

It could be a mistake, however, to assume that Americans do not make use of nonverbal markers and titles to provide context for guiding people in interpersonal interactions. The American Dietetic Association, for example, tried to dispense with the use of specific job titles to enhance a teamwork ethic in the organization. Reportedly, many people experienced quite a bit of discomfort, resulting in problems, such as how to celebrate Secretaries' Week when technically there were no longer any secretaries.[13] Occasionally, there are problems dealing with outside agencies, such as backers and donors who feel a need to deal with the top people of an organization, which is typically indicated by job title.

Similarly, the size and accoutrements of one's office have long been used as context or nonverbal markers to help reduce uncertainty regarding the other person's status and potential power. Dilbert and his fellow engineers in their small cubicles know where they stand in a relationship with an executive with a private, corner office.

Organizational Socialization

People come to understand how to function in organizations through a process of learning over time, a process that theorists refer to as *socialization*.[14] This assimilation into organizations, interestingly, follows a developmental sequence reminiscent of the developmental theory of social penetration for describing interpersonal communication. A person begins with generic information concerning the kind of organization she or he is entering, just as a person first uses available cultural-level information about a prospective communication partner. As they gain more experience within the new organization, they develop a deeper understanding of the organization's way of doing things, just as one person gradually learns sociological- and psychological-level information about a partner.

A useful model describing the process of organizational socialization has been developed by Frederic Jablin.[15] First, Jablin makes the point that the experience of organizational assimilation is relatively common in our society because of the turnover in American occupations. Even in stable industries, the average tenure with a given organization is under ten years.

The assimilation process comprises four stages, according to Jablin: anticipatory socialization, initial encounter, "metamorphosis," and exit (see Figure 9.2). The socialization process thus begins even before one officially enters the organization, as one begins to anticipate and plan for making adaptations to a new environment. Often, these expectations are somewhat unrealistic. The encounter phase refers to a breaking-in period, frequently consisting of a series of small shocks or surprises as the reality begins to look different from the expectations. Much of the communication in this phase is ambient in nature, meaning that the newcomer picks up information randomly from fellow workers and superiors, even though there is usually an initial effort at some sort of planned orientation or training program.

In the metamorphosis stage, the newcomer takes on new expectations and begins to use communication rules adaptive to the situation. In this phase, the member also begins to *individualize* his or her role in the organization, so that the adaptation occurs in two directions: As the individual adapts to the organization, the organization adapts to the individual. The exit stage is a period of disengagement as the member prepares to leave the organization and anticipates a new kind of environment.

This socialization provides people with the kinds of information that they need in order to understand and develop interpersonal relationships within organizations. As a person becomes more socialized or assimilated into an organization, one might expect that he or she would feel more comfortable knowing how to develop relationships with coworkers, superiors, and subordinates within it.

The customary paths or themes of interpersonal communication in some organizations may be different from the paths and themes in other organizations. A great

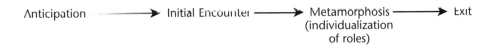

Anticipation ⟶ Initial Encounter ⟶ Metamorphosis ⟶ Exit
(individualization
of roles)

FIGURE 9.2 Stages of organizational socialization, according to Jablin; individualization of roles, as the individual adapts to the organization and the organization adapts to the individual, occurs in the third stage.

deal of joking or teasing between dyad partners may be the norm in one organizational culture, whereas another emphasizes formality and decorum in such relationships. Police officers in patrol cars, for example, often work in pairs, or dyads. The development of an interpersonal relationship through interaction in this dyad could conceivably have life-or-death consequences. The development of trust and respect are especially important in this relationship. A new officer's socialization into a police organization depends largely on the interpersonal communication experienced in the partner dyad.

A couple of caveats regarding this view of organizational socialization are in order. First, there is the tendency to see the organization as an entity, existing in a relationship as part of a person–organization dyad. This tendency is a form of organizational reification, which we have discussed earlier, particularly in Chapter 2. The organization is actually personalized in terms of the real-life human beings one encounters, and it is these human beings who pass on the culture and communication patterns of the organization. In addition, socialization messages are received from possibly depersonalized sources, such as handbooks, manuals, orientation materials, annual reports, and other similar written or video materials. Still, the actual hints concerning how to communicate with other organizational members undoubtedly come through person-to-person interaction.

Second, the process of organizational socialization may be experienced differently by different organizational members depending on their individual characteristics. Feminists have pointed out that organizations traditionally have been more attuned to socializing men than women. The organization has been unsure how to bring women into what perhaps had been an "old boys' club." If interpersonal communication patterns call for discussions of sports laced with expletives and sexual stereotypes, women may feel marginalized or treated as outsiders.[16]

The third caveat regarding organizational assimilation is to remember that what constitutes the organization may appear different to people in different parts of the organization. For some, the important socialization is into a particular professional identity rather than into a local organization. Thus, research faculty members at large universities may look to their professional societies and associations for unofficial guidelines regarding rules of interaction. These guidelines may be picked up at conferences, conventions, and graduate schools before one becomes a member of the faculty of a particular university organization.

Review of Relationship Development

Interpersonal communication between people in an ongoing, two-person relationship develops over time. As the relationship becomes more interpersonal, each partner is able to tailor his or her communication more closely to the individual needs and style of the other person. Two kinds of theories about interpersonal communication have helped to explain how this process works: attribution theory and uncertainty reduction theory. In an organization, these theories help us to understand how people go about learning how to communicate with a significant other person, such as a co-worker, mentor, superior, or subordinate. The organization itself socializes people in

AN ISSUE OF COMMUNICATION ETHICS

A Feminist Critique of Organizational Socialization

A basic question concerning organizational socialization has to do with the extent to which one surrenders one's own individuality in order to assimilate, to become a good team player. The process can be read as assuming that organizations shape and in fact dominate people's lives—that people exist for organizations instead of the other way around. Feminist critiques of the theorizing about organizational assimilation point to issues of this sort.

What has been termed "liberal feminist theory" criticizes organizational socialization from the point of view that such processes deny women the opportunity to rise in organizations because they are not allowed to participate fully in socialization processes. The discussion later in this chapter regarding mentoring touches on the difficulties encountered by women being mentored by higher-ranking men in organizations. A later development in feminist theory, however, called standpoint theory, questions even the assumptions of liberal feminism.*

*C. Bullis (1994), *Feminism and organizational socialization.* Paper presented at the annual conference of the Speech Communication Association, New Orleans.

This method holds that research and theorizing cannot help but be conducted from a particular standpoint, which excludes other possible standpoints. The standpoint from which organizational socialization is described assumes that the actual experience of women in the real-life world can be discounted as they assume roles in organizational life. For example, the present reality is that women still are seen as primarily responsible for child care and housework, despite gains in recent years. Organizational socialization can be communicated in such a way that these functions outside the organization are discounted or seen as only marginally important. One's true life is seen to be that of the organization.

Such critiques can raise questions regarding the organization's hold over people's lives, whether men or women. To what extent do organizational messages, aimed at socializing newcomers, imply that life outside the organization is secondary? How can people within organizations respond to messages, intentional or unintentional, of this sort?

terms of the type of interpersonal communication expected or considered normal within that organization. Organizational socialization is thus a major determiner of the way in which relationship development works out in specific organizational contexts.

INTERPERSONAL RELATIONSHIP MAINTENANCE

The dyad, once formed, is like a small system, consisting of two elements (the participants) within their immediate organizational environment. How the relationship is maintained influences the level of satisfaction experienced by each party, their willingness to be flexible with each other, and, in general, how well they work together. For superior–subordinate or leader–member pairs, relationship maintenance is important for the subordinate in that it may affect his or her career goals. In addition, the leader and member may be expected to be more well disposed toward each other in a well-maintained relationship, and the subordinate more successful in attempting to influence the superior.

Relational Communication

Theories of *relational communication* suggest ways in which the relationship system maintains equilibrium, or *homeostasis,* as discussed in the context of systems theories in Chapter 6 of this text. Relational communication grows out of the early work of Gregory Bateson, Paul Watzlawick, and their colleagues in the Palo Alto Group, based at the Mental Research Institute in Palo Alto, California. The foundations of relational communication are presented in the early, influential work *The Pragmatics of Human Communication.*[17] These foundations are communicated in five axioms, as presented earlier in the discussion of the transactional perspective in Chapter 3:

    1. "One cannot not communicate,"[18] which means that any behavior emitted in the presence of another person has the potential of being interpreted as having message value by that other person.

    2. Each act of communication contains both *content* and *relationship* information, which indicates that in addition to the manifest content, a message posits some sort of relationship between the interactants.

    3. Each interactant *punctuates* the series of communication exchanges in a relationship from his or her own perspective. In other words, each person sees any one message as part of a larger sequence, a context for interpreting it or assigning "the real meaning" to it.

    4. Communication is carried on through both *digital* and *analogic* coding. Digital coding is characterized by discrete units (symbols, words), which are arbitrary and conventional units of meaning. Analogic coding is representational, such as facial expressions or gestures, which cannot be reduced to discrete units.

    5. Interaction can be *symmetrical* or *complementary.* Symmetrical interchanges are characterized by similarity, indicating a basic equality between the two participants; complementary exchanges emphasize a difference in status or dominance between the two.

Applications of Relational Communication

These five axioms suggest several points at which there may be strains or problems in interpersonal communication. The dimensions of this relational component have been studied at some length in an effort to isolate the types of relational messages that are significant for relationship maintenance communication.[19]

    First, one may not be aware of the interpretations that another places on one's own behavior (the impossibility of not communicating). Even not sending a message sends a message. Japanese negotiators are much more comfortable with periods of silence in a conversation than are their American counterparts. Americans feel uneasy during such periods of silence and may try to fill what appears to them to be empty conversational space with chatter, perhaps unnecessarily giving in on points being negotiated.

Second, the relationship implied by the communication exchanges may outweigh the simple content intended to be conveyed. For example, prior to the nuclear accident that became known as Three Mile Island in Pennsylvania, a young engineer had alerted a supervisor in the nuclear operations division of the company running the power plant that an accident of the sort that happened was possible. The supervisor responded to the engineer's memo by seeing it as an implied criticism of his division rather than as a warning of what actually happened; that is, the relationship message took precedence over the content.[20]

The axiom concerning complementary and symmetrical exchanges has generated most research interest, with special focus on the issue of control in the relationship.[21] A symmetrical interaction is one in which both partners communicate as equals, whereas complementarity involves a dominant and a submissive partner. Any single interchange, or interaction consisting of a message and response, can be judged symmetrical or complementary, but whether the pattern that develops over time is seen as symmetrical or complementary is of more interest. For example, if one partner usually accepts a suggestion for action made by the other, the pattern is a complementary one, even though occasionally the second partner may successfully get the dominant partner to accept one of her or his suggestions. Competitive symmetry represents the situation in which the two interactants are competing for dominance. This situation may characterize a relationship between coworkers or one between organizational members whose relative status or authority is unclear. Typically, the superior–subordinate relationship results in complementary patterns of interaction. The relationship between mentor and protégé also can be expected to follow a complementary pattern (as can that between teacher and student).

Deborah Tannen is a sociolinguist (a person who studies the relationship between language use and social roles) who has analyzed the problems of communication between men and women. In her book on communication in the workplace, *Talking from 9 to 5*, she gives several examples of how interpersonal communication can exhibit misunderstandings of this sort. In one case, two colleagues are heading home following their presentations at a national conference.[22] Deidre compliments William on his presentation, intended to initiate a symmetrical exchange of compliments (she assumes she is sending a message to be interpreted as between two people on an equal footing, in a symmetrical relationship). William says "thanks," but does not otherwise respond with the expected return compliment, so Deidre prompts him, "Well, what did you think of mine?" He proceeds to deliver a lengthy critique instead of the expected compliment. In terms of the axioms of relational communication, William interpreted this as a complementary exchange, in which he was in the one-up position. Instead of seeing the situation as calling for a symmetrical exchange of compliments, he interpreted her compliment as a one-down message acknowledging his superiority by praising him. He heard her question as that of someone in a subordinate position literally asking for a critique. His mistake is almost like that of a person who responds to the normal American greeting, "How are you?" as a literal request for a medical report.

Serious consequences can result from such misunderstandings on the content–relationship and complementary–symmetrical dimensions, as the Three Mile Island

Aircraft personnel must maintain excellent communication rapport with one another, especially in hazardous conditions.

case shows. Similarly, on January 20, 1982, Air Florida's Flight 90 attempted to take off from Washington, D.C., National Airport during a freezing rain. Icing led to an immediate crash and the loss of the lives of all but five of the people aboard. The black-box recording of the conversation between pilot and copilot before takeoff showed how the copilot tried through the use of indirect comments to warn the pilot of the danger. He commented on the icicles hanging on other planes, for example, and how the deicing equipment could give one a false sense of security. The content of his messages was shaped by the relationship (subordinate talking to superior) in such a way that the copilot avoided directly suggesting that he might be questioning the pilot's competence by pointing out that surely he was aware of the situation.[23]

Punctuation of the sequence of interchanges can be a problem when one does not take into account what has gone on before in a relationship. Perhaps the supervisor in the Three Mile Island example had recently been buffeted by a series of unwarranted criticisms of his management of his department. The message from the engineer warning about a potential accident would be punctuated as part of that series of criticisms, a punctuation of which the engineer would be completely unaware.

Sequencing or timing of messages, in other words, may often determine how they are interpreted. Just after the boss has been dressed down by her superiors is not a good time to go ask her for a raise.

The content of messages is assumed to be carried by digital or symbolic means, at least in our low-context culture. In high-context cultures, as described previously, much content may be transmitted by nonverbal means and by the setting. Still, in Western culture, the messages that indicate relational information tend to come in the more ambiguous, analogic form of nonverbal communication. The danger here is that the emotion-laden relationship messages are carried in the more ambiguous channel and are thus more subject to potential misinterpretations.

Once an interpersonal relationship, or dyad, is established, it does not remain static. There may be attempts by one or both partners to change the rules or the nature of their relationship. Over time, that relationship can change. Both partners thus work to maintain or manage an ongoing relationship. Such maintenance can be revealed in the communication patterns between them. Maintaining an interpersonal relationship depends on both partners knowing and following the rules that they have negotiated for their interactions. The ability of the participants to maintain a productive and satisfying pattern of interactions depends on their coordinating these rules during their communication. For this reason, Philip Clampitt has suggested a metaphor of "dance" for capturing the essence of successfully executed dyadic communication.[24] Two dancers coordinate their movements and the specific rules governing their dancing; similarly, two persons who are communicating effectively coordinate effortlessly their movements and messages, following unique rules for negotiating any changes that either may wish to introduce into the pattern.

This brief theoretical background provides a basis for considering in more detail the research literature concerning significant face-to-face relationships in organizations. As noted, the most important relationships are those of superior and subordinate (or leader–member exchanges) and mentor and protégé.

IMPLICATIONS FOR LEADER–MEMBER COMMUNICATION

The relationship and the communication between superior and subordinate, or leader and member, are perennially major topics in the study of organizational communication. As organizations move increasingly toward work teams and self-managed teams, the terminology for this relationship has begun to shift from the classical, hierarchical notion of superior–subordinate toward the less hierarchical situation implied by the term leader–member. The terms are used interchangeably in this section, partly because of the wide acceptance of the superior–subordinate terminology in so much of the research literature.

This relationship is often central in determining one's satisfaction and motivation in the organization. Superiors spend a good deal of their time communicating with their subordinates—approximately one-third to two-thirds of their work time. Most of this communication is interpersonal, face-to-face, and typically concerned with task-related matters.[25] The leader–member link provides for most of the upward and downward vertical communication in the organization, as discussed in Chapter 8. Also bear in mind from the discussion of organizational climate in Chapter 5 that communication between superior and subordinate has been found to be a major determinant of people's perception of these climates. Supportiveness, fairness as perceived in evaluation and treatment, and participation in decision making were significant factors in one's satisfaction with organizational climate.

Relational Maintenance in Leader–Member Communication

Dyad partners negotiate their relationship and its procedural rules over time. The effectiveness of this negotiation is determined by perceptions of openness, trust, and warmth. Recent research suggests that the relationship between superior and subordinate may be characterized by either *leadership exchanges* or *supervisory exchanges*.[26] Leadership exchanges are characterized by the communication interaction one would expect of people within the same in-group. Supervisory relationships, on the other hand, are marked by more formal exchanges and depend on positional authority to induce the desired behavior in the subordinate. Leadership exchanges are thus characteristic of relationships that can be termed interpersonal, using the developmental perspective described above.

The case of an office administering a state trade association helps to clarify this distinction. The staff of the association consisted of a president, who was the chief executive, a director administering meeting and conference planning, a director of educational programs, and a secretary. For many years, the conference planner had a very good relationship with the highly efficient secretary. They developed a relationship that was truly a working relationship, in which the secretary, technically the subordinate, often came up with good meeting ideas, had an excellent feeling for the way the director liked to have things done, and had the same sense of humor. The secretary felt comfortable making suggestions and occasionally disagreeing with some of the director's recommendations and ideas. The communication between these two people, leader (the director) and member (the secretary), was characterized by what is called here leadership exchanges, as they worked as a cohesive, two-person team. When this secretary was lost to a better-paying job at a large corporation, the new secretary and the director were never able to develop this same kind of rapport. More and more the director found that she was issuing direct orders to the new secretary, that is, engaging in more supervisory exchanges than had been the case with the former secretary.

A relationship that is characterized as "high LMX" (high on leadership exchanges) is described as being based on trust, mutual respect, and agreement or convergence concerning goals.[27] Such relationships also imply a transformational form of leadership in that subordinates are motivated by factors beyond simple self-interest.

Subordinates or members have some control in regard to relationship maintenance. One communication researcher, Vincent Waldron, maintains that "in organizational settings, maintenance of an acceptable relationship with a supervisor may be the most critical communication objective."[28]

Subordinates' tactics in this regard depend on the leadership climate prevalent in a given organization. Where leadership exchanges are the norm, members tend to rely on informal, personal communications in order to maintain a positive, friendly relationship with superiors. This was certainly the case with the secretary and the association director described above. But in relationships characterized as more supervisory, emphasizing formal authority, the members tend to use "regulative," or strategic, communication tactics, such as the following:[29]

Avoiding delivering bad news

Checking on the mood of the superior before initiating communication

Avoiding appearing too ambitious

Appearing enthusiastic regardless of true feelings

In other words, in cases characterized by formalized supervisory exchanges, the members tend to be more cautious and less willing to stick their necks out. Members are thus less likely to take chances and initiate changes or recommendations on their own. Another result of such a relationship can be that, when only good or expected news is passed along to the leader, distortions can interfere with the organization's overall effectiveness.

A significant communication variable related to perceptions of leadership versus supervisory relationships is the element of *immediacy,* which is often conveyed nonverbally. Immediacy is defined as "any communication that indicates interpersonal warmth and closeness."[30] Verbal communication of immediacy includes messages indicating bonding or togetherness, providing relevant and timely feedback, and reinforcing the worth of the other person.[31] Nonverbal indicators of immediacy include appropriate eye contact, physical closeness, and attentiveness.

A study based on focus group interviews with employees concerning their supervisors' communication found that messages that indicate "having 'confidence in subordinate ability' had the most influence on subordinate satisfaction with supervision."[32] Other indicators of positive immediacy include encouraging subordinates' input concerning job or personal matters, attentiveness (being a "good listener"), showing personal interest in subordinates, and providing appreciation for subordinates' efforts. The flip side of these messages are those that reveal a superior's lack of immediacy toward subordinates: inattentiveness, lack of confidence, and, especially, "put-downs" of the subordinate. Subordinates' reports show that they are quite attentive to subtle, nonverbal cues in this regard, such as shuffling papers, appearing distracted, blank looks, and so on.[33]

Finally, subordinates' satisfaction with superiors' performance is often related to the *upward influence* the superior is able to exert in the organizational hierarchy. This relationship is termed the *Pelz effect,*[34] and it has a long history in organizational theory. The theory is based on the notion that a boss with such influence is able to deliver favorable outcomes for people reporting to him or her, thereby increasing their general feelings of satisfaction. Later research suggests that there is some interaction among the superior's perceived upward influence and other factors. These other factors include the extent to which subordinates perceive the supervisor to be open and supportive toward them and the status differential that seems to exist between superior and subordinates.[35]

Thus, in summary, subordinates show higher levels of satisfaction with superiors who both are supportive and have upward influence than with superiors who are less supportive but still have upward influence. One generalization from these factors appears to be that leaders with moderate upward influence in the organization can increase subordinates' satisfaction and openness by developing more supportive relationships with subordinates, rather than trying to politic for more upward influence.[36]

Evaluation and Feedback

One of the most important kinds of communication between leader and member consists of feedback to and evaluation of the subordinate. This feedback does not occur in a vacuum. Feedback is always interpreted in the context of the ongoing interpersonal relationship and in relation to previous messages and experiences. While the formal evaluation may occur only once or twice a year, a typical superior–subordinate or leader–member relationship continues throughout the year.[37]

In the terminology of relational communication, feedback contains both content and relational information, which is to say that it provides both information concerning one's performance and information concerning the nature of the personal relationship between leader and member. The maintenance of a positively valued relationship is generally conducive to a positive organizational climate, higher levels of satisfaction on the part of both parties, and usually higher levels of productivity.

Feedback can be characterized along five dimensions.[38] The first dimension has to do with whether the feedback is interpreted as *positive* (keep doing what one is doing) or *negative* (desist from current behavior). The interpretation of the feedback as positive or negative nature may not always be clear-cut. A pay increase, which may be intended as a positive sign, may be seen as negative if it is less than the increase that the subordinate anticipated or hoped for. A compliment may be interpreted negatively if nonverbal signs suggest that it is grudgingly or reluctantly given.

The second dimension is the *timing* of the feedback: Does it occur immediately after some behavior, or is it delayed? For example, while hurrying by to attend a committee meeting, a manager may observe a subordinate incorrectly handling an order or customer inquiry. A couple of days later, the manager and the subordinate are meeting to discuss scheduling upcoming projects over the next several weeks. Out of the blue, from the subordinate's point of view, the manager starts berating him or her for something that happened earlier and is not relevant to the discussion at hand. The subordinate may think the manager is "gunnysacking," or saving up negative points about a person. Suddenly, these matters are pulled out of the gunnysack when the victim is unprepared and unsuspecting.

The third dimension is *specificity,* concerning the amount of detail and concreteness that accompanies the feedback message. Vague messages, such as "Keep up the good work" or "Try to pay a little more attention to detail," do not provide enough concrete information to allow someone to know what is really expected. Again, someone receiving such vague messages can attribute negative relational messages—"They really are not noticing what I do," the recipient might think. On the other hand, members can attribute falsely positive messages as well. One sales department found itself facing some lawsuits claiming wrongful dismissals because supervisors had fallen into the habit of giving vaguely positive feedback messages rather than confronting poorly performing associates with specific, negative information. The vague, possibly positive comments were cited in court as indications that the dismissals were arbitrary.

Frequency is the fourth dimension. In many organizations, employees complain about the infrequency of both positive and negative feedback, leading to a general unease about not knowing where one stands. In many organizations, feedback on performance is given only as part of a formal, annual review process. This process can be quite elaborate, with both superior and subordinate filling out multipage forms and then meeting for formal conferences or evaluation interviews. One complaint members often voice concerning this type of evaluation process is that leaders feel relieved of having to give any feedback at other times during the year; consequently, the members can feel that they are in the dark much of the time. The relational message one could conceivably get from this situation is that the organization or the superiors do not highly value the person or his or her function.

The fifth dimension concerns the *sensitivity* with which the feedback is given: Does the superior show concern for the feelings of the subordinate when giving feedback or evaluation? The relationship that is already established or developing between the two people can affect interpretations of sensitivity. Tannen again provides a good example of how gender style differences can affect this dimension. A woman manager, given the fictional name Amy, was disturbed about the poor quality of a report submitted by a male subordinate, Donald. She called him to her office to discuss the report. To soften the criticism, she began with some positive comments in the hope that he would listen more acceptingly to the negative points. His minor revisions rather than the major ones she expected revealed that he had heard the positive comments as the main message, while hearing the negative comments as faint suggestions that he could safely ignore.[39] In this example, an analysis based on relational communication would suggest that *punctuation* differences led to the misunderstanding as well. Donald was able to punctuate the sequence of messages in such a way as to give more value to the early comments and less to those that came later in the conversation, opposite to the punctuation intended by Amy.

Attribution theory also provides some insights into communication of feedback between leader and member in an organization. First, a leader's feedback to a subordinate may depend on the kinds of *attributions* he or she makes concerning motives or causes of behavior. As we saw, a supervisor can attribute a worker's performance to internal or external causes. If a supervisor tends to give more weight to internal causes, his or her feedback will probably be directed toward the personal traits or characteristics of the supervisee; if external causes are credited, the feedback will be directed more toward aspects of the situation. Similarly, the nature of positive reinforcing feedback will be affected by this perspective.

A supervisor who believes in external causes or motivation will favor external rewards or motivators, such as pay bonuses or prizes. One who believes in internal motivators will emphasize feelings of competence or accomplishment as rewards.

Finally, the *credibility* of the superior as perceived by the subordinate is a major factor in the response to feedback. Feedback from highly credible sources is given more credence and weight than feedback from less credible sources. The perceived competence and positive characteristics of the leader are hence quite important in determining the effectiveness of his or her feedback to subordinates.

Interpersonal communication theories, such as attribution theory, hence play a role in the effectiveness of feedback and evaluation in the leader–member dyad. Notably, those giving feedback and evaluation may differ in terms of whether they tend to credit internal or external causes as motivators for peoples' actions. The credibility of the person giving the feedback, including perceptions of warmth as well as of competence, is also a significant factor in its effectiveness.

INTERPERSONAL COMMUNICATION IN THE MENTORING RELATIONSHIP

The idea of mentors helping to show younger members the ropes of a new organization or institution is a very old idea. In Greek mythology, Mentor was the name of a wise, trusted adviser of Odysseus (Ulysses), the hero of the *Odyssey*. Mentor stayed home while Odysseus accompanied the other Greek heroes in their famous war against the Trojans, as told by Homer. Odysseus's young son, Telemachus, also stayed home, and Odysseus asked the older man to be a guide and teacher for the boy. When the goddess Athena wished to communicate with either Odysseus or his son, she often took the form of Mentor. Therefore *mentor* became a common noun meaning a giver of sage advice. Today, a more experienced organization member who assists a younger or inexperienced member is called a mentor. The younger person who is thus mentored is variously referred to as a protégé or a mentee.

A mentor is thus an experienced person who develops a one-to-one relationship with a person new to the organization for the purpose of informal guidance, protection, and help. The purpose of the relationship lies in "aiding in the organizational socialization of the less experienced individual and passing along knowledge gained through years of living within an organization."[40]

In the past, the mentoring relationship developed informally, often as a result of circumstances or luck. Family connections or the so-called old-boy network meant that some people were favored over others because of accidents of birth or region or school attended. An uncle or cousin in a business might be asked to look after a relative who had joined the firm. Graduates of a particular college might have made a special effort to become mentors to younger alumni from the same school. Occasionally, an older person might simply take a liking to a younger, new member and become his or her mentor. More recently, organizations have made a systematic effort to create mentor relationships as a part of orientation or development programs.

A mentor is usually a person higher in the structure of the organization who is not a direct superior of the person being mentored, although occasionally one's boss is also one's mentor. Thus, the mentor is usually not in a position to formally evaluate or supervise the protégé. Standing outside the direct line of command over the protégé is thought to allow for more open, less defensive communication between the two people involved. The protégé can try out new ideas, for example, in front of the mentor without fear of direct repercussions if the ideas are not really good. The mentor can give advice to the mentee without the appearance of a superior showing favoritism toward a subordinate, because the two do not really stand in that kind of relationship.

Mentors can provide other advantages for the younger people, as well. They can sponsor their ideas or advancement by "talking them up" in front of other senior people in the organization. They can take protégés with them to important events, conferences, or meetings, thus giving the less experienced people more exposure within the organization.

In her study of the mentoring relationship, Kathy Kram suggests several functions that mentors perform for protégés, breaking them down into *career* and *psychosocial* functions.[41] The career functions are fairly straightforward and understandable; they include sponsorship, giving exposure and visibility, coaching, giving protection, and challenging the protégé. Psychosocial functions include being a role model for behavior that is rewarded in the organization, providing acceptance and confirmation of the protégé, counseling, and giving friendship.

Coaching, sponsoring, and giving visibility and protection by a more experienced colleague who is respected within the organization are clearly advantages for the person who receives them. The psychosocial functions help to build a new member's sense of self-worth and confidence. They help the protégé feel that she or he fits in and deserves a place in the organizational culture. These benefits can also be important advantages, especially vis-à-vis a colleague who does not receive them.

Left to form on their own, unguided mentoring relationships often developed along lines of "like seeking like." Uncertainty-reduction theory certainly suggests that there is more comfort in developing relationships with others similar to oneself: There is less uncertainty to reduce. In the past, males tended to form relationships with other males who were from a similar socioeconomic and educational class, thus putting at a disadvantage new members who were women, minorities, or from backgrounds notably different from those of senior members of the organization.[42] A kind of "glass ceiling" thus seemed to block the advancement of women and minorities in organizations, partly as a result of their exclusion from mentoring relationships.[43] As a result, many organizations began to develop systematic programs, linking mentors with every new entrant into the organization. In some cases, mentors are directly assigned, in others, mentors and protégés can develop voluntary associations, as long as every new member finds a mentor within a relatively short time.

As in most relationships, the advantages are not simply one-way. Mentors also usually gain from an effective mentor–protégé relationship. For example, senior members are able to keep up with what is going on at lower levels or at the cutting edge. Mentoring contacts can thus prevent ossification at the upper levels of an organization. Mentoring can also aid in promoting teamwork throughout the organization through the communication across hierarchical levels. A stable and coherent organizational culture can also provide benefits for mentors as well as other long-service members. Of course, mentors also derive personal and professional satisfaction from the leadership evinced through successful mentoring relationships with younger colleagues.[44]

There are some downsides to organizational mentoring, however. Socioeconomic factors have already been mentioned in regard to the voluntary formation of earlier kinds of mentor–protégé relationships. One study has found that positive outcomes from mentoring tended to be more significant for protégés who are from higher socioeconomic levels to begin with than for others.[45] This result suggests that protégés from higher socioeconomic levels were from the beginning more like higher-ranking mentors in outlook and values, and so benefited from a stronger relationship based on these initial similarities.

Gender differences between mentor and protégé can also confound the advantages of the relationship. In the past, men have tended to hold the higher positions in many organizations and, therefore, are more likely to be mentors to both men and women. Women have reported feeling at some disadvantage because male mentors treat them differently from the way they observe other male mentors treating their protégés who are men.

The same-sex pairs are more likely to socialize together after work, going out to play tennis or golf or to share a drink or dinner. Informal communication that occurs in these settings can be helpful in providing a protégé with insights into operations and other people; they become privy to important "inside" information. When the mentor is an older male and the protégé is a younger woman, there are potential charges of romantic or even sexual involvement; gossip can thus undermine an otherwise productive relationship.

Given the realities of the business world over the past several decades, not only are older, potential mentors generally male, but they are usually white males. *Racial and ethnic differences* are thus another potential barrier to the smooth operation of a mentoring relationship. One study, for example, found that white male mentors were unwilling or reluctant to discuss issues of discrimination even when African American protégés believed them to be highly relevant in an organization.[46]

Well-designed and sensitively executed mentoring programs can overcome the problems of gender and ethnic differences. One key lies in open communication about the potential problems in such relationships. It must be clear that all junior-level people are to receive the same benefits from mentoring.

In summary, the mentor–protégé relationship is intended to be somewhat different from the superior–subordinate relationship in that the mentor is usually not in a position to supervise, evaluate, hire, or fire the protégé. The relationship is felt to be less threatening, lacking the evaluative overtones of superior–subordinate relations. As the name implies, the mentor is a more experienced, established figure within the organization, whose job is to instruct, advise, and guide the younger employee. Many organizations have developed structured mentoring programs, in which mentors and protégés are often assigned to each other, rather than waiting for relationships to develop. For many new entrants into organizational life, mentoring programs mean that in addition to the significant dyad of superior–subordinate, there will also be the dyad formed with the mentor.

GENDER AND CULTURAL DIFFERENCES

Increasing ethnic and gender diversity in the workplace will have effects on interpersonal communication in the organization. Some demographic projections predict that 85 percent of the net increase in the American workforce by the year 2000 will be women and minorities; by that year, women will probably account for 63 percent of all employees.[47] As a result of these trends, it is increasingly likely that older white males will find themselves participating in interpersonal dyads with subordinates who are female or members of minority groups (or both). Naturally, the reverse situation will also become more likely, with white males reporting to female and minority superiors.

Do women have a different style of managing from men, especially in the one-on-one superior–subordinate relationship? There are conflicting views. A survey of men and women managers conducted by the International Women's Forum found some similarities—in pay and in conflicts in balancing work and home—and some differences in regard to management style.[48] Women tended to exhibit what was labeled "interactive leadership," based on collaboration with subordinates, as opposed to the male preference for seeing superior–subordinate interchanges as involving a series of rewards or punishments. Several popular works present arguments for gender differences in management, most notably John Gray's *Men Are from Mars, Women Are from Venus,*[49] and Carolyn S. Duff's *When Women Work Together.*[50] These authors hold that women rely on sharing and collaboration, in contrast to men's reliance on competition and status in getting things done.

The sociolinguist Deborah Tannen argues a similar point in her popular bestseller *You Just Don't Understand: Women and Men in Conversation,*[51] as well as in the work discussed above concerning on-the-job relationships, *Talking from 9 to 5.* She maintains that women are socialized by early play groups emphasizing collaboration, so that they are most comfortable with collaborative work, in which members are sensitive to the feelings of others. Men, on the other hand, are socialized in play groups emphasizing status and competition rather than collaboration and cooperation. Women are hence more likely to lead by indirect suggestion, implying what members should do rather than giving commands.

On the other hand, other research suggests that differences between men and women in management style can be accounted for by situational factors, such as the fact that until recently, women tended not to hold very powerful positions in many organizations. For example, a study concerning the compliance-gaining strategies of women and men managers found that most differences were explained by the perceived legitimacy of the action being requested rather than by the sex of the manager.[52]

Similarly, while other studies have found some slight differences in preferences for compliance-gaining strategies between men and women managers, the sex difference may not be the most significant factor. For example, women are slightly more likely to use altruistic appeals, whereas men are more likely to rely on threats or rewards, but the tendencies are not great in either direction.[53] In other words, as more women reach positions of authority in organizations, perceived differences between the sexes in management style may decrease.

DIVERSITY MATTERS

Regional Adaptations for Multicultural Differences

Intercultural training and awareness workshops are fairly new territory, as many firms are discovering. In many cases, these programs need to be developed in line with differing cultural patterns in different parts of the country.

In the American Southwest, for example, hotel and motel operators have found that language training, together with a sensitivity to language differences is good business. Hourly workers, many of them Spanish-speakers, are prevalent in the hospitality businesses in this region of the country.

The Wyndham Anatole Hotel and Sheraton Park Central, both in Dallas, Texas, have found that providing English classes for their staffs results in improved service, lower turnover, and higher rates of satisfaction among the staff.* In such regions of the country, it may also be increasingly a good idea for managers to become bilingual as well. Diversity training, including language learning, are proliferating in both the hotel and restaurant business.

In a different part of the country, multicultural awareness can reflect other cultural mixes. In Minneapolis, Minnesota, for example, the local area includes native Americans. American Express Financial Advisors has embarked there on a program cooperating with the "Eagle Project," a support-group for American Indians in business begun on the campus of the University of North Dakota at Grand Forks.** The company recognizes the need for responding to the multicultural community in which they are located.

Consider the different ethnic and cultural groups represented in your area. What sort of special communication needs might they represent? How could organizations develop programs that respond to those needs while valuing the diversity that such groups represent?

*Dallas Morning News, March 3, 1996, p. 1H.

**Star Tribune, December 18, 1995, p. 14A.

Intercultural differences may also confound interpersonal communication in the superior–subordinate relationship. Obviously the ability to make attributions concerning the causes of another person's behavior assumes a great deal of shared cultural understanding and value systems. Culture makes people's lives predictable. People who share the same culture are able to take many things for granted; it is assumed that everyone knows the rules and will follow them. The problem is that many of these rules are outside of conscious awareness; we are often completely unaware that we are even following cultural rules concerning matters such as appropriate eye contact, distance between conversation partners, appropriate topics for conversation, and so on.

Gudykunst's studies, based on the earlier work of Hall and Hofstede, alert us to the difficulties of uncertainty reduction and impression formation when partners in a relationship are from different cultures. Most recent attention has concerned communication between Americans, on the one hand, and people from Asian countries of the Pacific Rim, on the other, partly as a result of the impact of Japanese business success in the 1980s and 1990s.[54] The cultural values of Confucian societies, for example, are used to explain the organizational theories of many of the enterprises in the Pacific Rim area (Singapore, Hong Kong, South Korea, Japan, and China).[55]

Perhaps of more immediate interest for many American organizations are communication differences, or misunderstandings, that result from differences among subcultures and cocultures in the United States. The integration of minorities into higher managerial and executive levels in American organizations has seemed problematic, partly because of the racial or ethnic differences between superiors and subordinates; in their seminal work on corporate cultures, Deal and Kennedy saw this problem as a drawback to strong, shared corporate cultures.[56] In many corporations, mentor programs have been developed partly with the intention of easing the entry of women and minorities into executive ranks, as we have already seen.[57]

SUMMARY

The quality of life within organizations largely depends on the quality of interpersonal relationships and communication one experiences in interactions with other organizational members. This chapter reviews theories of interpersonal communication applicable to such experiences in organizations. Theories of relationship development and impression formation, particularly attribution theory and uncertainty-reduction theory, help explain how organizational relationships form and develop over time. Theories of organizational socialization indicate typical paths of assimilation into the patterns of relationships experienced in organizations.

Significant relationships that last over time, such as those between superior and subordinate, leader and member, or mentor and protégé, are especially important. Theories of relational communication suggest useful ways of analyzing how dyadic relationships form systems that evolve over time yet maintain a homeostasis or a set of expectations that shapes the general directions that such communication can take. Increasingly, people within organizations and those who theorize about organizational communication must take into account the cultural and gender differences affecting the development and maintenance of interpersonal communication in organizations.

EXERCISES AND QUESTIONS FOR DISCUSSION

1. Describe significant one-to-one relationships that you have experienced in campus organizations or work settings. What features have distinguished good experiences from bad experiences in these relationships? Can you make any generalizations concerning the consequences of the early stages of relationship development?

2. When you find that you are going to be working closely with another individual on a project

or job, how do you go about finding out "what makes that person tick"? What information is most useful for you when meeting new colleagues or coworkers?

3. Have you ever been a victim of a fundamental attribution error? Have you ever committed such an error yourself in commenting on or evaluating the mistakes or work of other people? How can one guard against making these kinds of attribution errors?

4. Can you describe experiences you have had entering a new organization, such as a student organization, living unit, work group, church, or similar organization? How did you find out the rules for functioning in this organization? Were your experiences successful or not? How can one get the organization to adapt to oneself as much as the other way around?

5. Have you ever experienced crossed communication of the sort that occurs when you and a partner do not agree on the nature of your relationship—symmetrical or complementary? How can such misunderstandings be dealt with?

6. Must there always be some distance between superiors and their subordinates, leaders and their followers, mentors and their protégés? Explain why you feel this way. What is the best way of maintaining respect between leaders and members in their one-to-one relationships (or is that necessary and important)?

7. Have you ever had a mentor? Explain the advantages and disadvantages of such a relationship. Why has it been difficult to assimilate women and minorities into relationships of this kind? Should a woman entrant always have a woman as a mentor? a member of a minority group a member of his or her minority group as a mentor? Why or why not?

SOURCES FOR FURTHER STUDY

Altman, I., and Taylor, D. (1973). *Social penetration: The development of interpersonal relationships.* New York: Holt, Rinehart & Winston.

Berger, C. R. (1986). Uncertain outcome values in predicted relationships: Uncertainty reduction theory then and now. *Human Communication Research, 13,* 35.

Berger, C. R., and Calabrese, R. J. (1975). Some explorations in initial reaction and beyond: Toward a developmental theory of interpersonal communication. *Human Communication Research, 1,* 99–112.

Bullis, C. (1993). Organizational socialization research: Enabling, constraining, and shifting perspectives. *Communication Monographs, 60,* 10–17.

Burgoon, J. K., and Hale, J. L. (1984). The fundamental topoi of relational communication. *Communication Monographs, 51,* 193–214.

Dansereau, F., and Markham, S. E. (1987). Superior-subordinate communication: Multiple levels of analysis. In F. M. Jablin, L. L. Putnam, K. H. Roberts, and L. W. Porter (Eds.), *Handbook of organizational communication: An interdisciplinary perspective.* Beverly Hills, Calif.: Sage.

Fairhurst, G. T. (1993). The leader-member exchange patterns of women in industry: A discourse analysis. *Communication Monographs, 60,* 321–51.

Gudykunst, W. B. (1988). Uncertainty and anxiety. In Y. Y. Kim and W. B. Gudykunst (Eds.), *Theories in intercultural communication.* Newbury Park, Calif.: Sage, pp. 123–56.

Gudykunst, W. B. (1989). Culture and development of interpersonal relationships. In J. A. Andersen (Ed.), *Communication yearbook 12.*

Hall, E. T. (1976). *Beyond culture.* New York: Doubleday.

Heider, F. (1958). *The psychology of interpersonal relations.* New York: Wiley.

Hofstede, G. (1980). *Culture's consequences.* Beverly Hills, Calif.: Sage.

Jablin, F. M. (1987). Organizational entry, assimilation, and exit. In F. M. Jablin, L. L. Putnam, K. H. Roberts, and L. W. Porter (Eds.). *Handbook of organizational communication: An interdisciplinary perspective.* Beverly Hills, Calif.: Sage.

Kelley, H. H. (1973). The process of causal attribution. *American Psychologist, 28,* 107–28.

Kram, K. E. (1988). *Mentoring at work.* Lanham, Md.: University Press of America.

Littlejohn, S. W. (1992). *Theories of human communication,* 4th ed. Belmont, Calif.: Wadsworth.

Miller, G. R. (1990). Interpersonal communication. In G. L. Dahnke and G. W. Clatterbuck (Eds.), *Human communication: Theory and research.* Belmont, Calif.: Wadsworth, pp. 91–122.

Miller, G. R., and Steinberg, M. (1975). *Between people: A new analysis of interpersonal communication.* Chicago: Science Research Associates.

Miller, G. R., and Sunnafrank, M. J. (1982). All is for one but one is not for all: A conceptual perspective of interpersonal communication. In F. E. X. Dance (Ed.), *Human communication theory*. New York: Harper & Row, pp. 220–42.

Pelz, D. (1952). Influence: A key to effective leadership in the first line supervision. *Personnel, 29,* 209–17.

Roesner, J. (1990). Ways women lead. *Harvard Business Review,* November–December, pp. 119–25.

Sunnafrank, M. J. (1986) Predicting outcome value during initial interactions: A reformulation of uncertainty reduction theory. *Human Communication Research, 13,* 12.

Tannen, D. (1994). *Talking from 9 to 5.* New York: William Morrow.

Waldron, V. R. (1991). Achieving communication goals in superior-subordinate relationships: The multi-functionality of upward maintenance tactics. *Communication Monographs, 58,* 291–92.

Watzlawick, P., Beavin, J., and Jackson, D. (1967). *The pragmatics of human communication.* New York: Norton.

NOTES

1. G. R. Miller (1990), Interpersonal communication, in G. L. Dahnke and G. W. Clatterbuck (Eds.), *Human communication: Theory and research,* Belmont, Calif.: Wadsworth, pp. 91–122.

2. Miller (1990), p. 97; G. R. Miller and M. Steinberg (1975), *Between people: A new analysis of interpersonal communication,* Chicago: Science Research Associates; G. R. Miller and M. J. Sunnafrank (1982), All is for one but one is not for all: A conceptual perspective of interpersonal communication, in F. E. X. Dance (Ed.), *Human communication theory,* New York: Harper & Row, pp. 220–42.

3. I. Altman and D. Taylor (1973), *Social penetration: The development of interpersonal relationships,* New York: Holt, Rinehart & Winston.

4. F. Heider (1958), *The psychology of interpersonal relations,* New York: Wiley; H. H. Kelley (1973), The process of causal attribution, *American Psychologist, 28,* 107–28; E. E. Jones and K. E. Davis (1965), From acts to dispositions: The attribution process in person perception, in L. Burkowitz (Ed.), *Advances in experimental social psychology, 2,* New York: Academic Press, pp. 219–66.

5. See C. R. Berger and R. J. Calabrese (1975), Some explorations in initial reaction and beyond: Toward a developmental theory of interpersonal communication, *Human Communication Research, 1,* 99–112.

6. C. R. Berger (1986), Uncertain outcome values in predicted relationships: Uncertainty reduction theory then and now, *Human Communication Research, 13,* 35.

7. M. Sunnafrank (1986), Predicting outcome value during initial interactions: A reformulation of uncertainty reduction theory, *Human Communication Research, 13,* 13; J. W. Thibaut and H. H. Kelley (1959), *The social psychology of groups,* New York: Wiley; H. H. Kelley and J. W. Thibaut (1978), *Interpersonal relations: A theory of interdependence,* New York: Wiley.

8. W. B. Gudykunst (1988), Uncertainty and anxiety, in Y. Y. Kim and W. B. Gudykunst (Eds.), *Theories in intercultural communication,* Newbury Park, Calif.: Sage, pp. 123–56.

9. E. T. Hall (1976), *Beyond culture,* New York: Doubleday.

10. G. Hofstede (1980), *Culture's consequences,* Beverly Hills, Calif.: Sage.

11. W. B. Gudykunst (1989), Culture and the development of interpersonal relationships, in J. A. Andersen (Ed.), *Communication yearbook 12,* p. 329.

12. Gudykunst (1989), p. 331.

13. *Wall Street Journal,* May 16, 1995, p. B1.

14. F. M. Jablin (1987), Organizational entry, assimilation, and exit, in F. M. Jablin, L. L. Putnam, K. H. Roberts, and L. W. Porter (Eds.), *Handbook of organizational communication: An interdisciplinary perspective,* Beverly Hills, Calif.: Sage, pp. 679–740.

15. Jablin (1987).

16. C. Bullis (1993), Organizational socialization research: Enabling, constraining, and shifting perspectives, *Communication Monographs, 60,* 10–17.

17. P. Watzlawick, J. Beavin, and D. Jackson (1967), *The pragmatics of human communication,* New York: Norton.

18. Watzlawick, Beavin, and Jackson, p. 51.

19. J. K. Burgoon and J. L. Hale (1984), The fundamental topoi of relational communication, *Communication Monographs, 51,* 193–214.

20. C. G. Herndle, B. A. Fennel, and C. Miller (1991), Understanding failures in organizational discourse: The accident at Three Mile Island and the Shuttle Challenger disaster, in C. Bazerman and J. Paradis (Eds.), *Textual dynamics of the professions,* Madison, Wis.: University of Wisconsin Press, pp. 279–305.

21. S. W. Littlejohn (1992), *Theories of human communication,* 4th ed., Belmont, Calif.: Wadsworth, p. 267.

22. D. Tannen (1994), *Talking from 9 to 5,* New York: William Morrow, pp. 68–69.

23. Tannen (1994), pp. 92–93.

24. P. Clampitt (1991), *Communicating for organizational effectiveness,* Newbury Park, Calif.: Sage.

25. F. Dansereau and S. E. Markham (1987), Superior-subordinate communication: Multiple levels of analysis, in F. M. Jablin, L. L. Putnam, K. H. Roberts, and L. W. Proter (Eds.), *Handbook of organizational communication: An interdisciplinary perspective,* Newbury Park, Calif.: Sage, p. 344.

26. V. R. Waldron (1991), Achieving communication goals in superior-subordinate relationships: The multi-functionality of upward maintenance tactics, *Communication Monographs, 58,* 291–92.

27. G. T. Fairhurst (1993), The leader-member exchange patterns of women leaders in industry: A discourse analysis, *Communication Monographs, 60,* 321–51.

29. Waldron, p. 298.

30. J. A. Sanders and R. L. Wiseman (1990), The effects of verbal and nonverbal teacher immediacy on perceived cognitive, affective, and behavioral learning in the multicultural classroom, *Communication Education, 39,* 341.

31. J. A. DeVito (1988), *Human communication: The basic course,* 4th ed., New York: Harper & Row, p. 227.

32. C. Koermer, M. Goldstein, and D. Fortson (1993), How supervisors communicatively convey immediacy to subordinates: An exploratory qualitative investigation, *Communication Quarterly, 41,* 277.

33. Koermer, Goldstein, & Fortson, 276–77.

34. D. Pelz (1952), Influence: A key to effective leadership in the first line supervisor, *Personnel, 29,* 209–17.

35. F. M. Jablin (1980), Superior's upward influence, satisfaction, and openness in superior-subordinate communication: A reexamination of the "Pelz effect," *Human Communication Research, 6,* 210–20.

36. Jablin, p. 219.

37. B. R. Nathan, A. M. Mohrman, Jr., and J. Milliman (1991), Interpersonal relations as a context for the effects of appraisal interviews on performance and satisfaction: A longitudinal study, *Academy of Management Journal, 34,* 352–69.

38. L. P. Cusella (1985), Feedback, motivation, and performance, in F. M. Jablin, L. L. Putnam, K. H. Roberts, and L. W. Porter (Eds.), *Handbook of organizational communication: An interdisciplinary perspective,* Newbury Park, Calif.: Sage, pp. 624–78.

39. Tannen (1994), pp. 20–21.

40. J. A. Wilson and N. S. Elman (1990), Organizational benefits of mentoring, *Academy of Management Executive, 4,* 88–94.

41. K. E. Kram (1988), *Mentoring at work,* Lanham, Md.: University Press of America.

42. W. Whitley, T. W. Dougherty, and G. F. Dreher (1991), Relationship of career mentoring and socioeconomic origin to managers' and professionals' early career progress, *Academy of Management Journal, 34,* 331–51.

43. K. Colburn (1992), Mentoring today, diversity tomorrow? *EDN, 37,* 81.

44. Kram, pp. 7–10; D. Jacoby (1989), Rewards make the mentor, *Personnel, 66,* 10–14.

45. Whitley, Dougherty, and Dreher, pp. 331–51.

46. D. A. Thomas (1989), Mentoring and irrationality: The role of racial taboos, *Human Resource Management, 28,* 279–90.

47. G. F. Dreher and R. A. Ash (1990), A comparative study of mentoring among men and women in managerial, professional, and technical positions, *Journal of Applied Psychology, 75,* 544; R. Knotts (1989), Cross-cultural management: Transformation and adaptations, *Business Horizons, 32,* 29–33.

48. J. R. Roesner (1990), Ways women lead, *Harvard Business Review,* November–December, 119–25; *New York Times,* August 15, 1993, p. F6.

49. J. Gray (1991), *Men are from Mars, women are from Venus,* New York: HarperCollins.

50. C. S. Duff (1993), *When women work together,* Berkeley, Calif: Conari Press.

51. D. Tannen (1990), *You just don't understand: Women and men in conversation,* New York: William Morrow.

52. Hirokawa, Mickey, and Miura, 434.

53. J. M. Dallinger and D. Hample (1994), The effects of gender on compliance gaining strategy endorsement and suppression, *Communication Reports, 7,* 43–49.

54. M. Zimmerman (1985), *How to do business with the Japanese,* New York: Random House; D. R. McCreary (1986), *Japanese–US business negotiations: A cross-cultural study,* New York: Praeger; B. M. Richardson and T. Ueda (1981), *Business and society in Japan,* New York: Praeger, among many others.

55. G. Chen and J. Chung (1994), The impact of Confucianism on organizational communication, *Communication Quarterly, 42,* 93–105.

56. T. Deal and A. Kennedy (1982), *Corporate culture: The rites and rituals of corporate life,* Reading, Mass.: Addison-Wesley.

57. G. F. Dreher and R. A. Ash (1990), A comparative study among men and women in managerial, professional, and technical positions, *Journal of Applied Psychology, 75:5,* 539–46; D. A. Thomas (1990), The impact of race on managers' experiences of developmental relationships (mentoring and sponsorship): An intra-organizational study, *Journal of Organizational Behavior, 11:6,* 479–92.

CHAPTER 10

Communication and Leadership in Organizations

CHAPTER OBJECTIVES

After studying this chapter, you should be able to:

- Explain why leadership has been an important topic for organizational studies.
- Explain different approaches to defining leadership.
- Describe the strengths and weaknesses of the trait approach to leadership.
- Explain behavioral or style theories of leadership.
- Discuss the contingency approach to leadership, explaining the Fielder model, Hersey and Blanchard's situational leadership, and path-goal theory.
- Define transformational leadership.
- Show the relationship of various kinds of organizational power to leadership.
- Discuss the communication implications of the study of leadership in organizations.

CHAPTER OUTLINE

THE CHANGING FACE OF ORGANIZATIONAL LEADERSHIP

As organizations become increasingly multicultural and global in their operations, ideas concerning leadership need to take more diverse theories or interpretations into account. American business has been much impressed recently with Japanese styles of management, which imply different approaches to leadership, for example. Some business leaders have recommended studying Chinese books as well, like the *Art of War* of Sun-tzu, to broaden Western understanding of leadership.[1] The Confucian ideal of leadership suggests a harmony of understanding between leaders and followers. This harmony is understood in terms of five relationships: ruler and follower, parent and child, husband and wife, elder sibling and junior sibling, and master and servant. The beneficial working of each relationship requires that both parties understand and perform the roles of superior and subordinate or elder and junior. This view of leadership stresses that leadership resides in a reciprocal relationship rather than in the actions of one person, the leader.

This chapter focuses on organizational leadership through a communication lens. The central importance of this topic is echoed by writers such as John Kotter, who maintains that the increasing complexity and diversity of modern organizations requires a sophisticated approach to organizational leadership, specifically "a sophisticated type of social skill."[2] The terms that are used today to describe leaders indicate this changing view. Effective leaders are seen as coaches, models, or mentors rather than as bosses or commanders. Team leadership is stressed, as is pointed out in the next chapter. The goal of such leaders is often to influence other members to develop and display leadership behavior of their own.

Leadership involves communicating with others to exercise influence, to gain their cooperation and commitment to the organization, and to induce them to engage in desired behaviors. This chapter first summarizes important theories concerning leadership and communication and then considers issues of influence, power, and compliance-gaining in organizations.

This topic overlaps with many others in this book. For example, an organization's culture leads to the development of certain kinds of leadership and expectations about leaders' communication. Leaders must foster effective horizontal as well as vertical communication within their organizations. Major functions of organizational leaders are fostering good decision making and dealing with conflict in constructive ways.

INTRODUCTION TO THEORIES OF LEADERSHIP

The earliest systematic studies of communication and leadership began in classical Greece as teachers of rhetoric known as Sophists traveled from city to city. The Sophists saw rhetoric as the key to leadership, and so, in teaching rhetoric, they advertised that they were teaching people how to become leaders. The Sophists' teaching was in this regard somewhat revolutionary, because early Greek thought held that the qualities of leadership were inherited and passed on through an aristocracy. Homer's heroes in the *Iliad* heralded their ancestry to substantiate their claims of virtue and heroism. In claiming that people could be taught to be leaders, the Sophists reinforced the democratic thinking then developing in Athens and elsewhere. In addition, the Sophists stressed the notion that skill in effective communication was directly related to the exercise of leadership.

Plato favored a new kind of aristocracy, one of the mind rather than ancestry, in opposing what he saw as the glib instruction of the Sophists. His criticism of Sophistic rhetoric was that it taught skill without substance; leaders thus developed did not have a solid basis in the philosophical understanding of the truth. Rhetoric could actually be dangerous, as leaders thus educated would not have the best interests of the city (the state, or society) at heart. The true and only appropriate training for leaders, according to Plato, was hence contemplation and deep philosophical study.

Aristotle, while influenced by his great teacher, Plato, believed in the possibility of practical training in rhetoric and politics while acknowledging the importance of ethics and philosophy underpinning the ideal statesman-orator. Aristotle therefore emphasized the importance of *ethos,* the character of the speaker, as a means for persuasion in its own right.

A few hundred years later, the Romans, very much impressed with Greek learning and arts, developed this notion of the skilled speaker who is, at the same time, an ethical and well-educated leader. This was Cicero's ideal in his later and more thoughtful works concerning the art of rhetoric. The clearest statement of this ideal is found in the writings of the greatest of the Roman educators, Quintilian, who defines the orator as the good (ethical) person speaking well. Classical rhetoric, as taught by the Romans and passed on through Western education, continued to equate training in rhetoric or communication with educating leaders.

Much of this early history of theories of leadership has a contemporary ring. There are still trait theories of leadership (leaders are born with certain personality traits)

Trait theories of leadership suggest that certain people are "born leaders."

and behavioral theories of leadership, which maintain that people can learn the requisite leadership skills. And we continue to find distinctions made concerning types of leadership that are similar to the Sophistic and Platonic dichotomy. For example, some writers distinguish between practical leaders, who are managers who know how to get things done, and "transformational" or "visionary" leaders, who are similar to the Platonic ideal of a philosopher-king.

Definitions of Leadership

There have been many attempts at defining leadership. First, one should distinguish the position or role of leader from the act or process of leadership. An individual can be designated a leader or be recognized informally by others as a leader, whereas *leadership* can be shared among many persons, positions, and roles within a group or organization. *Leaders* are people whom we expect to exercise leadership.

What makes a person a leader? What does he or she do in order to exercise what is called leadership? The answers to these questions have been elusive.

Some people focus on the power that leaders have, their ability to make other people do what these people might not otherwise choose to do. Others refer to the leaders' use of influence or persuasiveness rather than force, their ability to induce others to act in desired ways. Leadership has been described as an innate skill or characteristic, something that is possessed by an individual, or as a set of behaviors enacted by people, or as a relationship between people. We now turn to some significant attempts to define leadership; they tend to illustrate the tension between the idea of the leader as a certain kind of person and the relationship between leaders and followers.

Max Weber, whose theories concerning bureaucratic organizations are described in Chapter 4, discussed three "ideal types" of authority or leadership, which he labeled "traditional," "charismatic," and "bureaucratic." The first type refers to leadership conferred by traditional descent, usually through a family line, as with some chiefs or kings. The charismatic leader is owed loyalty and obedience because of some special aura, or *charisma,* that he or she has acquired, often through religious or divine revelation. There is no traditional or organizational basis for the authority of charismatic leaders. The third type of leader has authority because of the position he or she occupies in a rationally selected hierarchy. It is as if people owe obedience to the position, rather than to the individual who happens to be holding that position at a given time.

After reviewing several different although overlapping definitions, the *Handbook of Leadership* settles on the following definition: "Leadership is an interaction between two or more members of a group that often involves a structuring or restructuring of the situation and the perceptions of and expectations of members."[3] Although this definition emphasizes the relational nature of leadership, the leader is seen as acting as an *agent of change,* meaning that the leader's actions affect others more than their actions affect him or her.

James MacGregor Burns, in his Pulitzer Prize–winning study of leadership, similarly emphasizes the role of the leader as an agent of change. Although some define leadership as making others do what they might not otherwise choose to do, Burns prefers to stress the role of leaders as persuaders. He prefers to define leadership as "leaders inducing followers to act for certain goals that represent the values and the motivations—the wants and needs, the aspirations and expectations—of both leaders and followers."[4]

The leader, then, is a person who can mobilize, arouse, and engage others, one who can tap into various springs of motivation in order to activate others, the followers. Burns also distinguishes between *transactional* leadership, which is based on a leader exchanging desired goods with followers, and *transformational* leadership, which is based on the leader's raising the follower to a higher plane of justification for behavior (the leader "transforms" the follower and the follower's motives). This notion of transformational leadership is taken up later in this chapter.

These definitions of leadership stress the interactional nature of leadership, reiterating the point from the propositions in Chapter 2 that leadership is exercised through communication. Communication is essential to the leader's exercise of influence.

Trait Theories of Leadership

As already mentioned, the earliest theories concerning leadership were trait theories, implying that leaders are born rather than made. Traits are persisting and innate aspects of an individual's personality. Traditionally, early leaders had special prowess, especially in war, hunting, or rituals. Leaders hence often possessed traits of physical size, strength, and endurance, as well as intelligence.

Stogdill's exhaustive review of the literature concerning leadership was intended to discover the major personality traits of leaders that were supported by research. Early findings seemed to suggest that personal traits, such as physical, emotional, or mental characteristics, did not contribute as much to the emergence of leadership as other factors, such as the situation or the nature and the goals of the potential followers.

In reviewing later follow-ups to these studies, Bernard Bass, in the third edition of what began as Stogdill's handbook on leadership, suggests that there may have been too much of a tendency to downplay the role of personality factors. Characteristics such as intelligence, the need for achievement, a sense of responsibility, initiative, and ability to deal with stress are positively related to leadership emergence throughout the reported research.[5] Strictly physical characteristics, such as age, height, weight, and appearance, are not as clearly related to the emergence of leaders, although since the original survey of studies in 1948, little research has been concerned with these factors.

Interestingly, the Stogdill-Bass reviews did not consider the factor of sex as related to leadership. More recent studies have begun to look at this factor as it relates to types of leadership behavior.

Bass concludes that personality continues to be a factor in differentiating leaders from nonleaders; however, this is not a return to the old-fashioned trait approach, but rather a modification of what he terms the "extreme situationalist point of view," which denies the influence of any individual differences in favor of events and demands of the environment.[6]

Some traits that appear predictive of leadership involve teachable skills. Skills that a person can learn seem different in kind from personal traits that one is born with or inherits, such as body type or family status, or that are essentially beyond one's control, such as age or sex. For example, education, communication skills and fluency of speech, and technical competence emerge in the research as traits of people who become leaders. These findings support the Sophists' notion that leaders can be educated for leadership.

Research involving multinational organizations has sought to discover certain *organizational universals* that are applicable across national and cultural lines to any complex organization. Such studies have occasionally posited the existence of *universal leadership traits* that apply regardless of national or cultural setting, including a sense of humor, flexibility, patience, resourcefulness, and consideration for others.[7] A multicultural perspective usually leads us to look for cultural differences, and certainly they do exist with regard to expectations about leadership styles and behaviors. Research of this sort reminds us of the importance of looking for constants in human behavior and values as well.

The idea that some people have more aptitude for leadership positions than others has contributed to the development of *assessment techniques* that organizations can use to select people for management and leadership positions. Search and screening committees in business, government, and universities continue to operate on the assumption that committees can determine which candidates have the skills or traits needed for a leadership position. Many organizations have set up assessment centers to develop systematic methods for selecting people for promotion to higher managerial positions.

The case of Priscilla: Put yourself in the place of Priscilla, an upcoming executive with a growing environmental testing firm. She has been asked by the head corporate officers to select two of her subordinates for a special leadership training program. Looking over her team, she sees that there are about five people who could be considered for such an opportunity. How does she go about deciding which two of the five she will recommend? She will have to decide whether she will give more weight to technical skills, as laboratory techniques are involved in much of the testing conducted by the company, or to communication or so-called leadership skills. Priscilla is not alone in her problem; many managers find that they are constantly trying to determine which of their subordinates are capable of assuming leadership positions.

In many cases these assessments are based largely on intuition, as they seek to measure the unmeasurable, such as "vision" or initiative. Other methods have shown some ability to predict later success. An eight-year study of candidates' performance after selection by an AT&T assessment center found a positive relationship between their scores on assessment tests and their later performance, as measured by subsequent promotions.[8]

The highest correlations were found between success and the following two traits measured:

1. Oral communication skills
2. Human relations skills

Other highly related personal traits included a need for advancement, resistance to stress, tolerance of uncertainty, and organizing and planning ability.

The two most highly rated skills, then, were communication skills and are largely teachable. The next two traits, dealing with stress and tolerance for uncertainty, are more particularly personality characteristics, and are arguably less teachable.

That personal skills are important is supported by the well-respected study of the leadership of American presidents by Richard E. Neustadt.[9] Although Neustadt accepts that presidents operate from a base of enormous prestige and status or authority, the effectiveness of a president, he maintains, ultimately depends on the ability to persuade people and to negotiate with other power holders. Presidents may enhance or weaken the credibility they start with by either wise or infelicitous exercise of persuasion and negotiation skills.

In summary, we have largely abandoned the older notion that leaders are born for leadership, possessing unique personal powers denied to lesser people. Researchers still continue to find, however, that certain traits and skills are related to the emergence of leadership, such as intelligence, need for achievement, and communication skills. Priscilla would be wise to begin to look for these qualities in her candidates. But other considerations may be as or more important. She must also take into account the situations in which these people will be asked to exercise leadership. The next set of theories suggests that these factors can be more important in leadership effectiveness than the personal skills and traits of the individual.

Leadership Behaviors and Styles

A second approach to the study of leaders focuses on the behaviors they perform rather than looking at their personal traits. Historically, one of the earliest approaches to this view of leadership was developed by Niccolò Machiavelli, whose Renaissance work prescribing behaviors that would maintain a prince in power has come to be considered a masterpiece.

His work has given us the adjective Machiavellian to describe someone who cynically manipulates others with no regard for any goal other than keeping control of power. However, the popular view of Machiavelli, as represented by this famous adjective, overlooks many of the subtleties in his theories, which include warnings to the "prince," the leader, concerning what we would today call upward organizational communication. Many of his instructions, in fact, deal with acquiring and managing internal and external communication.

In a very different vein, Kurt Lewin and his associates, starting in the 1930s, began to investigate group dynamics. One aspect of Lewin's work was to study the effects of different styles of leadership on the performance of groups. The classic study was conducted by Lewin along with his associates, Lippitt and White, in 1939.[10] The groups in the study were subjected to three styles of leadership: *authoritarian, democratic,* and *laissez-faire.*

Authoritarian leadership is highly directive, emphasizing top-down communication. The leader unilaterally determines the goals of the group and the methods for reaching those goals. The authoritarian leader dominates the flow of information and the interaction within the group. Such a leader must supervise the followers' actions nearly all the time in order to ensure compliance and productive behavior. Without such continuous surveillance, the leader assumes that followers will not stay on task. Compare the assumptions of Theory X.

The laissez-faire type provides no direction or real leadership of any kind. Laissez-faire implies letting people do whatever they want. Hence, a laissez-faire leader avoids much interaction with the group, allowing people to set their own goals and decide how to reach them. He or she will provide suggestions or opinions only if asked for them directly.

In contrast to the laissez-faire leader, the democratic leader takes an active role in helping the group achieve its goals. The democratic leader differs from the authoritarian type, however, in allowing for group discussion of and participation in setting goals and selecting methods. Such a leader is therefore more of a facilitator who suggests lines of inquiry or investigation and tries to stimulate followers to find their own best solutions for problems. The democratic leader expects people working together in a group to come up with better solutions than an individual, even a remarkable individual, working alone. The democratic style was thus close to the ideal of the most effective kind of group leader in the early group dynamics movement.

These and later studies concerning these three leadership styles suggest that each type has a clearly different effect on working groups. The authoritarian style is effective in achieving productivity and solving problems when the problems are fairly well understood and methods for solution are also well known. The authoritarian style, however, has deleterious effects on morale, commitment, and member satisfaction, as one would expect. The Lewin, Lippitt, and White study, for example, found that group productivity dropped dramatically when the authoritarian leader left the room, suggesting that this style is costly and ultimately inefficient in the long run, because it is more cost-effective if followers internalize values that lead to productive behaviors. Then no one has to stand over the followers constantly to monitor their behaviors.

The modern version of this thinking is revealed in commitment to the team approach in programs such as Total Quality Management. The assumption is that if team members are committed to high quality, they will build quality into the product in the first place.

The democratic style is efficient in problem-solving situations, if occasionally more time-consuming than autocratically led groups. Groups with democratic leadership are more effective, however, in dealing with complex problems in environments of high uncertainty than are authoritarian-led groups. The participative approach allows for consideration of more points of view and novel approaches to problem solving. Such teams tend to show more commitment to their decisions and are also more innovative, probably for the reasons indicated. The advantage of the participative approach lies in the willingness of group members essentially to motivate themselves; there is thus less need for direct supervision and surveillance. Higher rates of satisfaction and commitment also translate into lower rates of turnover among group or organizational members. Recruiting and training costs (for replacements) are thus lowered in the long run.

The laissez-faire style of leadership is usually seen as the least effective of the three types. The leader seems to have little interaction with the followers, so there is dissatisfaction owing to insufficient feedback concerning performance, goals, and methods. Another problem is that laissez-faire leaders tend to avoid conflict rather than deal with it, which organizational members find to be the least satisfactory manner for handling conflict.

On the other hand, one can think of settings and organizations in which the laissez-faire style may be appropriate. A team of highly motivated scientists or artists may appreciate this style and be most productive in such a nondirective setting.

The group dynamics movement led to another related insight regarding styles of leadership. An enduring generalization from these studies is that two kinds of leadership tend to emerge in groups: *task leadership* and *relationship leadership*, often referred to as socioemotional leadership.

The first kind of leadership is concerned with getting the task accomplished; the other, with ensuring the group's cohesiveness, morale, and commitment. This insight from group dynamics was reinforced through a series of studies during the fifties and sixties that looked at the behaviors of existing leaders in ongoing organizations. Because much of this research was based at Ohio State, that university has given its name to these and related leadership studies.

The Ohio State studies conclude that organizational leadership can be described in two dimensions: "initiating structure" and "showing consideration." Initiating structure is basically the same as task orientation, whereas consideration is essentially concern for human or social relations. An effort was then made to investigate a relationship between leaders' scores on these dimensions and organizational performance and output. Although early results suggested a positive relationship between managers' concern for consideration (human relations) and productivity, later results were mixed.[11] A response to these mixed results was to reinterpret the relationship between the two dimensions—to see them as working in combination rather than in an either-or fashion.

The Blake and Mouton grid system, described in some detail in Chapter 5, represents an extension of research flowing from the Ohio State approach to leadership. The two dimensions in this grid are described as "concern for production" (the task orientation) and "concern for people."[12] The most recent work in this long tradition focuses on leadership, conflict management, and motivation and refines many of the earlier grid concepts. More attention is given to the responses of followers to leaders' initiatives and to the interactional nature of leadership.

Whereas the Ohio State series had earlier seen the two dimension as separate factors, assuming that a leader would be high on one or the other, the Blake and Mouton system aims at developing leaders that are high on *both* concern for people and concern for production.

In the grid system, leadership is seen in terms of handling the "three Rs," resources, relationships, and results. Resources represent the various attributes, skills, and knowledge that people bring to a situation. The results are the outcomes in terms of production, profit, creativity, services, or whatever goals sought by the organization. The key part of the process is found in the second R, relationships, the interactions among the people involved. In a recent work, Blake and McCanse point out, "This is where an excellent organization succeeds over a mediocre one because how well an organization uses the resources available to it is directly related to the results achieved."[13] The most important function of a leader is to achieve cooperation among the members of his or her organization in order to maximize the application of their human resources to the problem or job at hand.

The most effective leaders are consequently those who can develop effective teamwork with and among subordinates. These kinds of leaders can be developed, according to Blake and his associates. By the addition of a fourth R, reflection, people can learn where their style falls on the grid, and then act to move toward the team orientation, high on both concern for people and concern for production.

In summary, emphasis on leadership styles or behaviors shifts attention from relatively immutable personal traits to teachable skills of leadership. This approach grew from observations of the effects of different leadership styles, labeled as authoritarian, democratic, and laissez-faire. Both the Ohio State studies and early group dynamics stressed that there were two dimensions to leadership: concern for task or production (initiating structure) and concern for people (showing consideration). The Blake and Mouton managerial grid represents a tradition of research and leadership development that seeks to produce team-oriented leaders who are high on both dimensions.

Contingency Theories of Leadership

The perceived inadequacies of the trait approach to leadership and the mixed research regarding leadership styles led to contingency models of leadership. The underpinnings of contingency theories and their relationship to systems theory are described in Chapter 6 of this text. Contingency theorists look at the leadership styles and to the question of which is preferable, respond, "It depends."

Contingency theories of leadership essentially hold that there is no one best or most appropriate style of leadership. One must match leadership style with the exigencies of the organization's environment, the task, and interpersonal relationships between leader and members.

Fiedler's Contingency Model. Fred Fiedler's model, introduced in Chapter 6, takes as its starting point the concept of "least preferred coworker," or LPC.[14] A leader's LPC score is based, to an extent, on the notion of leadership traits. The assumption is that a leader's description of the person he or she least prefers (or preferred) to work with is directly related to that person's innate style of leading. In Fiedler's research, therefore, leaders fill out a semantic-differential questionnaire in which they are asked to describe a person with whom they have the most difficulty accomplishing a task. Scales include items such as Pleasant–Unpleasant, Boring–Interesting, Helpful–Frustrating, and so on. People at the positive end of the scale are scored 8 (for example, the most pleasant), with numbers decreasing to 1 (the most unpleasant).

People with high LPC scores are leaders who give generally high ratings or positive scores on these scales; low-LPC leaders give mostly low scores to their least preferred coworkers. In other words, high-LPC leaders are lenient even toward the people they least like working with. Note that in seeming to rate subordinates or other coworkers, the leader is actually providing a rating of him- or herself. Fiedler thus attempts to get around the criticism that people are notoriously inaccurate in giving self-ratings by disguising them as ratings of others.

The difference between Fiedler's approach and the Ohio State studies is that he maintains that the appropriate type of leader is not invariant but depends on the *favorableness* of the situation, which must now be explained. The favorableness of the situation depends on three factors: the clarity or complexity of the task (the task structure), the position or legitimate power of the leader, and the nature of the leader's interpersonal relationships with followers. The task can be clearly structured or unstructured, the authority of the leader can be strong or weak, and the relationships between leader and followers can be good or poor. The combination of these variables results in eight possible kinds of situations, ranging from the most favorable for the leader, when his or her authority is strong, the task is clearly structured, and the relationship with subordinates is good, to the least favorable, when authority is weak, the task is unstructured, and interpersonal relationships are poor.

An example of a favorable situation would be that of a strong military commander, popular with the troops, who must take possession of an unoccupied position with no enemy resistance. All three factors are positive for the leader.

An unfavorable situation is that of a person from one department appointed to chair a task force of people of the same rank from different departments to develop ways to "improve quality," with no guidelines concerning what is meant by quality. In this case, the task is unclear and, because quality can concern so many different aspects of production, is also very complex. Add to this scenario departmental rivalries, or fears that one department is trying to encroach on the turf of others. The task force members thus could be jealous of or lack respect for the appointed leader because they see him or her more as a representative of a department than as a representative of the whole organization. The team leader, as an appointee from one of the departments, has no particular authority beyond that of any other group member. In this case, then, the three main factors of task clarity, relationships between leader and members, and leader power are all unfavorable.

In these extremely favorable and extremely unfavorable situations, Fiedler's theory holds, the task-oriented, low-LPC leader is more effective than the high-LPC leader. In other words, his theory maintains that if relationships and all other factors are already favorable, the leader can dispense with working on relationships and concentrate on getting the task accomplished. If all factors are against the leader in a situation, the task orientation is again most preferred. In between these extremes are situations in which only one or two of the factors are positive. For example, leader–member relationships are good and the task is clearly structured, but the leader's authority is weak. Or, leader–member relationships are poor and the leader's authority is weak, but the task is well structured. In all intermediately favorable situations, Fiedler maintains that the high-LPC leader, who is relationship-oriented, is usually more effective.

An unexpected result of Fiedler's studies is the preference for the task-oriented leader in *both* highly favorable and highly unfavorable situations. This conclusion is at variance with the claims of the various human relations theories, such as McGregor's Theory X and Y or Blake and Mouton's team-oriented leader who is high on both task and human dimensions. Fiedler suggests that because leaders' personalities cannot be changed easily, leaders should be selected to match the three contingencies determining the favorableness of the situation.

There has been considerable criticism of Fiedler's model over the years. One problem has been confusion over just what it is that the LPC score is measuring. As it became clear that LPC scores fluctuated widely even for the same person completing the questionnaire at different times, Fiedler began to move away from the earlier notion that the LPC score reflected some enduring quality of personality.[15] Nor is it clear that the leader–member relationships are not affected by the LPC of the leader, meaning that they might be dependent on the LPC rather than being a separate aspect of the environment.

For these and other reasons, Fiedler has continued to revise his theory, tending toward a new approach called cognitive resources theory. The new approach takes into account leaders' intelligence (a personal trait) and treats the LPC as a more complex mix of preferences.

Hersey and Blanchard's Situational Leadership. Hersey and Blanchard, in their popular situational leadership theory, focus on the maturity of the followers, both job experience (job maturity) and psychological maturity. These two types of maturity determine the workers' "readiness" to perform effectively.[16]

Follower readiness can be low, moderate, or high. If it is low, the followers lack the needed skills (they are inexperienced) and are not willing to perform adequately (they exhibit a low personal maturity level). In the condition of high readiness, the followers are skilled, willing, and confident. The intermediate stages are those in which the followers may be willing but not skilled, or skilled but not as willing or confident as they should be. The same person can exhibit different levels of readiness on different tasks or assignments, as a person may feel confident about a well-learned skill but not about another operation. So in different circumstances the same group of people could be rated either high or low in readiness.

Each of the four conditions calls forth a different type of leadership style; these are designated *telling, selling, participating,* and *delegating.* In the first situation, low follower experience and maturity, telling, which is direct guidance, is the preferred management style. In the second, in which followers are willing but unskilled, the leader should be selling the idea that the skills can be acquired. When followers are skilled but not committed to performance, the leader involves them in participative decision making in order to gain their commitment. In the favorable situation of skilled and ready followers, the leader can delegate the task to them.

The first two styles, telling and selling, emphasize task behavior, whereas the second two emphasize relationship behavior. In other words, as followers increase in maturity or readiness, leaders should increasingly stress relationship behaviors over task behaviors (in contrast to Fiedler's prescription for the most highly favorable situations, in which he prefers task leadership). Hersey and Blanchard maintain that leaders should intervene in an effort to upgrade followers' maturity and readiness by gradually delegating more responsibility as they gain experience.

Hersey and Blanchard have not offered research support for their theory.[17] It is really more in the realm of popularized business literature than of research literature. The model is said to be based more on intuition from years of observation and consultation in business settings. The popularity of their approach with business practitioners suggests that the intuitive appeal of their model is strong.

Path-Goal Theory. This contingency theory represents an attempt to move away from personality measures, such as Fiedler's LPC, and has been supported by management research. Path-goal theory is based on a broader theory of motivation called *expectancy theory,* which holds that people are motivated to take certain actions when they *expect* them to lead to the realization of desired ends. The greater the perceived likelihood, or expectancy, that effort will be rewarded, the greater the motivation to expend the effort.

The role of leaders in organizations, according to this theory, is to induce followers to perceive that certain paths will lead to desirable goals. Leaders' communication hence should be directed toward clearly explaining what followers are expected to do (the *path*) and stressing the rewards to be expected (the *goal*) as a result of achievement.

A soccer coach, for example, might stress that long, hard practice drills are the most effective path toward a winning or championship season. Not only does she stress the goal, the winning season, but she must also convince team members that the drills are the most effective means to the end. On the other hand, she must also convince the team that each player's personal rewards from winning are worth the effort. Path-goal theory suggests that it would be insufficient to emphasize only one of these aspects of the situation, such as stressing only winning without also persuading players of the efficacy of the methods and the individual rewards to be realized.

Path-goal theory posits four possible leadership communication styles:

1. Instrumental or *directive leadership,* similar to the directive style of "telling" in the Hersey and Blanchard model or to the concern for production dimension
2. *Supportive leadership,* similar to behaviors high on the consideration dimension of the Ohio State studies
3. *Participative leadership,* which seeks to involve followers in decision making
4. *Achievement-oriented leadership,* which emphasizes excellence, setting challenging goals, and demonstrating confidence in followers

Two kinds of contingencies should be considered in determining which of the four styles is most appropriate in a given situation: the nature of the followers and the nature of the task environment. Relevant characteristics of subordinates include their needs (for achievement, recognition, being well liked, for example), their abilities and experience for the task, and aspects of their personalities (such as confidence and self-esteem). Task characteristics include how well the task is structured, the presence of formalized work rules, and the nature of the technology to be employed.

The relationships among these variables and the motivation and behaviors of followers are rather complex in the theory. In general, in situations in which there is a lot of uncertainty about expectations, uncertainty about how to perform the task, and a lack of experience, directive leadership is said to be most effective because it clarifies what is expected of each person and points to a direct relationship between performance and rewards. In situations in which followers are capable and clearly see what to do, such directive leadership would be unsatisfying and could thereby lower motivation.

According to path-goal theory, therefore, supportive leadership is best for situations in which followers perform tedious, repetitive, or seemingly unrewarding work.

The leader tries to make the performance of the necessary behaviors more pleasant and to minimize the negative aspects. This can be done by making a game out of parts of the task, such as having "teams" compete with one another to see which can stuff the most envelopes in a given amount of time, with the winners being treated to a pizza party. Supportive leadership can also enhance workers' confidence and self-esteem, leading them to believe that they can perform a difficult task that is seemingly beyond their capabilities, by increasing their belief in the efficacy of the path to some goal.

Participative leadership appears best for unstructured tasks and when individual roles are unclear. Taking part in discussion of the problem and in decision making increases subordinates' understanding of the task and should make them more confident of achieving their goals as a result. Such participation also adds to their satisfaction, making the effort more rewarding. For example, an organization was presented with the possibility of winning a sizable grant from an institution if it could come up with innovative programs to increase college enrollment in a community. Group members could not know at the start what role each might play in the new programs (individual roles were unclear), and the task was worded vaguely: increase college enrollment by community members.

Achievement-oriented leaders set high goals and then persuade followers that they have the abilities to reach them. This style is most effective for unstructured tasks that are neither boring nor repetitive. For clearly structured, repetitive tasks, setting higher and higher goals might be resented as quota setting, as when sales managers keep ratcheting up employees' sales goals or when supervisors demand faster and faster times on an assembly line. The result of setting higher goals in these repetitive task situations is higher stress levels.

Path-goal theory highlights the importance of the communication by leaders. Leaders tailor their communication messages and styles to fit the various factors covered in the theory.

The complexity of path-goal theory has been both its strength and its weakness. The strength derives from the theory's ability to show the relationships among many kinds of contingent variables. Note that the theory takes into account many kinds of contingent factors, more than the other contingency theories considered here. For example, the implication that achievement-oriented leadership is effective in unstructured, nonrepetitive situations but not in other situations is potentially quite useful. The complexity, however, also makes the theory difficult to test and to validate. The final verdict on the theory's validity is therefore not yet in.

In summary, contingency theories of leadership deny that any one set of personality traits or leader behaviors is appropriate in all circumstances. The key to effective leadership lies in matching the variables of each situation with the requisite style of leadership. Fiedler's model essentially suggests changing the leader him- or herself to match the contingent situation. Hersey and Blanchard's system and path-goal theory both suggest that the leader can alter his or her behavior in response to follower maturity (Hersey and Blanchard) or a wide range of environmental and follower characteristics. Path-goal theory most emphasizes the need for the leader to persuade and motivate followers through communication. Depending on the situation, the leader needs to

AN ISSUE OF COMMUNICATION ETHICS

Secret Taping

For many people in leadership positions in organizations, one of the most difficult tasks they face involves evaluating and even disciplining other members. The possibility of poor evaluations and even of dismissal can taint the relationship between leader and follower. One result of a dysfunctional relationship can be the secret taping by one side or the other of leader–member interchanges. As noted in an earlier ethics box, surveillance technology is becoming increasingly sophisticated and difficult to detect.

Employees who feel threatened have increasingly turned to the use of secret taping of this sort. One California attorney who handles many cases involving claims of wrongful dismissal claims that about one-fifth of his clients have secretly taped conversations with their supervisors.* Secret taping is allowed by federal law as long as one of the people involved in a taped conversation is aware of it. Even in cases in which state law forbids secret taping, when the tapes reveal definite wrong-

doing by the organization, they may still be admissible.

One of the most frequent problems brought to light by such secret taping is a superior's giving a subordinate a reason for dismissal or disciplining that differs from the official reason recorded in organizational documents. This difference may result from the superior's wishing to soften the blow or to avoid hurting the subordinate's feelings in a face-to-face encounter. This trend could be complicated by some courts' willingness to consider "compelled slander" claims by fired employees. This type of slander case results when an employee is given a reason for being dismissed; when interviewing for another job, when asked why he or she was dismissed by the former employer, the applicant is "compelled" to reveal possibly defamatory information about him- or herself.

What are ethical ways in which a leader can communicate with followers in order to avoid problems of secret surveillance? Do you feel that such secret taping can be justified under certain circumstances? How can leaders maintain a communication climate with followers that will reduce the chances that problems of this sort will occur?

*Wall Street Journal, November 3, 1992, p. B1.

persuade followers of their abilities and confidence, the efficacy of required efforts in reaching some goal, and the value of the goal to them and to the organization.

Transformational Leadership

The notion of transformational leadership is associated with James Macgregor Burns and his influential study of leadership. In recent management literature, a similar term has become popular: the visionary leader. A perusal of announcements for top executives or college presidents or deans these days will convince one of the widespread demand for a leader with "vision." The basic idea behind these concepts is that there is a substantial difference between a manager or implementer, who capably fulfills the everyday obligations and expectations of supervising or administering an organization, and a *leader*, who focuses on issues beyond administering.

Burns draws a sharp distinction between a leader and simply a "wielder of power." A leader is involved in a relationship with followers that takes into account motives and goals on both sides, whereas the power wielder need be concerned only with his or her own needs. Further, Burns distinguishes between two different forms of leadership itself: transactional and transformational.

Transactional leadership occurs in situations in which the leader trades valued items for the compliance or cooperation of followers. Political leaders who put together coalitions of interests so that various groups' interests appear to be met by supporting them are transactional leaders. One reason for concern about special-interest groups dominating local or national politics is the fragmentation and divisiveness that such appeals can cause.

On the other hand, transformational leadership "occurs when one or more persons engage with others in such a way that leaders and followers raise one another to higher levels of motivation and morality."[18] The transformational leader appeals to motives and needs of followers, as does the transactional leader, but a higher level of

Leaders are seen as transformational leaders when they appeal to higher motives among followers.

motives and needs. The leader may have to awaken followers to the existence of these motives and needs in themselves, because they may not be immediately apparent or conscious. For that reason, Burns speaks of this kind of leadership as "elevating leadership." Gandhi, for example, attempted to go beyond followers' grievances against the injustices they suffered under British rule and awaken in them a humane concern for peace, life, and justice even toward enemies and conquerors. Note also the reciprocal relationship between leader and followers in this formulation. The leader is partly transformed by the followers even while he or she is acting to raise or transform the followers.

Appealing to higher rather than lower motives or needs suggests the existence of a hierarchy of motives or needs, such as Maslow's famous hierarchy. A transformational leader tries to make salient—that is, bring to conscious awareness, needs at the top end of the pyramid, such as needs for esteem or for self-actualization, rather than appealing to survival or safety needs. Such a leader may also make followers aware of long-range or hidden values that could be overlooked by someone appealing to baser motives, such as ethnic hatred or clannishness. A transformational leader thus tries to bring out the social or human benefits of an organization's function instead of concentrating simply on profit or organizational survival (of course, the argument is that concentrating on higher motives is the best way to ensure survival).

Burns's ideas concerning transformational leadership can be compared to those writers in the management literature on human resource development. Chris Argyris, for example, was distressed that in most organizations, the maturity of the individual seems not to be compatible with the demands of the organization. An answer to this problem, Argyris believes, is to move from authoritarian styles of leadership toward more "democratic," "participative," "collaborative," "employee-centered" styles. Argyris draws on ideas from Maslow and appeals to higher needs, calling for more coaching and creation of more "authentic" relationships that evoke the higher values of both leaders and followers.[19]

These concepts have been reinforced in the popularized literature as well. Warren Bennis, for example, calls for visionary leaders, as he and Burt Nanus emphasize the oft-quoted epigram, "Managers do things right, leaders do the right things."[20] They speak of the need for such leaders to create focus for an organization by maintaining the group's attention on a vision. A major strategy for such leaders is to create a "compelling image of a desired state of affairs" through effective communication.[21] Leaders have the ability to visualize and reinforce positive goals for the organization; they are able to catch up others in their enthusiasm for or commitment to these goals.

Another term for this kind of leader is "corporate pathfinder," as used by H. J. Leavitt.[22] Leavitt regrets that "we have unintentionally neglected the visionary, pathfinding part of the managing process over the last 20 years."[23] He means that leadership training, primarily in management schools, has stressed analytical skills rather than persuasion skills, overlooking the emotional appeals that are necessary if other people's commitments and behaviors are to be changed. Leaders are first of all effective communicators rather than simply technical experts or financial geniuses.

The organizational culture literature similarly emphasizes the importance of transformational leadership. Deal and Kennedy focused on the important role of the "symbolic manager," who uses the cultural network and symbols to lead an organization toward higher levels of achievement. A symbolic manager thus is a leader who is able to tap into symbols of values that are important to followers, in the way that a transformational leader appeals to the higher motives of followers.

Trice and Beyer, whose system for analyzing cultural systems is described in Chapter 7, maintain that an important rule for cultural leaders is to "preserve and embody" organizational cultures.[24] They refer as well to "transformational leadership" as especially important for effecting organizational change.[25] Schein, as noted in Chapter 7, also emphasizes the role that leaders play in creating, maintaining, and changing organizational cultures.[26] Although he suggests that we can become obsessed with vision as a single criterion for leader effectiveness, if an organization's existing values or symbols are fuzzy or contradictory, emphasis on vision may lead the organizational culture to recognize this.[27]

A leader with vision, one who could be described as a transformational leader, is able to articulate a clearer sense of mission for such an organization. Such a leader can himself come to symbolize the organization or industry he represents, as Lee Iacocca has done for Chrysler and the American automobile industry. The CEO of Monsanto made it a point to spend at least one day a week in one of the company's chemical laboratories, learning firsthand about new products being developed.[28] His action symbolized the importance of research to the company and also the importance of leaders sticking close to the basic business of the enterprise.

Review of Leadership Theories

A leader is an individual; leadership, on the other hand, can be shared among many different people in an organization and exercised at different times in different ways. Most definitions of leadership stress that it implies a relationship between the leader and the followers. The leader becomes an agent of change when he or she is able to induce members to perform in ways that meet important goals. Early theories concerning leadership stressed that leaders were born, rather than made, and had to possess certain innate traits. Some leadership traits are acquired skills, such as effective communication. Many organizations seek to identify potential leaders through various kinds of assessment procedures and search-and-screen committees, which try to pinpoint individuals who may have the requisite traits or skills.

Later theories tended to move away from traits by focusing on behaviors enacted by people under different circumstances. These behaviors were seen as forming styles of leadership, such as democratic, laissez-faire, and authoritarian styles. Leadership styles were also categorized in terms of whether they furthered task functions or relationship functions for a group. The Blake and Mouton grid system, for example, hoped to move leaders toward a style that combined both concerns. Contingency models of leadership assume that there is no one best style of leadership; it depends on the situation, that is, the contingencies. Some theories, such as Fiedler's, call upon organizations to match leaders to the favorableness of the situation, whereas others assume that the same leaders can adapt their leadership styles to conform to the contingencies.

Transformational or visionary leadership is seen as a form of leadership that transcends even effective management. Transformational leaders call on the highest levels of motives and values of members. As a result, both members and the leader reach a higher level of performance than either may have thought possible.

POWER AND LEADERSHIP IN ORGANIZATIONS

Power is clearly a factor in exercising leadership. The effectiveness of a leader may depend on the leader's communicating to others his or her power to induce them to act in certain ways. People can exercise power without at the same time being leaders, however, as when a criminal robs someone at gunpoint; we would say the robber has power but has not necessarily been a leader in this instance. Power is distributed through a group or organization in such a way that leadership and power may be exercised by individuals at various levels of the organizational hierarchy. The bases for power in organizations hence provide for further understanding of how leadership works.

The concept of *power* has been interpreted in several different ways, emphasizing its different aspects. Some define power in terms of one person's getting another to do what the second person would rather not do.[29] This definition has a decidedly coercive connotation. Others define power more in terms of a relationship between two or more people, in which one person, who has power, is less dependent on the other(s) than vice versa. This second definition allows power to be exercised in both directions between leaders and followers: Leaders are to a certain extent dependent on followers following. In that sense, followers have some power vis-à-vis leaders. In modern organizations, coercive power, while certainly not nonexistent, is often less important than other forms of power based on organizational structure, expertise, or relationships.

Bases for Organizational Power

From the standpoint of communication studies, then, we are interested in power as it affects and is used in the communicating of leadership and influence. As one authority puts it, "Communication provides the means through which power can be exercised, developed, maintained, and enhanced."[30] *Power* is defined for these purposes as *the ability to persuade, induce, or influence others to act in ways desired by the person exercising it.*

When Weber developed three ideal types of legitimate authority, he focused our attention on a specific type of bureaucratic power associated with the modern organization. Unlike the traditional ruler or charismatic leader, the bureaucrat derives power from his or her position in the bureaucracy. This type of power is *positional power;* the position confers the power. Some people within organizations are able to exercise a different kind of power, not based on formal position in the hierarchy; such power can be based on knowledge, skill, popularity, interpersonal skills at building coalitions, and so forth. This second type of power is *personal power*. Over the years, some useful systems have been developed for categorizing more specifically the different kinds of positional and personal power available to people in organizations.

Amitai Etzioni, for example, has categorized the power of leaders of organizations in terms of whether compliance is gained through physical, material, or symbolic means.[31] Power obtained through physical means, the threat or use of force, is termed *coercive power*. Coercive power is characteristic of organizations such as prisons or some combat units. Material means lead to *remunerative power*, which is based on the power holder's control of desired resources and rewards, such as wages, salary, and fringe benefits. Remunerative power is obviously characteristic of most organizations in which people are employed and paid for their services.

The third means of exercising power, symbolic means, called *normative power* by Etzioni, is of most interest from the point of view of communication studies. Etzioni's definition of normative power is compatible with an organizational cultural analysis, he says that it "rests on allocation and manipulation of symbolic rewards and deprivations through employment of leaders, manipulation of mass media, allocation of esteem and prestige symbols, administration of ritual."[32]

He further distinguishes two types of normative power. The first type, which he labels "pure normative power," is that typically exercised by superiors over subordinates. This pure type is represented by the controlling of signs of esteem, prestige, and other symbolic rewards. The second type is "social power," which is characteristic of relations among equals, as in the exercise of cohesive or normative power in small, informal groups.

Although Etzioni's introduction of the notion of normative power is productive from a communication point of view, it does not go as far in identifying sources of informal or social power as the widely referenced scheme of John French and Bertram Raven.[33] The French and Raven typology allows us to see that power extends beyond the official organization chart's hierarchy. In any organization, individuals who are nominally subordinate nearly always possess some basis for power. The distribution of power in an organization is thus more complex than it may first appear when one considers positional power only.

French and Raven describe five types of power in an organization:

1. Coercive power
2. Reward power
3. Legitimate power
4. Expert power (or knowledge power)
5. Referent power

The first two bases for power are quite similar to Etzioni's coercive and remunerative power. Coercive power depends on the perception of others that the power holder has the capacity to administer punishments in order to gain their compliance. Reward power similarly depends on the perceptions of others that the power holder controls the distribution of desired rewards. In this case, the exercise of power represents an exchange of goods or other desirables.

Legitimate power is similar to Weber's notion of bureaucratic power. The subordinates in the hierarchy accept the power holder's exercise of power because they have internalized the rationality and legitimacy of the power structure of the organization. In the military, deference and unquestioning obedience is due to the person of the next higher rank than oneself, for example.

The fourth and fifth bases for power in French and Raven's typology are useful additions to the discussion of power and communication. First, *expert power* refers to the expertise and special knowledge of some members of the organization. Although they may not appear at the top of the hierarchy, experts who know how to perform tasks that are crucial to the operations or survival of the organization actually can wield considerable power. The mechanics who know how to keep the machinery operating are obviously in a position of this sort. Engineers, accountants, attorneys, physicians, and many others with special expertise are similarly able to exercise power, especially when a crisis or problem highlights matters in which they are the experts. When these experts are able to communicate to others the importance of their knowledge, they are able to influence those who appear to have legitimate or positional authority over them.

Expert forms of power can be balanced against position power so that negotiation and discussion become the preferred means for making decisions, setting policy, or settling conflicts in these kinds of situations. Expert power is usually seen as acceptable to followers, and is less likely to provoke resistance when the expertise is seen as relevant to the task.[34]

The fifth basis for power, *referent power,* has attracted considerable attention. Referent power is the power of identification, or of the role model. A person with referent power is a person whom others wish to be like, or wish to be associated with. If we want another person to like us, that person has this kind of power over us.

Referent power is hence mainly personal power exercised through social relationships, although one can imagine this kind of power manifesting itself through less direct means, as when a respected celebrity urges people to contribute to a cause, refrain from drugs or smoking, or the like. In these cases, the celebrity exercises referent power through the mass media. These indirect uses of referent power, however, are usually not relevant to internal organizational communication, in which the face-to-face relationship typically is the medium for its exercise. Referent leaders are of special interest in organizational culture analyses of organizational communication. Deal and Kennedy and Trice and Beyer point to the need to discover the symbolic leaders, or the informal leaders who represent or personalize the values of the organization's culture.

In organizations, bases for power can be combined, enhancing the ability of leaders to gain compliance. If a person has legitimate power because of her position, and also is well liked and has special expertise for the task at hand, she should be able to bring more power to bear than another leader who lacks some of these advantages. Note that this kind of combination of power bases is similar to Fiedler's notion of a highly favorable situation for a leader. Or, to recall the approach of path-goal theory, a leader with expert power would be effective when stressing his or her expertise in convincing followers that the path selected for reaching a goal is workable and will achieve a desired goal.

The concept of referent power reinforces human relations–oriented theorists' stressing of warmth and consideration in the treatment of subordinates. The theory put forth by Blake and Mouton suggests that the most effective leaders are those who combine what is here called referent power with expert and legitimate power. A leader communicates referent power, first, by showing consideration and concern for followers. Second, if people are to identify with the leader, it is essential that the leader set the kind of example necessary to be a role model.

There are, however, potential disadvantages to relying on referent power in all situations. First, identification seems to work best among people who share the same values and other characteristics. The "other characteristics" may often include similar background, ethnicity, culture, and gender. One of the weaknesses of some mentor programs for example, has been that they tend to rely on mentors and protégés sharing the same social and cultural background. Women and minorities have had trouble being enculturated into some tightly knit organizations for these reasons, as we saw in Chapter 9.[35] Identification, or referent power, hence may not be effective or even desirable in some situations.

Second, referent power is usually exercised through a leader making personal appeals to followers ("Do this for me," "Follow my example"). Such appeals can be overdone or overused, thus losing their effectiveness over the long run. In a sense, one can go to the bank too often when using personal capital. Furthermore, ethical questions arise when followers are asked to identify with values or outcomes favorable to leaders as individuals, but inimical to the best interests of the followers and the organization. And, finally, referent power is not useful when followers do not respect the leader's knowledge or expertise or legitimate authority.

In summary, power is an important variable relating to organizational leadership. Power is largely manifested or enhanced through communication. Classifications of types and bases of power remind us that there are different kinds of power and that the distribution of power in most organizations is shared and complex. Power operates through relationships and on the basis of organizational members' perceptions. Etzioni's classifications point to the significance of normative power and its functioning through the use and manipulation of symbols. French and Raven provide a more detailed and widely used system for classifying the bases of power. Their system highlights the existence of different kinds of power distributed throughout an organization. Expert and referent power especially direct attention to power derived from a person's credibility, or *ethos,* in an organization. People at various levels in the organization can possess and use expert and referent power vis-à-vis superiors as well as subordinates. Leaders can enhance their effectiveness by communicating in ways that remind followers of their expert and referent power in addition to their legitimate power. There are, however, potential drawbacks to reliance on referent power in all situations.

Power and Organizational Politics

The foregoing argues that organizations, especially large, complex organizations, are as much political as rational in nature. To say that an organization is political is to say that decisions are taken as a result of choosing among competing alternatives, championed by competing groups and interests within the organization. Obviously, there is nothing necessarily irrational about such a process.

The direction that an organization takes, the decisions made, and the actions taken are thus the result of the interplay of essentially political forces and communication. (*Political* is used here not in the sense of governmental politics, but in the sense of this internal competition.) That decisions are justified in terms of their apparent rationality depends on someone's getting others to accept his or her definition of "rationality." Although many people may deprecate institutional politics, playing organizational politics, like conflict itself, is probably inevitable and not necessarily negative in most complex organizations. Where politics is played for the purpose of furthering an individual or group at the expense of others, however, the game can have deleterious effects.

One of the images of organization that Gareth Morgan develops in his book on organizational theories is that of the "organization as political system."[36] Each organization, either intentionally or otherwise, works out how decisions are going to be made and carried out, who has authority, and how that authority is exercised. These are essentially political issues. Some organizations are autocratic (rule by one), some are democratic, and there are various alternatives in between. A special kind of authority or rule applicable to modern organizations is that of the bureaucracy (rule by the "office" or bureau), as analyzed by Max Weber (see Chapter 2). Companies dominated by an all-powerful founder-owner represent autocracies; organizations allowing for rule by consensus or vote, such as some universities, volunteer or charitable organizations, or social organizations or clubs, are democracies.

John P. Kotter summarizes the situation of many contemporary, complex organizations when he points to two distinctive features of such organizations: diversity and interdependence.[37] Diversity means that organizational members exhibit competing values, goals, and objectives, and that there are differing interpretations of problems and solutions. The amount of diversity, Kotter suggests, is directly related to the potential for conflict and the amount of effort required to deal with such conflict. If the membership of an organization is fairly homogeneous, conflicts that do arise are dealt with more quickly and easily than in organizations with diverse memberships. Interdependence means that the operations of a complex organization require the cooperation of many different elements. No one person or group in such an organization is in a position to carry out major organizational functions unilaterally; hence, others may be in a position to block, retard, or modify courses of action taken in other parts of the organization. Interdependence thus requires that conflict be resolved or handled in some way.

The combination of these factors, diversity and interdependence, implies that conflict is likely, that it must be dealt with (in order to get on with the business of the organization), and that it may be difficult to deal with.

The types of organizational power and how they are communicated therefore become relevant aspects of an analysis of organizational politics. Morgan provides a list of the various sources of personal power available in complex organizations that can be used to participate in institutional politics.[38] Naturally, several of Morgan's sources of power overlap with those of French and Raven:

- Formal authority, similar to legitimate or position power
- Control of scarce resources, quite similar to reward power
- Control of technology, and control of knowledge and information, quite similar to expert power
- Interpersonal alliances, networks, and control of the "informal organization," similar to referent power

In addition, his list includes some other levers of political influence that may be overlooked. The following potential sources of influence are interesting in this regard:

- *The use of an organization's structure, rules, or regulations.* One who has detailed knowledge concerning the procedures or rules to be followed in various cases can have more power over decisions than one who is less familiar with them. New managers, for instance, may not know that there are precedents or standing rules for dealing with certain kinds of issues. Similarly, a person with extensive knowledge of "Robert's Rules of Order" can wield some power in an organization bound to follow these procedures.

- *Control or influence over decision processes.* Organizational politics often involves attending meetings and even more meetings. It is possible at these meetings to have some influence over the agenda, to bring certain problems to the attention of others, and perhaps to suggest certain alternatives for consideration. Some wits have suggested that 80 percent of success in life is simply showing up. Knowledge of the premises and values underlying a particular organizational culture can suggest the ways in which decisions are normally taken; such information can be a source of some power in the organization.

- *Ability to cope with uncertainty.* Complex organizations are subject to various sorts of internal and external uncertainties, such as market changes, unpredictable weather, accidents, breakdowns, and international incidents. Those who can deal with such uncertainties can thereby accrue some power. As a simple example, maintenance people who can fix machinery breakdowns have this sort of power. Robert Dilenschneider, CEO of Hill and Knowlton, reports an experience he had when making a recommendation to a tough manufacturing CEO that the company recognize the legitimacy of striking union workers' claims. The manufacturing president became so enraged at one point that he threw a glass ashtray through a plate glass partition behind Dilenschneider. In the shock, on some sort of automatic pilot, Dilenschneider asked if he could pull the drapes, hiding the shattered glass, in order to keep out the draft. The other CEO was so impressed by this cool handling of the unexpected that he gave in.[39]

- *Control of symbolism and management of meaning.* Persons who are particularly verbal and are able to create images or metaphors that describe what the organization aspires to derive some power from their skill. Symbolic leaders pick up on such images as well as on the dress or style associated with influential people in the organization. Morgan reports that people with access to powerful leaders such as the president of the United States frequently show up early for appointments with the leader in order to communicate to others their access. This access in turn becomes a lever for enhancing their own power.[40] The discussion of cultural symbols in Chapter 7 indicates how someone can acquire influence through the manipulation of the proper objects, signs, and furnishings. The presence or absence of computers, cellular phones, and pagers, for instance, can communicate status and possibly enhance one's power.

Bear in mind that in most circumstances, these last four sources of power may be incremental and even marginal in their effects. If one lacks the basic positional power or expert power, manipulation of symbols, meeting agendas, and the like may be fairly inconsequential. But given some other basic elements of organizational power, awareness and use of these additional factors can make the difference among opponents who may otherwise be rather evenly matched.

Organizational politics are often a fact of life, and they are not necessarily a bad thing. Competition for attention and resources can be healthy in an organization. Those who would exercise leadership in most complex organizations must be aware of internal politics and know how to compete effectively, if for no other reason than self-defense or group defense.

MOTIVATION AND COMPLIANCE GAINING IN LEADER–MEMBER COMMUNICATION

The shift away from classically managed organizations toward team approaches places more emphasis on the mutual influence that each partner in a leader–member dyad has on the other. Rather than giving orders, leaders are more likely to turn to persuasion strategies; similarly, members attempt what can be called upward influence, persuasion directed at leaders. In professional organizations, for example, the nominal subordinate may retain a good deal of professional expert power and autonomy. Charitable or public organizations often depend on voluntary or willing compliance of subordinates. Even strictly hierarchical businesses find that motivating or appealing to the needs and desires of subordinates is more effective in the long run than relying on coercive orders for gaining compliance.

Compliance-Gaining Strategies

In the subfield of interpersonal communication, the rubric of *compliance gaining* refers to a body of research concerning interpersonal strategies for gaining another person's willingness to comply with one's wishes, usually in one-on-one settings.

The notion of compliance gaining as a topic of research goes back to an article in a psychology journal in 1967, written by G. Marwell and D. R. Schmitt.[41] More than

100 research articles have appeared since, many of them concerned with developing a taxonomy, or classification system, for the various strategies one can use.[42] Despite all these efforts, most schemes fail to provide exhaustive lists of potential strategies, perhaps because they are simply lists of informal strategies people have observed. Typical strategies include the following:

- *Positive altercasting.* Point out that a good person would do what you want the other person to do. When the chair of a trade association convention was trying to get other committee members to work late on some difficult planning to coordinate panels, he named some particularly respected members of the association who had performed just such tasks for earlier meetings. He thereby hoped that the other members would infer that they could also be highly respected and liked by other members in the same way.

- *Negative altercasting.* Point out that only a bad person would not do what you want. The chair of the planning committee in the example above could have pointed out that the members would lose the respect of fellow members if the planned meetings do not go well because of their spending inadequate time and effort in preparation. He then emphasizes the negative results of their not complying with his directives.

- *Bargaining.* Agree to do something for the other person if he or she will comply. Often a leader can rely on trading favors or the promise of such favors to get the compliance of the other person. If you do this for me now, I will look favorably on your request for a more flexible work schedule in the future.

- *Self-feeling.* Suggest that the members will feel better (or worse) about themselves if they do (or do not) comply. Regardless of what others may think about them, the leader may here suggest that the members will feel unfulfilled if they know that they could have achieved something but did not.

And so on. As many as sixty-four different specific strategies have been identified.[43]

One way to bring order to this chaos of lists is to distinguish between positive and negative strategies. Positive, or "pro-social," strategies include positive altercasting and appealing to positive moral qualities or values to obtain compliance. Negative strategies include negative altercasting and appealing to authority or potential harm or punishment that will result if the other person does not comply. In line with research concerning transformational leadership, communication climate, and contingency theories, the use of positive compliance-gaining strategies results in the leader's being perceived as more competent and effective than is the case with the use of negative strategies.[44] The use of positive strategies allows the superior to maintain a good interpersonal relationship with subordinates.

Compliance-gaining strategies can also be direct or indirect. Direct strategies involve spelling out exactly what the consequences or rewards are for complying with one's wishes. Indirect strategies are more subtle, hinting of the consequences or rewards. An example of an indirect strategy would be for the leader to begin to refer to Jones or Smith, who lost favor in the organization when he or she failed to carry out some assignment or, on the other hand, moved swiftly up the organizational ladder. The direct comparison between the actions of Smith and Jones and the current situation is never drawn but is left to be inferred by the target of this indirect strategy.

Two other variations in the use of compliance-gaining tactics have been shown to be fairly effective.[45] One technique involves beginning by asking for more than the other person can probably be expected to do. When this request is refused, follow up with a more reasonable request, which is really the behavior desired in the first place. This technique is sometimes referred to as the "door-in-the-face" tactic.

The other, complementary technique is to begin with small, fairly inconsequential requests, leading up to a request for a more significant commitment to action on

DIVERSITY MATTERS

The Problem of Defining Race and Ethnicity

There are many forms of diversity within organizations today. One of the important questions concerning leadership communication and the establishment of leadership relationships has to do with the effects of ethnic or gender differences between leaders and followers.

Differences based on race and ethnicity are potentially quite emotionally charged but have not been widely studied in the research concerning organizational communication.*

First, it is useful to explain these terms more fully. *Race* has been used as a basis for categorizing people in terms of presumed biological differences. The scientific basis for categorization is somewhat illusory, however. *Ethnicity,* on the other hand, is assumed to relate to cultural differences among identifiable groups, usually of national or regional origin. A related term often used in the United States for discussing different categories or groups of people is "minority" groups, implying the existence of some sort of "majority" group. Significant minority groups in the United States include African Americans, Chicanas (fem.) and Chicanos (masc.), Chinese Americans, Japanese Americans, Filipinas (fem.) and Filipinos (masc.), Native Americans, and Puerto Ricans.**

In official organizational discourse, these groups can become marginalized and the differences between them glossed over by the use of the general term *minorities,* implying "others" or, more particularly, "not us." The cultural richness of the different heritages represented by these groups may not be affirmed by such generalizations. Informal organizational communication may also serve to separate and stigmatize members of these groups, given the "insider" role of long-time organizational members. Inside jokes and references can serve to emphasize a separateness between the insiders and the out-groups. Again, the result can be to lump all minorities into one negative group, outsiders, instead of recognizing their individuality and the individuality of their distinct cultural backgrounds.

What has been called leadership in this chapter, especially transformational leadership, must be exercised in ways that show awareness of these problems. More importantly, transformational leadership is called for in developing positive responses to these problems leading to a positive endorsement of all individuals and ethnic or minority groups present in the organization.

*B. J. Allen (1995), "Diversity" and organizational communication, *Journal of Applied Communication Research, 23,* 143–55.

**Allen, p. 144.

the part of the other person. This tactic is known as the "foot-in-the-door" technique. These techniques thus involve a series of compliance-gaining requests over a short or long period of time, more like a campaign to gain compliance than like the one-shot requests of earlier compliance-gaining research.

Some experienced veterans of organizational life are aware of these methods, however, and may therefore be wary of giving an inch, fearing "foot-in-the-door" sequences. Unions in some industries, for example, are resistant to small changes in work rules or conditions for fear that they are invitations to larger changes down the road.

Gender differences in the use of compliance-gaining strategies have also been studied. One question concerned the relationship between a leader's gender and the use of direct versus indirect techniques. In sum, research supports the generalization that power or legitimate authority is a better predictor of the use of direct versus indirect compliance-gaining tactics than gender, but that there is some effect of gender. In other words, both male and female managers who have the authority to legitimately request a behavior of a subordinate tend to use direct strategies, such as direct requests or warnings, but women managers show a greater tendency to forgo reliance on power tactics.[46]

Review of Compliance-Gaining Communication

Many leaders rely on informal, face-to-face requests in order to get members to take actions desired by the leader. Such informal and interpersonal influence attempts have been labeled compliance gaining in the communication research literature. As organizations move away from emphasis on using authority and giving orders to gain compliance, there will be more use of such informal methods of personal persuasion as leaders try to motivate members.

The many efforts to categorize compliance-gaining strategies have been disappointing, but it is possible to look at some aspects of the way such strategies are employed in organizational settings. For example, positive strategies are seen as more effective and satisfactory than negative ones. While it has been thought that women leaders may be more likely than male leaders to use influence strategies in indirect rather than direct ways, research has not provided strong support for this hypothesis. The legitimate basis for authority or for requesting compliance is a better predictor than gender for use of direct rather than indirect tactics.

SUMMARY

Leadership is enacted, enhanced, and maintained through communication. The theories and principles covered in this chapter imply several generalizations concerning leadership and organizational communication.

• Traits associated with leadership include communication skills. Although trait theories of leadership, especially those emphasizing innate personality factors, are losing their appeal, certain traits, such as intelligence and communication skills, are correlated with leadership emergence. Neustadt's studies of presidential leadership reinforce the conclusion that communication skills such as negotiation and persuasion are important.

• The communication style that leads to both high levels of satisfaction and relatively effective problem solving is the democratic style. Democratic leaders differ from laissez-faire leaders in that they actively involve followers in the processes of decision making and discussion of alternatives. Directive leaders, using an authoritarian style of leadership, may be effective in simple, clear problem-solving situations, but they do not contribute to members' satisfaction.

• Organizational members interpret leadership behavior as emphasizing either task performance or human relations and consideration. Task leaders' communication emphasizes giving directions, orders, or instructions on how to do a job. Leaders perceived as high on the consideration dimension are more likely to maintain a nondefensive climate for communication.

• Contingency theories of leadership direct attention to the personal relationships between leaders and followers as a significant factor influencing the appropriate leadership style. Although Fiedler takes the view that leadership style is the result of relatively unchanging personality traits, other contingency models assume that the leader can select among different approaches to fit different situations. Hersey and Blanchard, for example, suggest the different communication modes of selling, telling, participating, and delegating. Each style represents a different kind of communication between leader and follower.

• Path-goal theory implies that leaders must be sensitive to a range of situational conditions in order to modulate their communication to fit each set. To be successful in motivating followers, a leader must emphasize both the rewards of achieving a goal and the means of accomplishing the goal, or the path. No one communication style is best, however, for carrying out the leadership function. Leaders cannot apply a set formula, in other words. Emphasizing achievement and high goals, for example, would probably be counterproductive for boring, repetitive tasks, the theory suggests. In this situation, supportive leadership should be more effective.

• The theory of transformational leadership stresses the importance of leaders' appealing to followers' higher levels of motivational goals or needs. Essentially, transformational leaders seek to make followers aware of significant, worthy, and ethical bases for their actions. Transformational leaders tend to be innovative and even revolutionary.

• Leaders draw on different sources of power in order to carry out leadership activities. This power is derived either from the nature of the position the person occupies or from sources associated with the individual's personality, relationships, knowledge, or skill. French and Raven describe five bases of power: coercive power, reward power, legitimate power, expert power (or knowledge power), and referent power.

• Coercive power tends to be the least satisfying for followers and requires more effort and surveillance on the part of the leader. When the leader can demonstrate that coercive power is legitimately demanded by the situation, as in an emergency or crisis, however, it may be accepted and effective.

• The effective communication of reward power requires clear explanation of the association between the desired behavior and the reward. Herzberg's motivator-hygiene theory, as well as other studies of workplace motivation, suggests that rewards in themselves are insufficient for inducing high motivation, however. One communication task of a leader may be to convince others of the value of symbolic or nontangible rewards when material rewards are too costly or simply unavailable.

• Legitimate power is generally reinforced by the norms of the culture and the organization. A leader exercising this kind of power thus needs to refer to these sanctions. Unsupported by other bases for power, such as expertise, credibility, or warm relations with followers, this kind of power is not conducive to high levels of motivation over the long term.

• The exercise of expert power requires, first, communicating that one's expertise is especially relevant to the task at hand. The leader must persuade others that his or her knowledge is correct and useful. The notion of expert power also reminds us that power, like leadership, is situational. Someone lacking legitimate power in an organization can suddenly become very powerful when his or her skill becomes critical. Both expert power and referent power are reminiscent of the rhetorical prin-ciple of credibility, or *ethos*.

• Of the five types of power, referent power is probably the most dependent on communication for its expression and maintenance. In comparison to other forms, this kind of power takes more time to develop. In essence, referent power represents a kind of ethos or source credibility, based on one's reputation, attractiveness, or popularity. Exercis-ing referent power involves communicating accep-tance of and identification with followers. Its use often requires making personal appeals to follow-ers, and hence it can be overused and lose effec-tiveness.

When Robert L. Dilenschneider, president and chief executive officer of Hill and Knowlton, con-cludes, "Communications has become the number one aptitude of the CEO," he reinforces the link between communication and leadership.[47] This chapter has demonstrated that the exercise of lead-ership is an important aspect of organizational com-munication.

EXERCISES AND QUESTIONS FOR DISCUSSION

1. Make a list of people you admire as leaders. Share your list with others in your group. Do some of the same people appear on these differ-ent lists? Select those people that most of the group agree are good examples of leaders. Ex-plain what it is about each person that makes him or her an effective leader.

2. Why is it difficult to come to a single definition of leadership? List various synonyms or near synonyms that you can think of. What distinc-tions in the meaning of leadership can you find in these various possible synonyms?

3. How important are leaders in organizations? In giving attention to leaders, are we tending to personalize events and impersonal factors? To what extent can leaders make a difference? Does it depend on the nature of the organization? of the situation? of the environment?

4. Do you agree that there are personality traits that leaders must have in order to become ef-fective leaders in organizations? List the traits you think are essential for good leadership. As in Question 1, compare your list with others' and try to achieve a consensus regarding the necessary traits. Are these traits innate, or are they learned? If they are learned, how would this learning occur?

5. Have you experienced leaders exhibiting the three styles associated with the early leadership studies: authoritarian, democratic, and laissez-faire? If so, how does your experience fit with the generalizations concerning these styles made in the text?

6. Consider the contingency theories of leadership. Do the contingent factors referred to appear to represent all the substantial possibilities? What kinds of factors influence the kind of leadership required for different situations?

7. Does transformational leadership seem realis-tic to you in most of the organizations with which you are familiar? What would be poten-tial advantages and disadvantages of serving un-der a leader of this sort? If possible, refer to some of the popularized works, such as those by Bennis and Nanus listed in the Sources for Fur-ther Study below. Would you want to work with visionary leaders of the sort described? Why or why not?

8. Discuss the relationship between power, lead-ership, and communication. Describe tactics that a leader can use to communicate his or her special kind of power. What are the advantages and disadvantages of each of the types of power categorized by French and Raven?

SOURCES FOR FURTHER STUDY

Argyris, C. (1990). *Integrating the individual and the organization.* New Brunswick, N.J.: Transac-tion Publishers.

Bass, B. M. (1990). *Bass & Stogdill's handbook of leadership.* New York: The Free Press.

Bennis, W., and Nanus, B. (1985). *Leaders: The*

strategies for taking charge. New York: Harper & Row.

Blake, R. R., and McCanse, A. A. (1991). *Leadership dilemmas—grid solutions.* Houston: Gulf Publishing.

Buller, D. B., and Aune, R. K. (1992). The effects of speech rate similarity on compliance: Application of communication accommodation theory. *Western Journal of Speech Communication, 56,* 36–53.

Bullis, C. (1991). Communication practices as unobtrusive control: An observational study. *Communication Studies, 42,* 254–71.

Burns, J. M. (1978). *Leadership.* New York: Harper & Row.

Dahl, R. A. (1957). The concept of power. *Behavioral Science, 2,* 201–15.

Dilenschneider, R. L. (1990). *Power and influence: Mastering the art of persuasion.* New York: Prentice-Hall.

Eblen, A. L. (1987). Communication, leadership, and organizational commitment. *Central States Speech Journal, 38,* 181–95.

Etzioni, A. (1961). *A comparative analysis of complex organizations.* New York: The Free Press.

Fiedler, F. E. (1967). *A theory of leadership effectiveness.* New York: McGraw-Hill.

Frost, P. J. (1987). Power, politics, and influence. In F. M. Jablin, L. L. Putnam, K. H. Roberts, and L. W. Porter (Eds.), *Handbook of organizational communication: An interdisciplinary perspective.* Newbury Park, Calif.: Sage.

Hackman, M. Z., and Johnson, C. E. (1991). *Leadership: A communication perspective.* Prospect Heights, Ill.: Waveland Press.

Hersey, P., and Blanchard, K. (1982). *Management and organizational behavior.* Englewood Cliffs, N.J.: Prentice-Hall.

Kotter, J. P. (1985). *Power and influence.* New York: The Free Press.

Leavitt, H. J. (1986). *Corporate pathfinders.* Homewood, Ill.: Dow Jones-Irwin.

Lewin, K., Lippitt, R., and White, R. K. (1939). Patterns of aggressive behavior in experimentally created social climates. *Journal of Social Psychology, 10,* 271–99.

Mintzberg, H. (1973). *The nature of managerial work.* New York: HarperCollins.

Nanus, B. (1992). *Visionary leadership: Creating a compelling sense of direction for your organization.* San Francisco: Jossey-Bass.

Neustadt, R. E. (1980). *Presidential power: The politics of leadership from FDR to Carter.* New York: Macmillan.

O'Keefe, B. J., and McCornack, S. A. (1987). Message design logic and message goal structure: Effects on perceptions of message quality in regulative communication situations. *Human Communication Research, 14,* 68–92.

Schein, E. H. (1992). *Organizational culture and leadership,* 2d ed. San Francisco: Jossey-Bass.

Smith, P. B., and Peterson, M. F. (1988). *Leadership, organizations and culture: An event management model.* London: Sage.

Trice, H. M., and Beyer, J. M. (1993). *The cultures of work organizations.* Englewood Cliffs, N.J.: Prentice-Hall.

Wiseman, R. L., and Shuter, R. (1994) (Eds.). *Communicating in multinational organizations.* Thousand Oaks, Calif.: Sage.

Yukl, G. A. (1981). *Leadership in organizations.* Englewood Cliffs, N.J.: Prentice-Hall.

Zorn, T. E. (1991). Construct system development, transformational leadership and leadership messages. *Southern Communication Journal, 56,* 178–93.

Zorn, T. E., and Leichty, G. B. (1991). Leadership and identity: A reinterpretation of situational leadership theory. *Southern Communication Journal, 57,* 11–24.

NOTES

1. *The art of war, by Sun Tzu,* Ed. J. Clavell (1983), New York: Delacorte Press.
2. J. P. Kotter (1985), *Power and influence,* New York: The Free Press, p. 11.
3. B. M. Bass (1990), *Bass & Stogdill's handbook of leadership,* New York: The Free Press, p. 19; the ideas mentioned in this text are developed on pp. 19–20. This handbook developed originally from the work of Ralph

Stogdill, stretching back to the 1940s, when he began to compile information concerning the characteristics of leaders and leadership.

4. J. M. Burns (1978), *Leadership,* New York: Harper & Row, p. 19.

5. Bass, pp. 83–86.

6. Bass, p. 87; G. A. Yukl (1981), *Leadership in organizations.* Englewood Cliffs, N.J.: Prentice-Hall, p. 70.

7. R. Shuter and R. L. Wiseman (1994), *Communication in multinational organizations: Conceptual, theoretical, and practical issues,* in R. L.Wiseman and R. Shuter (Eds.), *Communicating in multinational organizations,* Thousand Oaks, Calif.: Sage, p. 4.

8. Yukl, pp. 72–73.

9. R. E. Neustadt (1980), *Presidential power: The politics of leadership from FDR to Carter,* New York: Macmillan.

10. K. Lewin, R. Lippitt, and R. K. White (1939), Patterns of aggressive behavior in experimentally created social climates, *Journal of Social Psychology, 10, 271–99.*

11. P. B. Smith and M. F. Peterson (1988), *Leadership, organizations and culture,* London: Sage, pp. 9–13, provides a useful summary of this research.

12. R. R. Blake and A. A. McCanse (1991), *Leadership dilemmas—grid solutions,* Houston: Gulf Publishing.

13. Blake and McCanse (1991), p. 3.

14. F. E. Fiedler (1967), *A theory of leadership effectiveness,* New York: McGraw-Hill.

15. Smith and Peterson, pp. 18–19.

16. P. Hersey and K. Blanchard (1982), *Management and organizational behavior,* Englewood Cliffs, N.J.: Prentice-Hall.

17. Yukl, pp. 143–44; Smith and Peterson, p. 23.

18. Burns, p. 20.

19. C. Argyris (1990), *Integrating the individual and the organization,* New Brunswick, N.J.: Transaction Publishers.

20. W. Bennis and B. Nanus (1985), *Leaders: The strategies for taking charge,* New York: Harper & Row; B. Nanus (1992), *Visionary leadership: Creating a compelling sense of direction for your organization,* San Francisco: Jossey-Bass.

21. Bennis and Nanus, p. 33.

22. H. J. Leavitt (1986), *Corporate pathfinders,* Homewood, Ill.: Dow Jones-Irwin.

23. Leavitt, p. 2.

24. H. M. Trice and J. M. Beyer (1993), *The cultures of work organizations,* Englewood Cliffs, N.J.: Prentice-Hall, p. 276.

25. Trice and Beyer, p. 287.

26. E. H. Schein (1992), *Organizational culture and leadership,* 2d ed., San Francisco: Jossey-Bass.

27. Schein, p. 383.

28. R. L. Dilenschneider (1990), *Power and influence: Mastering the art of persuasion,* New York: Prentice-Hall, p. 82.

29. R. A. Dahl (1957), The concept of power, *Behavioral Science, 2,* 201–15.

30. P. J. Frost (1987), Power, politics, and influence, in F. M. Jablin, L. L. Putnam, K. H. Roberts, and L. W. Porter (Eds.), *Handbook of organizational communication: An interdisciplinary perspective.* Newbury Park, Calif.: Sage, p. 507.

31. A. Etzioni (1961), *A comparative analysis of complex organizations,* New York: The Free Press.

32. Etzioni, p. 5.

33. J. R. P. French and B. Raven (1959), The bases of social power, in D. Cartwright (Ed.), *Studies in social power,* Ann Arbor: University of Michigan.

34. Bass, p. 233.

35. G. F. Dreher and R. A. Ash (1990), A comparative study among men and women in managerial, professional, and technical positions, *Journal of Applied Psychology, 75,* 539–46; W. Whitley, T. W. Dougherty, and G. F. Dreher (1991), Relationship of career mentoring and socioeconomic origin to managers' and professionals' early career progress, *Academy of Management Journal, 34,* 331–51.

36. G. Morgan (1986), *Images of organization,* Newbury Park, Calif.: Sage.

37. J. P. Kotter (1985), *Power and influence,* New York: The Free Press, pp. 17–22.

38. Morgan, p. 159.

39. Dilenschneider, pp. 19–20.

40. Morgan, p. 177.

41. G. Marwell and D. R. Schmitt (1967), Dimensions of compliance-gaining behavior: An empirical analysis, *Sociometry, 30,* 350–64.

42. K. Kellerman and T. Cole (1994), Classifying compliance gaining messages: Taxonomic disorder and strategic confusion, *Communication Theory, 4,* 3.

43. Kellerman and Cole, pp. 7–12.

44. G. Johnson (1992), Subordinate perceptions of superior's communication competence and task attraction related to superior's use of compliance-gaining tactics, *Western Journal of Communication, 56,* 54–67.

45. J. P. Dillard and J. L. Hale (1992), Prosocialness and sequential request compliance techniques: Limits to the Foot-in-the-door and the Door-in-the-face? *Communication Studies, 43,* 220–32.

46. R. Y. Hirokawa, J. Mickey, and S. Miura (1991), Effects of request legitimacy on the compliance-gaining tactics of male and female managers, *Communication Monographs, 58,* 422–23.

47. Dilenschneider.

CHAPTER 11

Decision-Making Teams and Groups

CHAPTER OBJECTIVES

After studying this chapter, you should be able to:

- Explain the problems with the rational actor model of decision making.
- Describe factors leading to bounded rationality and satisficing.
- Define and explain the effects of simplified decision heuristics.
- Describe the effects of framing on problem solving and decision making.
- Explain groupthink and bolstering as barriers to effective group decision making.
- Describe factors in selecting decision strategies.
- Describe the process of vigilant problem solving.
- Discuss methods for dealing effectively with group conflict.

CHAPTER OUTLINE

The Nature of Decision Making

Importance of Team Building and Group Communication

Decision Making in Organizations
    The Limits on Rational Decision Making
    Simplified Decision Rules
    Groupthink
    Bolstering
    Review of Simplified Decision Rules
    Power and Politics in Decision Making
    Highlights of Problems of Decision Making

Factors in Selecting a Decision Strategy

Decision-Making Systems
    Vigilant Decision Making

THE NATURE OF DECISION MAKING

Communication is an important element in organizational decision making that is often overlooked.[1] At each stage of a typical decision-making process in an organization, communication is essential. Decision making requires an ability to work with other people to develop understanding of a problem, to formulate the issues involved, and to predict possible outcomes. Implementing a decision, especially inducing others to carry it out, obviously requires communication as well. As organizations increasingly turn to programs of participative decision making in efforts to decentralize authority and empower organizational members, the widespread use of quality teams emphasizes skills in group communication.

IMPORTANCE OF TEAM BUILDING AND GROUP COMMUNICATION

Team building is becoming an important goal in modern organizations.[2] Charles Manz and Henry P. Sims, in the 1993 book *Business Without Bosses,* point out, "Today teams are often seen as a critical element to a total quality management (TQM) program."[3] Boeing Company of Seattle, Washington, embarked on a concerted Continuous Quality Improvement (CQI) program based on team building beginning in the 1980s. In

Boeing has embarked on a special program to improve organizational culture and communication.

1992, the company redoubled efforts to become a "world-class corporation" through the CQI program. This program emphasizes team building in decision making and ensuring quality at all levels of production.

Team building and CQI at Boeing are seen as more than merely the application of certain methods and techniques. The intent is to achieve a real change in organizational culture. As one Boeing document put it, "CQI represents a significant cultural change and shift in the fundamental philosophy of doing business. We will achieve the mindset required to attain world-class quality when we begin to believe that perfection is possible."[4] To achieve such cultural and philosophical changes, the company relies on the development of team leadership and team-building skills.

Boeing holds that there are five critical areas of decision making requiring team involvement:[5]

1. In preparing a mission statement, people use consensus to create a vision that is intended to unify the group and guide the actions of each group member.
2. In making day-to-day decisions concerning how the work will be performed, team involvement is needed.

3. In implementing process improvement, changes are to be made in a team environment.
4. In problem solving, involvement is essential so that everyone will feel committed to carrying out solutions.
5. In implementing organizational change, participation by all involved is seen as vital.

Team interaction should be conducted in "an open and supportive environment," in which "everyone is expected and encouraged to do, discuss, and say what they believe to be right regardless of the person they are speaking to, the subject they are discussing, or the 'politics' of the situation."[6] Kimball Fisher reports on the effects of this effort: "Boeing 777 design teams are another example of empowered teams being used to improve the speed and quality of product delivery."[7] And the *Seattle Times* has pointed to the use of teams in the development of the 777 as an example of a major corporate cultural change at Boeing.[8]

Furthermore, Boeing maintains that reliance on group or team management requires skillful group leadership, meaning that understanding of the dynamics of group communication is essential. An analysis of several case studies focusing on self-directed work teams similarly reports, "While technical expertise is useful and appropriate (especially to establish baseline credibility), the social skills of the coordinator seem to be much more critical."[9] The implication is that technical skill is not enough; communication skills are necessary in equal or even greater measure.

In a similar vein, Robert Waterman has popularized the term *adhocracy* in management circles as an organizational response to changing organizational demands.[10] The basis for "managing adhocracy," Waterman believes, lies in the formation and utilization of ad hoc project teams and task forces. The four attributes of well-run ad hoc teams are as follows:[11]

- They cut across conventional lines and boundaries, bringing together individuals who might not otherwise communicate regularly given the nominal structure of the organization.
- They require broad participation in order to facilitate implementation of solutions and decisions.
- Participants become advocates of change, because of their involvement in decision making throughout the process.
- They are characterized by authentic teamwork.

These principles echo Boeing's team-building approach, in that team building highlights process skills as being "as important as knowledge of the problem under scrutiny," Waterman argues.[12] This emphasis indicates a growing awareness of the centrality of effective group communication in organizational life.

Central to the team approach is the notion that an individual's responsibility is defined in terms of team or group responsibility: The individual's basic responsibility is to recognize what action needs to be taken at any given time to meet team objectives and goals, regardless of the individual's job title or classification. For example, in modern hospitals, floors and wings of patient rooms are assigned to teams of nurses, medical technicians, respiratory therapists, pharmacists, and supervisors. Rather than any one nurse or therapist being responsible for a specific room or patient, team members are expected to pitch in and help one another to provide whatever care is required. The team meets regularly to plan their shifts and to evaluate their performance. All team members are equally responsible for the quality of care in the team's unit.

The emphasis on teams leads to the designation of group leaders as team builders. One management text suggests the term *superleaders,* who encourage others to learn how to lead themselves.[13] In a sense, team builders are intended to serve more as trainers or facilitators of group processes than as traditional chairpersons or supervisors. Team leaders are therefore evaluated in terms of how well they succeed in developing leadership behavior on the part of other group members.

Finally, a note of caution regarding enthusiasm about organizational teams may be in order. While the team concept is often presented as a program for empowering workers, Gareth Morgan provides an alternative view. In the early stages of industrialization in this country, he points out, assembly lines, although intended to enhance the power and control of management, contributed to the power of workers.[14] Standardized procedures led workers to see their common interests and similarities; the sequential nature of the line meant that concerted action by the workers could shut down the entire operation. The move to autonomous teams can have the effect of reducing the power of collective groups of workers in that teams lead to a fragmentation of concerns and interests.

The first section of this chapter describes and analyzes some of the major problems encountered in organizational decision making. First, the "rational actor" model of decision making does not describe the real world of decision making, in which real-life limitations often detract from high-quality decisions. The second section discusses the factors affecting group decision situations, calling for differing levels of effort, or vigilance, in making effective decisions. Group decision making in complex organizations involves conflict of various sorts, and so issues of communicating in conflict situations are important. Finally, we turn to questions raised by the growing use of computerized and media technologies by decision-making groups.

DECISION MAKING IN ORGANIZATIONS

Despite the huge amount of scholarly attention and a significant popular literature on decision making, the feeling remains that much decision making in modern organizations is haphazard and flawed. Decisions are made without careful analysis of the problem, all potential alternatives, or all relevant data bearing on the decision. Many decisions are the result of "top-of-the-head" intuitions or in response to political or personal pressures within the organizations.[15] While there are many prescriptions available for rational problem solving, they are often not applied in the real, everyday world. Understanding the problems limiting systematic approaches to decision making begin with an analysis of the limitations of the notion of the "rational actor."

The Limits on Rational Decision Making

The so-called rational actor model of decision making is derived mainly from economic theory. This model assumes that when faced with a need to make a decision, an individual or a group systematically analyzes the alternatives and then selects the course of action resulting in the greatest utility, or good. In theory, the selection of a decision is thus relatively simple and apparent: The decision resulting in the greatest subjective expected utility (SEU) is selected. The SEU model is based on the concept of how an ideal market works. In such a market, buyers and sellers are fully aware of all prices, levels of supply, needs, and so on, and buyers and sellers therefore make buying or selling decisions that will maximize their returns. Such a situation is, obviously, an *ideal* one that is not often encountered in real life.

The rational actor, or SEU, model assumes that it is possible to lay out and quantify the values of all potential alternatives. A typical decision process following this sort of model would set forth the steps or stages in decision making as follows:[16]

1. Define the problem, gathering data and searching the relevant literature.
2. Identify the alternatives, making a list of solutions that meet certain predefined criteria and the desired goals and outcomes of the individual or group.
3. Quantify alternatives, including risks or potential costs and, short-range and long-range benefits.
4. Apply decision aids, possibly including decision grids or trees, programmed models, or the like.
5. Make the decision, that is, select one of the alternatives.
6. Implement the selected alternative.

This model can rarely be applied to real decision situations that organizational members typically face. This difficulty has been analyzed by the decision theory group of organizational theorists associated with Carnegie-Mellon University (formerly Carnegie Institute of Technology). This school, under the leadership of Herbert A. Simon, maintains that administrative or organizational decision makers do not have sufficient time and information available to them to follow the SEU model. Not only that, organizations, unlike individuals, are social complexes in which there are conflicting views regarding each stage in the prescribed process.

First, the process begins with establishing goals and objectives, but consider the problem of defining these goals. Typical complex organizations comprise factions or groups who disagree concerning the organization's goals, purposes, and desired outcomes. In a university, for example, the faculty may see the main goals of the organization in terms of teaching and research, whereas the business office may see goals in terms of income and expenses. Furthermore, the goals of an organization are not always quantifiable. How does one quantify the goals of a church or of a university?

Different factions may emphasize short-term or long-term goals and objectives, further complicating the search for organizational goals. For example, some managers of a firm may emphasize quarterly profits and immediate gains in stock values, whereas others may be more concerned about long-term investment in research and development, which could delay profits to later quarters or years. Lack of agreement on the relative importance of these goals could obviously lead to different weightings of expected outcomes.

Hence, decision theorists remind us, "Organizations are social constructs made up of the interaction of individuals and groups holding a variety of ideas (beliefs and values), which may be very difficult to define and harder to predict."[17] The point is that organizational decision making requires a balancing and negotiating among competing views and priorities represented by different parties and groups.

Second, it is rare for all the information required for a completely rational decision to be available or even obtainable. In real organizations, managers are under pressure to make decisions quickly and to make more than one decision at a time. The number of possible alternatives is too big and the amount of data that are possibly relevant, too vast for any one person or group to consider them all, especially given time constraints.[18] The widespread use of computers to generate data and information has contributed to information overload and made it even more difficult for organizational decision makers to study carefully all the data and all the ramifications.

In place of maximizing or optimizing decisions, Simon and his colleagues at Carnegie-Mellon contend, decision makers engage in satisficing, which means searching only until a minimally satisfactory solution appears and then accepting it. The notion of satisficing is part of what Simon refers to as *bounded rationality,* which means that the rationality we can apply in real-life organizational settings is not unlimited or ideal but is limited, or "bounded."

Some decisions that need to be made in an organization are fairly routine and straightforward. These situations call for *programmed decision making,* in which one simply applies certain well-known rules to a situation; the typical troubleshooting case is an example. For instance, if an appliance does not work, the first rule is to check to see if its electric cord is plugged into an outlet. A set of step-by-step procedures of the "if this, then try that" variety then follow. The Internal Revenue Service, for example, uses a programmed method of selecting returns for audit, based on factors such as level of charitable deductions, unusual expense claims, and the like (in addition to randomly selected returns).

Unprogrammed decisions are those for which there is no set of preexisting guidelines to follow; the problem is new or complex or little understood. Perhaps the organization lacks sufficient experience with this kind of problem to have worked out a set of simple decision rules to deal with it. Unprogrammed decisions are often more subject to satisficing, which means that groups do not employ a fully rational scheme for problem solving as assumed in the rational actor model.

Finally, the range of potential alternative decisions actually considered may be predetermined by the nature of the organization itself. Marketing organizations, for example, will usually come up with solutions that involve marketing; educational institutions will most likely come up with solutions involving teaching or curricular changes. The organizational culture and history similarly constrain searches for data and alternatives.

In other words, decision makers strive to use methodical, rational forms of decision making, but their rationality has real-life limits. The result is a rough-and-ready kind of intuitive decision making that may or may not be appropriate for a given problem. The next section takes up the kinds of rules and processes that often underlie this sort of real-life group decision making.

Simplified Decision Rules

Heuristics are decision rules or guidelines that people carry around in their heads to simplify or rationalize decisions. For example, a recruiter who decides that she will hire the next interviewee who does not bring up the issue of salary is employing a simple (if ill-advised) decision heuristic. Heuristics, then, are essentially rules of thumb that are used routinely, usually without conscious reflection. Like individuals, groups frequently adopt heuristics for their decision making, and these heuristics can become habitual patterns for them. Often, such simple decision rules are quite adequate for routine or relatively insignificant policy decisions, but problems ensue when more important decisions are also subject to simplifying rules.

Heuristics usually depend on the *framing* of a problem in a particular way, meaning that the problem is perceived in a specific context and presented as having particular characteristics. For example, a decision situation can be framed in terms of emphasizing the losses that may be incurred or the gains that can be realized. Two psychologists, Amos Tversky and Daniel Kahneman, have extensively researched these effects on how people perceive decision situations.[19]

The following case is typical of several examples that they have used in their studies of the effects of framing on decision making.[20]

> Case: An anticipated flu epidemic is expected to kill 600 people; two programs have been proposed to deal with it.
>
> If Program A is adopted, 200 people will be saved;
>
> If Program B is adopted, there is a one-third probability that 600 people will be saved, but a two-thirds probability that no people will be saved.

When the problem is worded this way, a majority of people favor the first decision; that is, most people given this frame are *risk-averse*, which means that they select the sure prospect of saving 200 lives over the risky proposition of a one-third chance of saving all lives. On the other hand, when the case is presented in the following manner, most people shift their choices:

> Case: The same anticipated flu epidemic as above; two programs have been proposed.
>
> If Program C is adopted, 400 people will die; but,
>
> If Program D is adopted, there is a one-third probability that nobody will die, and a two-thirds probability that 600 will die.

Faced with the sure prospect that 400 people will die under Program C, a majority of people prefer the solution in Program D, which is identical with Program B, which a majority reject when the first wording of the problem is used. When the losses were emphasized, people were risk-seeking. Tversky and Kahneman go on to point out that these results are consistent for different kinds of groups and professions: "We have observed this reversal in several groups of respondents, including university faculty and physicians."[21]

These findings have very significant implications for organizational communication. The manner in which a problem is framed, or communicated, can bias the choices people make.

Other types of framing heuristics are the availability heuristic, analogizing, and the nutshell briefing rule. The *availability heuristic* depends on the presentation of a reference point or alternatives, so that certain probabilities or outcomes are made available to the decision makers—that is, they are brought to their attention.

Consider the case of having a salient reference point. Tversky and Kahneman report that if given the choice of driving across town 20 minutes to save $5 on the cost of a store item (a jacket or calculator), people respond differently when the $5 saving is on an initial price of $15 or $125. People are more likely to drive 20 minutes to save $5 on a $15 item than on a $125 item.[22] The actual saving in either case is exactly the same. In a similar experiment, people were told that they are going to a theater to see a play for $10 admission; upon arriving at the theater, they discover that they have lost a $10 bill. Would they still pay the $10 admission for the play? Although 88 percent said yes to the question when it was framed this way, when told that what they had lost was a prepurchased $10 ticket for the play, only 46 percent said that they would buy another ticket for $10.[23] Again the total cost was $20 regardless of the way the problem was worded. Making a kind of reference point available, in other words, changed the way people made their decision.

In addition, the *number of alternatives* made available or salient for decision makers tends to alter their responses. When more alternatives are suggested, people are more likely to consider a wider range of solutions. Otherwise, decision makers usually restrict themselves to a few readily available solutions. In a celebrated murder trial of several years ago, a jury was unable to agree on whether the verdict should be first-degree murder, second-degree murder, voluntary manslaughter, involuntary manslaughter, and so on. Even though they agreed on the defendant's guilt, their failure to settle on the degree of guilt resulted in a hung jury. In this case, the range of available decisions overwhelmed their decision-making powers.

Similar to the availability heuristic is the decision rule that Irving Janis calls *analogizing*.[24] In such a case, when no readily available standard operating procedure comes to mind, decision makers search their memories for a well-known analogy that appears to fit the current circumstances. For example, the Truman administration interpreted North Korea's apparent invasion of South Korea in terms of the analogy of Hitler's invasions of Czechoslovakia and Poland. The Kennedy and Johnson administrations used the same analogy for interpreting the events in South Vietnam in the early 1960s. The analogies suggested the decision to be made in each case: major military operations against the perceived aggressor. Decision makers are often swayed by recent, catchy, or especially memorable analogies, whether these are actually appropriate or not.

Similarly, decision makers may seek out *adages* or *aphorisms* that seem to fit the circumstances of the current problem. Typical adages used to make decisions include,

"If it ain't broke, don't fix it," and "Let sleeping dogs lie." Occasionally, the adages available may be inconsistent, as is the case with the sayings, "Look before you leap" and "A stitch in time saves nine" or "He who hesitates is lost."

The analogy or adage thus made salient often depends on the organizational culture. Some organizational cultures favor more risk-taking approaches, and hence the available adages will favor such approaches ("A stitch in time"). In more risk-averse, process-oriented cultures, the available sayings and analogies will usually support more cautious decisions ("Look before you leap" or "If it ain't broke, don't fix it").

Janis discerned the *nutshell briefing rule,* which is widely employed in decision making concerning United States foreign policy.[25] In this situation, the group asks a subcommittee or task force, presumably well informed, to boil down the facts and considerations in a complex problem to a one-page memo, to sum it all up "in a nutshell." The danger of relying on such memos or briefings arises when they become the sum total of the information considered in the decision-making process. The complexity and information overload associated with many modern policy issues explains the power of lobbyists in Congress and other legislatures: The lobbyists put things "in a nutshell" for overworked legislators. Essentially, the decision makers have delegated the responsibility for making the decision to those who provide the summary and its interpretation of the problem.[26]

Again, note the impact that communication has on the process of organizational decision making. The way in which a problem is framed, the analogies brought to the attention of decision makers, or the summary in nutshell briefings biases the problem-solving process. Janis points out that relying on these heuristics "might generally work out well when an executive is making routine choices or dealing with minor policy issues."[27] They are not always bad, in other words, but they are inappropriate when a group is dealing with important, complex problems.

Some decision rules do not even have the quasi-rational appearance of the decision heuristics just discussed. One example is the *avoid punishment* rule.[28] In these cases, elements extraneous to the specific issues of a problem become more important than the actual substantive issues confronting decision makers. The first step in this process is to find out whether a powerful person in the organization already desires a certain solution. Someone applying the avoid punishment rule then short-circuits the rest of the rational problem-solving process and searches for information supporting this desired result. Note that the process is equally subverted whether the decision maker's perception of the powerful person's preferences is correct or not. The author has seen a group paralyzed into inaction because it could not agree on what powerful authorities in the organization "really wanted."

A variation on the avoid punishment rule involves the fear that if one disagrees with powerful others, one will "lose effectiveness" in future discussions. A reason often given by policy makers for going along with decisions to escalate American involvement in Vietnam, even when they personally disagreed with that policy, was the fear that they would be thought of as "soft" and lose any influence over other aspects of the policy. The organizational culture and the history of leadership actions can affect perceptions leading to the use of the avoid punishment or lose effectiveness rule. If there is a history of people being punished for making the wrong decision, such rules may come into play.

Groupthink

Groupthink occurs when members of a group or team or department place a higher value on their harmony and personal relationships than on achieving high-quality decisions.[29] If a group is very attractive to members and they obtain desired social support from it, there is a temptation to go along with group decisions rather than to risk controversy by challenging other members' assumptions or facts. Whereas the avoid punishment rule is concerned with the fear of retaliation, groupthink is concerned with maintaining the benefits that members derive from their group membership.

Cohesiveness, conformity, and deviance are closely related patterns in group communication that can be linked to groupthink. A *cohesive* group is one that "sticks together," to rely on the root meaning of the word. Individual members are strongly attracted to the group and derive a great deal of satisfaction from their membership. *Conformity* is the extent to which all group members go along with the norms and decisions of the group as a whole. As a group develops its norms and rules of interaction, it will exert pressure on individual members to conform to these norms and rules. *Deviance* occurs when members do not go along with a particular norm or decision of the group. Typically, the dissenter or deviate receives a lot of communication from the other members, as they try to induce him or her to conform. If they are not successful, they may reduce or eliminate their communication with the deviate after a time; the deviate thus becomes an isolate or nonparticipating member.

The pressure for conformity may weigh differently on individual members, depending on other factors. High-status individuals, who occupy positions of leadership, may be given more leeway than other members. Similarly, deviates and isolates may also not be expected to follow group norms as closely. When representing the group to other constituencies outside the context of a group meeting, however, leaders or group representatives may feel the pressure of group norms even more strongly.

Successful groups tend to be highly satisfying to their members; there is a strong "team feeling," or sense of cohesiveness. Hence, many organizations encourage being a "team player." But too much group conformity can be a dangerous thing. An overly cohesive group may put positive group feelings ahead of successful completion of the task. To be effective, groups must balance the competing needs of task achievement and social relationships.

Groupthink arises when a group insulates itself from outside criticism, and there is pressure within the group to create and reinforce a sense of group unanimity and agreement. Because members value their membership in the group highly, each member is reluctant to call attention to shortcomings in the group's problem-solving process. As a result, groups experiencing groupthink tend not to analyze the problem fully or to consider all options carefully. Potential pitfalls in proposed solutions are discounted or ignored, as is the likelihood of resistance or opposition from other groups in the larger organization. The appearance of group cohesiveness hence takes precedence over task-related communication intended to enhance rational decision making.

Groupthink results when certain structural and cultural factors are characteristic of an organization. Some of the major characteristics include the group's having the ability to insulate itself from internal criticism, perhaps because of the power or prestige of its members, or an organizational culture that lacks norms for systematic problem-solving procedures. Symptoms of groupthink include intragroup communication that reinforces an image of the group's special expertise or inherent wisdom while derogating or stereotyping other groups. The group also tends to put pressure on members in order to create the illusion of unanimity and harmony. As a result of these tendencies, groups suffering from groupthink omit relevant information or evidence from consideration, fail to examine all options or resist reconsidering options originally rejected, and fail to examine all potential risks and contingencies.

Groups may be subject to other sorts of simplified decision rules as well. Group members may want to exhibit high morale or confidence, for instance, leading them to be overly confident about making risky decisions. This tendency may in part explain the phenomenon of *risky shift,* a preference for groups to shift toward decisions that are more risky than the decisions that individual members would generally make on their own. Janis refers to this tendency as the "can do" or audacity decision rule.[30] Groups may urge members to take actions that they might not undertake upon cool reflection if they were left to their own devices. Thus the members of some teams involved in bargaining urge one another to take a strong "all-or-nothing" stand, although a more conciliatory position might be more appropriate. Positive enthusiasm for a solution that suddenly appears out of nowhere may lead to an equally sudden decision, made without thinking through all ramifications, especially if the group feels under time pressure.

Bolstering

An additional problem in organizational decision making results from efforts to seek out information or reasons to justify a decision resulting from an inadequate problem-solving process. Leon Festinger's theory of cognitive dissonance posits a tendency toward "bolstering" in order to rationalize decisions after making them. A major application of Festinger's theory deals with postdecision situations in which the decision maker tries to reduce possible dissonance by seeking out information that specifically supports the decision that was made while avoiding evidence that supports options that were not selected.

Cognitive dissonance theory holds that the tendency toward bolstering is especially pronounced in situations in which the decision has been complex, difficult, or uncertain, as when two alternatives are very similar. Studies of decision making in organizations suggest that such bolstering not only occurs in postdecision situations, to support a decision once it has been made, but also occurs during the processes, to bolster or support the steps in the process being used to reach a decision.[31]

At some stage in the decision-making process, a group may decide that, for some reason, they no longer wish to search for more data or alternatives. At that point, they may begin to bolster an interim decision to limit the search for more information or alternatives. Group members may say to one another, "We've spent enough time (or 'wasted' enough time) on this already—it's time to make a decision." Bolstering occurs when they look for rationalizations to support the notion that "enough time" has indeed been spent. Within departments or work groups, one can see how this kind of interpersonal communication can lead to such predecisional bolstering. Deciding that it is time to "fish or cut bait" can even lead decision makers to search for information that will make an undesirable option look less unattractive ("Well, maybe it's not as bad as we thought at first").

Such bolstering can take several forms, often involving wishful thinking.[32] First, the group might exaggerate possible favorable consequences and minimize potentially unfavorable ones. For example, people rationalize taking on a burdensome assignment by playing up the prestige or influence to be gained, while hoping that some of the work can be delegated to others. Or, people may emphasize the remoteness of the consequences, which may be postponed until later. Of course, people can redefine possible bad effects as good effects, as when people decide to procrastinate on an important project by claiming that they work better under pressure and relish the challenge.

Janis and Mann give several historical examples of decision makers engaging in bolstering to avoid a more involved, complex problem-solving process. For instance, the naval commander at Pearl Harbor in December 1941, Admiral Kimmel, received several fairly explicit warnings of the danger of a Japanese attack, but he and his staff found ways to interpret the repeated warnings that allowed them to assure themselves that the danger was not imminent. Their discussions tended to bolster less threatening interpretations of the intelligence and their decision not to take significant precautions.[33]

Cognitive dissonance can thus make it difficult to correct some of the problems of decision making described above. For example, after a decision has been made in accordance with simplified heuristic or groupthink decision rules, the decision makers look for evidence and arguments to support, or bolster, their decision. Bolstering in order to reduce cognitive dissonance can in this way reinforce an inadequate problem-solving procedure.

Review of Simplified Decision Rules

In summary, the possible reliance on heuristics and emotional decision rules can derail sequential and systematic problem-solving processes. The application of one rule early on, such as the avoid punishment rule, can cut short the route to the best decision. One step may set off a train of thought or discussion that bypasses a more rationally defensible process. Groupthink can cause problems at various points in the decision-making process as the group avoids potential disharmony or conflict by smoothing over possible points of opposition or dissent.

Power and Politics in Decision Making

Complex organizations are no longer thought of as single-motive collectives, in which all members share the same goals and objectives. In universities, as we have seen, the goals of the faculty are seldom identical to the goals of administrators in the school's business office or admissions office or athletics office. In industrial organizations, labor and management often disagree over fundamental matters. And, managers from different divisions of the same corporation often do not share the same objectives when it comes to decisions about production or budget allocations (especially those concerning which division is to produce what and get how much budget). Decisions in these circumstances are not made by a single decision maker who coolly weighs the quantifiable factors and performs systematic calculations. Rather, decisions are the result of the interplay of power and influence among competing internal interests and groups.

Decisions resulting from the influences of power and organizational politics are not necessarily unwise or flawed decisions. The point here is that unrestrained or ineffectively managed conflict and political maneuvering can detract from optimal decision-making processes. When politics are pursued mainly for personal interests or those of a self-interested group, decisions may be based on inappropriate considerations. Turf battles are a good example of how an emotional decision heuristic can enter into a problem-solving process: One group vows to fight a particular decision for no other reason than that it appears to favor a rival group. Typically, bolstering can be expected, as "rational" reasons are sought to reinforce an alternative that favors one faction over another.

The role and function of conflict management is further considered later in this chapter.

Highlights of Problems of Decision Making

The realities of time constraints, information loads, and complexity mean that decision makers in organizations must often follow simplified decision-making processes, satisficing instead of optimizing. These processes rely on the prepackaging of information and on decision rules as simplifying strategies. Occasionally, these decision rules become questionable, as when decisions are based on stereotypes, personal biases, rumor, and simple appeals to authority or to supposed expert opinion, or when institutional politics take priority.

Recall the case of the launch leading to the explosion of the space shuttle *Challenger*. Many of the flaws that can affect important decisions were present in that case, as the presidential review panel discovered. The pressures of time (perceived by the NASA executives) and the complexity of the available data to be considered in that short time represent the kinds of pressures and complexity that affect organizational decision makers.

The *framing* of the problem and alternative solutions led to a reversal of the usual burden of proof in such launch decisions: The engineers were placed in the position of trying to prove that the shuttle would explode rather than the proponents of launching having to prove that it was safe to do so. The many previous successful launches undoubtedly led to a feeling of invulnerability or superiority often characteristic of *groupthink*, and the in-group of managers felt themselves to be in a better position to make the decision than the engineers. Also, the final decision makers at NASA were insulated from the concerns and even strong objections that had been voiced by the Thiokol engineers. As noted previously, flawed decision making is often marked by *bolstering* and a tendency to cut the discussion and get on with it, as when NASA executives complained, "Well, when do you want to me launch, in April?"

FACTORS IN SELECTING A DECISION STRATEGY

Of course, not every decision requires highly vigilant and careful decision making. Given the demands on time and information overload in modern organizations, one must set priorities to determine which problems require heroic efforts and which do not. Distinguishing among types of decision situations may be as important as knowing how to apply effective and rational decision-making processes. Factors that often distinguish decision situations include the following:

• *Importance.* Some problems are more important than others. One temptation facing organizational decision makers is to focus on problems that can be dealt with quickly and easily, while putting off more difficult but more important ones. A less important but well-understood problem often offers better prospects for success and perceived achievement.

• *Routine versus nonroutine problems.* Presumably routine problems call for a programmed response, but occasionally a group tries to make a nonroutine problem conform to a routine one in order to simplify decision making. Confusing nonroutine problems with routine ones is typically a mark of *analogizing,* or searching for a familiar problem that superficially resembles a current but nonroutine one.

• *Uncertainty.* The outcomes of some decisions are more difficult to predict than the outcomes of others. A rapidly changing environment, with turbulent or unclear information and inconsistent messages, contributes to such uncertainty. Framing of the problems by emphasizing potential gains or losses can threaten problem solving in these circumstances.

Furthermore, uncertain information tends to lose its perceived uncertainty as it moves from one point in the organization to the next. What began as someone's estimate or projection (or guess) becomes certain information or fact as it reaches other parts of the organization, where the tentative nature of an original estimate is no longer realized.

• *Risk.* Some kinds of uncertainty involve trivial or insignificant differences in outcomes, and groups tend not to worry about this kind of nonrisky uncertainty. Risk coupled with uncertainty is more threatening. In the face of threat, decision makers may be tempted to fall back on simple rules that seem familiar or habitual. The avoid punishment rule may become significant when decision makers face risky decision situations.

• *Time factors and limits.* Executives and similar decision makers work in fragmented and pressure-filled conditions. Several problems may be competing for a group's attention simultaneously, and deadlines are a real factor. The amount of time available to devote to a problem-solving process can thus limit that process's thoroughness.

• *Information availability, load, and turbulence*. Information needed for making a decision often comes with many different limitations: First, there is not enough available; or, second, there is too much available (overload); or, third, what is available appears to be complex, inconsistent, or continually changing in meaning (turbulence). Problems of information may therefore call for a group's exercising special care and vigilance in working through a problem.

• *Organizational culture*. The culture of the organization may direct a group's attention to certain problems and deemphasize others. Problems directly related to the organization's product or service are naturally more readily obvious than others. The climate may be conducive to open questioning of authorities or may incline toward groupthink or the avoid punishment rule.

• *Personality, cognitive styles, and information-processing ability*. Various personality factors may also determine how people handle problem-solving situations. Some people (or cultures) may have more tolerance for ambiguity and uncertainty than others, for example. Such tolerance for ambiguity may allow for a more relaxed approach to risky and uncertain problem situations.

Combinations of these factors influence the nature of group decision-making processes in organizations. The mix of circumstances, organizational culture and practices, and individual tendencies leads to the selection of a variety of decision-making approaches. It is thus not always possible to predict on the basis of only one type of factor the kind of process that will be initiated. In general, more important decisions, dealing with nonroutine problems with high degrees of risk or uncertainty, elicit careful problem-solving processes. But the organizational culture, climate, and individual personalities may lead to other approaches under these same circumstances.

DECISION-MAKING SYSTEMS

The typical model for rational decision making on page 251 lists the steps that are usually recommended for a systematic problem-solving process.

Systems of this sort provide a *checklist* for decision makers. Such a system represents a program for problem solving and decision making. Several real-world problems, as discussed above, prevent the simple application of this type of quantitative, programmed decision making in many instances. Nonetheless, the rational model represents an ideal when factors indicate that an organization is facing a highly consequential decision. Several other systems have been developed to meet the ideals of a rational model while recognizing the constraints of real-world situations.

Vigilant Decision Making

Irving Janis's *vigilant* process involves four steps.[34] One moves back and forth among the four steps while working through a problem; in other words, the four steps may be taken sequentially, but a wise decision maker is prepared to return to earlier steps to ensure a thorough analysis.

The four steps include the following:

1. *Formulate the problem.* The management guru Peter F. Drucker believes this step to be crucial in the process. Drucker takes issue with the admonition to "get the facts" at the beginning stage, because, he points out, "There are no facts unless one has a criterion of relevance. Events by themselves are not facts."[35]

The first part of formulating the problem, then, deals with determining the *requirements for a good solution,* the criteria for evaluating the problem and possible solutions. Groups thus begin with questions concerning what dangers are to be avoided, what costs are to be minimized, or what possible gains will be lost if the problem is not solved.

After completing the first step, decision makers should have a good idea about the importance of the decision and the necessity of proceeding with a painstaking analysis or applying a simpler or programmed approach.

2. *Scan available data or seek new information.* Like Drucker, Janis recommends that data gathering follow careful analysis of the criteria or requirements for a good solution. Relevant information may already be available in the organization. Other units of the organization may have dealt with this or a similar problem before: Can these resources be applied in the present situation? Organizations can have short or long memories, because of the pace of personnel turnover or the corporate culture. Long institutional memories are required for finding information regarding past experiences with similar problems.

After looking at existing information, decision makers determine what new information is needed. This research stage depends on the earlier steps. The search for new information should be guided by the analysis of criteria, possible directions a decision might take, and a survey of existing knowledge bearing on the issue.

3. *Analyze and reformulate the problem.* Possibly the information gathered in the second step has indicated that the original criteria formulated in Step 1 need to be refined. Research may also suggest alternative directions for a solution not thought of in the first place. The search for information can disclose that there are yet more data out there that need to be obtained before going further.

The analysis at this stage may lead the decision maker to go back to Step 1 or 2 or both. This *recursive* nature of problem solving is a central element in Janis's approach.

4. *Evaluate possible solutions and select one.* This stage requires careful consideration of the benefits and costs of each alternative in an effort to select what appears to be the best solution. Groups ask whether any criteria or requirements for a good solution are left unmet by this choice. What are the costs and risks associated with the preferred choice? Finally, one should determine whether there is a need for additional plans for implementing and monitoring the solution. In this stage, the decision maker needs to lay out the contingencies that could cause deviations from the proposed plan; how will these contingencies be dealt with? For example, can one anticipate strong opposition to the plan? If so, how is that opposition to be handled or answered? This stage further requires that decision makers plan for ways to evaluate the results of the decision; how can they demonstrate that it has worked and has met the requirements or criteria established in the first place?

Following these steps does not necessarily guarantee vigilant problem solving unless some of the usual defects of flawed processes are absent. These defects include major omissions of important objectives or criteria or failure to consider all possible alternatives; grossly incomplete data gathering, looking only for certain kinds of information, or selectively choosing information that bolsters a preferred solution; and failure to reconsider alternatives that were earlier rejected or set aside, failure to examine the risks and costs of the proposed solution, or failure to work out steps for implementing or evaluating the solution or dealing with contingencies.

Drucker reinforces these principles and emphasizes that dissent and disagreement are vital signs of effective problem solving, vital signs that are suppressed in groupthink or in defensive decision making. As he puts it, "Decisions of the kind the executive has to make are not made well by acclamation."[36] Challenging one's preconceptions necessitates well-reasoned and documented support for those preconceptions or, perhaps more importantly, reveals the absence of such support. Drucker maintains that in many cases, only disagreement or dissent can lead to a group's considering alternatives. Such disagreement can also stimulate imaginations to find creative solutions to problems.[37]

Functional Model of Group Decision Making

Randy Hirokawa and associates have focused their research on processes that seem to have the most effect on the quality of group decisions. Hirokawa believes that earlier research on decision-making groups did not really identify the task-relevant functions that groups had to perform in order to arrive at a high-quality decision.[38] He also notes that much of the group communication research has failed to demonstrate a causal relationship between group communication and the quality of the group's product.[39]

Are there certain issues that a group should deal with, certain functions that it should perform, to increase the possibility of arriving at "good" decisions? This is the question that led Hirokawa and others to consider a functional approach for analyzing group decision making. This approach is based on three assumptions: First, there are certain tasks that are critical in making decisions; second, successfully completing these critical requirements increases the likelihood of successfully making good decisions; and third, group communication is the means by which a group satisfies these critical requirements.[40]

Successful groups fulfill these functions more effectively than others, with success being defined in terms of what is perceived to be the quality of the group's decision. In a series of research studies, Hirokawa and his associates isolated four critical requirements that the group must meet:[41]

1. Establishing *complete and accurate understanding of the problem,* its extent and seriousness, its possible causes, and the potential consequences of not dealing with it effectively
2. Understanding of the *requirements and criteria for an acceptable solution,* involving the objectives to be satisfied and the standards for evaluating a good decision
3. Appropriate *assessment of positive and negative qualities of alternative solutions,* in order to identify the alternative with the most positive outcomes
4. Gathering and using *quality information* in regard to the other three areas

The functional analysis of group processes thus highlights critical requirements that groups must meet in order to achieve high-quality decisions. The order in which these requirements are met can be straightforward or not. Groups may recycle through some of these issues, going back to reanalyze the problem situation, for example, after considering positive and negative qualities of alternatives. Hence, Hirokawa's perspective emphasizes fulfilling decision functions rather than following prescribed sequences or steps.

A further question concerns to what extent communication variables uniquely account for a decision-making group's effectiveness. It is possible that more effective groups consisted of members who happened to be more intelligent or had access to better information than members of less effective groups. Regardless of their communication processes, the group with more initial potential would have been more successful. Carefully constructed studies have recently demonstrated, however, that groups with similar potential (in terms of beginning information and expertise) differed in their success in reaching high-quality decisions according to the amount and openness of group communication allowed.[42]

In other words, groups with the same potential that were permitted to conduct free and open discussions produced better decisions than otherwise similar groups that were permitted only limited discussion. This finding powerfully supports the idea that well-conducted group discussions lead to superior decisions.

Successful resolution of organizational and group problems must take account of the presence of conflict within and among groups in the organization. We now turn to the issue of conflict management for that reason.

ORGANIZATIONAL CONFLICT AND DECISION MAKING

Increasingly, organizational theorists conceive of conflict as pervasive and natural in most complex organizations.[43] The mixed goals and objectives within organizations mean that decision making and conflict resolution are often based on political considerations as well as "the facts." Moreover, the definition of the facts is often in dispute, and the determination of the method for discovering the facts is often the subject of covert or overt conflict.

Industrial relations theory, in contrast to earlier organizational theories, took the mixed motives of industrial organizations for granted. Although labor and management differed in some of their goals, notably in terms of workers' wages and working conditions, they shared other goals, such as the continued existence and profitability of the enterprise. Conflict took place within a context of shared mutual interests. Recently, the balance of power has tended to shift away from traditional, organized labor unions toward management, especially when the joint interests of labor and management are emphasized over their competing ones.

Conflict, even in industrial organizations, tends to concern areas other than traditional labor-management disputes. In nonindustrial organizations, such as educational, governmental, nonprofit, professional, or service organizations, conflicts are more likely to be about organizational goals, objectives, principles, structures, and methods than about wages and working conditions. Thus, although labor relations once provided the fundamental perspective on conflict, at least in industrial organizations, the nature of modern organizations requires a broader and more general analysis of organizational conflict.

Causes of Organizational Conflict

When a large number of people, with different backgrounds, trainings, and specialties are brought together, disagreements naturally result. Conflict is an expected part of doing business in certain organizations, such as court systems with prosecution versus defense or legislatures with two parties. Departments of the same organization may compete for assignments, personnel, or funding. In the Roman Catholic Church, "devil's advocates" are appointed when a person is being considered for sainthood, reflecting the belief that truth is best tested in an adversarial situation. One may need to look no further than the nature of the organization itself and its rules of operation in order to discover basic causes for conflict. There is, then, institutionalized conflict.

Some conflicts are the result of competing interests of different groups or parts of an organization. For example, teachers in a public school system have interests different from those of school board members and those of school administrators. Teachers' priorities are usually job security and sufficient pay, good teaching conditions (such as reasonable class sizes, facilities, hours for preparation, and so on), and student learning. Administrators may be more concerned about holding down costs while raising money for new construction. School board members may have priorities dictated by community pressure groups or interests, and so on.

Competing interests may range from superficial or transitory, on the one hand, to fundamental, on the other. Some conflicting interests may be so fundamental that a permanent state of conflict, latent or manifest, is nearly inevitable. For example, a Marxist analysis of society posits a fundamental and permanent conflict between the interests of capitalists and of workers. This view holds that the material position one finds oneself in determines one's permanent sense of being in the dominant or the exploited class in society. This divide cannot be bridged or resolved, according to Marx, until a revolution has overthrown the dominant capitalist interest. More recent interpretations of the Marxian view continue to maintain that economic class is fundamental, but allow for political resolutions other than the violent overthrow of the current dispensation. And, the dominant, or hegemonic, class may be defined in terms other than economic, such as those of gender, race, or culture.

Another sort of fundamental or intractable set of differing interests is that based on moral commitments, leading to a deep-seated "moral conflict."[44] This situation arises when organizational members find themselves divided over fundamental grounds for determining what is moral or valid. Members of an advertising agency, for example, may feel that it is fundamentally wrong for their firm to represent a company whose product they see as wrong or immoral. Some antismoking advocates may feel that way about representing a tobacco company, for instance. Or, some groups in a broadcasting organization may oppose running ads for condoms as part of a public campaign for AIDS prevention. People who find themselves on opposing sides of the debate concerning abortion are involved in this kind of moral conflict. Because the opposing parties argue from value premises, they even find it difficult to discuss or confront the conflict directly ("It's just impossible to talk to 'those people,'" advocates may claim). In these cases, people are committed to "mutually exclusive moral orders," leading to the failure of many normal dispute resolution techniques.[45]

Organizational conflicts may also be caused by so-called personality clashes, or *affective conflict,* engendered by mutual hostility or dislike between two individuals in the organization. Such affective conflicts may be the product of previous rivalries or earlier conflicts. When earlier disputes are left unresolved or end ambiguously, there is a special tendency for participants to dwell on the problem. Such mulling over the situation may lead one or both parties to attribute negative motives or hostile feelings to the other, exacerbating later conflicts and adding negative personal feelings to the other issues.[46]

Causes of conflict hence may be built-in or institutionalized in the organization; they may be the result of competing or conflicting interests; or they may result from personal clashes, or affective conflict. A final area of conflict could involve disputes about the methods to be used to deal with the conflict itself. There is, then, the potential for *metaconflict*—that is, conflict about what to do about conflict. The different approaches to conflict resolution are discussed next.

Conflict Strategies

Conflict is expressed and enacted through communicative behaviors. Through communication, the parties initiate and carry out strategies for dealing with conflict. Conflict strategies are "those communicative behaviors, both verbal and nonverbal, that provide a means for handling conflict."[47] These approaches to dealing with conflict range from extreme aggressiveness, on the one hand, to accommodation or avoidance, on the other. In either case, the strategies can be characterized as either tough or conciliatory, hard or soft.

A popular method for categorizing conflict strategies has been derived from the grid concept of Blake and Mouton, described earlier. The grid designates managerial styles in terms of two concerns: concern for production and concern for people. Similarly, one can map approaches to conflict on two dimensions: concern for one's own outcomes and concern for the outcomes of others. These two dimensions differentiate conflict strategies that emphasize *competition* from those that emphasize *cooperation*. In this way, five major conflict styles or strategies can be described:

Avoiding (low on both concerns)

Accommodating, or smoothing (low on concern for own outcomes, high on concern for others')

Compromising (moderate on both concerns)

Forcing (high on concern for own outcomes, low concern for others')

Confronting, or problem solving (high on both concerns)

"Confronting" here is used in the sense of confronting the conflict, bringing it and attendant issues out into the open so that they can be dealt with constructively.

These five conflict strategies can be cast in terms of the familiar win versus lose dichotomy, as well. The *win-lose* approach takes what is called a *distributive* view of conflict. In the distributive view, there is a fixed pie to be divided up among competitors; what one person wins, another person must lose. For this reason, this view is also described as a zero-sum game (gains and losses always cancel out, or add up to zero). People who see a situation as a win-lose conflict are likely to exhibit a forcing, aggressive style, viewing the conflict as something to be won at all costs.

Accommodating, essentially giving in to the other side, represents a *lose-win* approach. In a particular case, one faction in a group may be willing to give in to the other side, perhaps because the other side is too powerful, the stakes involved do not seem significant, or there is a prospect later on for a reciprocal accommodation by the other side on another matter.

Both compromising and avoiding can be described as *lose-lose* strategies. When compromising, each side must lose some of what it had hoped to achieve; the situation could also be described as "half-win–half-lose." Participants may both lose if the conflict goes unsettled as a result of an avoiding conflict style. On the other hand, if conflict on one matter is avoided, a coalition may be held together in order to achieve some other valued outcome. The factors of a given situation may often determine whether smoothing or avoiding styles have positive or negative outcomes.

The so-called confronting approach, also known as problem solving, is characterized as a *win-win* style. The view that both sides could win, in terms of realizing their actual or underlying interests, is known as *integrative* conflict management. In contrast to the distributive approach, this integrative style assumes that the conflict is really a nonzero-sum game, meaning that gains and losses do not have to total zero. Instead of envisioning a fixed pie to fight over, the participants try to find ways to expand the pie—to discover alternative solutions beyond the apparent limits. Participants approach conflict as problem solvers rather than as battlers.

In an effort to construct an instrument to measure conflict strategies, Linda Putnam and Charmaine Wilson developed an Organizational Communication Conflict Instrument (the OCCI).[48] Statements were developed based on the five conflict styles or strategies described above, and subjects were asked to respond on a seven-point scale from "strongly agree" to "strongly disagree" to questions about how they would act in a given conflict situation. Results indicated that the five categories were not necessarily mutually exclusive, nor did they discriminate clearly among different strategies. Revisions and statistical tests of the results suggested that the five categories could be reduced to three: *nonconfrontation*, which includes avoiding and smoothing; *solution orientation*, which involves direct confrontation of the problem and possible solutions and can involve willingness to compromise; and *control* strategies, which include forcing and unwillingness to solve problems or compromise.

The work of Putnam and Wilson suggests that it may be simpler and more useful to think of three kinds of strategies: *distributive* (control strategies, win-lose, forcing), *integrative* (problem solving, compromising, open), and *avoidance* (smoothing or ignoring).

Those using distributive strategies will debate and argue for their position, will build coalitions to gain allies for the fight, and will describe the conflict in terms of winning and losing. People using integrative methods rely less on personal confrontation and belligerency, are more likely to describe the situation as joint action, and search for a solution to a problem. More open discussion of conflict issues and nonobvious solutions also characterizes the integrative approach. Avoidant approaches involve skirting the issues of the conflict, changing the subject, directing attention to other matters, and the like.

Factors in Selecting Conflict Management Strategies

Given the various ways of characterizing possible responses to conflict situations, the next question concerns what determines or influences a person's selecting a particular strategy. As was the case with leadership, it is possible, in simple terms, to look to two alternative explanations: personality factors and situational contingencies.

The first alternative implies that each person has a *preferred style* of dealing with conflict. In other words, deep down a person tends to be an aggressive, tough battler or tends to be a compromiser who shies away from any kind of conflict. This kind of explanation assumes that people have embedded in their personalities a fairly permanent, "programmed" way of responding to conflict. As in leadership studies, explanations based on personality factors have largely given way to more behavioral explanations, giving weight to environmental or situational conditions. Still, some personal attributes are tied up with the identification of leaders: intelligence, characteristic responses to risk and uncertainty, verbal facility, and so on. Similarly, it may not be possible to dispense entirely with personality-based explanations for preferences in dealing with conflict.

The second kind of explanation, termed *situational* or *contingent,* is more widely accepted among theorists today. Even though personality factors may lead someone to prefer a particular conflict strategy, the variables in the situation may suppress or redirect that preference. Thus a supposed "tough battler" may use compromising or smoothing conflict behaviors during a given conflict episode. Ongoing patterns of communication, the history of interaction in a given relationship or organization, and expectations concerning these elements are central factors in selecting a particular conflict strategy. The point is made forcefully by Putnam and Wilson when they assume that "the decision to use a particular conflict strategy is largely governed by the situational rather than personality constraints."[49]

Situational factors that appear to be especially relevant in choosing a conflict style or strategy include the following:

1. *Structural factors.* Patterns of communication established in a relationship or in an organization (structural factors) can influence strategy selection. As might be expected, superiors often rely on their position power and a forcing style in conflicts with subordinates. First-line supervisors, however, who must continue in a closer re-

lationship with workers, show a greater preference for problem solving than their superiors. Subordinates in conflicts with superiors show more preference for avoiding and smoothing than for confronting.[50]

2. *Expectations about the relationship.* Expectations concerning an ongoing relationship are an important consideration in selecting a conflict style. When both parties believe that they will have to cooperate in the future, there is more tendency to select cooperative or problem-solving strategies. If no such future relationship is anticipated, more forcing or control strategies may be expected. Also deceptive tactics are less likely when participants anticipate the need for a continuing relationship. Thus, it may make a difference whether a team is permanent or merely an ad hoc one. Even in the latter case, team members may perceive that they may be working with other members again in some future arrangement.

3. *Reciprocity.* People may change an initially selected conflict strategy in response to the strategy used by people on the other side. If conciliatory methods do not seem to work, then they may switch to a more controlling or forcing style.[51] Switching from a cooperative style to a more competitive one leads to a kind of escalation of conflict, which is typical, according to the systems theorists Katz and Kahn: "One of the best-established findings about conflict interaction is the tendency toward similar or reciprocal behavior and the consequent escalation of the conflict process."[52]

4. *Shared goals.* A factor that mitigates animosity and competitiveness in a conflict is agreement on goals or objectives. Presumably, the members of an organization share some overall organizational goals that could offer the basis for a solution to a conflict. Kotter reminds us that modern organizations are likely to be especially diverse, meaning that conflicts are likely to be more serious than in more homogeneous organizations. Moral conflicts, also alluded to earlier, are instances in which fundamental beliefs and, consequently, goals are in conflict, making cooperative resolutions more difficult to achieve.

5. *Setting and awareness of audiences.* Conditions surrounding the conflict can determine the kind of conflict strategy selected by participants. One study of the factors in dispute escalation suggests that organizational conflicts tend to move from a "grievance expression stage" to outright "disputing," which is much more public, involving more elements of the organization than early stages.[53] The more public stages of disputing involve intensified efforts at seeking third-party support or intervention. The presence of an audience or constituents can lead group members to adopt aggressive conflict behaviors. For example, a representative of a group may feel that she must be seen to fight hard for her constituents, so as to be accepted by them as a "hero" rather than rejected as a "traitor." Positions taken publicly are harder to retract, upon reflection, without losing face. The presence of an audience or constituents during public phases of disputing can therefore lead to more combative conflict styles.

The perceived effectiveness of a particular conflict strategy depends largely on the situation, even though earlier studies have suggested that one strategy, the confrontational or problem-solving strategy, was the most preferred method for handling conflict.[54]

DIVERSITY MATTERS

Gender and Cultural Differences in Conflict Strategies

The gender or culture of the parties in a dispute can lead to differing conflict strategies. Research supports the hypothesis that women tend to adopt cooperative strategies more than men, who seem more likely to adopt coercive or forcing styles.* That is, women may look for tactics that allow the other side to save face or that acknowledge the legitimacy of the other side's concerns. On the other hand, this difference may stem from traditional power and status differences, given that in the past, women have tended not to hold positions of authority as often as have men. This apparent gender difference may reflect an embedded hierarchical difference, described above under structural factors.**

*M. Dowd (1991), Power: Are women afraid of it—or beyond it? *Working Woman,* November 1991, pp. 948–49.

**B. M. Gayle (1991), Sex equity in workplace manage-

National cultural factors appear likely to influence the selection of conflict strategy as well. The Japanese, for example, prefer to deal with intraorganizational conflict in ways that reinforce group harmony and consensus more than presumably individualistic Americans do. Some American negotiators, for example, have been frustrated by their experience that Japanese counterparts never say no in a direct or clear way (from the perspective of the Americans). Rather than giving a direct negative, the Japanese prefer to delay, suggest difficulties, or even remain silent. Differences in cultural style can themselves become factors leading to conflict within diverse organizations, as Kotter points out above, as different national or background cultures are increasingly represented within the same multicultural organization.

ment, *Journal of Applied Communication Research, 19,* 156–69.

A series of studies has investigated the relationship between conflict strategy and perceptions of communicators' competence.[55] This work shows that our views concerning people's competence and their conflict strategies can be explained in terms of *attribution theory* (see Chapter 9). Recall that attribution theory holds that we strive to explain the behavior of other people who interact with us by searching for plausible causes for this behavior. Knowing the causes, we assume, allows us to predict their behaviors in future situations. In this way an element of control and predictability is secured. Other people's communication strategies, including their strategies for dealing with conflict, are basic indicators of the sort of causes sought for. Are certain ways of dealing with conflict judged to be more competent than others? In general, distributive strategies are seen as less competent than integrative strategies. Avoidant strategies may be judged as more or less competent depending on the situation.[56]

Judgments concerning the competence of conflict strategies are no doubt partly dependent on an observer's vantage point. The perceptions of third-party observers differ from the perceptions of those directly involved in the conflict. Communicators often tend to judge themselves as more competent than observers judge them. Negative actions and conflict strategies are typically attributed more often to the other side than to one's own. People tend to judge the other side's strategy in terms of its perceived *appropriateness* and their own in terms of its *effectiveness*, whether it seemed to work or not. In other words, if the other side wins (is effective) but seems to be aggressive or manipulative in doing so, we judge them to be less competent. If we use similar tactics, we are likely to excuse them on the basis of their effectiveness in the dispute at hand. Disputants are likely to recall apparently negative or distributive conflict strategies on the part of others more readily than positive or integrative behaviors.[57] Personal perspective thus shapes our view of the conflict strategies and behaviors of others, depending usually on our own role in the conflict.

Review of Organizational Conflict

Conflict is pervasive in most complex contemporary organizations. Although early organizational theories tended to consider conflict as dysfunctional, or as a problem to be solved or eliminated, recent theories view organizational conflict as natural, expected, and potentially functional. Whether conflict has positive or negative effects depends on how the conflict is dealt with rather than on whether it was avoided or smoothed over.

The issues in conflict can include the goals and objectives or purposes of the organization, problem definition, values or criteria for solving problems, policies or solutions to the problems, and their outcomes. Causes for conflict can be built-in expectations or structures of the organization, competing interests, or fundamental value differences. Competing interests are widely present in complex, interdependent organizations, and they can range from superficial to concrete. The strategies people employ when involved in a conflict can be distributive, integrative, or avoidant. Which strategy is selected depends on many factors, even though personality factors may dispose one to prefer one style over another. These factors include structural location in a hierarchy; expectations concerning the participants' relationship; reciprocity; the presence of shared goals; setting, especially commitment before an audience; and gender and cultural differences.

The next section takes up the use of negotiation, bargaining, and mediation as communication solutions for dealing with group or organizational conflict.

NEGOTIATION, BARGAINING, AND MEDIATION

Methods of conflict management in organizations range from the coercive to cooperative, problem-solving ones, as we have just seen. The interdependence of most organizations and the need for component groups to maintain good working relationships place a premium on cooperative communication strategies, such as negotiation, bargaining, or mediation. Arbitration and litigation are related methods, but the decision is made by a third party who is not directly involved in the dispute. Informal arbitration occurs when disputing parties turn to a superior for a decision. More formal types of arbitration are legal or quasi-legal procedures for dispute resolution, as in labor-management, community, or domestic disputes. Litigation involves recourse to courts of law and the employment of legal counsel. The formal processes of arbitration and litigation are essentially beyond the scope of this work.

Negotiation is an option when disputing parties see some benefit in working together to find a jointly satisfying solution. Negotiation occurs "when two or more parties within one or in different organizations jointly make decisions and do not have the same preferences."[58] "Bargaining" is often used interchangeably with "negotiation," although bargaining implies a specific kind of negotiation featuring the trading of valued resources or services.[59] Mediation involves a third party, but one who does not have the power to impose a solution on the disputants. The mediator, rather, serves as a process consultant to help the parties negotiate their own outcome.

Communication in Negotiation and Mediation

The process of negotiation is conducted mainly through communication, often face-to-face but increasingly through interactive, mediated channels. In many organizations, negotiation is initiated because of formal procedures established as part of a contract. Informal or voluntary negotiation is probably more widespread, however. Organization members may find themselves involved in some kind of negotiation nearly every day, as they negotiate with other members regarding workload or distribution, budget matters, personnel evaluations, and access to organizational resources.

By implication, a negotiated settlement usually integrates the original intended outcomes of the two parties. If one side succeeds in forcing its original desired outcome on the other, the result is due more to the successful side's reliance on authority or power, persuasion, or payments to the other side.

The communication styles involved in bargaining and negotiation can again be divided into "tough" and "soft" categories, or the distributive and integrative categories described earlier in discussion of conflict styles. A popular work developed from the Harvard Negotiation Project prefers a trichotomy of "hard," "soft," and what is called "principled" styles of negotiating. Hard negotiators focus on winning, perhaps by manipulation and even deception. The soft category is similar to the accommodating conflict style, in which a negotiator smooths over differences as much as possible in order to maintain good interpersonal relations.[60] Principled negotiators are most concerned with discovering creative solutions that manage to allow both sides to satisfy their major needs or interests. In other words, such negotiators basically seek "win-win" solutions. Similarly, a mediator is likely to be most successful in getting both sides to accept a solution when each can perceive that the solution meets its needs or interests.

Successful negotiations, then, follow the principles of effective problem solving. The aim is to induce both parties to see the dispute as a joint problem, to be solved by working together.

Certain conditions must be present for this redefinition to occur. First, both parties must perceive a need to cooperate with each other and share a recognition of their interdependence. Second, each side should have some power relative to the other. If the power balance is quite lopsided, the outcome is likely to be the result of the exercise of power rather than negotiation. The categories of types of power developed by

French and Raven or by Gareth Morgan are useful in making salient the different kinds of power that seemingly weaker groups may have in relationship to others.

Problems in Negotiation and Mediation

The communication problems that can hinder effective negotiation are similar to the kinds of problems that can hinder effective decision making, compounded by the competitiveness that conflicts engender. Reliance on simplified decision heuristics that can sidetrack decision making can be exacerbated by a need to win and to beat the other side.

The typical barriers to successful integrative negotiation include the following:

- Overemphasis on winning, a distributive or "win-lose" orientation
- Lack of perspective taking, the inability to visualize the problem from the viewpoint of other parties
- Overconfidence in one's own judgment, exacerbated by a competitive atmosphere
- Escalation and the effects of public commitment
- Misleading framing of alternatives
- The use of deception

An emphasis on winning can lead to the concealing of one's genuine interests and needs in a dispute, leading to a style of negotiating known as *positional bargaining*. In this situation, one emphasizes the articulation of positions or demands instead of discussing the reasons behind the positions or demands. Positional bargaining typically results in compromising, in which neither side is satisfied, or other kinds of suboptimal solutions. If it were possible to discover the real needs or interests that led to the stated positions, the two sides could possibly discover new ways of satisfying these needs. The "win-lose" orientation assumes a fixed pie, whereas integrative bargaining assumes that it is possible to find ways to expand the pie or substitute alternatives for pie. An effective communication strategy, therefore, is to persuade each side to explain the rationale for positions or demands in terms of the real needs that underlie them. The discussion then can turn to exploring alternative ways to meet those needs.

The second barrier points to the need for a negotiator or a mediator to bring out the perspectives of the two sides and to make each other's perspective palpable to the other. A mediator, for example, could use role playing to induce each side to verbalize the needs and perspectives of the other side.

Research supports the common observation that people tend to overestimate their own fallible judgment (everyone sees him- or herself as "above average"). In negotiation situations, negotiators typically overestimate the extent to which a neutral third party or arbitrator will agree with their own position and award them a victory.[61] As a result, negotiators often tend to hang tough rather than discuss an integrative settlement. A successful negotiator or mediator needs to provide a reality check in this situation, by finding examples of similar situations in which objective third parties have not supported similar positions. It may be possible to apply a test by seeking out the opinions of others not involved in the conflict to indicate the existence of this kind of overconfidence.

Escalation of conflict often occurs when one side plays to an audience of committed constituents. Negotiations typically take place within a complex context involving not just the two parties directly involved but constituents with whom the negotiators must communicate as well.[62] Negotiators are engaged not only in communicating with each other but also in communicating with constituent groups. The negotiator takes on the roles of both advocate (persuader) and representative (information giver) and must balance the give-and-take with the other side against the need to uphold the interests of constituents. In this circumstance, a mediator can help negotiators balance these needs and allow sufficient opportunites for communication between negotiators and their constituents to avoid the risk of an integrative settlement being rejected

AN ISSUE OF COMMUNICATION ETHICS

Lying in Negotiations

Deception or lying can become a special barrier to discovering integrative solutions. Deceptive tactics are more likely, of course, in situations defined as "win-lose" or intensely competitive. Naturally, some lack of candor is typical in a conflict or bargaining situation. Negotiators often face a dilemma between openness and giving away too much, between trust and being taken advantage of. A negotiator would probably not be effective if he or she began by revealing that those on his or her side did not really agree on their position or needs, or by revealing that they really did not need as much of the resources as they are demanding. On the other hand, if a negotiator is completely untrustworthy—communicated by not disclosing anything—it will also be hard to get to a settlement.

The use of deceptive or unfair bargaining tactics seems to depend on situational factors, although some attempts have been made to draw a relationship between personality tendencies and the use of deception. Cultural factors, particularly organizational cultural ones, may be relevant at this point.* There are some indications that views of

lying or deception may depend on gender or gender relationships. One study found, for example, "Not only did women rate lying as a less acceptable form of behavior than did men, but women were more likely to view the act of lying as significant," and to respond with more negative reactions to lying.**

In general, the bigger the prize and the greater the emphasis on competition and winning, the more likely are deceptive tactics. Perceived power differences also seem to lead to the more powerful employing deception against the weaker. The perception of the relationship between the two parties, especially the perception of the need for a continuing, workable relationship, seems to reduce the tendency toward deceptive tactics. An effective negotiator or mediator, therefore, needs to emphasize the nature of this relationship and the value of open discussion of real needs and interests to discover the most viable solution to a problem.

90; S. Bok (1968), *Lying: Moral choice in public and private life*, New York: Pantheon.

*R. J. Lewicki (1983), Lying and deception: A behavioral model, in M. H. Bazerman and R. J. Lewicki (Eds.), *Negotiation in organizations*, Beverly Hills, Calif.: Sage, pp. 68–

**T. R. Levine. S. A. McCormack, and P. B. Avery (1992), Sex differences in emotional reactions to discovered deception, *Communication Quarterly, 40,* 294.

by the constituent groups. These groups, in all likelihood, will not have gone through the brainstorming or problem-solving discussions that led negotiators to their solution.

Highlights of Negotiation and Mediation

Conflict management in organizations often relies on the processes of negotiation and mediation. Negotiation requires that the two parties in conflict recognize their interdependence and that each side hold some power vis-à-vis the other. In negotiation, the two sides work together without outside intervention to come to a mutually acceptable resolution. Mediation involves recourse to a third party, who serves primarily as a process consultant to help the two parties come to a solution. In summary, in negotiating or mediating a dispute, communication that emphasizes the interdependence of the parties and the problem-solving nature of the situation is most likely to result in integrative solutions.

As noted at the start of this section, team discussion and dealing with conflict and negotiation usually involve face-to-face communication. Increased use of communication technologies allows for mediated group decision making as well. The final section of this chapter concerns potential effects of communication and computerized technology on these processes.

GROUP DECISION MAKING AND TECHNOLOGY

Computerized electronic media in organizational communication, computer-mediated communication (CMC) systems, are being used in place of or as supplements to face-to-face decision-making groups. There are important questions concerning the effects that the use of such forms of media will have on group decision-making processes.

First, *computer conferencing* occurs when group participants are linked through computer lines rather than being face-to-face (FtF). Such conferences can be *asynchronous,* meaning that participants can log on and read what others have contributed, then add their own comments at any time, regardless of whether other members are currently on-line or not. Or, computer conferences can be in real time, which means that all the participants are actually on-line at the same time, responding to one another as in a regular FtF situation, although without the physical aspects of the group setting such as the nonverbal elements.

Second, computer technologies can be used to supplement or assist a live, FtF group discussion; these technologies are referred to as group decision support systems, or GDSS.[63] When using GDSS, a group meets together as in a traditional group meeting, but several communication and computer tools intended to aid their discussion are available. For example, the group is seated at a horseshoe-shaped table with an overhead projector and screen at the front of the room, where instant vote tallies or brainstorming lists can be displayed.

Software can be used to display decision trees, structured group agendas, and similar prepared decision aids. The software package typically includes suggested rules

A room set up for using a group decision support system, or GDSS.

regarding handling of straw votes, the use of decision aids, and the like. The group, of course, usually develops its own rules or norms regarding the use of the technological aids.[64] In addition, information stored on computers can be readily accessed by the members in the course of the discussion, making large amounts of information instantly available to the participants.

GDSS can also be combined with *videoconferencing* technologies, allowing a GDSS discussion to be conducted among participants who are at remote locations. The overhead screen at the front of the room is replaced by video monitors that allow the participants to see one another in the videoconference, as well as displaying the information seen on the projector screen in the nonvideo setting.

Effects of Computerized Communication on Group Decision Making

Cutting across spatial and time boundaries, newer varieties of communication technologies, particularly CMC, allow for wider participation in organizational decision making. The effects can significantly alter the possibilities for group communication within an organization.[65] The full extent of these effects is not yet known and is still being worked out because of the rapid introduction and modification of these communication technologies in organizations. For the two kinds of group situations, computer conferencing and computer-assisted GDSS discussions, effects appear as tentative propositions regarding advantages and disadvantages.

First, regarding computer conferencing, advantages and disadvantages tend to fall into the following areas:

Asynchronous Communication. Although computer conferences do not have to be asynchronous, they often are. Individual members do not have to coordinate their schedules in order to meet at the same time, there are fewer restrictions on involving participants in different time zones, and geographical separation ceases to be a problem in bringing the group together. Presumably, absent time and distance constraints, people with the best or widest possible variety of information or access to information can constitute the group.

A possible disadvantage to asynchronous communication is that the order or sequence of comment and response can be lost, as participants log on at different or irregular intervals. Some of the synergistic effects of the flow of FtF discussion groups are thus lost. Not all members of the group can be expected to be "on the same page" at the same time.

Nonverbal Elements of Communication. One of the most often noted effects of computerized communication is the loss of the nonverbal cues available in FtF meetings. CMC is said to represent a *leaner* form of communication, lacking the richness of the variety of messages, both verbal and nonverbal, available in FtF situations. The advantages of reduced nonverbal cues include the softening of status and authority cues, thereby lessening possible inhibitions or constraints on members' contributions. Ideas can be analyzed in terms of their content separate from their source, which should lead to more attention to rational elements of arguments, such as the use of evidence and reasoning.

Disadvantages of the loss of nonverbal elements include corollaries to these advantages. The loss of leadership cues can result in the group's floundering about, without a clear sense of direction (this can be exacerbated in the asynchronous situation in which the order and sources of messages are unclear). One reason advanced for the observation that computer-mediated groups often take longer to solve a problem than FtF groups is this loss of the nonverbal cues of leadership.[66]

Without cues such as vocal tone and inflections, facial expressions, and gestures, the intended meaning of comments may be lost as well. Hence, it may take longer to explain the ramifications of members' contributions. The lessening of inhibitions may also lead to the well-known computerese phenomenon of "flaming," in which people use stronger and more outrageous language than they would if they were actually face to face. Finally, the lack of face-to-face cues can mean that conflict is more difficult to manage. Nonverbal cues, the way things are said, can soften messages that might otherwise seem hostile or angry, and such cues can provide a context for understanding the way in which verbal messages are to be interpreted.

The advantages and disadvantages of *GDSS* programs fall into the areas of idea generation and communication and decision making.

Idea Generation and Communication. GDSS is designed to overcome some of the disadvantages of computer conferencing delineated above. For example, displaying written lists, proposals, vote tallies, and the like on a screen tends to focus discussion more on content than on the source, especially if contributions are displayed anonymously. The nonverbal cues that help people interpret others' meanings are still present, however, as the group interacts. Contributions can be more evenly distributed among group members because the written displays allow quiet members as well as more voluble members to communicate their suggestions. One intended result of GDSS is that this will make more ideas available. Disadvantages that may detract from effective communication include an overemphasis on the technology, its rules, and uses. The "bells and whistles" can overshadow the normal flow of discussion.

Decision Making. GDSS systems provide for immediate access through computer links to vast amounts of relevant information. Through the computer link, members can call up data that would not normally be available during a group meeting. The system can also make expert systems available, indicating how experts would approach the kind of problem the group may be dealing with. A potential drawback is that groups may use inappropriate models or an inappropriate agenda as a result of overreliance on the system rather than using their own judgment and knowledge of the immediate situation. Again, the members may be so taken with the technology that they rely on it to the exclusion of their own resources.

Highlights of the Effects of Technology on Decision Making

Whether advantages or disadvantages predominate in a group's use of these technologies depends on the group's experience and interaction. Poole and DeSanctis point out that "the technology alone cannot guarantee improvements . . . these are tied to how the groups appropriate the technology into the interaction system."[67] In other words, the effectiveness of GDSS depends on the ways in which groups choose to use them. George Huber believes that with increased experience, groups will learn to use the systems more effectively, and hence the disadvantages will tend to be outweighed by the advantages in the long run. Furthermore, he believes that these decision-aided technologies will tend to be used appropriately because of the comparative advantages they will give to organizations that do so over those that do not.[68]

Over time, the disadvantages that seem to be present in computer-mediated discussion systems may fade away as group experience with the technology grows. The finding that groups using computer conferencing take longer to solve a problem than face-to-face groups may disappear with this kind of experience.

SUMMARY

Organizational decision making relies on communication. At several points, communication variables influence the direction and outcomes of problem-solving processes. The communication implications of decision making can be summarized in the following points:

• *Credibility.* The source of information within an organization can sway the decision-making process in important ways. Source credibility determines what sorts of problems are noticed and taken seriously. Inside sources of information are typically given more credibility by other members. Powerful sources have the ability to set agendas for problem solving. Source effects can lead to several problems detracting from high-quality decisions, as when members are reluctant to challenge an authority, leading to the decision rules associated with self-protection. A highly attractive group can be subject to the groupthink phenomenon described by Janis.

• *Structural effects.* As information relevant to decision making moves through the network of an organization, it tends to take on more certainty than may be warranted. Information used for problem solving may therefore be misinterpreted by decision makers, who assume that there are facts when, in reality, there are only estimates or projections. Recall that increasing the number of steps through which a message must pass increases the likelihood of distortion of that information.

• *Information processing.* Communication lines or networks within organizations may determine certain kinds of information processing. The first two points above remind us that internal sources of information have more credibility and that information loses uncertainty as it moves away from its initial source. Organizations may differ in their ability to process complex information.

In less than optimal situations, complex information may be dealt with by the application of *simplified decision heuristics.* While the use of such rules may not result in serious harm in the case of routine or trivial decisions, they are less likely to produce high-quality decisions in important matters.

• *Framing of problems and solutions.* The way in which a problem is presented to decision makers often determines the directions they take and the alternatives that receive serious consideration. The work of Tversky and Kahnemann makes it quite clear that how problem situations are communicated significantly influences the decision-making process. One framing may suggest or make available certain solutions that would not be as salient given a different framing. For example, a small decline in sales in one month could call forth quite different solutions depending on whether the overall economic health of the organization was robust or weak. In the robust context, rather mild or minor changes in response to a one-month decline would be most likely, whereas in the weak context, people might turn to more drastic alternatives.

• *Organizational culture.* Chapter 7 has detailed the effects of organizational culture on organizational communication. The culture of an organization goes a long way in determining what kind of problems are considered important and how they are to be handled. The culture also determines, to some degree, the communication associated with problem solving. Some cultures may habitually rely on full participation, whereas others tend to employ autocratic decision-making practices.

• *Group and interpersonal dynamics.* Janis, Hirokawa, and others have made it abundantly clear that group processes shape the discussion of problems, what is considered relevant information, and the directions taken in considering potential solutions and outcomes. Interpersonal dynamics may also be operating when a subordinate fears to suggest all possible alternatives because of a desire to avoid punishment.

The rational actor hence does not play the role in organizational settings that may seem appropriate to decision theorists. The rational actor model is individualistic in orientation; that is, it assumes that a single actor, or the organization acting as a single individual, can consider all relevant information and all possible alternative solutions before making a decision. In real-life organizational settings, however, decisions are the result of complex interaction among many different individuals, groups, and interests. Decisions are shaped through ongoing transactions of interpersonal and group communication.

The importance of group communication in modern organizations is highlighted by the trend toward self-directed teams and team building. There is a widespread belief that shared decision making and team efforts are the key to enhanced efficiency and productivity. This trend places renewed emphasis on understanding the processes of group communication. Research on small-group communication supports the notion that a group is a unique environment for human communication.

EXERCISES AND QUESTIONS FOR DISCUSSION

1. Think of group projects or committees that you have participated in. Have you observed cases that illustrate bounded rationality and satisficing? Describe the reasons that seemed to justify satisficing in these cases. In what kind of situations is optimal decision making more important than satisficing? Should all major decisions be based on rational and objective grounds?

2. Can you identify decision heuristics that are operative in an organization to which you belong (or a company where you work)? How would one determine what the decision heuristics are in your school or university? What kinds of questions could one ask to discover important decision rules?

3. Framing, or the reliance on decisional heuristics, indicates the importance of the way in which a problem is communicated. Give examples of framing emphasizing gains versus losses, analogizing, misleading adages, or nutshell briefings that can lead to biased or less than rational decision making. Do you rely on certain adages or analogies when confronted with a decision, such as "If it ain't broke, don't fix it"? If so, what can you do to avoid overreliance on such heuristics?

4. Have you observed examples of emotional decision rules, such as statements of competitiveness, overconfidence, or the like? How can one confront reliance on emotional decision rules when they arise in groups or committees?

5. Discuss ways to determine when a decision requires a vigilant or especially careful analysis. What kinds of problems can be handled relatively quickly, perhaps by relying on simple heuristics? What factors tend to indicate a significant problem situation that requires a careful decision process?

6. Compare the features of problem-solving systems, such as those proposed by Hirokawa or Janis. What elements of these systems do you find especially useful or attractive? Which systems could you usefully apply to decision-making situations you face or have faced? Explain what factors are important in your choice. Can you analyze or evaluate a decision made by a group that you observe or have observed in terms one of these systems?

7. What are societal conflicts that today tend to affect conflict within companies or other organizations? To what extent do social concerns over equal opportunity, nondiscrimination, and sexual harassment lead to internal organizational conflicts? How should social conflicts be dealt with when they surface within an organization? When should they be smoothed and when should they be confronted? Are some social conflicts within organizations unresolvable? If you think so, discuss examples of what appear to be irreconcilable conflicts. How should an organization deal with these kinds of conflicts?

8. Consider your experience with group conflict. Do you find that you tend to exhibit one of the styles for dealing with conflict described in the chapter? Do you tend to be aggressive or combative in conflicts? Why or why not? Do you

prefer to avoid or smooth over conflict? Why or why not? When is it best to confront a latent conflict and bring it out into the open? Are there times when conflict should be avoided? If you think so, discuss the special features of those circumstances.

SOURCES FOR FURTHER STUDY

Barker, J. R., Melville, C. W., and Pacanowsky, M. E. (1993). Self-directed teams at Xel: Changes in communication practices during a program of cultural transformation. *Journal of Applied Communication Research, 21,* 297–312.

Bazerman, M. H., and Lewicki, R. J. (Eds.) (1983). Preface. *Negotiating in organizations.* Beverly Hills, Calif.: Sage. p. 7.

Blake, R. R., and Mouton, J. S. (1984). *Solving costly organizational conflict.* San Francisco: Jossey-Bass.

Bok, S. (1968). *Lying: Moral choices in public and private life.* New York: Pantheon.

Burrell, N. A., Donohue, W. A., and Allen, M. (1990). The impact of disputants' expectations on mediation: Testing an interventionist model. *Human Communication Research, 17,* 104–39.

Canary, D. J., and Spitzberg, B. H. (1987). Appropriateness and effectiveness perceptions of conflict strategies. *Human Communication Research, 14,* 93–118.

Canary, D. J., and Spitzberg, B. H. (1989). A model of the perceived competence of conflict strategies. *Human Communication Research, 15,* 630–49.

Canary, D. J., and Spitzberg, B. H. (1990). Attribution biases and associations between conflict strategies and competence outcomes. *Communication Monographs, 57,* 139–50.

Cherrington, D. J. (1989). *Organizational behavior.* Boston: Allyn & Bacon.

Cloven, D. H., and Roloff, M. E. (1991). Sense-making activities and interpersonal conflict: Communication cures for the mulling blues. *Western Journal of Speech Communication, 55,* 134–58.

Conrad, C. (1991). Communication in conflict: Style-strategy relationships. *Communication Monographs, 58,* 135–55.

Cyert, R. M., and March, J. G. (1963). *A behavioral theory of the firm.* Englewood Cliffs, N.J.: Prentice-Hall.

DeTurck, M. A., and Miller, G. R. (1990). Training observers to detect spontaneous deception: Effects of gender. *Communication Reports, 4,* 81–89.

Donohue, W. A., Weider-Hatfield, D., Hamilton, M., and Diez, M. E. (1985). Relational distance in managing conflict. *Human Communication Research, 11,* 387–405.

Drucker, P. F. (1974). *Management: Tasks, responsibilities, practices.* New York: Harper & Row.

Fisher, K. (1993). *Leading self-directed work teams.* New York: McGraw Hill.

Folberg, J., and Taylor, A. (1984). *Mediation: A comprehensive guide to resolving conflicts without litigation.* San Francisco: Jossey-Bass.

Freeman, S. A., Littlejohn, S. W., and Pearce, W. B. (1992). Communication and moral conflict. *Western Journal of Communication, 56,* 311–29.

Hill, P. H., et al. (1979). *Making decisions: A multidisciplinary approach.* Reading, Mass.: Addison-Wesley.

Hirokawa, R. Y. (1988). Group communication and decision-making performance: A continued test of the functional perspective. *Human Communication Research 14,* 487–515.

Janis, I. L. (1972). *Victims of group think.* New York: Houghton Mifflin.

Janis, I. L. (1989). *Crucial decisions: Leadership in policymaking and crisis management.* New York: The Free Press.

Janis, I. L., and Mann, L. (1977). *Decision making: A psychological analysis of conflict, choice, and commitment.* New York: The Free Press.

Kahneman, D., Slovic, P., and Tversky, A. (Eds.) (1982). *Judgment under uncertainty: Heuristics and biases.* New York: Cambridge University Press.

Kotter, J. P. (1985). *Power and influence.* New York: The Free Press.

Levine, T. R., McCormack, S. A., and Avery, P. B. (1992). Sex differences in emotional reactions to discovered deception. *Communication Quarterly, 40,* 289–96.

Ma, R. (1992). The role of unofficial intermediaries in interpersonal conflicts in Chinese culture. *Communication Quarterly, 40,* 269–78.

MacCrimmon, K. R., and Taylor, R. N. (1983). Decision making and problem solving. In N. D. Dunnette (Ed.), *The Handbook of organizational psychology.* New York: Wiley.

Manz, C. C., and Sims, H. P. (1993). *Business without bosses.* New York: Wiley.

Moore, C. A. (1986). *The mediation process.* San Francisco: Jossey-Bass.

Morgan, G. (1986). *Images of organization.* Newbury Park, Calif.: Sage.

Morrill, C., and Thomas, C. K. (1992). Organizational conflict management as disputing process: The problem of social escalation. *Human Communication Research, 18,* 400–28.

Newton, D. A., and Burgoon, J. K. (1990). The use and consequences of verbal influence strategies during interpersonal disagreements. *Human Communication Research, 16,* 477–518.

Papa, M. J., and Natalle, E. J. (1989). Gender, strategy selection, and discussion satisfaction in interpersonal conflict. *Western Journal of Speech Communication, 53,* 260–72.

Pfeffer, J. (1981). *Power in organizations.* Marshfield, Mass.: Pitman.

Putnam, L. L., and Poole, M. S. (1987). Conflict and negotiation. In F. M. Jablin, L. L. Putnam, K. H. Roberts, and L. W. Porter (Eds.), *Handbook of organizational communication: An interdisciplinary perspective.* Beverly Hills, Calif.: Sage, pp. 549–95.

Rahim, M. A. (Ed.) (1989). *Managing conflict: An interdisciplinary approach.* New York: Praeger.

Renz, M. A., and Greg, J. (1988). Flaws in the decision-making process: Assessment and acceptance of risk in the decision to launch Flight 51-L. *Central States Speech Journal, 39,* 67–75.

Roloff, M. E., and Campion, D. E. (1987). On alleviating and debilitating effects of accountability on bargaining: Authority and self-monitoring. *Communication Monographs, 54,* 145–64.

Salazar, A. J., Hirokawa, R. Y., Propp, K. M., Julian, K. M., and Leatham, G. B. (1994). In search of true cause: Examination of the effect of group potential and group interaction on decision performance. *Human Communication Research, 20,* 529–59.

Simon, H. (1957). *Administrative behavior,* 2d ed. New York: Macmillan.

Turner, D. B. (1990). Intraorganizational bargaining: The effect of goal congruence and trust on negotiator strategy use. *Communication Studies, 41,* 54–76.

Tversky, A., and Kahneman, D. (1974). Judgment under uncertainty: Heuristics and bias. *Science, 185,* 1124–31.

Waterman, R. H., Jr. (1990). *Adhocracy: The power to change.* New York: W. W. Norton.

Weeks, D., and Whimster, S. (1985). Contexted decision-making: A socio-organizational perspective. In G. Wright (Ed.), *Behavioral decision-making.* New York: Plenum Press.

Witteman, H. (1988). Interpersonal problem-solving: Problem conceptualization and communication use. *Communication Monographs, 55,* 336–59.

Witteman, H. (1992). Analyzing interpersonal conflict: Nature of awareness, type of initiating event, situational perceptions, and management styles. *Western Journal of Speech Communication, 56,* 248–80.

NOTES

1. R. M. Cyert and J. G. March (1963), *A behavioral theory of the firm,* Englewood Cliffs, N.J.: Prentice-Hall, p. 67.

2. J. R. Barker, C. W. Melville, and M. E. Pacanowsky (1993), Self-directed teams at Xel: Changes in communication practices during a program of cultural trans-

formation, *Journal of Applied Communication Research*, 21, 297–312.

3. C. C. Manz and H. P. Sims (1993), *Business without bosses*, New York: Wiley, p. 8.

4. "Managing for World-Class Competitiveness," internal document, Boeing Company, August 10, 1992, p. 3–5.

5. Boeing document, p. 3–25.

6. Boeing document, p. 3–25.

7. K. Fisher (1993), *Leading self-directed work teams*, New York: McGraw-Hill, p. 33.

8. A. Byron, "Boeing's bold switch toward Japanese-style work teams: 777 is focal point of move to put system into effect company-wide," *Seattle Times*, April 7, 1991, p. 1.

9. Manz and Sims, p. 60.

10. R. H. Waterman, Jr. (1990), *Adhocracy: The power to change*, New York: W. W. Norton.

11. Waterman, pp. 19–20.

12. Waterman, p. 35.

13. Manz and Sims, p. x.

14. G. Morgan (1986), *Images of organization*, Newbury Park, Calif.: Sage, pp. 172–73.

15. See I. L. Janis and L. Mann (1977), *Decision making: A psychological analysis of conflict, choice, and commitment*, New York: The Free Press, p. 24.

16. P. H. Hill et al. (1979), *Making decisions: A multidisciplinary approach*. Reading, Mass.: Addison-Wesley, p. 22.

17. D. Weeks and S. Whimster (1985), Contexted decision-making: A socio-organizational perspective, in G. Wright (Ed.), *Behavioral decision-making*, New York: Plenum Press, p. 173.

18. H. Simon (1957), *Administrative behavior*, 2d ed., New York: Macmillan, p. 79.

19. A. Tversky and D. Kahneman (1974), Judgment under uncertainty: Heuristics and bias, *Science, 185*, 1124–31; D. Kahneman, P. Slovic, and A. Tversky (Eds.) (1982), *Judgment under uncertainty: Heuristics and biases*, New York: Cambridge University Press.

20. A. Tversky and D. Kahneman (1985), The framing decisions and the psychology of choice, in G. Wright (Ed.), *Behavioral decision-making*, New York: Plenum Press, pp. 26–27.

21. Tversky and Kahneman (1985), p. 27.

22. Tversky and Kahneman (1985), p. 37.

23. Tversky and Kahneman (1985), pp. 36–37

24. I. Janis (1989), *Crucial decisions: Leadership in policy-making and crisis management*, New York: The Free Press, pp. 35–40.

25. Janis (1989), pp. 40–42.

26. Janis (1989), p. 42.

27. Janis (1989), p. 43.

28. Janis (1989), pp. 46–47.

29. I. L. Janis (1972), *Victims of group think*, New York:

Houghton Mifflin; I. L. Janis (1982), *Groupthink: Psychological studies of policy decisions and fiascoes*, 2d ed., Boston: Houghton Mifflin.

30. Janis (1989), pp. 71–85.

31. Janis and Mann (1977), pp. 82–120.

32. Janis and Mann (1977), pp. 91–92.

33. Janis and Mann (1977), pp. 121–24.

34. Janis (1989), p. 90.

35. P. F. Drucker (1974), *Management: Tasks, responsibilities, practices*, New York: Harper & Row, p. 471.

36. Drucker, p. 472.

37. Drucker, p. 473.

38. R. Y. Hirokawa (1982), Group communication and problem-solving effectiveness I: A critical review of inconsistent findings, *Communication Quarterly, 30*, 134–41.

39. R. Y. Hirokawa (1988), Group communication and decision-making performance: A continued test of the functional perspective, *Human Communication Research, 14*, 487–515.

40. Hirokawa (1988), p. 489.

41. Hirokawa (1988), p. 511.

42. A. J. Salazar, R. Y. Hirokawa, K. M. Propp, K. M. Julian, and G. B. Leatham (1994), In search of true cause: Examination of the effect of group potential and group interaction on decision performance, *Human Communication Research 20*, 529–59.

43. L. L. Putnam and C. E. Wilson (1982), Communication strategies in organizational conflicts: Reliability and validity in a measurement scale, in M. Burgoon (Ed.), *Communication yearbook 6*, Beverly Hills, Calif.: Sage, p. 629; L. L. Putnam and M. S. Poole (1987), Conflict and negotiation, in F. M. Jablin, L. L. Putnam, K. H. Roberts, and L. W. Porter (Eds.), *Handbook of organizational communication: An interdisciplinary perspective*, Newbury Park, Calif.: Sage, p. 549.

44. S. A. Freeman, S. W. Littlejohn, and W. B. Pearce (1992), Communication and moral conflict, *Western Journal of Communication, 56*, 311–29.

45. Freeman, Littlejohn, and Pearce, p. 315.

46. D. H. Cloven and M. E. Roloff (1991), Sense-making activities and interpersonal conflict: Communication cures for the mulling blues, *Western Journal of Speech Communication, 55*, 136–37.

47. Putnam and Wilson, p. 622.

48. Putnam and Wilson.

49. Putnam and Wilson, p. 633.

50. Putnam and Poole, p. 558.

51. C. Conrad (1991), Communication in conflict: Style-strategy relationships, *Communication Monographs, 58*, 135–55.

52. D. Katz and R. L. Kahn (1978), *The social psychology of organizations*, 2d ed., New York: Wiley, p. 634.

53. C. Morrill and C. K. Thomas (1992), Organizational conflict management as disputing process: The problem of social escalation, *Human Communication Research, 18,* pp. 401–3.

54. Putnam and Poole, p. 558.

55. D. J. Canary and B. H. Spitzberg (1987), Appropriateness and effectiveness perceptions of conflict strategies, *Human Communication Research, 14,* 93–118; D. J. Canary and B. H. Spitzberg (1989), A model of the perceived competence of conflict strategies, *Human Communication Research, 15,* 630–49; D. J. Canary and B. H. Spitzberg (1990), Attribution biases and associations between conflict strategies and competence outcomes, *Communication Monographs, 57,* 139–51.

56. Canary and Spitzberg (1990), p. 140.

57. Canary and Spitzberg (1990), pp. 141–42.

58. M. H. Bazerman and R. J. Lewicki (Eds.) (1983), Preface, *Negotiating in organizations,* Beverly Hills, Calif.: Sage, p. 7.

59. Putnam and Poole, p. 563.

60. See R. Fisher and W. Ury (1981), *Getting to yes: Negotiating agreement without giving in,* Boston: Houghton Mifflin; and W. L. Ury, J. M. Brett, and S. B. Goldberg (1988), *Getting disputes resolved: Designing systems to cut the costs of conflict,* San Francisco: Jossey-Bass.

61. M. H. Bazerman and M. A. Neale (1983), Heuristics in negotiation: Limitations to effective dispute resolution, in M. H. Bazerman and R. J. Lewicki (Eds.), *Negotiating in organizations,* Beverly Hills, Calif.: Sage, pp. 58–59.

62. D. Turner (1990), Intraorganizational bargaining: The effect of goal congruence and trust on negotiator strategy use, *Communication Studies, 41,* 54–75.

63. Other terms for this kind of technology include "groupware," computer-supported cooperative work (CSCW), and electronic meetings systems (EMS). N. S. Contractor and D. R. Seibold (1993), Theoretical frameworks for the study of structuring processes in group decision support systems, *Human Communication Research 19,* 528–63.

64. M. S. Poole and G. DeSanctis (1992), Microlevel structuration in computer-supported decision making, *Human Communication Research, 19,* 5–49.

65. G. P. Huber (1990), A theory of the effects of advanced information technologies on organizational design, intelligence, and decision-making, *Academy of Management Review, 15,* 47–71.

66. S. Kiesler, J. Siegel, and T. W. McGuire (1984), Social psychological aspects of computer-mediated communication, *American Psychologist, 39,* 1123–34.

67. Poole and DeSanctis, p. 43.

68. Huber, pp. 50-51.

CHAPTER **12**

Public Communication

CHAPTER OBJECTIVES

After studying this chapter, you should be able to:

- Describe the main characteristics of the public communication setting that differentiate it from other communication settings.
- Explain why public communication studies usually follow functionalist and transmissional perspectives in organizational communication.
- Explain how reification of the organization makes it difficult to identify sources for many public communication messages.
- Explain the presence of a persuasive element to most organizational public communication.
- Define the characteristics of public messages aimed at organizational socialization.
- Give examples of each of the message strategies of identification, framing, and symbolic convergence.
- Discuss the effects of available channels or media on public communication.
- Summarize some of the legal considerations on organizational public communication.

CHAPTER OUTLINE

THE NATURE OF PUBLIC COMMUNICATION

The Fed announces a one-quarter of a point increase in interest rates, a university sends a letter to students and their families to explain an increase in tuition for the coming academic year, lobbyists for the electric power industry issue a position paper for state legislatures on the industry's financial structure, and so on.

Organizations are the sources of many kinds of messages. The ubiquity of advertising is no doubt the most obvious effect of public organizational communication. Increasingly, advertising is omnipresent in other countries as well as in the United States. Public relations departments are also becoming more sophisticated in ways of getting an organization's messages before a public.

Additionally, organizations constantly send messages to their own members through public communication. Upon arriving at work on the first day, a typical employee is ushered into an orientation meeting with other new associates, followed by training meetings, and perhaps a lunch addressed by one of the top executives of the corporation. In this instance, the messages are basically internal to the organization, while the first paragraph of this section provides examples of external communications.

Public communication is characterized by a *speaker–audience* setting. Interpersonal communication and small-group communication both assume a continual give

Public communication stresses the speaker–audience situation.

and take among the participants, with no one person expected to hold the floor to make a prepared or formal-sounding presentation. In public communication settings, the roles of "speaker" and "audience" are more clearly demarcated, however. Some distance and a clear distinction between speaker and listener are implied. The speaker may be physically present with a gathering of listeners, or his or her message may be broadcast through some medium, such as microwave, CATV, or computer link-ups. The speaker may be identifiable as an individual, or the source may be seen as an organization or institution (as in the example of a university or a federal agency making an announcement).

Approaches for the Study of Public Communication

The analysis of public communication draws on the principles and theories of traditional, classical rhetoric, the basic discipline underlying the preparation and production of persuasive messages. The rhetorical perspective is especially concerned with the analysis and explanation of the effects of messages intended to advocate some position. Whereas useful perspectives for analyzing interpersonal communication or group communication stress mutual turn taking and interactional sharing, the point of view for studying public communication stresses communicator intentionality and message effects.

The focus on public communication emphasizes the view of communication as strategic action, intended to bring about some desired result. Scholars looking at organizations' public communication in this way often subscribe to an interpretivist perspective, as described earlier, especially in Chapter 2. In other words, they are interested in developing an understanding of different rhetorical choices and strategies and the effects of these choices and strategies.

Public communication directs communicators' attention to the transmissional perspective of communication study, described in Chapter 3. The transmissional perspective focuses on the effects of channel and media in carrying or transmitting a coded message. This perspective stresses the fidelity of message transmission and the potential effects of noise that detracts from the receipt of a message as originally formulated at a source. This view also emphasizes the intentional nature of public communication, its concern with audience effects, and its strategic nature. The transmissional model of communication is normally compatible with a functionalist perspective of organizational communication, because this view of communication emphasizes making the process run "right"—that is, right from the point of view of someone in charge in the organization.

Critical theorists look at organizational public communication in terms of how it strengthens or reinforces a particular power relationship. One of the main purposes of internal public communication, from this point of view, is to inculcate a particular organizational ideology. Critical theorists tend to ask, beyond how something works, the question of who benefits from the operation. Thus critical analysts would look at ways in which attempts to change organizational culture represent attempts to control the value judgments of organizational members, even though the organization's values may not be in the members' best long-run interests.

Internal and External Public Communication

The term *public communication* is here defined in terms of the setting and the perceived relationship between a speaker and an audience. Thus, some public communication is primarily directed toward members within the organization, whereas other messages are directed at external audiences. Public communication relies on identifying the audience or multiple audiences for messages, and the production of public messages is therefore based on audience analysis and audience adaptation. Presumably, there are *internal* and *external* audiences.

The indoctrination and training of an organization's own members, for example, represent internal communication, whereas pronouncements directed to the general public or competitors or government agencies, for example, represent external communication. Of course, some messages may be aimed at both internal and external audiences; in fact, it is highly likely that external messages will be received and interpreted by organizational members. That internal messages will similarly be received by the general public is less likely but not impossible. Some messages will thus have multiple and overlapping audiences. In fact, the distinction suggested here is somewhat artificial, but it is useful for analyzing differences between rhetorical efforts directed primarily at different audiences.

Internally directed public communication is considered first, in terms of identifying and analyzing the source of these messages, their purposes, the intended audiences, and message strategies. The subsequent section takes up the same points regarding externally directed organizational communication.

INTERNAL PUBLIC COMMUNICATION

A significant amount of organizational rhetoric is directed toward internal audiences. This effort typically begins with the orientation and indoctrination of new members. In fact, such attempts at indoctrination often precede hiring, beginning with recruiting interviews. Good recruiters realize that part of their function is to create in people a positive attitude toward the company or institution, regardless of whether an interviewee is eventually inducted.

After a person becomes part of an organization, the organization's rhetorical effort naturally continues. Chapter 9 includes a discussion of the process of organizational socialization, pointing out that members typically are assimilated into the organization in stages over time. That discussion also pointed out that much of the communication that contributes to socialization is interpersonal and informal in nature.[1] Still, organizations often make a concerted effort to assimilate or socialize new members through various forms of formal and public programs. Many organizations have formal entry and orientation programs that are designed not only to train new members in specific job-related skills but also to win them over to the values of the organizational culture, at least as it is envisioned by the people in charge of the indoctrination. New members are therefore exposed to speeches, videotapes, and other kinds of presentations to begin the intended assimilation process. New hires at Disney World, for example, are introduced to the Disney way of doing things in the first stages of orientation. The employees' entrance to the grounds from Lake Buena Vista pointedly welcomes "cast members," providing an image of how new employees are to think of themselves.

Settings for internal public communication thus include training lectures and presentations, and also meetings to explain work processes, rules, benefits, updates of organizational objectives, financial standing, and innovations. Other meetings or presentations may stress the importance of quality and innovativeness, perhaps, or other current programs developed by upper management. In some organizations, other groups besides upper management have access to public communication settings; the most typical such group is a recognized labor union or other collective bargaining organization. Still, most of the "airwaves" for formal internal communication are often controlled by the higher levels of management. The question of identifying the sources for public communication messages within organizations is the next topic for analysis.

Sources for Internal Communication

The *source* of organizational messages is not always readily apparent. The tendency toward *reification* of the organization is mentioned in Chapter 2. Reification makes it possible for the real, human sources of messages to remain indeterminate. The "administration" is the source for a message concerning tuition increases, for example; or the "company" announces the decision to relocate its plant in Mexico, resulting in the layoff of several hundred local workers. The organization rather than an individual becomes the source in these circumstances. Even an individual spokesperson claims to be speaking not in his or her own name, but in the name of the organization. Institutional rhetoric thus has a sort of anonymous quality and is presented as the voice of the collective.

Several implications flow from this nature of organizational sources. First, the definition and boundaries of the organization may be rhetorical constructs themselves. That is, when we say that an organization is the source of a message, who is included or implied as part of that organization? For example, when a university announces a tuition increase, are the students seen as part of the organization, "the university"? When a plant is being relocated, is the labor union representing the line workers seen as part of the organization that is making this announcement? Are patients considered to be part of the organization designated as the hospital? These kinds of questions have no clear answer. At times, students are considered part of the organization known as the university; for other purposes, they may not be. Who or what, then, is understood to be the speaker in cases of organizational rhetoric? Certain groups within the organization are typically empowered to speak in the name of the entire organization on different issues or at different times.

A second important issue is the credibility of the perceived source of the communication. Classical rhetorical theories referred to this credibility as the *ethos* of the speaker. The ethos was the character of the speaker as perceived by the members of the audience. Organizations are endowed with *collective credibility* or ethos. This implication raises questions concerning what is the "character" of the organization as perceived by the rank and file, the intended audience for the message. For individuals, ethos is thought to be influenced by whether the audience sees the speaker as competent and trustworthy. An organization's ethos is shaped, similarly, by perceptions concerning the organization's effectiveness and openness or trustworthiness.

Anecdotal evidence and survey research suggest that organizational credibility is often not high, especially on matters related to organizational change and restructuring.[2] A survey of over 90,000 employees of the Internal Revenue Service found that only 24 percent believed that upper management communicated with them honestly, only about a third felt that they received enough information about other parts of the agency, and only 40 percent said that internal communication about organizational change was handled well.[3] Another survey of 32,000 employees in 26 different firms found that only half of the respondents thought that internal communication was either candid or accurate; "two-thirds said communication was incomplete, and more than half said communication was strictly top down, with no opportunity provided for feedback."[4] Perceptions of source credibility are thus tied up with perceptions of openness as well as of accuracy. Timeliness is undoubtedly an important factor as well, as organizational members trust information that correctly warns or alerts them concerning upcoming events or crises. In the case of a large electrical utility that was preparing to merge with another, equally large utility in a different state, the author observed that there was widespread concern about receiving information regarding the merger in a timely fashion. Many employees seemed to feel that they were often in the dark regarding the impact of and timetable for the steps in completing the merger. In a different merger situation in California, employees reported feeling that they were receiving contradictory messages: On the one hand, they were to develop self-directed teams to work through problems of merging the two operations, but these teams, on the other hand, were kept in the dark about decisions affecting the merger.[5]

Third, internal public communication is usually a form of downward communication, as the source is usually located at a higher level of the hierarchy than the intended audience (see Chapter 8 regarding downward communication). Hence, discussion of the nature and problems of public communication in organizations appears to have a strong management bias. Problems with downward communication, such as those of credibility, lack of contact, semantic distance, or perceived cultural or gender differences, can thus affect public communication as well.

On the other hand, as noted in Chapter 8, people do prefer personal or face-to-face channels for information from higher levels; a live presentation or a speech by the CEO or another top executive can personalize downward communication messages, and can thus be more effective than written or other impersonal channels. For example, Bob Crawford, the energetic founder and CEO of a leading furniture rental company, often surprises newly hired sales associates by leading some of their training sessions himself.[6] The use of face-to-face presentations that personalize messages and emphasize the importance that top managers place on communication can improve on the perceived weaknesses of organizational source credibility.

Purposes of Internal Communication

Presenters of internal public communication often distinguish between two basic purposes, information giving and persuasion, although these categories can be misleading. One person's "information" may be another person's propaganda. Information giving is linked with persuasion in that giving information is necessary in order to effect persuasion, and a speaker must persuade listeners that the information given is relevant, important, true, and so on, in order to inform. In the organizational context, critical theorists would argue that all communication is in some way persuasive, noting that even job training makes certain assumptions regarding perpetuation of the power structure or the value of the organization's work or product.

Consider the following topics, which may be seen as mainly informative from a managerial point of view:

Orientation to company policies, products, work processes

Job training

Job instructions and directions

Explanation of benefits and compensation policies

Description of safety procedures

Presentations on organizational structure and reorganization

From a presenter's point of view, these topics may seem completely neutral, just a matter of giving information. Still, even a so-called informative presentation will try to indicate that there is a right way and a wrong way to do things. Safety presentations, for example, are concerned with convincing people that safety is an important matter, in the first place, and then convincing them to behave in certain ways.

The increasing complexity of internal communication can be seen in the case of benefits communication. For many Americans, the organizations for which they work provide not just a salary but access to various other kinds of social benefits, such as health insurance and care, that are not readily available through other means. More companies and people with communication and marketing backgrounds are entering the field of employee benefits because of the need for improved communication with employees regarding benefits programs.[7] Explanation of fringe benefits is thus becoming a subfield of internal communication in its own right. These messages not only provide information about how benefits packages work, but often are aimed at convincing organizational members that a particular package is the best one—that it should be selected or voted for, for example. Hence, there is a persuasive component to this communication as well as an informative one.

Some rhetorical purposes are described as being more definitely persuasive, such as the following:

Gaining compliance with directives and policies

Motivation and morale building

Indoctrination in regard to organizational ideology and goals

Building support for changes or new initiatives

While most of these presentations aim at giving audience members new information, skills, or understanding, usually in areas of technical competence, they intend to induce in listeners new, reinforced, or changed beliefs and attitudes. Beliefs, in this sense, are statements that a person thinks are true or false, such as "exposure to radon is associated with increased incidence of lung cancer." Attitudes are beliefs that contain a significant evaluative component inclining one to some action, such as "exposure to radon is dangerous and should be avoided." A speaker can try to create a new belief or attitude, as when listeners are unfamiliar with radon or had never heard of its purported health risk. One can try to reinforce an existing belief or attitude: "You're right to avoid exposure to radon and here are even more reasons to do so." Or, the speaker can try to alter existing beliefs and attitudes: "Radon exposure is not as harmful as you may think."

In addition, efforts at "managing" or changing organizational culture rely on persuasive communication. The case of Boeing in the previous chapter is a good example; the company hopes to create among the workers a new belief and attitude system concerning the way to achieve quality in work processes and products. Campaigns calling for "zero defects" intend to create the belief that it is possible to work to a standard that allows for no defects; this may require changing certain existing beliefs, such as, "some waste is to be expected." Efforts at creating or changing a corporate culture are hence rhetorical efforts, advanced through public presentations, media events, or meetings.

The emphasis on organizational culture, related movements to enact Total Quality Management (TQM), and team-building programs highlight the persuasive nature of internal communication. These persuasive efforts combine ideological and motivational appeals with technical training and information giving by linking the rewards of a positive organizational culture with technical performance and expertise. Notice how this contemporary trend contrasts with the traditional internal communication envisioned by Taylorism or classical management theory, in which managers simply give directions and orders for workers to carry out. TQM and emphasis on organizational culture assume that it is important to explain the rationales for decisions and directives and to inculcate attitudes and beliefs that allow workers to be self-directed or self-motivated. Of course, such teams can develop a form of mutual monitoring, which itself becomes quite pervasive and controlling, as members continually are present to "look over each other's shoulders."[8] When a self-directed team buys into the organizational message in this way, managerial control is tightened.

Internal communication is thus often directed toward "socializing" organizational members, bringing them to feel and behave as insiders rather than outsiders. Orientation and training, for example, often represent attempts at socialization and therefore at creating certain preferred beliefs, attitudes, and values.[9] Not only do members learn requisite procedures and skills, they also learn to identify with a particular organizational culture. Stories, myths, rituals, and ceremonies reinforce the messages from training and orientation, communicating to new members preferred roles and norms of behavior. Much of internal communication is thus concerned with inducing people to identify with and be committed to the organization, its goals, and its values. Consequently, the rhetorical critic George Cheney concludes, "In fact, persuasion is inherent in the process of *organizing*."[10]

Effects

Finally, a concern with purpose implies a concern with the effects of rhetorical messages, specifically with determining whether the intended effects were produced. First of all, the ability to determine whether a message has had an intended effect depends on the clarity and specificity of the objective. Some effects are easier to observe than others. If you ask someone to shut the door, that person either does or does not do so: The effect of the message can be immediately and directly known. Most organizational messages are more complex and subtle than this. When a company launches an internal campaign built around the slogan "quality is job one" or "zero defects," as in the Boeing case, the effects of any one message cannot easily be sorted out.

An outcome of a concerted communication campaign for improving plant safety could be observed in terms of a decrease in the number of accidents and injuries; improvements in product quality can be measured in terms of defects per unit of product. It may not be easy, however, to ascribe the improvement in safety or quality directly to specific public communication messages. Other factors could have led to the changes, including group pressures, interpersonal influence, changes in the workforce, and so on. Similarly, when an organization is trying to change its corporate culture through a campaign designed to get people to commit to a new set of values, the results are much more difficult to discern and to measure.

Clearly, in many organizations today, an important desired outcome for internal organizational communication is *organizational commitment,* which refers to the extent to which individuals are committed to the goals, values, and purposes of the organization. A questionnaire has been developed for the purpose of measuring this kind of positive attitude toward the organization.[11] It may thus be possible to measure this particular effect, organizational commitment, and relate it to programs of internal public communication. Research concerning organizational commitment indicates that positive commitment is generally related to features of the organizational climate and to certain styles of leadership or leader communication.[12] Specifically, communication that emphasizes the importance of the individual in the organization or that shows consideration for the individual member is directly related to members' commitment to the organization.

Audiences

Internal communication depends on identifying and adapting to the appropriate audience or audiences. Questions about defining organizational boundaries, touched on previously, can be quite relevant at this point. Who constitutes the internal audience for organizational messages? For different purposes or for different messages, there may be different definitions of who and what groups make up the internal audience. When are students considered part of the organization "the university," and when are they considered to be "clients" or "consumers"? Determining who constitutes the "we" implied in internal messages may be in part a rhetorical consideration itself. Certain messages can imply that some people are insiders and others are not. Internal public communication may thus define organizational boundaries, and in so doing inadvertently alienate or exclude some potential audiences.

Furthermore, there are various ways to *segment* potential internal audiences into groups for whom different persuasive appeals or communication strategies would be appropriate. Orientation programs for new members clearly segment or differentiate new members from veteran or experienced members. In many organizations, newer members serve a kind of apprenticeship or probationary period before being inducted into full membership: university faculties, certain skilled crafts, law firms, and some arts organizations, for example. A message that deals with advancement from one status to another within the organization will obviously be received differently by the two audiences. Say that a law firm decides to announce that only four partnerships will be available for the twenty probationary associates in the firm. The associates will obviously respond to that message very differently from full partners, as the associates will feel more threatened by it.

Many large corporate organizations segment internal audiences in terms of unionized versus nonunionized members, often categorized as "bargaining unit" and "nonbargaining unit." For purposes of team building, quality control, safety consciousness, and the like, both groups may be treated as constituting the same audience. When matters touching on union contracts, wages, or working conditions are the topic, however, these groups represent different kinds of audiences. The unionized members may suddenly feel that they have become an external audience for these kinds of messages.

Internal audiences may be further segmented in terms of the nature of the work they perform within the organization. Some members' work, for example, may depend on a highly technical competence or expertise: computer specialists, electrical engineers, chemists, architects, faculty teachers, and researchers are examples. These organizational members may identify as much with a professional association as with the organization in which they are currently employed. Loyalties to the profession can compete with loyalties to the specific organization, so that these people may interpret appeals in organizational messages based on commitment to the organization differently from the way those in less technical areas in the organization interpret them. Those with professional affiliations may feel more mobile and thus identify less with the fate of an individual organization.[13]

Implied in some of these distinctions are differences of status. In large corporations, there are often vast differences in pay, lifestyle, and consequent status as one moves from the bottom of the hierarchy to the top. Creating the feeling that people of such different status levels are somehow all part of the same team (or family or whatever similar metaphor is chosen) can be difficult. Communication that appeals to people of high status in the organization may have little appeal to or relevance for audiences composed of people of lower status. It is more likely that people will identify with smaller subsets of the larger organization and thereby potentially constitute different kinds of audiences for internal messages.

These differences—based on organizational boundaries, seniority or rank, unionization, nature of work, and status—are only illustrative. Many other bases for segmenting internal audiences exist. As organizations increase in size and complexity, therefore, one cannot assume that there is a single or unified audience within a single organization; rather, there are usually multiple internal audiences. The more complex the organization, the more distinct internal audiences there are likely to be.

Channels

Many of the channels for internal organizational communication were presented in Chapter 8:

- *Written or print channels,* such as:
   handbooks
   instruction manuals
   job descriptions
   work rules
   internal newsletters
   memoranda
   pay inserts

letters (to members' homes)
print advertising (aimed partly at organizational members)
bulletin boards, posted notices, posters
information racks, pamphlets, and handouts
annual reports

- *Interviews or face-to-face meetings,* such as:

employment interviews
performance evaluations
disciplinary interviews
on-the-job training, giving instructions
conferences
chain-of-command (serial transmission of messages through steps in the hierar-
    chy)
mentoring

- *Group meetings,* such as:

orientation and training groups
department meetings
committee meetings
quality circles
mass meetings, speeches

- *Media channels,* such as:

video presentations, films
telephone "hot lines"
computer bulletin board messages, E-mail
fax messages
voice mail
videoconferences
external advertising on radio and television

Clearly not all of these media are relevant for public communication involving a speaker–audience situation. Generally, the channels in the third and fourth sections above—various kinds of meetings addressed by a speaker and several kinds of media messages—can be relevant. Video presentations and films, addresses to videoconferences, and media messages directed to an audience can also represent instances of public communication. Usually, voice mail, telephone hot lines, bulletin boards, E-mail, and fax do not have the dynamics implied by the speaker–audience nature of public communication. Nonetheless, persuasive messages on voice mail, E-mail, hot lines, or bulletin boards, as well as those in print media, often make use of many of the same kinds of rhetorical strategies employed in public settings.

Meetings are the most obvious setting for public communication, especially when the meeting is addressed by a speaker. The organizational culture school draws attention to the fact that there are rhetorical elements in other kinds of organized meetings as well. There are, for example, rallies, celebrations, awards ceremonies, seminars, and training meetings, all of which can provide opportunities for public messages to internal audiences. Rallies for Mary Kay cosmetics representatives are excellent examples of extravaganza meetings with primarily rhetorical intent. The meetings of self-help or support groups, such as Alcoholics Anonymous, are also meetings in which speakers exemplify and reinforce the mission and values of the organization. Company picnics and retirement dinners are ceremonies at which public communication takes place with similar purposes.

When the organization is too large or is geographically dispersed, the same kind of setting can be approximated by the use of various media. For example, executives can address the membership through a video link using cable or broadcast systems. Videotapes can be distributed to remote locations to be viewed by the local members seated in front of the VCR, simulating an audience being addressed in a meeting. Remote locations can be directly linked in real time, as in videoconferencing, allowing a speaker to address conferees (as in the classrooms in "distance education"). In real-time link-ups, the speaker can be aware of actual audience responses as they occur, instead of relying on delayed feedback as in other mediated situations, such as direct or delayed broadcast.

Message Strategies

Public communication settings are typically the most obviously strategic of all the types of organizational communication (other types are often strategic as well, but less obviously so). A speaker consciously selects a strategy in order to bring about a desired effect among audience members. In classically managed organizations, there was less concern with persuasion as a means of motivating or controlling the behavior of organizational members. The formal authority of the hierarchy or the superior technical knowledge of the "expert" was sufficient to induce the desired behaviors; there was little concern for inculcating organizational values and attitudes.

Modern organizations, however, tend more toward motivating their members to perform in desired ways. We have already noted the importance of socialization as a means of getting members to accept the value system of an organization. Just as youth are socialized into a particular national culture by instruction and example, organization members are taught to internalize the organizational culture and its values. Presumably, members who are thus socialized are committed to the same goals as the other members and the goals of the organization as a whole; what they want individually is the same as what is desired for the collective. In those organizations with very strong cultures, therefore, members do not need much supervision and direction, because they have accepted the organization's goals and methods as legitimate and as nearly identical with their own.

Organizational communicators hence increasingly rely on *rhetorical strategies* aimed at socializing internal audiences into a desired culture. The basic strategy is that of *identification,* in which the speaker hopes to induce the listeners to identify their own needs and interests with those of the organization.[14]

The Swedish organizational theorist Mat Alvesson stresses the use of cultural values and ideologies in internal organizational rhetoric.[15] These strategies rely on the ability of one group to *frame,* or define, reality or important domains of reality for organization members, a second kind of rhetorical strategy.

In a third type of strategy, often referred to as *symbolic convergence,* common visions of organizational reality become the basis for organizational persuasion.[16]

Identification. The rhetorical strategy of *identification* is associated with the critical theories of Kenneth Burke.[17] George Cheney delineates three subtypes within this general category of identification: the common-ground appeal, appeals based on a common enemy or threat ("identification through antithesis"), and the use of the assumed "we."[18]

1. *The common-ground appeal* attempts to show that the interests of the organization are the same as those of the individual members, as when a manager tells workers, "We are all in the same boat here." For example, management argues that workers, even labor union members, have the same interest in corporate profitability as the chief executives. Or, an appeal is made based on the common identification of workers and management as all being American, or parents who are concerned about family values, or people concerned about physical health and well-being. Because the interests of the group and of the individual coincide, the individual is persuaded to accept the group's interests as his or her own.

In terms of corporate culture, common-ground techniques can be based on an idealized collective identity. Efforts are made to hold up this organizational identity as a source of pride, as in statements such as "IBM people" are proactive self-starters. It is hoped that the individual will take on this identity as a certain kind of person and therefore enact the desired behaviors and espouse the desired attitudes. The message is that you are a special kind of person whose identity is caught up in the identity or image of the organization. Boeing Company, for example, stresses the identification of being "world class" in its communications to motivate managers to implement the Continuous Quality Improvement (CQI) program, as shown below.

2. *Contrasting insiders with outsiders,* or the "enemy," is the second application of the identification strategy; instead of saying who or what we are, the speaker stresses who or what we are not. Collective identity is extolled in contrast to its opposite, those who are outside, different, or the enemy. Perceiving a common threat becomes a way to build collective identification. Typical threats or enemies have been defined as "foreign competition," as when a leader such as Lee Iaccoca points an accusing finger at the Japanese car manufacturers. Other typical enemies have been identified as "environmentalists" or "government regulators" or "bureaucrats." Political organizations build their collective identity around opposition, of course, as when Republicans call for party unity in order to prevent the Democrats from taking advantage of the Republicans' broken ranks. Occasionally a group may find unity only in collective opposition to some other group or practice.

This technique can lead to the practice of "scapegoating" or stigmatizing others in order to draw attention away from the organization's own shortcomings. Thus, some companies that are charged with polluting the environment through their processes may scapegoat environmentalists, trying to identify them as some kind of radical, fringe element. An effort is made to stigmatize the environmentalists as irrationally more concerned with spotted owls and snail darters than with real, live working people, whose jobs are portrayed as threatened by environmental protectionism. The ethical implications of techniques of this sort are further considered in Chapter 14 of this text.

3. *The assumed "we"* is the third technique perceived by Cheney, who views it as a powerful strategy because of its unstated and subtle nature. The language implies that all members of the organization participate in and accede to the message. A typical effort at changing a corporate culture, in this case at Boeing, uses this technique:

> *We* visited world-class companies and listened to the quality experts. *We* started educating our employees and *we* started to focus on problem-solving and process improvements. But CQI means far more than the application of practices and techniques. CQI represents a significant cultural change and a shift in the fundamental philosophy of doing business. *We* will achieve the mindset required to attain world-class quality when *we* begin to believe that perfection is possible. *We* will make this necessary shift when *we* know that *we* can go for years without defects or mistakes in out processes.[19] (emphasis added)

This technique relies on indirect suggestion by implying a list of characteristics that *we* all share. The strategy of identification can be most effective when its evocation goes unnoticed. Lincoln at Gettysburg, for example, contended that "we are engaged in a great Civil War." In fact, many people in the North did not then support the war, and many militarily eligible men found ways to evade or buy their way out of the draft. Were these nonparticipants part of the "we" engaged in that war? When a large corporation announces that "we" must close an unprofitable plant, are the workers to be laid off part of the implied "we"?

Framing. *Framing* is a rhetorical strategy based on defining situations in certain ways so that some issues are highlighted and others are implied to be irrelevant. The frame provides the context within which actions are to be judged. We say, "Honesty is the best policy," and that one should always tell the truth, but should one tell the truth to a kidnapper or to a terrorist threatening to blow up a high-rise office building? We can frame such situations, setting them off from normal experience, and say that within this frame, or definition of the situation, normal rules are suspended; it's OK to mislead or misinform the kidnapper or the terrorist in order to save lives. Public communicators use framing when they attempt to show that what they are advocating should be evaluated within a special context or that a situation should be defined in a particular way, often at variance with how such a situation would be defined in "everyday life."

The organization and its internal cultural values provide the frame for guiding and directing action. Within the frame of business, it is said to be rational to discount personal feelings and considerations—"business is business." In order to ensure profit

and survivability, the organization can resist pollution controls or costly safety measures, perhaps. People are asked to split their personalities, with approved behavior
and attitudes in private life separated from approved behaviors and attitudes in their
institutional lives. The expanding use of beepers, cellular phones, and networked
home computers means that this bifurcation extends into "private" or "off" time more
and more. Some organizations, such as hospitals and physicians' practices, police and
fire departments, military organizations, and other governmental agencies, can demand an extraordinary commitment of members' time and loyalty because of the
extremely high importance attached to their operations. This commitment is especially expected in situations that are framed as emergencies.

Framing tends to be ideological or cultural, in that it defines reality for specific
groups of people. *Ideology* here refers to "an integrated set of values, ideals, and understanding about a particular part of social reality that justifies certain commitments
and actions."[20] The values, ideals, and interpretations of the relevant part of reality are
determined by the organizational culture. A speaker tries to justify a certain belief or
course of action by framing it in terms of an accepted belief or value in the corporate
culture. Chapter 7, dealing with organizational cultures, indicated some of the basic
schemes for categorizing such cultural messages. The categories of Trice and Beyer,
for example, include the following forms of cultural communication:[21]

- Symbols (objects, settings, performers, or roles); nonverbal communication
- Language (jargon, humor, metaphors, slogans, gestures); verbal communication
- Narration (stories, legends, sagas); verbal communication
- Practices (rituals, taboos, rites, ceremonials); both verbal and nonverbal communi-
  cation

Clearly, a speaker can refer to cultural symbols, use language (jargon, humor,
metaphors, slogans) characteristic of the culture, or tell stories that illustrate the culture. The presentation can be placed within the framework of a ritual, rite, or cer-
emony. Stories or narratives are particularly popular for internal organizational
discourse.[22] By telling a story or referring to one that is already well known to his or
her listeners, the speaker frames what is being talked about, that is, suggests the culturally appropriate way to interpret it.

Mumby analyzes the well-known story of Tom Watson at IBM and the woman
who refused to admit him to a restricted area because he lacked the proper identification badge. The story can be used to illustrate the unique values of this particular
organization, as well as the singular characteristics of the founding hero, Watson.
According to the story, the woman, described as "a twenty-two-year-old bride weigh-
ing ninety pounds," recognizes the head of IBM, Watson, as he strides toward her area
with his entourage. There is a moment of high drama as the woman denies him clear-
ance while the rest of the entourage gasps. Watson says nothing, but holds up his
hand until someone is able to rush off and procure the appropriate badge. One moral
of this story is that at IBM, the rules apply to everybody; another could be that all
employees must do their duty regardless of who is involved. A speaker can use this

DIVERSITY MATTERS

Framing and Sexual Harassment

Robin Patric Clair has pointed out that various framing techniques can be used to rationalize away the seriousness of sexual harassment in the workplace.* For example, the harassment can be framed as "simple misunderstanding," or "flirting," or it can be framed as human nature, suggesting that this is "just the way things are." Stories may be used to show that women who are "good team players" shrug off such advances and do not rock the boat.

Various surveys and other studies suggest that sexual harassment is still widespread in American organizations; nevertheless, organizational rhetoric tends to downplay the seriousness of this issue. While the top levels of the organization may tend to frame sexual harassment in ways that discount its presence or its seriousness, even women and men who are subjected to what is arguably harassment may also develop framing devices in order to avoid confronting the power structure and bringing formal charges. According to Robin Patric Clair's article there are several frames that thus discount sexual harassment.**

1. Accepting the "best interests" of the organization. Stories may support the "good employee"

who refrained from making formal charges because that was "best for everyone" or "best for the company."

2. Claims of simple misunderstanding. Perhaps the supposed harasser was just flirting. In these days of more open sexuality, perhaps one shouldn't be too sensitive, this frame may argue.

3. That's just the way things are, the "human nature" frame. There are some things that you just can't expect to change—boys will be boys and men will be men, this frame may explain.

4. Seeing the charges as joking, humorous behavior, not to be taken seriously. This frame may also be used to make light of the alleged harassment. People should be able to take a joke, or a little teasing, are forms this frame may take.

5. The demarcation between public (organizational) and private domains. Dealing with unwanted sexual advances is something between the two people involved, this frame argues; they should work it out themselves.

Narratives within the organizational context that are part of organizational socialization can thus be used to place various experiences in a desired context. While this process can be useful for inculcating positive values, such as commitment to public service or quality, it can be detrimental in denying organizational problems, such as sexual harassment. How can the frames described above be overcome or neutralized in trying to deal effectively with issues such as sexual harassment?

*R. P. Clair (1993), The use of framing devices to sequester organizational narratives: Hegemony and harassment, *Communication Monographs, 60,* 113–36.

**See Clair, pp. 119–21.

story by telling it in detail or by merely referring to it if he or she feels that the audience members are already familiar with the details. Different speakers can use the story for a variety of purposes to evoke desired values and attitudes.

The simple moral of a story may mask more subtle interpretations. Mumby points out that beneath its surface, the story about Watson teaches that rules, as made by the top executives, must be upheld at all costs. The story gets its force from the hidden contradiction that Watson upholds the principle because he, among all others, is powerful enough to break it, should he choose to do so.[23]

Symbolic Convergence. *Symbolic convergence,* or "fantasy theme analysis," refers to a system for analyzing communication developed by Ernest G. Bormann. This analysis originally grew out of observations of task-oriented groups. Robert Bales and then Bormann noted what appears to be a typical phenomenon experienced by such groups: a break from task-related discussion for a period of "sharing group fantasies."[24] Such breaks usually begin with an individual injecting a dramatic image or, more typically, a dramatic story into the discussion. Another member takes up the imagery or story line, elaborating on the theme; others then join in, developing the same theme or story. In sharing the fantasy, the group members share similar emotions and responses. Their symbolic pictures of the world or a particular part of the world begin to converge through this sharing process, hence the term *symbolic convergence*. In this manner, a group consciousness is developed and shared; puzzling or worrisome aspects of the environment are clarified and explained for those sharing the fantasy. Note that the term *fantasy* is used in a technical sense here by Bormann; it does not necessarily refer to a fantastic or unreasonable story—the story may actually be fairly accurate and true to life. In the same way, a myth is not necessarily untrue; it is a story intended to explain some problematic aspect of life to those who share it. Fantasies, therefore, like myths, have important explanatory functions. Usually they portray heroes overcoming obstacles or hardships in order to conquer or defeat some enemy or villain.

Although the theory was originally applied to small group communication, Bormann has shown that it can be applied to communication experiences in organizations, public address, and political rhetoric as well. The organization, or a division or subset of the organization, over time develops various fantasy themes that portray valued characteristics or values of members. The story about Watson and the young bride, described in the previous section, is an example of a fantasy theme, a story that could be retold and cast in different ways in order to make the point that even the founder and head of the organization respects the organization's rules and regulations. In an organization with developed fantasy themes, one need only allude to the story almost in code, using just a person's name or some other loaded term. "Remember the WIN buttons," someone may say, to remind in-group members of an earlier, unsuccessful attempt at some sort of public campaign.

Bormann also describes fantasy types, rhetorical visions, and rhetorical communities. *Fantasy types* serve as recurring plot lines, in which the situations and characters change but the point remains the same. For example, during the 1970s and 1980s, the Chinese government urged people to emulate Lei Feng, a young soldier killed in an accident in 1962 who was an exemplar of all the virtues the Chinese leaders hoped to reinforce in the population. Lately a new twenty-two-year-old soldier has replaced Lei Feng: Xu Honggang fought off a group of three thugs trying to attack a woman on a Beijing bus. Although stabbed several times in the fight, Xu drove off the attackers and led the police to them. Like Lei, Xu turned out to embody all the correct virtues that Chinese leaders extoll.[25] Whether the protagonist is Lei Feng or Xu Honggang, the story of the courageous young soldier represents a fantasy type used in the public rhetoric of the Chinese government. In organizations, there are often fantasy types about the dedicated worker who comes up with some great new invention on his kitchen table or in his garage or basement on his own time; or there is the fantasy type showing that the boss is only human, or has a warm or humorous side; and so on. Thus, the CEO who works one day a week in the company's laboratory is portraying a commitment to research and development, emphasizing a fantasy type that is important to the organization.

A *rhetorical vision* usually portrays an image of the group sharing the fantasies. The vision can often be described in a metaphor or analogy. For example, the vision may be that the organization is all one big family, or a well-oiled machine, or a winning sports team. Military imagery is often popular as well, as organizations refer to task forces, to people assigned to "take the point," to the need for reconnaissance, and the like; people are encouraged to be "good soldiers." The vision is often cast in sports jargon: The leadership develops a "game plan," while still having the flexibility and skill to "call an audible." The organization knows how to "play hardball," especially when the "clock is running down," or the game goes into "overtime." The use of the theatrical metaphor for Disney employees has been alluded to before. The idea that people selling soft drinks, running the rides, and cleaning up the grounds are cast members implies a vision of the organization's work. Even sales associates in stores selling Disney products are now referred to as cast members, who dress in "costume," certain prescribed styles. These people are engaged in show business, not just ordinary retail.

A group or organization that shares the same fantasy themes, types, and visions represents a *rhetorical community*. Large and complex organizations probably include several, often overlapping, rhetorical communities. The engineering department, for example, may develop into its own rhetorical community in the larger organization. The sales staff see themselves as somehow separate and special, as shown in their shared consciousness and identity revealed in their shared fantasies. If an organization has several internal groups with different rhetorical visions, there will usually be continual disagreement over mission, goals, allocation of resources, and the like. There will probably be many meetings to try to hammer out mission statements, future plans, and vision statements.

Shared fantasies, types or themes, and visions can be used by public communicators as they to evoke a desired response from their internal audiences. Bormann's theory thus provides a way of describing and explaining the strategies used for such communication.

Highlights of Internal Public Communication

The organization itself, or at least those higher-level members in control of the organization, is the source of public communication aimed at internal audiences. Identifying the actual sources of such messages is not always a simple matter. Messages may in fact imply the boundaries of a particular organization, indicating who is or is not part of the organization. Internal public communication is downward communication and is thus subject to the distortions and credibility problems characteristic of that form of communication.

Most such communication is intended to be persuasive in some way, even though some intentions are framed as primarily informative rather than persuasive. A great deal of internal communication concerns efforts at organizational socialization or gaining organizational commitment. Efforts at remaking organizational culture also involve campaigns of internal public communication.

There may be different audiences for internally directed messages, as the members can be segmented in different ways for different rhetorical purposes. Such segmentation may depend on length of service, unionization, or nature of work performed. Therefore, one may not assume a single, monolithic audience for internal messages. Similarly, there are many different channels and media available for internal public communication, although presentations before meetings (face-to-face or mediated) are most characteristic of public messages.

Message strategies are often based on the techniques of rhetorical identification, framing messages and contexts, or symbolic convergence. These strategies involve creating a sense of an in-group (the organization members) versus out-groups and a commitment to a common vision or metaphor for the members.

EXTERNAL PUBLIC COMMUNICATION

Two preliminary points should be understood at the outset of this section. First, external public communication, in which the organization becomes the source for messages directed to audiences outside the organization, is often the function of specialized groups within an organization and usually falls under the heading of advertising, public relations, lobbying, or issues management. These fields are specialized subjects or communication disciplines in their own right, and, except for perhaps lobbying, are extensively covered in other texts and courses. An assumption of this text is that organizational communication is primarily concerned with internal communication activities. For that reason, this section provides only an overview of external communication.

Second, often a definite relationship exists between internal and external communication. As a result of internal messages, organizational members become committed and motivated to being sources for communicating an organizational message to outsiders. Thus, if members feel good about their organization, they will present it in a favorable light to neighbors, family members, and friends. These people may, in turn, tell their friends that they know someone who works for this or that company, and that person is really enthusiastic, so it must be a very good organization. Effective internal communication programs can therefore lead directly to more effective external programs.

Sources for External Communication

As in the case of internal communication, identifying the source of externally directed organizational messages is not always a simple matter. The reification of the organization, as well as the legal fiction that corporations are persons, may obscure the real sources of organizational messages, typically individuals with decision-making authority within the organization. Even when the president or CEO is personally addressing an audience, the notion that she or he is a spokesperson or representative of the organization, and not really speaking for him- or herself, is maintained. One frequent defense of the employment of speechwriters to compose such addresses is based on this notion. The speechwriter is not seen as composing words for other individuals to pass off as their own; rather, the speechwriter is part of a collective, organizational team composing the message for the institution, not the individual. The writer is one part of the team; the actual speaker, another part; the legal department that approves the language, a third part; and so on.

The source for organizational messages is therefore perceived as a collectivity. The source of the message thus becomes the NRA or the NAACP or the Brightwood School Corporation or Quaker Oats Corporation. In everyday language and news reports, one typically hears, "Chrysler Corporation announced today . . . ," "The Sierra Club says . . . ," and the like.

The process by which this message was agreed to by constituencies or stakeholders within the organization is usually hidden from public view. The message itself may reflect the views of only a small group within the larger organization; there may, in fact, be many internal dissenters. Individuals may or may not feel bound by the organization's public pronouncements, depending on the nature of the organization. Many Republicans and Democrats, for example, often feel that party platforms adopted for political campaigns do not need to express their own views on the various matters covered. Many church members feel themselves part of the organization even when they dissent from doctrinal positions on issues such as euthanasia or abortion. Whistle-blowers, as described earlier in the text, are good examples of internal dissenters in businesses. However, whistle-blowers are unusual; there are undoubtedly many more dissenters within an organization who may not agree with the company message but go along because "a job is a job."

The organization as a source of communication also has its own credibility or ethos, as discussed under internal public communication. Organizational ethos is associated with a particular image projected by the organization. The projection of a desired image has become an important objective of many organizations. For example, think of the image or ethos typically associated with the following:

Greenpeace

Rotary International

The U.S. Postal Service

Ben & Jerry's Ice Cream

AT&T

University of Notre Dame

Your college's alumni association

A local church

A local fire department

The FBI

The CIA

Amnesty International

As you look over this list, there is a good chance that some image or associations spring to mind. When one thinks of Notre Dame, for example, football and Lou Holtz may come to mind. There may be negative as well as positive associations for many of these organizations. These images and associations constitute the organizational ethos, which can affect how people process messages ascribed to the organization. The FBI, for example, probably has strong positive ethos—that is, credibility—when it is the source of messages regarding crime statistics in the United States.

Purposes of External Communication

Internal communication is often aimed at gaining commitment from, compliance of, or control over organizational members. External communication, excluding product advertising, is usually concerned with engendering a favorable opinion of the organization on the part of the general public or specific agencies in order to facilitate achieving some objective. As the previous discussion makes clear, a major purpose of organizational messages is to create a favorable public image of the organization, or to overcome what may be a negative one.

Rhetorical purposes of organizations thus may be specific or general. The first is related to a specific proposal or issue. If a public utility wishes to convince ratepayers of the necessity for a proposed rate increase, the purpose is a specific one. When the same utility, in other years, sends messages to the public that are intended to create a climate of opinion favorable to the organization, this represents a general purpose. The creation of a favorable climate may be expected to facilitate acceptance of the more specific messages when the time for the rate increase comes around.

Public relations and *advertising* are major types of external public communication; as noted above, they are not extensively covered in this text. Additional types include *image advertising, public affairs* and *government relations,* and *issues management* or *issues advocacy.* Sometimes falling within the purview of one or more of these areas are cases involving *risk communication* and *crisis communication,* situations that often clearly reveal the rhetorical strategies preferred by an organization.

Image advertising is intended to foster a favorable attitude toward the organization, on the part of the public, rather than focusing on one of the organization's specific products or programs. *Image* may be thought of as nearly the same thing as organizational *identity,* although some people prefer to make a distinction. Organizational identity can be defined narrowly in terms of public name recognition and a general understanding of what the organization does. The graphic design of logos and widespread media advertising can develop such name recognition and understanding. Given extensive corporate acquisitions, mergers, and takeovers, many corporate executives are concerned that people will not know what business their particular organization is really in—hence the tendency toward more abstract acronyms and names so that people will be less likely to identify a newly formed conglomerate with the simpler product line of the old days. International Harvester becomes Navistar, for example, just as, years ago, Standard Oil of Indiana became Exxon. Pepsi Cola, as a company, takes on the abstract name of PepsiCo in an effort to remind people that the company sells tacos, chicken, and many other products besides soft drinks.

Organizational image, on the other hand, is usually thought of in terms of provoking an evaluative response—favorable or unfavorable attitudes toward the organization.[26] Thus a corporation will try to project an image as a caring or innovative or "can-do" kind of organization. An image can be seen as something more changeable than an identity, in that one can try to change a negative image, while holding to the basic identity of an organization.[27] Dow Corporation, which had a negative image in the eyes of many during the Vietnam War because of its production of napalm, has succeeded in changing this to a positive image of a corporation that is eager to receive college graduates in order to make a difference in the world (according to recent advertising campaigns).

In its "view books" sent to prospective students, a university presents an image of itself, one that is intended to be attractive to potential students and their parents. The image is presented through pictures of happy students and professors having a good time (not stuffy) while learning. The books typically picture a campus that is a combination of tradition and up-to-dateness, large enough to provide many opportunities, but small enough to care about each individual.

Public affairs and *government relations* are functions that recognize the special importance of various funding and regulatory bodies as audiences for external communication. These functions require, first, a monitoring of the relevant environment. This means that some large organizations assign individuals to keep track of news reports, media coverage, and pending hearings and legislative sessions that could deal with some aspect of the organization's activities. Some have full-time legislative liaisons and lobbyists who serve such a function. Utilities, such as electric power companies, need to cultivate public support when public service commissions are preparing to conduct hearings on the rates the utilities may charge customers, for example. The companies may conduct full-scale media campaigns to develop such support, and also send out members of speakers' bureaus to support their position in speeches to service clubs or other local meetings. The author was involved a few years ago in consulting with a statewide utility company, which set up focus groups in major cities served by the corporation. These groups provided a setting for public messages intended to promote a favorable, caring image of the utility among consumers and business leaders in its service area.

When it is obvious that proposed legislation might affect a particular organization, it may gear up for a campaign of public communication to influence lawmakers. Proposals relating to health care reform and financing, for example, have resulted in many public messages from health care providers, hospitals, insurance companies, retired persons' organizations, and so on. These public messages were all intended to have some effect on the legislative process. Lobbying is, of course, one of the major avenues for organizations' exercising influence over governmental processes, but such activities are typically conducted more in face-to-face and small-group settings than through public communication. Typical venues for lobbying, outside of the legislative halls or offices themselves, include receptions and social events that bring together organizational members and legislators. Legislators or their aides are also invited to conferences or conventions to hear speakers and programs that are intended to cast the industry or organization in a favorable light.

Issues management is closely related to the public affairs and government relations functions, but is usually more general in scope. The intent is to shape public response to or understanding of a public issue, preferably before the issue has been taken up by legislative or regulatory bodies. On environmental issues, for example, a corporation tries to communicate its careful management of resources; this should eliminate the need for governmental action, the corporation hopes to imply. One coal company published photographs of a nature setting, with animals peacefully grazing around a lake jumping with trout, challenging the viewer to pick out where the coal strip mine had been. As another example, hospitals publicized their programs of cost containment well before the Clinton administration sent health care proposals to Congress.

Some organizations exist primarily to conduct *issues advocacy*. Examples include anti-abortion groups such as Operation Rescue as well as organizations on the other side of this issue, such as the National Organization of Women. Increasingly, organizations whose roots lie in membership services, such as the National Rifle Association and the American Association of Retired Persons, find more and more of their efforts moving in the direction of full-time issues advocacy. The National Conference of Catholic Bishops is a religious organization that has become very much involved in issues advocacy, beginning with the group's pastoral letter on war and peace in 1983.[28] The Moral Majority and the American Council of Churches similarly are religious organizations that are increasingly involved in issues advocacy. A recent controversy surrounding the leadership of the National Association for the Advancement of Colored Persons (NAACP) involved debate about which issues the organization should be advocating in public communication. The purposes of issues management or advocacy can hence become central concerns in many modern organizations.

Risk communication is a growing area of concern for many public and private organizations. Because of growing public worry about radiation, ozone depletion, and carcinogenic agents, many organizations find that they must address such fears and explain any risks that their operations or products might entail. For example, over the past several years, public concern about the possibility that proximity to power lines could increase cancer risks, especially in children, has increased. Electric utility companies have had to address these concerns through public risk communication. The utilities need to understand how people perceive these kinds of risks in order to develop messages to deal with their concerns. *Crisis communication,* on the other hand, deals with situations in which a risk has been transformed into an actual disaster: an explosion at a chemical plant or a fatal fire at a factory or the disintegration of a space shuttle. Crisis communicators do not have the luxury of researching and carefully developing messages; crisis communication therefore depends on foresight and preparation in advance for a possible emergency. The special problems in considering questions of audience, channel selection, and strategies for risk and crisis communication are further discussed in the following sections.

Audiences

External public communication depends on analysis of the audience and adaptation to it. Multiple audiences are possible and often probable. Externally directed messages are received by organizational members as well as the external public. External audiences for a for-profit corporation include clients or customers, stockholders, competitors, government regulators and legislators, and suppliers, as well as a more vaguely defined "general public." These different audiences often exhibit competing interests as they sit in judgment on the messages delivered by the organization. Nonprofit organizations have external audiences comprising clients, patients, or others who receive their services, governmental agencies, perhaps licensers, professionals, other similar organizations, funding bodies such as the United Way, and boards of directors or trustees, as well as the general public. One could similarly segment the potential audiences for educational institutions, government and political organizations, and advocacy groups. For example, audiences for a university include students and potential students and their families, members of boards of trustees, state legislators (especially relevant for public institutions), alumni, faculty, support staff members, administrators, and potential donors or funding agencies, as well as the general public.

Efforts can be made to tailor messages to these different audiences within the general environment. In fact, failure to distinguish among different kinds of audiences can be a fundamental cause of organizations' communication failures. A second problem can result when the messages designed for one audience are inconsistent with or contradict messages intended for others, especially when multiple audiences receive such mixed messages. A corporation may want to communicate to stockholders that it will hold down the costs of safety monitoring while also communicating to customers that safety is its number-one priority. Cases such as this obviously raise ethical questions, as well.

Organizations may also have problems conducting an effective analysis of specific audiences for their external messages. Obviously, some smaller or less well funded organizations lack the resources for a full-scale marketing analysis or polling of their publics. Of more theoretical concern are assumptions that organizational communicators may make in regard to audience perceptions of their messages.

Risk and crisis communication are especially instructive in this regard. Experts and technically oriented organizational members often have different perceptions of risk than do lay members of the general public. Technical experts are accustomed to thinking of risk in statistical or probabilistic terms; hence, they will say that there is less risk from emissions from a chemical plant than from driving your car to work or eating hamburgers. In fact, the author, as well as many others, has heard airline pilots remind people that they are in more danger, statistically, driving to and from the airport than flying. Utilities, to return to the perceived risk of power lines causing cancer, mentioned earlier, point out that the danger, if any, is statistically quite small.

The problem is that the lay public simply does not interpret risks this way, and so the messages are often ineffective. Public perception of risk usually includes issues such as fairness, voluntary versus involuntary exposure to risk, and knowing versus unknowing exposure, as well as the potential for catastrophic loss. There may be far fewer airplane crashes than automobile accidents, but the potential for catastrophic loss of life is far greater in each airplane crash than in each automobile accident. Of course, far more people in the United States are killed in automobile accidents than in airplane crashes, but these accidents happen singly or in small numbers, spread out over time and geographic space, so that the cumulative effect is less. People feel that they can choose to drive to work or to eat a hamburger, but may not feel that they have any control over toxic emissions or power lines. It is worse when the consequences are something as generally frightening as cancer rather than what are perceived as more remote threats, such as those posed by fat and cholesterol. Notice that there is no claim that the public perceptions are accurate in a scientific sense; rather, these perceptions must be understood by a communicator who must explain risks to the general public.

Crisis communication must deal with the same kinds of perceptual differences between insiders and external publics. In addition, crisis communicators must operate, as implied by the designation, under the pressures of stress, emergencies, and unexpected public scrutiny. When the space shuttle *Challenger* exploded in full view of national television audiences in 1986, NASA found it difficult to follow through on communication scenarios developed in advance. Audience analysis may be short-circuited, then, by unexpected events and lack of preparation for emergencies or crises. That is why there is such a powerful predilection toward "stonewalling," or avoiding saying anything at all, when an emergency does arise.

Channels

In general, fewer channels are available for external public messages than for internal messages because an organization usually does not control as many external media as internal media. Channels for public communication are those involving speaker and audience or simulating such a speaker–audience situation through media. Print media and advertising are of course ways in which organizations present themselves to various publics, although these channels typically have less of the feel of a speaker–audience setting.

The selection of a particular channel for an organization's message may be dictated or at least influenced by cost considerations. Smaller or less well financed organizations may not have the option of launching expensive media campaigns and must therefore rely on more immediate and face-to-face channels. Even larger, better endowed organizations prefer a mix of mediated and face-to-face means of putting out their messages. In addition to financial constraints on media selection, there are the norms and traditions characteristic of a particular organization or organizational culture. For years there has been the tradition that law firms do not openly advertise in popular print or broadcast media, although that constraint appears to be weakening. Similarly, other professionals, such as physicians, have not used communication channels associated with consumer products. More recently, however, one sees public service announcements (advertisements?) that publicize the services of health organizations and hospitals.

A large corporation may opt for a speakers' bureau, for example, even though the audiences that any one speaker may address are quite small compared to that corporation's entire base of customers or clients. The individual speakers personalize the organization and its message for these audiences, however, and members of these audiences may in turn influence others, so that a ripple effect is created. Speakers' bureaus aim at audiences composed of people who may be seen as opinion leaders in their communities and circles of friends. Similarly, speeches by top executives may be scheduled for conferences or conventions. Thus, while individual public speakers may not appear to be a cost-effective way to get an organizational message across to a larger public, they can have important effects in terms of personalizing a corporate image and influencing opinion leaders. In addition, there is the hope that the press will cover a major executive's speech and thereby disseminate the message even more widely.

Many organizations that have the resources to do so combine various types of channels to send mutually reinforcing messages. Thus the American Medical Association may provide speakers for service clubs and community organizations, place issues-oriented advertisements in publications, and prepare broadcast spots for television and radio in a concerted effort to influence the public debate on health reform. Tobacco companies may be involved in similar campaigns, often intended to rebut some charges made about their product by health-related organizations. In a well-coordinated campaign, the speakers would develop the same themes that are presented in the media. Many corporations have now turned to the use of "video news releases," which are like written news releases except that they are presented as video. A Nielsen survey in 1993 of 92 local television stations found that all had at one time or another broadcast such video news releases received from corporations, often implying that they were actually news stories prepared by the station's news department.[29] Such efforts are often combined with lobbying as well.

On-line channels of communication are of growing importance. Companies such as Dell Computer Corporation and Gateway 2000 deploy people to surf the Internet full-time, watching for information that could have an impact on their products and services.[30] Internet chat rooms, for example, can bring to the surface questions or problems that users may have concerning a particular product or program. Obviously, the monitors can also discover in this way when competitors' products are having problems, giving them information that is possibly useful in gaining a marketing edge. When such messages appear, they are prepared to answer through E-mail or electronic bulletin board, in order to get their message before the growing cyber-public. Private on-line services such as America Online, Prodigy, and Compuserve can provide venues for organizations' public communication.

Many companies are setting up "home pages" on the World Wide Web of the Internet as a way of bringing messages before an expanding public audience. Universities, government agencies, and other institutions similarly offer public communication through the use of home pages.

Hidden Organizational Messages

The example of the use of video news releases (see p. 311) raises several kinds of ethical questions regarding the use of what are essentially cloaked channels for organizational messages to external publics. In the case of video news releases, one can fault the local media outlet, rather than the organization providing the release, for taking a prepackaged video provided by an interested party, such as a corporation, and passing it off as the station's own reporting. The station is taking the easy and inexpensive route of filling broadcast time with canned programming purporting to be news.

Other techniques of issues management that may seem questionable include the use of orchestrated telephone, letter-writing, or fax campaigns to bring pressure on regulators or lawmakers with regard to a pending decision or legislation that affects an organization's interests. This form of organizing, known as "grass-tops" (as opposed to "grass-roots") organizing, actually goes all the way back to the 1930s. The idea is for an organization, working from the top down, to fund and stage-manage what appears to be a grass-roots, spontaneous outpouring of public expression on a particular topic. For example, when automakers were concerned about pending federal legislation regarding pollution controls, a public relations firm was able to generate letters from senior citizens and even parents of Little Leaguers expressing the fear that controls would eliminate the larger vehicles and vans that they relied on for transportation.*

Computer communication systems, on-line services, E-mail, and similar technologies can of course now be used to facilitate these kinds of grass-tops efforts more quickly and with more sophisticated messages than was possible using only mail or telephone. Elsewhere in this section (see p. 311) is an indication of some of the ways in which computer-communication systems are being developed as public communication channels.

Ethical questions arise when the organization attempts to avoid attribution as the source for public messages. The intent is to create the impression that its message is really being sent by an independent news source or by ordinary members of the public. Discuss examples of hidden organizational messages. How can they be detected by the general public?

*New York Times, March 20, 1994, p. F13.

Organizations may find that at times they wish to open some channels for communication with the public and close others. As already noted, in times of crisis, organizations often close or restrict certain communication channels, as when they require that all media inquiries go through a specific office or public relations officer. An effort may be made to restrict access to certain locations or operations in order to control the channels for communication at such times.

Message Strategies

Rhetorical strategies for public communication include those used for internal communication. Identification and scapegoating, framing and narratives are widely used strategies for public image building and issues management. In addition, symbolic convergence, or fantasy theme analysis, provides a useful way to describe and analyze themes of public organizational messages. Product advertising, which is beyond the scope of this text, is not covered; rather, the focus is on various strategies for impression management in order to project a particular organizational image or influence views of public issues. One must note, however, that the line between public service announcements and advertisements is not always clearly drawn.

In using identification strategies, organizations project a type of image by associating themselves with cultural endeavors or particular charities. Mobil Oil, for example, provides funding for public television dramas, and Texaco has long been associated with opera broadcasts. McDonalds Corporation supports the Ronald McDonald Houses for families of children suffering from cancer. Athletics represents another area of corporate identification. Increasingly the Olympics depend on corporate sponsorship. As a result, all kinds of products can project themselves as the official "fill-in-the-blank" (peanut butter, radial tires, or fried chicken) of the U.S. Olympic team. Similarly, college football bowl games now mostly have corporate sponsors, which represents a type of image advertising for the sponsors. Of course, nonprofit organizations also become identified with charitable activities, such as the Lions Club's association with vision and eye care or the Shriners with children's hospitals.

Identification strategies, as described earlier, include techniques of establishing common ground and, in contrast, of scapegoating, that is, dissociating the organization from outsiders or even enemies ("identification through antithesis").[31] Hence, organizations appeal to patriotism when stressing their reliance on American workers or suppliers or when identifying with patriotic goals. During the Gulf War in the early 1990s, for example, many organizations highlighted their support for Desert Shield and then for Desert Storm. Of course, support for a national Olympic team similarly can be seen as an appeal to patriotism. In scapegoating, the message intends to dissociate the organization from some outsider or enemy. Thus, American corporations try to portray a threat from foreign competitors as a threat not just to themselves but to the nation as a whole. This technique is therefore similar to the assumed "we," described in the discussion of internal communication.

Framing strategies are those in which the communicator attempts to construct a favorable context for interpreting events. Part of this context is the image developed for the organization. Johnson & Johnson, following the panic that occurred when Tylenol™ capsules were tampered with and poisoned in the 1980s, developed a corporate image as a leader in concern for product and consumer safety.[32] In contrast, NASA's less successful handling of the aftermath of the *Challenger* accident tarnished its image of technological efficiency and skill. Possibly Johnson and Johnson's success in dealing with the earlier tampering scare has helped it to deal with more recent alleged health problems associated with this product, after the publicizing of the harmful effects that acetaminophen (the basic ingredient of Tylenol) might have on the liver and kidneys. Johnson and Johnson had failed to place warnings on the product indicating that moderate alcohol consumption could lead to damage even when the pain reliever is taken in small or moderate doses. While the company's ad campaigns to counter this crisis were seen as less successful than those in the tampering case, the public outcry has been muted.[33]

Framing strategies are efforts to define the nature of the issue or to limit discussion to a particular aspect of the issue. The Clinton administration, for example, attempted to frame the discussion of health care reform in terms of fairness and concern for people who were not adequately covered by health insurance. Many health care delivery organizations, on the other hand, attempted to frame the debate in terms of quality of health care and the American value of an individual's freedom of choice. The intent of such framing is to rule certain arguments or messages out of order as outside the frame. Hence, organizations that are opposed to medical abortions attempt to place legalistic or constitutional arguments as beside the point by placing abortion within the frame of murder. Pro-abortion groups counter by asserting that the applicable frame is that of freedom of choice and women's rights.

Symbolic convergence strategies tend to rely on narratives that highlight a hero or a struggle involving overcoming obstacles. Public messages may therefore rely on identifying an organization with a spokesperson, or hero. Such a hero need not always be human, or even real. For years, the U.S. Park Service, in its campaigns about preventing forest fires, has featured a mythical bear, Smokey. Presumably, Smokey got his start when some forest rangers discovered a real, live cub in the smoldering aftermath

Organizations can be identified with well-known spokespeople.

of a fire, the only survivor of a family of brown bears. From this factual beginning, the symbolic character was developed. Occasionally, the spokesperson can gain as much exposure as the organization represented: Ronald Reagan became famous as the spokesperson for General Electric in the 1950s, and went on to a successful political career as a result.

In internal communication, the community sharing the rhetorical vision is supposed to be the organization itself; when this strategy is used for external communication, the rhetorical community is extended to include the intended audience. The organization's message can therefore be presented in the form of a story that draws on values that are presumably shared by the organization and the larger community of the audience. Messages for the United Way may thus present vignettes of sports heroes and their families contributing their time and talents to one of the United Way–supported agencies. The audience does not simply hear an endorsement of the agency or of the umbrella United Way organization, but actually sees a short film of the athlete taking part in one of the agency's programs. Advertising for the Saturn division of General Motors often focuses on employees of an assembly plant rather than on the car itself. In one case, we see employees returning to the plant after it has been cleaned up and refurbished by the company. A basketball goal has been set up for recreation time, and each employee has been given new safety eye protection glasses. The intended message is: If we care this much about the well-being and safety of our workers, think how much we care about the quality of the car and its service. We are a different kind of automobile manufacturer, one that you would want to be associated with (as a customer).

A newer approach to analyzing external organizational communication is described as *institutionalism*.[34] This theory applies particularly to cases of crisis communication, in which an organization needs to repair a possibly damaged image. The organization is seen as a "corporate actor," who must follow "social rules" that obtain for it and other similar organizations operating within the same environment. The key objective in such a case is for the organization to maintain "legitimacy" in the eyes of the other actors and stakeholders who have some control or influence over that organization's prospects for success or even survival. When a crisis threatens this perceived legitimacy, the organizational actor needs to communicate to relevant audiences (stakeholders, regulatory agencies, customers, and the like) that its structures and operations are legitimate and capable of dealing with the problem.[35] As noted above, the previous success of Johnson & Johnson in dealing with a public scare about tampering may have provided the company with sufficient institutional legitimacy to weather later crises that raised questions about the safety of Tylenol.

While the general strategies can fall within the categories of identification, framing, or symbolic convergence, the institutional approach suggests a different way of envisioning organizational rhetoric when the organization faces a challenge to its legitimacy or a crisis. Two choices are available to an individual or an organization in such a case: to deny fault or the existence of a problem, or to mitigate the seriousness of the problem.

The first strategy involves showing that the organization in fact fits with the norms and values of those who would be its judges or critics; this strategy, known as *ingratiation,* attempts to show conformity with the audience's values, beliefs, and norms. This strategy is thus much like identification. The second approach implies an admission but tries to excuse or rationalize or apologize for the perceived fault. The difficulty is that the actor may wish to maintain the image of complete competence or faultlessness, while at the same time apologizing for what would appear to be a failure of competence or a fault. The conflicting objectives can result in mixed messages, as when a government agency "takes responsibility" for a crisis, as the Justice Department did for the assault on an armed fundamentalist religious group in Waco, Texas, but at the same time denies any mistake or poor judgment. Ultimately, the theory hypothesizes that in such a situation, the organization will direct its major efforts at impression management toward what it perceives to be the most influential or powerful stakeholder among potential audiences. For corporations, this may be stockholders or government regulatory agencies.

Legal Considerations

Many external corporate messages are subject to review or control by governmental regulators. Such regulation is fairly obvious in the realm of advertising, where the Federal Trade Commission (FTC) is mandated to prevent misleading or fraudulent claims. Other agencies may become involved in regard to the areas of image and issues advocacy. For example, the Federal Communication Commission (FCC) formerly oversaw the "Fairness Doctrine," intended to ensure that broadcast media provide "balanced" coverage of controversial issues. An organization's message on such an issue may need to be balanced by an opposing view or edited in such a way as to allow for such balance.

In a study of corporate advocacy communication, Robert Heath and Richard Allen Nelson point out that the Internal Revenue Service can also become involved in these matters through regulations indicating which kinds of communication expenses may be tax deductible.[36] They point out that Shell Oil Company decided not to engage in issues advocacy on proposed legislation concerning windfall profits taxes because the IRS has held that the costs of campaigns regarding pending legislation are not deductible.[37]

Other government agencies may also affect organizational communication strategies. The Securities and Exchanges Commission (SEC) may be involved in determining whether messages project a misleading picture for investors or could be construed as providing insider information to only certain groups. The Equal Employment Opportunity Commission (EEOC) is concerned with messages regarding the presentation of an organization as following nondiscrimination guidelines or projecting itself as an equal opportunity or affirmative action employer.

Highlights of External Public Communication

Sources for external communication are often reifications of the organization, obscuring the real sources of messages. There is often an assumption that the organization is like a person and has a monolithic viewpoint shared by all members. Organizations can thus have an ethos, just like individual speakers. Many familiar organizations are associated with images or personalities that spring readily to mind.

The purposes of external communication, apart from advertising a product or service, include image advertising, public affairs and government relations functions, issues management or issues advocacy, and risk and crisis communication. There are many different kinds of external audiences for these messages, sometimes with competing interests and points of view. Audience analysis and adaptation may therefore be difficult for an organization because competing audiences may receive the same public message. Risk and crisis communication is problematic because the ways members of the general public usually perceive and interpret information about risk are different from those of experts and organizational insiders.

Message strategies for external communication are similar to those available for internal messages, as communicators rely on identification, framing, and symbolic convergence. One view of external communication concerns institutionalism, involving the organization's demonstrating its legitimacy as a social actor in dealing with the issue at hand. Success at earlier persuasion efforts or campaigns may reinforce efforts of this sort.

SUMMARY

Public communication implies a speaker–audience relationship and thus highlights organizational rhetoric. Prepared, somewhat formal messages are presented to audiences in face-to-face or mediated settings. Messages may be intended primarily for either internal or external audiences, although such a distinction is not always clear or precise.

Although internal public communication can be about many different topics—orientation, job training, procedures, organizational plans, and so on—an underlying theme tends to be organizational socialization of members. Therefore, internal communication is often about organizational values and commitment, at least at some level. Sources of organizational messages are less clear and definite than in cases in which an individual is speaking for him- or herself, because of the reification of the organization as an actor or speaker. One can thus speak of an organizational ethos or credibility.

One can delineate different internal audiences for organizational messages, depending on the na-

ture of the organization (such as whether it is unionized or not). It is possible for some messages to include certain groups as members while others seem to exclude the same groups. The boundaries of the organization may themselves thus be rhetorical constructs.

The message strategies for internal communication can be analyzed according to rhetorical principles. Three kinds of strategies can usefully be discerned: rhetorical identification, framing, and symbolic convergence.

Much of organizations' external public communication may be seen as falling beyond the scope of organizational communication, which is largely concerned with communication within an organization. In overview, we can see that many of the rhetorical principles discussed in regard to internal communication apply in some ways to external messages as well. Leaving advertising, marketing, and public relations for other texts and courses, it is possible to discuss the general rhetorical stance of organizations in the areas of image advertising, public affairs and governmental relations, issues management or advocacy, and risk and crisis communication.

In these areas, the issue of reification of organizations as sources arises, along with organizational credibility and ethos. Audiences are again seen as segmented and often competing with one another. Organizations must be wary, therefore, of sending and receiving incompatible messages. Audience analysis is usually more complex because of the complexities of these different kinds of audiences. Often organizational experts have difficulty understanding how external audiences may perceive their messages. Problems involving the perception of risk communication are good examples of problems of this type.

The message strategies used for external communication can usefully be analyzed using the same rhetorical perspectives that were used for internal communication: seeking to establish identification between the organization and an external audience; attempting to establish a frame or context for presenting the organizational message; and seeking to use the strategies of fantasy themes, rhetorical visions, and rhetorical communities of symbolic convergence theory. Legal ramifications may affect organizational rhetoric, as federal and local regulatory agencies, such as the FCC, Securities and Exchange Commission, FDA, and others, may monitor these public messages.

EXERCISES AND QUESTIONS FOR DISCUSSION

1. Try to collect examples of internal public communication in which an organization, such as your school or work organization, is the source. Is it always clear who the real source of such messages is? Do you feel that people occasionally wish to avoid attributing organizational messages to any one individual or group? Is this avoidance necessarily good or bad?

2. Why does the study of public communication, whether internal or external, tend to appear to be pro-management? Are there avenues in organizations for public communication, as defined here, that can give lower-level members an effective voice?

3. In the organizations in which you participate, is the use of electronic or computer-mediated public communication increasing? Describe examples of the use of such media for public mes-

sages. What are the effects of the use of these mediated channels that may be different from those of the use of face-to-face channels?

4. Collect examples of organizations' public communication messages that make use of the strategy of identification. Discuss why the identification attempts were or were not successful, and with what audiences. Repeat the exercise for the other two strategies, framing (and framing narratives) and fantasy themes.

5. Consider the college or work organization with which you are most familiar. For the public messages of this organization, how many internal audiences can you identify? How many significant external audiences can you identify? Discuss the difficulties of adapting messages to fit the competing interests of these different audiences.

SOURCES FOR FURTHER STUDY

Allen, M. W., and Caillouet, R. H. (1994). Legitimation endeavors: Impression management strategies used by an organization in crisis. *Communication Monographs, 61,* 44–62.

Alvesson, M. (1987). *Organization theory and technocractic consciousness.* Berlin: Walter de Gruyter.

Alvesson, M. (1993). Cultural-ideological modes of management control: A theory and a case study of a professional service company. In S.

A. Deetz (Ed.), *Communication yearbook 16*, pp. 3–42.

Bormann, E. G. (1983). Symbolic convergence: Organizational communication and culture. In L. L. Putnam and M. E. Pacanowsky (Eds.), *Communication and organizations: An interpretative approach*. Newbury Park, Calif.: Sage, pp. 99–122.

Bullis, C. (1993). Organizational socialization research: Enabling, constraining, and shifting perspectives. *Human Communication Research, 60,* 10–17.

Cheney, G. (1995). Democracy in the workplace: Theory and practice from the perspective of communication. *Journal of Applied Communication Research, 23,* 167–200.

Cheney, G., and Vibbert, S. L. (1987). Corporate discourse: Public relations and issue management. In F. M. Jablin, L. L. Putnam, K. H. Roberts, and L. W. Porter (Eds.), *Handbook of organizational communication: An interdisciplinary perspective*. Newbury Park, Calif.: Sage, p. 176.

Clair, R. P. (1993). The use of framing devices to sequester organizational narratives: Hegemony and harassment. *Communication Monographs, 60,* 113–36.

Eblen, A. L. (1987). Communication, leadership, and organizational commitment. *Central States Speech Journal, 38,* 181–82.

Heath, R. L., and Nelson, R. A. (1985). Image and issue advertising: A corporate and public policy perspective. *Journal of Marketing, 49,* 58–68.

Howard, L. A., and Geist, P. (1995). Ideological positioning in organizational change: The dialectic of control in a merging organization. *Communication Monographs, 62,* 110–31.

MacCarthin, E. Z. (1989). Beyond employee publications: Making the personal connection. *Public Relations Journal,* July, p. 15.

Meyer, J. C. (1995). Tell me a story: Eliciting organizational values from narratives. *Communication Quarterly, 43,* 210–24.

Morgan, B. S., and Schiemann, W. A. (1983). Why internal communication is failing. *Public Relations Journal,* March, pp. 15-17.

Mumby, D. K. (1987). The political function of narrative in organizations. *Communication Monographs, 54,* 113-27.

Mumby, D. K. (1988). *Communication and power in organizations: Discourse, ideology and domination*. Norwood, N.J.: Ablex.

Porter, L. W., Crampon, J. W., and Smith, F. J. (1976). Organizational commitment and managerial turnover: A longitudinal study. *Organizational Behavior and Human Performance, 15,* 87–98.

Scott, W. G., and Hart, D. K. (1979). *Organizational America*. Boston: Houghton Mifflin.

Treadwell, D. F., and Harrison, T. M. (1994). Conceptualizing and assessing organizational image: Model images, commitment, and communication. *Communication Monographs, 61,* 63–85.

Trice, H. M., and Beyer, J. M. (1993). *The cultures of work organizations*. Englewood Cliffs, N.J.: Prentice-Hall; see Chapter 7 of this text, pp. 134–38.

NOTES

1. J. C. Meyer (1995), Tell me a story: Eliciting organizational values from narratives, *Communication Quarterly, 43,* 210–24.

2. *Wall Street Journal,* November 2, 1993, p. B1; *Wall Street Journal,* September 3, 1993, p. B1; B. S. Morgan and W. A. Schiemann (1983), Why internal communication is failing, *Public Relations Journal,* March, pp. 15–17.

3. *Wall Street Journal,* August 17, 1994, p. A1.

4. E. Z. MacCarthin (1989), Beyond employee publications: Making the personal connection, *Public Relations Journal,* July, p. 15.

5. L. A. Howard and P. Geist (1995), Ideological positioning in organizational change: The dialectic of control in a merging organization, *Communication Monographs, 62,* 110–31.

6. F. Rice (1991), Champions of communication, *Fortune,* June 3, p. 112.

7. J. L. Laabs (1992), The many faces of benefits communication, *Personnel Journal, 7,* 58.

8. G. Cheney (1995), Democracy in the workplace: Theory and practice from the perspective of communication, *Journal of Applied Communication Research, 23,* 167–200.

9. C. Bullis (1993), Organizational socialization research: Enabling, constraining, and shifting perspectives, *Human Communication Research, 60,* 10–17.

10. G. Cheney (1983), The rhetoric of identification and the study of organizational communication, *Quarterly Journal of Speech, 69,* 144.

11. L. W. Porter, J. W. Crampon, and F. J. Smith (1976), Organizational commitment and managerial turnover: A longitudinal study, *Organizational Behavior and Human Performance, 15,* 87–98.

12. A. L. Eblen (1987), Communication, leadership, and organizational commitment, *Central States Speech Journal 38,* 181–82.

13. Eblen, p. 181.

14. Cheney (1983), pp. 144–47.

15. M. Alvesson (1993), Cultural-ideological modes of management control: A theory and a case study of a professional service company, in S. A. Deetz (Ed.), *Communication yearbook 16,* pp. 3–42; M. Alvesson (1987), *Organization theory and technocratic consciousness,* Berlin: Walter de Gruyter.

16. E. G. Bormann (1983), Symbolic convergence: Organizational communication and culture, in L. L. Putnam and M. E. Pacanowsky (Eds.), *Communication and Organizations: An interpretive approach,* Newbury Park, Calif.: Sage, pp. 99–122.

17. K. Burke (1945), *Grammar of motives,* Berkeley: University of California Press and (1950), *Rhetoric of motives,* Berkeley: University of California Press.

18. Cheney (1983).

19. Boeing Company internal document (1992), *Managing for World-Class Competitiveness,* pp. 3–5.

20. Alvesson (1993), p. 8.

21. H. M. Trice and J. M. Beyer (1993), *The cultures of work organizations,* Englewood Cliffs, N.J.: Prentice-Hall; see Chapter 7 of this text, pp. 134–38.

22. D. K. Mumby (1987), The political function of narrative in organizations, *Communication Monographs, 54,* 113–27.

23. Mumby, p. 123.

24. Bormann, pp. 103–4.

25. *Christian Science Monitor,* July 7, 1994, p. 20.

26. D. F. Treadwell and T. M. Harrison (1994), Conceptualizing and assessing organizational image: Model images, commitment, and communication, *Communication Monographs, 61,* 63–85.

27. G. Cheney and S. L. Vibbert (1987), Corporate discourse: Public relations and issue management, in F. M. Jablin, L. L. Putnam, K. H. Roberts, and L. W. Porter (Eds.), *Handbook of organizational communication: An interdisciplinary perspective,* Newbury Park, Calif.: Sage, p. 176.

28. Cheney and Vibbert (1987).

29. *New York Times,* March 20, 1994, p. F13.

30. *Wall Street Journal,* September 15, 1994, p. B1.

31. Cheney.

32. Cheney and Vibbert.

33. Los Angeles Times, January 5, 1995, p. D2.

34. M. W. Allen and R. H. Caillouet (1994), Legitimation endeavors: Impression management strategies used by an organization in crisis, *Communication Monographs, 61,* 44–62.

35. See Allen and Caillouet, p. 46.

36. R. L. Heath and R. A. Nelson (1985), Image and issue advertising: A corporate and public policy perspective, *Journal of Marketing, 49,* 58–68.

37. Heath and Nelson, p. 63.

Capstone

Part Four deals with matters of general interest for the entire field of organizational communication. First, Chapter 13 takes up the problems of assessment of internal organizational communication. There are quantitative and qualitative approaches for evaluating the quality and effectiveness of communication activities and programs in organizations. Both functionalist methods, such as the communication audit, and interpretivist techniques are discussed.

Critical studies provide a third type of evaluation of organizational communication, although the purpose of these studies is usually not enhancing the everyday functioning of the organization, but rather emancipating or empowering people involved in organizational life. Many of the issues often raised by critical analysts of organizational life and communication are alluded to at various points in the text, especially in the sections "An Issue of Communication Ethics" and "Diversity Matters" in each chapter. Because these issues are covered extensively in this final part, Chapters 13 and 14 contain no further special sections on ethics and diversity. Chapter 14 in particular attempts to address many of the issues that represent the interface of organizational life with societal and cultural issues.

As this introductory survey of the field of organizational communication comes to a close, it seems particularly important to take stock of the impact that organizations have on so many aspects of our lives. Communication scholars, as they contemplate this area of their discipline, have a special concern with many of these issues, for they often concern activities, techniques, and processes that clearly involve the focus of their discipline: human communication.

These two chapters, covering assessment and the confrontation of vital issues of the social and cultural meaning of organizations in our lives, constitute the capstone for this study of organizational communication.

CHAPTER 13

Assessing Organizational Communication

CHAPTER OBJECTIVES

After studying this chapter, you should be able to:

- Explain the concepts of proprietary and applied research for internal assessment of organizational communication.
- Discuss the reasons why communication assessment usually follows a functionalist perspective.
- Indicate the different kinds of questions asked by interpretive and critical researchers, in contrast to functionalists.
- Define the concept of communication audit, particularly the ICA audit.
- Discuss the uses of the various assessment tools in a communication audit.
- Explain the interpretive approach to methodologies for research on organizational communication.
- Describe several interpretive methods for the assessment of organizational communication.

CHAPTER OUTLINE

CONCEPTS OF ASSESSMENT AND EVALUATION

Earlier chapters suggest various ways of looking at communication in organizations; in other words, they are intended to provide an overview of the domain of organizational communication. This chapter is concerned with systematic ways of analyzing internal organizational communication, preferably for the purpose of diagnosing problems and designing interventions that can improve communication. This internal research can analyze such things as leadership behaviors, group and team processes, superior–subordinate communication, processes and structures for upward–downward communication links, systems for dealing with conflict, and many other issues derived from the topics of this book.

For example, a manufacturer of plumbing fixtures approached the organizational development department of a business administration college with a problem. Upper-level management was aware of poor communication between headquarters and remote plants and other locations. The problem was vaguely presented as a delay in responding to queries from the corporate office, misinterpretation of work or product orders that resulted in insufficient or incorrect shipments, and the like. The general feeling was that because of the geographical dispersal of the firm's operations, there tended to be breakdowns in internal communication.

There are many ways of responding to a problem presented in such a vague fashion. Obviously, the first step is to follow up with questions in order to get more focus on exactly how the perceived problem manifests itself. In terms of the various topics of this book, the communication problem could have several different kinds of causes. And, the causes that might come to mind may depend on one's orientation toward organizational communication.

A functionalist concerned with information processing could begin by asking about channels and their capacities for carrying different kinds of information. This analysis would focus on the people and media used for carrying messages between corporate offices and the plants. Are there enough such channels? Are they capable of carrying the information with high enough fidelity? A network analysis, which is a related approach, could suggest that some of the liaisons or bridges in the network that are supposed to interconnect the geographically dispersed units of the company are overloaded. Who and where are the crucial links in the firm's networks?

An analysis concerned with organizational culture might ask about the elements of the culture that support or facilitate horizontal communication. Is communication between corporate offices and remote locations seen as a valued and rewarded activity for those who might carry it out? What are the traditions in regard to relations between the various locations? Does the climate support openness in the kind of communication that usually flows back and forth between the locations and headquarters? Similar questions may be raised by someone interested in looking at the interpersonal communication links that may facilitate or hinder this kind of communication. Are there breakdowns in the superior–subordinate links that could provide information flow from one location to another?

In other words, a simple-sounding problem, as when this manufacturer says, "We have trouble communicating with our plants in Alabama and Oregon," could be analyzed in many different ways. The actual causes of the problem could be quite complex, involving a combination of many of the factors referred to above plus others (latent conflict, inadequate computer communication or training in its use, and so on).

Finding the answers to these questions and solutions to the problems they raise requires research. Research is a systematic method for seeking answers to specific questions. This kind of research tends to be proprietary and applied. *Proprietary* means that the research is commissioned by a specific organization, in such a way that that organization essentially owns the results. *Applied* research, as opposed to pure research, means that the focus is on solving specific problems in a real-life situation, as in the case of the headquarters communicating with remote sites, rather than on discovering broad generalizations about the nature of communication. Of course, applied research can lead to insights that can generate pure research, as when the solving of a company's problem can lead researchers to look for a general principle behind that solution that can be tested in a variety of different settings.

Assessing Organizational Communication

In education, the current popular word for evaluating internal functioning is *assessment,* which implies assessing how well an organization is doing in terms of meeting desired goals and objectives. In doing a communication assessment, one begins by determining the desired goals and objectives (which may be implicit or vague; often organizations have not worked out specific goals and objectives for their internal communication system).

The implication is that assessment is normally concerned with improving some aspect of organizational communication. The improvement, of course, is from the point of view of someone in the organization. This someone is typically in the higher levels of the organization's hierarchy or structure. Upper management may feel that communication is improved if they have tighter control over processes and people at lower levels. Those at the lower levels may have differing views concerning whether this is improvement. On the other hand, improving communication can mean finding ways to allow people at all levels in the organization more freedom of expression and action or to allow for more candid upwardly flowing communication. Improvement can also be aimed at increasing the effectiveness of the organization in terms of the

A communication audit is often performed by an outside consultant.

quality of its service to clients, patients, consumers, or other members of the larger community.

The assessment is often performed by a communication manager or consultant, which means that the person carrying out the research may be internal or external to the organization. In either case, the person probably follows a "consultant model" in the approach to specific communication problems and needs. Such a model implies that the person doing the assessment is engaged in a process of helping or facilitating. In this case, he or she is helping the members of the organization to diagnose or analyze facets of internal communication, to develop programs to improve or resolve problems, and to maintain effective communication systems in the future.

Functionalist, Interpretivist, and Critical Approaches

Traditionally, *organizational development* has been the term for actions intended to improve the functioning of organizational processes, including communication. Organizational development (OD) refers to "planned change," which is intended to increase the effectiveness or health of an organization.[1] Efforts at organizational development are usually managed from the top down, as noted above.

For this reason, assessment techniques for organizational communication have typically been *functionalist* in approach. Recall that functionalism is concerned with isolating those elements of an organization that contribute to or inhibit smooth operations. The plumbing manufacturer in the above example was concerned with finding ways to improve the functioning of its methods of communication, in order to enhance its control over operations. Many of the assessment tools used in a communication audit, for example, are expressly designed to enhance the fidelity of the communications within an organization. These tools are based on social or behavioral science techniques, employing surveys, questionnaires, network studies, and similar instruments designed to elicit statistical, or at least quantifiable, information regarding communication practices.

Interpretive approaches, on the other hand, rely more on methods that are not intended to produce quantifiable data. Recall that just because research uses an interpretive approach does not imply that the sought-for outcome is not to improve communication for the benefit of management. Still, the interpretive perspective is also used to achieve an understanding of the lived experience of the people who constitute the organization at all levels. By its very nature, interpretive research is concerned with "bringing to life" the meaning of what it is to live and work in a particular organization day in and day out. Studies of organizational culture are most often associated with this kind of approach, as we have seen.

Critical studies are interested in questions of dominance and hegemony. Critical theorists look at the power structure of an organization and try to understand the ways in which it maintains itself. Critical theorists raise important questions concerning the very purposes for organizations of all sorts in modern societies. For example, their approach confronts the issue of whether a people can have a truly democratic society if the organizations in which they spend most of their time are not run on democratic principles. Because top management usually commissions assessments, critical theorists have been less likely than functionalists or interpretivists to carry out applied or internal communication research for organizations.

Whether one takes a functionalist, interpretivist, or critical perspective can thus determine one's approach to assessing an organization's internal communication system. The interpretivist, for example, may be more likely to apply an organizational cultural approach, or to attend to the organizational or communication climate. As we have seen in Chapter 7, culture can be envisioned as something that can be manipulated or changed in order to bring about organizational transformation, thereby implying a functionalist interpretation of the concept "culture." However, functionalists more typically consider information flows and loads, communication networks, and channels and media for handling communication. Critical theorists, including feminist scholars, are more likely to ask questions concerning the deep meaning of organizational symbols and practices that serve to maintain a certain group or class in power.

The functionalist and interpretive approaches to assessing organizational communication are taken up in this chapter. The themes of critical approaches to the study of organizational communication are discussed more thoroughly in the next chapter. It should be recognized that there may be some overlap among these categories, as some techniques, such as the critical incident technique described below, could arguably be described as either functionalist or interpretivist depending on the use to which the technique is put.

FUNCTIONALIST METHODS FOR COMMUNICATION ASSESSMENT

The Communication Audit

The basic method for assessing internal communication from a functionalist viewpoint has been the *communication audit*. A handbook for conducting audits defines a communication audit as "an objective report on the internal communication of an organization," with the purpose of allowing "management to improve the way in which the organization deals with the information necessary to its operation."[2]

This definition implies several things. First, it states that the audit is to be "objective," suggesting that it be conducted from the outside, whether that "outside" refers to external to the organization or external to the particular part (or subsystem or subculture) of the organization. The idea of scientific objectivity is of course a hallmark of the functionalist perspective. Second, in this definition, the primacy of the interests of management is explicitly accepted. That the purpose of the audit is to improve the functioning of the organization in terms of increasing productivity or efficiency is also implied.

An audit of an organization's communication is thus analogous to a financial audit or to an individual's medical checkup. A financial audit is intended to check over all the details of the financial transactions of an organization over a given period of time, usually a year. A medical checkup is intended to give a complete picture of all aspects of a person's health at a given point in time. Thus, a financial audit suggests following processes through a period of time, whereas a checkup provides a "snapshot" of one's condition at one point in time.

The communication audit is used for either or both purposes: to give a readout on the state of communication at a given time, such as how members perceive the communication climate, or to reveal bottlenecks or weaknesses in the networks of an organization's handling of the flow of information. The focus of a communication audit, it should be emphasized, is on evaluating the processes or systems of communication, not on evaluating individuals.

Several methodologies for conducting communication audits have been employed. Usually, those conducting the audit draw up a series of questionnaires or survey forms concerning communication activities to administer to organizational members. "Duty studies" and diaries are also popular; these typically ask organizational members to keep track of all communication contacts or activities occurring during a specific period of time. For example, one organization the author observed conducted a "brownpaper study." The exercise was given this name because the consultants had each staff department of the organization stretch large pieces of brown wrapping paper along a wall in each office. When any person in that office sent or received a phone call, opened or answered mail, or dealt with a walk-in request for information, that person was to run over to the wall and, with a marking pen, write in the details of time, number of people involved, duration of action, and so on. Needless to say, the brown paper came in for a lot of jokes as well as resentment during the study.

In some organizations, a communication audit is essentially a content analysis of the written communications produced by the organization over a stated period of time. Telecommunications consultants often look exclusively at the use of and need for telephone stations. The purpose of the audit can thus suggest the methods that are used.

Typical methods for focused and systematic observation can include the following techniques:

Focus groups

Interviews (directive or nondirective)

Questionnaires and surveys

Network analysis

Communication diaries or logs

Content analysis (of publications, manuals, handbooks)

Interaction analysis (of team or group meetings)

Nominal group techniques

Technology or media analysis

The International Communication Association (ICA), a professional association of communication professionals and academics, has developed a package of assessment instruments for communication audits. These instruments have been used in a variety of settings and organizations over time, meaning that they have certain advantages over assessment techniques developed for one use in one organization at one time.[3] For instance, because these instruments have been used in different organizations at different times, a large number of cases and a vast amount of data are available, and so results from one organization can be compared to norms established in others. Studies of the audit's usefulness suggest that it does succeed in locating communication problems and suggesting solutions for them.[4]

The ICA audit is based on a series of research techniques for observation, data gathering, and analysis that are standard in the social and behavioral sciences. These techniques are designed to obtain data, usually quantifiable, in real-life or field situations. Five different methods are used to gather information concerning communication within an organization: interviews, a survey questionnaire, reports of communication contacts for network analysis, descriptions of so-called critical incidents involving effective or ineffective communication, and communication logs or diaries.

An interesting aspect of these instruments, especially of the questionnaire, is the focus on comparing desired or needed communication with the communication actually received. For example, the questionnaire includes items on the following topics, among several others:

Pay and benefits

How I am being judged

Organizational policies

Job duties

Promotion and advancement policies

How technological changes affect my job

Mistakes and failures of the organization

For each topic, the respondent is asked to indicate on a scale from 1 (low) to 5 (high) two judgments: First, rate the amount or quality of the information you now receive concerning this topic; and, second, rate the amount or quality of the information you feel you need concerning this topic. The researcher can then compare the amount or quality of information received about a particular topic with the amount or quality that the members feel they need. People often receive a lot of information about job duties, for instance, although they would rather be receiving more information about pay and benefits or about how they are evaluated for promotions or raises. Significant discrepancies between the scores for what information is currently received and what is seen as actually needed can point to potentially serious problems in the organization's communication system or practices. Other items on the questionnaire deal with timeliness of information received, amount of follow-up or action taken or needed regarding information sent to others, and quality of communication relationships, as well as demographic information about the respondent.

The paper-and-pencil questionnaire form can be administered to large numbers of people in the organizations, possibly the entire membership of even quite large firms. The scoring can be facilitated by the use of machine-readable test forms and methods, allowing for a quick readout and simple statistical analysis of the responses. The other instruments of the audit, however, can flesh out the outlines of an organization's communication. Interviews, obviously, allow for more give and take and exploration of topics hinted at in the paper surveys. Usually, interviews can be administered only to selected members of a large organization, given limits on time. The researcher must therefore develop a rationale for selecting this sample.

Interviews can be of two types: open or closed format. In open interviews, the interviewer provides little direction, allowing topics to come up in any order and following various trains of conversation without any particular plan. Closed interviews, on the other hand, follow more strictly an interview schedule, which is a plan for a definite sequence of topics and types of question (hence, closed interview formats are said to be highly scheduled). The most closed form of an interview is basically an oral survey, in which the questioner merely asks items on the survey, allowing the respondent only a narrow range of answers: "On a scale of 5 (best) to 1 (worst), how would you rate the quality of the information you receive concerning your company's benefits package?"

The ICA audit interview schedule usually covers items such as the following. The respondent is asked to describe his or her job, elaborating on the kinds of decisions he or she makes and the sources and adequacy of the information received for making those decisions. The respondent is asked to describe the communication strengths and weaknesses of the organization and to describe the nature of the formal and informal channels through which he or she receives information. The interviewer then explores the issues of ways to improve information flow in the organization, typical decision making, and conflict resolution methods in the organization. The respondent is also asked to discuss his or her communication relationship with superiors, co-workers, middle management, and subordinates.

A more nondirective or open format for an interview would allow a trained interviewer to explore in more depth a problem or discrepancy that may have appeared in the analysis of the written questionnaires. For example, the interviewer may have noted that, on average, people rated information needed concerning safety procedures very high, but rated the amount of safety information received very low. The interviewer may also be aware that management feels that they provide a great deal of safety information. The interviewer could probe these discrepancies in perception. It may be that management's information, contained in written manuals concerning chemical qualities of potentially toxic substances, is not seen as readily accessible during day-to-day operations, or that they strongly emphasize the importance of safety-consciousness rather than factual information regarding chemical reactions.

A third instrument used in an ICA audit is the critical incident report. Like the survey, this instrument has a paper-and-pencil format. The respondent is asked to recall a recent incident involving communication in the organization in which the communication was perceived by the respondent as either very effective or very ineffective. The person is asked to write a fairly detailed description of that incident. The information thus received, it is hoped, will also help to flesh out some examples of communication problems that may have surfaced in the raw data from questionnaires and surveys. Obviously, these reports cannot be machine-scored and require much more time and effort to read and analyze. The results from this kind of instrument are much less quantifiable than the output from surveys or directive interviews.

The critical incident technique (CIT) can also be administered through interviews as well as through written surveys. In CIT interviews, the investigator is able to probe the descriptions of the incidents recounted by the subject, adding to the richness and understanding of the incident and the respondent's interpretation of it. The interviews can be tape-recorded so that written transcripts can be produced. These transcripts can be subjected to content analysis for the purpose of identifying types of incidents (positive or negative) and the nature of the producing cause (conditions, communication, or environmental factors, for example). One study of a health care facility using this method coded the content of the interviews according to whether positive or negative incidents involved features of the facility itself, the nature of the health care received, or communication with the facility's staff or others.[5] The results of this study revealed that communication was the most important factor in determining patients' satisfaction or dissatisfaction with the health care they received.

Like interviews in the ICA audit, interviews in the critical incident method require much more effort and time (and person power on the part of researchers) than paper-and-pencil administration. Analysis of the results is also time-intensive.

In a similar way, the flow of information through the organization may be tracked by choosing a specific incident (or manufacturing one, if appropriate) and following the dissemination of news about it through the organization; this process is sometimes referred to as ECCO analysis, from the pun on *echo* and from *episodic communication channels in organizations*. Respondents are asked to indicate whether or not they have heard of the incident. If they have, they are asked to describe it in as much detail as possible. Then they are asked to indicate the channels and individuals through which they received the information. The description can provide a measure of the accuracy with which the incident was communicated, and the other information indicates the location of the respondent in a communication network or clique, or his or her isolation from the network.

Network analysis is a standby of many communication audits, as networks have long been a staple interest of organizational scholars, especially functionalists.[6] Network studies are intended to produce a "map" of typical interconnections among members of an organization, pointing out heavily used communication channels, possible bottlenecks, gatekeepers, and positions that play important linking functions in the organization's communication patterns.[7] Network analyses are concerned not so much with the content of the information being passed through the organizations as with the identification and location of the links themselves. The researcher is trying to discover patterns of communication flow, albeit a one-time snapshot of these patterns.

Data gathering for network analysis typically begins with distribution of forms that ask each member to keep track of communication contacts with other people for a specific period of time, such as one day or one week. The brown-paper study mentioned above was thus a form of network analysis. Members who are to participate in the study will usually need some training in coding their entries so that they can be made quickly and easily. Some people prefer using a computer spreadsheet-like form to keep track of and code contacts, but that has the disadvantage of forcing people to switch back and forth among applications on their work computers whenever the phone rings or a visitor appears for a quick conference or conversation.

A typical network analysis form asks respondents to keep separate records for contacts with individuals and for meetings. The person will list all the people he or she expects to have contact with during the period of the study, leaving blanks for others and for external contacts that can be filled in as the need arises (these names can be coded for confidentiality later by the researchers). By each name on the form, the respondent logs the time and channel for each contact on a given day.

Thus if John S. phones at 10:00 A.M., the respondent logs that contact next to the name of John S., using a form such as "P 10:00"; the people conducting the study might instruct the respondent to circle or underline the P if the respondent him- or herself initiated the contact. Other codes would be used for faxes, E-mail, voice-mail messages, personal contact, and conferences.

The information from all the logs for a given number of days can be used to construct matrices showing the amount and kinds of contacts among individuals in the organization. The matrix should indicate who was in contact with whom, who handles lots of communication contacts and who has relatively few contacts, the most used channels, and patterns of regular interconnections. Data gathering can be expanded to include information regarding the purpose, duration, and content of the contacts, although recording such additional information can place undue strain on the respondents. They can become so busy or distracted that they do not make nota-tions, then try to reconstruct the information after the fact.

The fifth tool in the ICA audit is a diary or log of individuals' communication activities over a specified period of time. This sort of "duty study" is similar to and can be based on the logs used in network analysis. These diaries provide self-reports by respondents on the length of time spent in various communication activities, such as composing letters or memos, preparing notices for computer bulletin boards, down-loading feeds from listservers, conferring with other organization members, making and receiving phone calls, and so on. In addition, the respondent reports the people involved (where known or appropriate), the subjects or topics involved, and the ini-tiator of the message (self or others). These diaries give a more complete picture of the full range of communication activities than the network forms probably can. Again, the problem in collecting this kind of data lies in the strain that keeping records of this kind meticulously for any length of time places on the participants.

Data gathered through network analysis and communication logs can tell one a great deal about the channels and media through which people receive their informa-tion. These studies can thereby serve as analyses of the technologies and media used for communication in the organization as well as the human channels and contacts.

In summary, the five kinds of tools that make up an ICA-type communication audit are as follows:

1. Questionnaires (paper-and-pencil surveys)
2. Interviews
3. Critical incident reports (similar to ECCO analysis)
4. Network analysis
5. Communication diaries or logs

A communication audit is thus aimed at developing a fairly large database that indicates the range of communication activities within an organization. Most of the assessment techniques result in some kind of quantifiable data, although information gathered from open interviews is obviously less amenable to statistical treatment. The effort is intended to provide an objective picture highlighting potential or real break-downs or weaknesses in the flow of communication in the organization.

Assessment of Communication Climate and Culture

This section provides an overview of methods for the systematic description and analysis of organizational climate and culture. Several tools and methodologies have been de-veloped to allow researchers to analyze and evaluate both. The nature of the tools chosen, of course, reflects the perspective from which an individual researcher is op-erating.

For studying climate, the standard methods of description and analysis have been surveys and questionnaires. Several instruments have been developed and used over the years. Likert was one of the earliest organizational theorists to include specifically communication-oriented items on questionnaires concerning climate. The work of

Litwin and Stringer and their colleagues, mentioned in Chapter 5, led to the development of survey instruments intended to measure organization members' perceptions of warmth, support, and conflict. Following the suggestions of Redding concerning communication climate, Dennis put together a questionnaire concerned with the following dimensions:[8]

1. Quality of superior–subordinate communication
2. Quality and accuracy of downward communication
3. Perceived openness in superior–subordinate communication
4. Opportunities for effective upward communication
5. Reliability perceived in communication from subordinates and coworkers

The International Communication Association, as we have seen, developed one of the most extensive procedures that can be used for measuring communication climate in organizations: the ICA Communication Audit. Others prefer a more interactive and interpretive approach to studying communication climate.[9] Paper-and-pencil surveys and structured interviews, they feel, do not fully allow the researcher to test out his or her interpretations of the data by bouncing them off the organization members themselves. Communication (and organizational) climate, they believe, is likely to be unique to each organization, and consequently researchers should engage members in interaction, looking for key concepts related to climates to emerge. In this approach, the particular climates for subgroups or departments are discovered, and the "kernel" climate (the general one for the whole organization) can then be deduced from them.

Methodologies for describing and analyzing organizational culture from a functionalist perspective have been used and recommended, although the concepts are often associated with the interpretive viewpoint, as we have seen earlier.

First, survey instruments and techniques can be used to discover individuals' and groups' perceptions of the culture. The Organizational Culture Profile (OCP) is an example of this type of instrument.[10] Organization members are asked to respond to fifty-four items, indicating the extent to which each item is descriptive of their organization. Items focus on issues such as risk taking, aggressiveness, stability, conflict management, orientation toward action and achievement, emphasis on team or group versus individual responsibility, competitiveness, social responsibility, performance expectations, innovativeness, supportiveness, formality, security, and friendliness or cohesiveness. A respondent might rate his or her organization high on aggressiveness and risk taking, say, while rating it low on stability, and so on.

A study using this instrument reported that organizational culture had a stronger effect on retention in six public accounting firms than changes in the labor force or employee demographics.[11] Firms whose cultures emphasized interpersonal relationships, team orientation, and respect for others retained professionals for significantly longer periods than firms that emphasized task values such as detail and stability.

Geert Hofstede and his colleagues, referred to earlier with regard to the elements of organizational culture, based their results on interview and survey techniques derived from Hofstede's cross-national study of cultural dimensions as described in Chapter 7, p. 134.[12] Following interviews with key people in each organization, his team administered a questionnaire to random samples of people in each organization studied.

The questionnaire consisted of 135 items concerned with work goals, general beliefs, and work practices, such as attitudes toward meetings, promotion policies, and the like. Items from the cross-national surveys were also included. The study of firms in Europe indicated that values were more closely related to national culture and to demographic characteristics such as age than to corporate or organizational membership. Corporate cultures were differentiated by what they called "practices," the conventions, customs, and traditions unique to specific organizations. These findings are at variance with the usual claims that values are fundamental to organizational cultures.

Group discussion methods are a second technique for conducting functionalist analyses of organizational cultures. These methods are a refinement of the more informal methods recommended by Deal and Kennedy in their early popular description of corporate cultures. Recall from Chapter 7 that Edgar Schein emphasizes the importance of getting below the surface manifestations of culture to the underlying assumptions. As a result he prefers a "clinical research model," requiring high involvement on the part of both the researcher and the participants in the organization being studied. This involvement can include a lengthy period in which the researcher is a participant-observer, following the field study approach of a cultural anthropologist.

Group meetings can begin the search for identifying key cultural elements.

Schein recommends a large group meeting of selected or key members of the target organization to identify and analyze underlying assumptions.[13] Following a brief lecture by the "process consultant," or researcher, the group is asked to describe cultural artifacts or practices, such as dress codes, physical layout of space, the kinds of emotions typically encountered, and so on. The consultant then moves on to "espoused values," the reasons for doing the things described in the first exercise (which are displayed on flip chart sheets or the like around the room). As conflicts between practices and espoused values develop, such as a stated value on innovativeness running contrary to the practice of documenting careful following of all rules, attempts are made to articulate more basic assumptions. The large group may break into subgroups at this point to refine and discuss these assumptions. Obviously, this method is quite time-consuming and requires complete commitment and support from leadership.

Highlights of Functionalist Methods

The functionalist perspective emphasizes generating social scientific data that are useful in detecting weaknesses in the functioning of some aspect of an organization's communication system. The standard methods are encompassed in a communication audit, which is intended to provide objective, often quantified data about an organization's communication activities.

These methods consist of paper-and-pencil surveys and questionnaires, focused interviews, network analysis, critical incident reports, and communication diaries or logs. Functional assessments of communication often make use of these and similar tools. For example, there are several ways to conduct critical incident studies, including the CIT method and ECCO analysis. These are similar to various kinds of network analyses intended to trace the routes and connections for the flow of information through formal and informal channels.

Functionalist methods can also be employed for studying the communication climate and culture of an organization, as there are examples of surveys and questionnaires focusing on aspects of organizational climate and culture. Focus group techniques can also be used to try to discern the deep structure of the organization's culture.

Studies of organizational cultures, however, have typically been more closely associated with those who follow an interpretivist perspective. This is taken up in the next section.

INTERPRETIVIST METHODS FOR COMMUNICATION ASSESSMENT

The interpretive perspective is concerned with discovering and understanding what it means to experience the organization from the inside. The interpretivist analyst is hence more concerned with understanding organizational communication from the point of view of participants than with manipulating it for practical aims of the organization.[14] Interpretivists therefore follow an approach to research or assessment of communication that is often labeled phenomenology or ethnomethodology. Either term suggests that the researcher does not begin with a preordained methodology or set of categories to impose on the data to be discovered. Rather, the researcher immerses him- or herself in the experiences or culture of the organization. Eventually, patterns emerge and become discernible, and the researcher then interprets these patterns in an effort to give them meaning.

This last point does not mean that the interpretive scholar always proceeds with no method or plan of study at all. The point is that the interpretivist is not limited to any particular methodology or theoretical approach, but lets the material suggest the best or most appropriate techniques. What marks the interpretivist is thus more seen in what he or she does with the data rather than in how it is gathered.

Interpretivist Methodologies

One type of interpretive communication study is referred to as *naturalist research,* because the researcher observes natural events in an organization without attempting to intervene by using intrusive instruments such as surveys or similar data-gathering techniques.[15] Charles R. Bantz, who is an advocate of this approach, suggests that researchers can gather data for naturalist research by becoming participant-observers, studying messages produced by the organization, interviewing participants, and analyzing organizational documents, including training manuals, orientation materials, and memoirs of organizational members.

In addition to gathering verbal material, then, the researcher looks at written materials. When studying the documents or other written materials, however, the researcher uses more the techniques of a rhetorical critic than those of a content analyst, who is interested in finding quantified characteristics of the content. Content analysis is a technique that relies on counting instances of verbal phenomena, such as the number of negative references to a group in a document. Content analysis is often used to analyze the readability or educational level of materials, by recording details such as average word and sentence length, word familiarity and novelty, and so forth. Rhetorical analysis is more concerned with describing and interpreting the symbols or themes or point of view of the materials. Orientation materials for new members, for example, can be a source for discovering the values espoused by the organization, as when the family metaphor is used to describe the organization.

The result of naturalist analysis is intended to be descriptions and interpretations of the meanings of organizational messages, leading to an understanding of organizational life that would be accepted by members as valid and understandable.[16] Thus, if someone produces a description of the communication methods at Disney World that results in an explanation of "good mickeys" and "bad mickeys" or reveals how ride directors communicate with one another to deal with difficult "audience members," and Disney World employees (or "cast members") recognize these interpretations as valid, then the research goals of this type of analysis have been met.

A second research technique associated with the interpretivist approach is the study of *organizational narratives,* or stories. We generally know what a story is, of course, although a narrative can be more precisely defined as any account describing a sequence of events that make sense in this sequence.[17]

The brown-paper study described earlier in this chapter became the basis for a narrative within the organization that experienced it. Upper management felt that they had to appear to do something about annual deficits in operational budgets, and so they hired a consultant to help them locate places for making cuts. The purpose of the brown-paper study was thus seen as providing ammunition to justify cuts in personnel in various offices. In some versions, the story concludes a year later, when all the positions that had been eliminated as a result of this study had been gradually restored or refilled. The story, even in this brief form, does much more than simply recount a series of events. A certain cynicism is evident in the imputation of motives for the brown-paper audit from the very beginning. Throughout the story, the idea of a hidden (albeit not well-hidden) agenda appears: The communication audit was actually a cover for the "real motive," to cut jobs. The conclusion suggests the futility of the original motive, as all the cuts were eventually restored. The story thus provides a way for organizational members who lived through the period to interpret and make sense out of their experiences.

Stories can thus be used to help members explain conflicts or contradictions that they perceive in the organization's policies or actions. In this way, stories can provide resistance to organizational changes initiated at higher levels that appear threatening at lower ones. Stories can become especially important at times of organizational dislocation or uncertainty. As one analysis put it, such narratives can help fill in the "betwixt and between position which develops when previous structural arrangements have been terminated, but new ones have not yet been established."[18]

Narratives have hence been especially interesting to interpretive scholars, who see stories as attempts to make sense of and give meaning to organizational events. Storytelling is pervasive in organizations, and the stories affect the way people see the organization and their roles in it. Of course, stories tend to perpetuate a particular interpretation of past events and present reality. In addition to the informal stories, such as the one about the brown-paper study, there are more formal organizational stories that are intended to present organizational founders or leaders in a favorable light and to support sanctioned organizational values. Stories about a founding hero who overcame many kinds of obstacles and disadvantages to establish the company abound. Trice and Beyer (see Chapter 7) refer to these kinds of official stories as organizational sagas. Seemingly stuck in a dead-end job, the founder stays up nights working on his or her kitchen table or out in the garage to put together the new invention that will launch a meteoric rise.

"Official" stories are often used to legitimate leaders' authority and control, as we saw with the famous IBM story about Watson and the young woman security guard who refused him admittance to a restricted area because he lacked the proper badge. As Dennis Mumby and others point out, these stories have a political function in that they create a picture of reality and encourage one interpretation over others.[19]

In addition to narrative analysis, interpretivists may also employ *metaphor analysis,* which involves analyzing the metaphors that are used to characterize the organization and its activities. The research tries to discover the metaphors that are widely used in the organization both in formal presentations and documents and in the everyday conversations of members. Discovering these metaphors can require immersing oneself in the organization as a participant-observer.

Typically, metaphors are of several kinds. First, there are those metaphors that have to do with a particular orientation to space and time. The organization stakes a claim to a certain territory, surveys its landscape, is moving forward, is located on the cutting edge, and so on. Second, there are metaphors that have to do with the activities of the organization or the leaders of the organization. A new CEO or administration is seen as "breathing new life into the organization," for example. Or, the organization is embarked on a new journey, heading down a different road or a new path. Another type of metaphor is one that projects a certain image of an organization, as a team, an extended family, a well-oiled machine, a starship "boldly going where no one has gone before," a cast for a movie, an army, or a religious crusade.

Entertainment and sports metaphors are widely popular, as when the leadership "calls an audible," meaning that it adapts to changing circumstances, just as a quarterback of a football team changes the prearranged play at the line of scrimmage to exploit an unexpected change in the defense. The organization aspires to be a "world-class act" or a "superstar," or to come up with a product or service that is a "smash hit" or that "goes gold" or "goes platinum."

Both narratives and metaphors can serve to reveal underlying beliefs that are often articulated in stories and symbols. These stories and metaphors are more readily observed than the basic assumptions themselves. A set of themes reflecting basic assumptions has been discerned for these narratives and metaphors.[20] These themes include the following:

- *Persecution.* The organization is portrayed as a victim or as subject to a hostile environment. The brown-paper story can be interpreted this way by the staff members in the offices affected by it. Arts organizations have portrayed themselves that way in the face of governmental cuts in funding for PBS or the National Endowment for the Arts.

- *Exorcism.* Some part of the organization is to blame for organizational troubles and needs to be exorcized.[21] This theme can take the form of scapegoating, with particular individuals singled out for sacrifice, as when the coach of a losing team is fired instead of the entire team.

- *Dependency.* The organization is described as depending on a unique CEO or leader, a product, or a certain technology. Thus Chrysler stories recounted the importance of Lee Iacocca, and AT&T stories stressed the importance of long distance to the company's operation for many years.

- *Grandeur or power.* Stories emphasize that the organization has great power, or that leaders and members exhibit confidence in special abilities or powers. The stories surrounding leaders such as Ted Turner or Ross Perot could include such themes.

- *Philosophic or moral missions.* Stories emphasize the role of the organization in improving the environment or others. Organizations such as Doctors without Borders (*Les Medicins sans Frontieres*), Greenpeace, and Habitat for Humanity stress the moral nature of their activities.

- *Guilt.* Large corporations that have been associated in the past with pollution or dangerous products, such as manufacturers of chemicals, napalm, or petroleum products, emphasize support for the arts, public broadcasting, or educational foundations.

A special kind of story or narrative is the *reflexive account,* which is a narrative, often formulated after the fact, that explains or accounts for earlier behaviors. Researchers using this technique ask organizational members to explain the reasons for the organization's past actions. These accounts tend to describe the earlier activities as supporting legitimate or current goals and objectives of the organization, whether that was in fact true or not. Such reflexive accounts are thus good sources for identifying what the current goals or values are, rather than good explanations for past events.

In a related vein, Ernest Bormann suggests the applicability of fantasy theme analysis, or convergence theory, for interpreting shared organizational cultures.[22] A fantasy theme is similar to what Trice and Beyer term a "myth," a story intended to explain events or values. The stories are presented in terms of people acting out a scenario or standard script. The message is therefore dramatized, with heroes and villains. Several such themes or stories are put together to provide an overall shared group identity in what Bormann calls a "rhetorical vision," often implying an organizational image, such as a family or Disney World's cast members. The direction that the "chaining out" of fantasy themes may take is not easy to predict, and therefore the method of convergence theory, or fantasy theme analysis, helps one to understand an organizational culture but not necessarily to predict or control it.

A final approach to the study of organizational culture is that of *ethnographies of communication.* This approach involves deep involvement of the researcher as a participant-observer, immersed for some time in the target organizational culture. The researcher is looking for patterns of communication use that indicate the kinds of competencies necessary to be able to function within a given speech community.[23] For example, greetings in the workplace typically follow certain standard patterns in specific organizations. The kinds of *topics* that can be discussed *with whom* on *what occasions* lead to the discovery of other kinds of observable patterns. The uses of *language* and *rituals* as described by Trice and Beyer and discussed in Chapter 7 are the sorts of observable behaviors that lead to the identification of such patterns. This method is highly descriptive in its approach and would be the most time-consuming of the methods summarized here, as it usually involves total immersion in the organization for an extended period of time.

Highlights of Interpretivist Methods

In assessing organizational communication, the interpretivist scholar is concerned with understanding the experiences of organizational members and the interpretations they place on those experiences. The interpretivist thus does not try to impose a method or set of categories on the phenomena of communication in the organization. Rather, the interpretivist immerses him- or herself in the everyday activities of the organization for purposes of observation and of developing qualitative explanations of those observations.

Interpretivists may choose from a range of qualitative research techniques in approaching their data and experiences. These techniques include those of naturalist research, relying on naturally occuring communication events or documents of the organization; narrative analysis, looking for underlying themes and meanings of organizational stories and storytelling; metaphor analysis, or determining the images or metaphors that members use to describe their organization and their situation within it; fantasy theme analysis; and ethnographies of communication, taking the perspective of a participant-observer in the organization.

SUMMARY

Organizations and their members are often interested in an assessment of the effectiveness of the organization's internal communication activities. Usually the leadership or upper management of the organization is interested in this analysis in order to enhance their control over the organization's processes and to allow the organization to function or meet its goals more effectively. Functionalist perspectives on organizational communication and research have most often been used for the kind of communication assessment conducted under these circumstances. The functionalist approach is most concerned with figuring out how the organization as a system works and finding ways to improve its functioning.

Functionalist methods of communication assessment have most often taken the form of a communication audit, such as the ICA communication audit. The audit is intended to provide objective, often statistical data on the state of communication and information processing in the organization, and relies on several social scientific data-gathering instruments. The ICA audit itself is based on five such instruments or tools, which are similar to other kinds of data-gathering methods used for communication assessment. These tools include a survey or questionnaire, which can produce quantitative data, interviews, critical incident methods, network analysis, and communication logs or diaries. Related tools that are not part of the ICA audit protocol but are used for other kinds of communication audit are the CIT, or critical incident technique, ECCO analysis (episodic communication channels in organizations), focus groups, and content analysis of organizational documents.

Interpretivist approaches to assessment of communication in organizations are more concerned with understanding than with control. Some analyses of organizational and communication climate and culture lie between the functionalist and interpretivist approaches, although those based on surveys or questionnaires are placed in the functionalist camp because of their quantified results. Usually, however, interpretivists aim at analyzing the meaning or quality of organizational life and communication through systematic analysis of organizational stories or narratives, metaphors, fantasy themes, and their underlying symbolism. Ethnographers of communication study organizational communication by prolonged immersion in the organizational culture, usually as participant-observers, so that they can offer "thick descriptions" (that is, detailed descriptions) of what it means to communicate as an insider.

EXERCISES AND QUESTIONS FOR DISCUSSION

1. Reread the problem of the plumbing fixture manufacturer that was introduced early in the chapter. Discuss the various problems that could be among the causes of the difficulties being experienced in communication among distant facilities and the corporate office. Working in a group, and based on the material in the earlier chapters of the text, list all the potential kinds of breakdowns. Next, discuss methods that could be used to discover the presence of any of

these problems. If you were a consultant to this company, what preliminary steps would you suggest to begin to uncover the nature of their problem of communication.

2. Consider the problems caused by the brown-paper study discussed at several points in the chapter, especially the narrative that placed a cynical interpretation on the purposes of the study. What kinds of communication problems are probably present in this organization that would lead to these kinds of interpretations? How could management proceed to overcome the cynicism or mistrust that seems to be revealed in this narrative?

3. How would you assess the communication climate of a company or an organization with which you are familiar? Discuss the advantages and disadvantages of using functional or interpretive instruments or approaches in your assessment.

4. Some situations or communication problems may call for a functionalist approach, while others may appear more amenable to an interpretive perspective. If you were asked to analyze the corporate culture of a local marketing and public relations firm, how would you propose to proceed? Try to construct a plan for discovering the nature of this culture—what should you do first? How would you gather preliminary data? What things should you look for on a first visit to the site?

5. Discuss metaphors that are used by insiders to describe their organization, a business, university, team, or whatever. What do these metaphors imply about how people relate to one another in the organization? Discuss the advantages and disadvantages of the use of each of these metaphors.

6. What organizational stories or narratives are particularly widespread in the school, university, or other significant organization in which you participate? What are the underlying themes of these stories? What do they reveal about the climate within these organizations?

SOURCES FOR FURTHER STUDY

Bantz, C. R. (1983). Interpretivist approach. In L. L. Putnam and M. E. Pacanowsky (Eds.), *Communication and organizations: An interpretive approach*. Newbury Park, Calif.: Sage, pp. 55–72.

Bantz, C. R. (1993). Ethnographic analysis of organizational cultures. In S. L. Herndon and G. L. Kreps (Eds.), *Qualitative research: Applications in organizational communication*. Cresskill, N.J.: Hampton Press, pp. 107–20.

Bormann, E. G. (1983). Symbolic convergence: Organizational communication and culture. In L. L. Putnam and M. E. Pacanowsky (Eds.), *Communication and organizations: An interpretive approach*. Newbury Park, Calif.: Sage, pp. 99–122.

DeWine, S. (1994). *The consultant's craft: Improving organizational communication*. New York: St. Martin's Press.

Eisenberg, E. M., and Goodall, H. L., Jr. (1993). *Organizational communication: Balancing creativity and constraint*. New York: St. Martin's Press.

Falcione, R. L., Sussman, L., and Herden, R. P. (1987). Communication climate in organizations. In F. M. Jablin, L. L. Putnam, K. H. Roberts, and L. W. Porter (Eds.), *Handbook of organizational communication: An interdisciplinary perspective*. Newbury Park, Calif.: Sage, pp. 195–227.

Feldman, S. P. (1990). Stories as cultural creativity: On the relation between symbolism and politics in organizational change. *Human Relations, 43*, 809–28.

Fisher, W. R. (1987). *Human communication as narration: Toward a philosophy of reason, value, and action*. Columbia, S.C.: University of South Carolina Press.

Hamilton, S. (1987). *A communication audit handbook: Helping organizations communicate*. New York: Longman.

Hofstede, G., Neuijen, B., Ohayv, D. D., and Sanders, G. (1990). Measuring organizational cultures: A qualitative and quantitative study across twenty cases. *Administrative Science Quarterly, 35,* 286.

Lindlof, T. R. (1995). *Qualitative communication research methods.* Thousand Oaks, Calif.: Sage.

O'Reilly, C. A., III, Chatman, J., and Caldwell, D. F. (1991). People and organizational culture: A profile comparison approach to assessing person-organization fit. *Academy of Management Journal, 34,* 487–516.

Poole, M. S. (1985). Communication and organizational climates: Review, critique, and a new perspective. In R. D. McPhee and P. K. Tompkins (Eds.), *Organizational communication: Traditional themes and new directions.* Beverly Hills, Calif.: Sage.

Query, J. L., and Kreps, G. L. (1993). Using the critical incident method to evaluate and enhance organizational effectiveness. In S. L. Herndon and G. L. Kreps (Eds.), *Qualitative research: Applications in organizational communication.* Cresskill, N.J.: Hampton Press, pp. 63–77.

Saville-Troike, S. (1989). *The ethnography of communication: An introduction,* 2d ed. Oxford: Basil Blackwell.

Schein, E. H. (1991). *Organizational culture and leadership.* San Francisco: Jossey-Bass.

Schneider, S. C., and Shrivastava, P. (1988). Basic assumptions themes in organizations. *Human Relations, 41,* 493–515.

Sheridan, J. E. (1992). Organizational culture and employee retention. *Academy of Management Journal, 35,* 1036–56.

NOTES

1. R. Beckhard (1969), *Organizational development: Strategies and models,* Reading, Mass.: Addison-Wesley.

2. S. Hamilton (1987), *A communication audit handbook: Helping organizations communicate,* New York: Longman, p. 3.

3. S. DeWine (1994), *The consultant's craft: Improving organizational communication,* New York: St. Martin's Press, p. 115.

4. DeWine, p. 115.

5. J. L. Query, Jr., and G. L. Kreps (1993), Using the critical incident method to evaluate and enhance organizational effectiveness, in S. L. Herndon and G. L. Kreps (Eds.), *Qualitative research: Applications in organizational communication,* Cresskill, N.J.: Hampton Press, pp. 63–77.

6. E. M. Eisenberg and H. L. Goodall, Jr. (1993), *Organizational communication: Balancing creativity and constraint,* New York: St. Martin's Press, p. 271.

7. Hamilton, p. 57

8. R. L. Falcione, L. Sussman, and R. P. Herden (1987), Communication climate in organizations, in F. M. Jablin, L. L. Putnam, K. H. Roberts, and L. W. Porter (Eds.), *Handbook of organizational communication: An interdisciplinary perspective,* Newbury Park, Calif.: Sage, p. 201; pp. 200–203 summarize various research instruments used to measure climate.

9. M. S. Poole (1985), Communication and organizational climates: Review, critique, and a new perspective, in R. D. McPhee and P. K. Tompkins (Eds.), *Organizational communication: Traditional themes and new directions,* Beverly Hills, Calif.: Sage.

10. C. A. O'Reilly, III, J. Chatman, and D. F. Caldwell (1991), People and organizational culture: A profile comparison approach to assessing person-organization fit, *Academy of Management Journal, 34,* 487–516.

11. J. E. Sheridan (1992), Organizational culture and employee retention, *Academy of Management Journal, 35,* 1036–56.

12. G. Hofstede, B. Neuijen, D. D. Ohayv, and G. Sanders (1990), Measuring organizational cultures: A qualitative and quantitative study across twenty cases, *Administrative Science Quarterly, 35,* 286.

13. E. H. Schein (1991), *Organizational culture and leadership,* San Francisco: Jossey-Bass, pp. 149–56.

14. T. R. Lindlof (1995), *Qualitative communication research methods,* Thousand Oaks, Calif.: Sage.

15. C. R. Bantz (1983), Interpretivist approach, in L. L. Putnam and M. E. Pacanowsky (Eds.), *Communication and organizations: An interpretive approach,* Newbury Park, Calif: Sage; C. R. Bantz (1993), Ethnographic analysis of organizational cultures, in S. L. Herndon and G. L. Kreps (Eds.), *Qualitative research: Applications in organizational communication,* Cresskill, N.J.: Hampton Press.

16. Bantz (1983).

17. See W. R. Fisher (1987), *Human communication as nar-*

ration: *Toward a philosophy of reason, value, and action,* Columbia, S.C.: University of South Carolina Press.

18. S. P. Feldman (1990), Stories as cultural creativity: On the relation between symbolism and politics in organizational change, *Human Relations, 43,* 809–28.

19. Feldman; D. Mumby (1987), The political function of narrative in organizations, *Communication Monographs, 54,* 113–27.

20. S. C. Schneider and P. Shrivastava (1988), Basic assumptions themes in organizations, *Human Relations, 41,* 493–515.

21. Schneider and Shrivastava.

22. E. G. Bormann (1983), Symbolic convergence: Organizational communication and culture, in L. L. Putnam and M. E. Pacanowsky (Eds.), *Communication and organizations: An interpretive approach,* Newbury Park, Calif: Sage, pp. 99–122.

23. M. Saville-Troike (1989), *The ethnography of communication: An introduction,* 2d ed., Oxford: Basil Blackwell.

CHAPTER 14

Confronting Issues in Organizational Communication

CHAPTER OBJECTIVES

After studying this chapter, you should be able to:

- Describe major demographic changes affecting the makeup of organizational membership.
- Discuss the implications for organizational communication of increasing participation of women, the aging of the organizational workforce, ethnic and linguistic diversity, and health and safety issues.
- Explain the problems of dealing with technologically fueled information explosions in organizations.
- Discuss the problem of balancing the public good with the organizational good.
- Discuss the dilemmas of democracy in organizations.
- Explain the role of systematically distorted communication in organizations.

CHAPTER OUTLINE

TRENDS AFFECTING CONTEMPORARY ORGANIZATIONS

This book begins with the observation that organizations occupy a major part of our lives. Unfortunately, it appears that people are not widely satisfied with the roles that organizations play in their lives or the roles that they themselves play in those organizations. A national survey of nearly 3,000 American workers in 1993 revealed several interesting perceptions.[1] The results indicated that employees felt less loyalty to their organizations than workers had in the past, which is not surprising given the downsizing or right-sizing of the early and middle 1990s. The reasons given for taking or changing jobs did not emphasize pay and benefits, items that are often taken for granted as most important. Rather, workers rated open communication and the effects of the job on family life well ahead of concerns about pay and benefits.

Other trends at the end of the century support the notion that people are growing more wary of, if not overtly hostile to, the organizations that loom so large in their lives. Feelings of distrust of government and political leaders seem to be growing. Some people expressing this distrust feel that organizations, particularly bureaucracies, have too much control over people's personal lives. Although political leaders and governments suggest that the economy is better off than ever before, there is widespread nervousness and even malaise, as ordinary people measure what they are being told about these matters against their everyday experiences and feelings of insecurity.

Another trend that will have significant consequences for organizational communication is the expansion of the technologies for communication. On the one hand, these technologies mean that people will have access to more information than was ever possible before. On the other hand, others will also have access to information about them. Control over and access to the information in organizational databases and information systems raises questions concerning the privacy and security of that information.

These matters lead to questions concerning possible trade-offs between an organizational good and the public good. What responsibility do organizational communicators assume regarding public policy? In the West, public life is presumably conducted along the lines of a political democracy. We are gratified and heartened by the turn toward democratic politics in Eastern Europe, Africa, and Latin America, but how do we feel about democracy in our organizations, democracy in the workplace?

Someone who would embark on the informed study of organizational communication must be aware of the issues that concern the people who make up the organizations being studied. These organizations do not exist in a laboratory; they exist within the real social, economic, and political conditions of their societies and cultures. At several points in the text, issues have been encountered that need to be considered in the context of these real-life organizations. Many but not all of these issues have been discussed in the boxes dealing with communication ethics and diversity in organizations. This chapter is intended to bring together many of these issues as a way of providing a capstone summary of the nature of organizational communication today and in the future.

THE PEOPLE, THE COMMUNICATORS, IN ORGANIZATIONS

Who are the people who make up the organizations that we study? In the United States, the people working in most organizations are growing increasingly diverse, a fact that must be taken into account when making generalizations about how they communicate in organizational settings. The most recent report on the American workforce by the United States Department of Labor points out that, over the period since 1969, it "has undergone a gradual but very significant transformation, with the proportions accounted for by women and members of racial and ethnic minorities expanding considerably."[2]

During that time, the number of people employed in the United States grew by 60 percent, from about 81 million in 1969 to more than 128 million in 1993. This significant growth in the labor force was due to the coming of age of the "baby boomers," born right after World War II, and the very rapid increase in the number of women, especially younger married women, seeking employment. The average age of the labor force has begun to inch back up, after dipping as the boomers first joined its ranks. The trend of younger women, especially those with young children, entering the workforce, however, has not abated, nor is it likely to. In fact, much of the growth in the number of the employed workers in the 1980s was due to the increasing rates at which women joined the workforce. Figure 14.1 (on p. 348) shows the trends in male and female participation in the labor force very clearly.

These trends are likely to continue into the future, as both the Labor Department and the *Workforce 2000* report of the Hudson Institute, referred to earlier, project. As we begin the next century, the Hudson Institute report predicts that the "workforce will grow slowly, becoming older, more female, and more disadvantaged."[3] Growth in the number of people employed by organizations in the United States will also be accounted for by growing numbers of minorities, African Americans, Hispanics, as well as immigrants (see Table 14.1 on p. 349).

These trends should have several important implications for organizational communication. These implications can be considered under the headings of the increasing proportion of women in organizations, the aging of the organizational workforce, increasing ethnic and linguistic diversity, and growing concerns over health and disabilities.

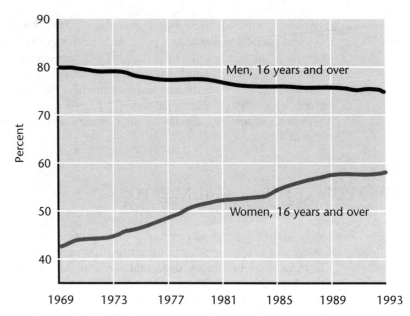

FIGURE 14.1   Trends in labor force participation for men and women, 1969–93 annual averages. (*Source:* U.S. Department of Labor, Report on the American Workforce, 1994, Washington, D.C.: U.S. Government Printing Office, p. 7.)

Increasing Participation of Women

In 1993, 45.6 percent of all people employed in the United States were women. This percentage should trend upward into the first decade of the next century. This situation is quite different from the one that existed in the 1960s, 1950s, or earlier. Typically, in these earlier times, married women stayed at home to take care of the home and children, while the men tended to be gainfully employed. Women who did hold jobs were usually in occupations such as nurse, public school teacher, or secretary. The two-income family is now much more the norm. While some of these couples entered the ranks of the more affluent as "dinks" (dual incomes with no kids), many others found two incomes to be a necessity.

Some implications of these changes include the following:

• More emphasis will be placed on child care as an organizational issue. One of the trends noted has been the growing percentage of women with young children entering the labor force. Women moving along the same career path as men will not want to postpone advancement for stay-at-home child rearing. The two-parent family is no longer the norm, in any case. Accommodation will have to be made for single-parent families, whether the parent is male or female. Even in two-parent families, it is increasingly true that both partners have to remain employed for economic reasons.

TABLE 14.1   Labor force participation rates for major population groups, annual percentage averages, selected years, 1969–93

Group	1969	1973	1979	1983	1989	1993
Total, 16 years and over	60.1	60.8	63.7	64.0	66.5	66.2
Men	79.8	78.8	77.8	76.4	76.4	75.2
16 to 19 years	55.9	59.7	61.5	56.2	57.9	53.1
20 to 24 years	82.8	85.2	86.4	84.8	85.3	83.1
25 to 54 years	96.1	95.0	94.4	93.8	93.7	92.6
55 to 64 years	83.4	78.2	72.8	69.4	67.2	66.5
65 years and over	27.2	22.7	19.9	17.4	16.6	15.6
Women	42.7	44.7	50.9	52.9	57.4	57.9
16 to 19 years	43.2	47.8	54.2	50.8	53.9	49.9
20 to 24 years	56.7	61.1	69.0	69.9	72.4	71.3
25 to 54 years	49.1	52.3	62.3	67.1	73.6	74.7
55 to 64 years	43.1	41.1	41.7	41.5	45.0	47.3
65 years and over	9.9	8.9	8.3	7.8	8.4	8.2
White	59.9	60.8	63.9	64.3	66.7	66.7
Men	80.2	79.4	78.6	77.1	77.1	76.1
Women	41.8	44.1	50.5	52.7	57.2	58.0
Black	(¹)	60.2	61.4	61.5	64.2	62.4
Men	(¹)	73.4	71.3	70.6	71.0	68.6
Women	(¹)	49.3	53.1	54.2	58.7	57.4
Hispanic origin	(¹)	(¹)	(¹)	63.8	67.6	65.9
Men	(¹)	(¹)	(¹)	80.3	82.0	80.0
Women	(¹)	(¹)	(¹)	47.7	53.5	52.0

¹Not available.

Source: U.S. Department of Labor, Report on the American Workforce, 1994, Washington, D.C.: U.S. Government Printing Office, p. 8.

Furthermore, the parents may have to hold down more than one job apiece. Some organizations may provide child care facilities themselves, whereas others will need to consider child care arrangements in matters such as scheduling meetings or other work. At any rate, organizations probably cannot continue to operate as if children of members do not exist.

• Family concerns will increasingly take precedence. One finding from the 1993 study cited above is that people are now more likely to turn down promotions or to refuse relocation because of the impact this may have on family life or children. The aging of the baby boom generation may mean that people will assume more responsibility for care of elderly parents as well as young children.

• Telecommuting may become more prevalent as a response to these issues. In order to gain the flexibility and time to handle child-rearing responsibilities or to take care of elderly parents, more people, men as well as women, may resort to the use of

Organizations must increasingly take into account members' roles in families.

interactive telecommunications and computer links to stay in touch with the organization. As a result, organizational members may find that more of their interpersonal interactions are mediated electronically. The effects of electronic interfaces rather than face-to-face communication between superior and subordinate or among coworkers will become more important. One question for future studies could be the possibilities for and effects of electronic mentoring, for example.

• Organizations will become more flexible in defining what it means to be an organizational member. In addition to increased use of computer and electronic technologies to allow telecommuting, organizations will become more flexible in defining organizational roles, locations, and positions. Organizations that have traditionally been somewhat regimented will turn to flextime, shared positions, or similar innovative work arrangements.

• The nature of motivation or incentives in the organization will undergo changes. The 1993 survey of American workers suggested that open communication had become the most important determinant of satisfaction on the job. A growing emphasis on family and personal relationships could lead to changing definitions of success.[4] People may rethink what it means to "get ahead" in the organization.

• Women will occupy positions of leadership in more and more organizations. As women attain the highest leadership positions in organizations, different styles of leadership may become the norm. Throughout the text, we have seen that there is some debate concerning whether women and men really have different methods of communicating leadership. It has been suggested, as noted earlier, that women as leaders exercise more shared leadership, with more concern for community and for allowing all members of the organization to maintain face. Regardless of the outcome of this debate in the literature of organizational communication, the emergence of women leaders in major organizations will undoubtedly shift more attention toward discussion of the kinds of health and family concerns these differences imply.

While these trends may seem to suggest a liberalization of the organization and organizational life, the effects may also run in a different direction. The expansion of telecommuting or sharing of careers or positions could lead to a further blurring of the lines between organizational and private life. Telecommuters appear to be freer than their counterparts who are physically at some organizational location, but they may experience even more work pressure. Since the office is at home, there is never a sense of separation; some work may always be calling to them from another room in the house or apartment while they are cooking, entertaining, or relaxing. They never physically get away from the office. Cellular telephones and pagers can have the same kind of effect, creating a sense of never quite being off duty.

Some of these same issues will be growing in prominence outside the United States as well. In the *maquiladora* belt of American-owned manufacturers along the American border in Mexico, the proportion of young women workers tends to be high; they are often a majority in assembly operations. Textile and clothing manufacturers in Asia, such as in Thailand and the Philippines, likewise rely on a young, female workforce. As women become more prominent in managerial and government positions in the United States and other countries, concerns about the abuse or exploitation of these worker populations may receive more attention. Child care, nutrition, and health programs may become more important topics for organizational discussion.

The Aging of Organizational Membership

The second trend affecting the American workforce is the aging of the employed population. The baby boomers will continue to be the "elephant moving through the boa" among organizational members. The so-called baby bust generation followed the boomers into the nation's schools and workforce, making up a much smaller percentage in both. In this instance, the American and Western European experience is counter to that of much of the rest of the world, where working-age populations are growing significantly *younger* rather than older.

As the Department of Labor report puts it, "The past trends in the birth rate will have an overriding impact on the growth and makeup of the working-age population over the next decade."[5] By 2005, the members of the baby boom generation will have started to retire, meaning that the ratio of retired persons to employed workers will increase markedly, possibly leading to social discontent as younger workers grow to resent the burden of service for the elderly. These issues may thus become significant in organizational discussion and discourse.

Several scholars have pointed to the advantages that could inhere in an aging organizational population. Older members tend to be more experienced, more loyal to their organization, and more interested in quality of workmanship or service.[6] Such members are often concerned about the quality of life and relationships within the organization as well. They can serve important roles as mentors to less experienced members. Days Inn Corporation has been particularly successful in recruiting older workers to handle telephone reservations in its Atlanta and Knoxville offices and elsewhere. Days Inn has found that the more mature workers show less turnover, less absenteeism and lateness, and more loyalty, and exercise more care in taking and processing reservations.[7] McDonalds is another corporation that has benefited from efforts at recruiting retired persons to staff its restaurants.

Implications of an aging organizational population include the following:

• Organizations will show more concern for health-care issues. The aging membership in many organizations will put some pressure on organizations to address concerns about health care, health insurance, and similar matters, such as the future of Social Security, and could thus lead to wider involvement of the organization in political issues. The Days Inn case, by the way, has shown that health-care costs do not necessarily increase when older workers are recruited.

• Organizations may rely more on temporary or part-time members. As mentioned in regard to women in organizations, hiring older workers may allow for more flexibility. Rather than needing or wanting full-time employment, many retired persons may prefer to fill in and handle special projects as needed. Again, the definition of organizational members may undergo change. These changes could have implications for interpersonal and network communication, as membership fluctuates over time and from project to project.

• Mentoring may receive added emphasis. In taking advantage of the experience of older executives and other members, organizations may find the ranks of potential mentors increased, especially for entering female and minority members.

Ethnic, Racial, and Linguistic Diversity

The third trend is increasing rates of participation by ethnic, racial, and national minorities. Not only will the percentage of African Americans and Hispanics in the workforce increase, but immigration will add approximately 880,000 new workers a year to the American population between now and 2005.[8] Much of this new immigration will be from Asia and Latin America, presenting the "melting pot" with new educational and linguistic challenges. The fastest-growing ethnic group in the American workforce has been the Hispanic population; this group also goes against the trend of the aging of the workforce, as its average age is trending downward. The rapid growth of this group is attributable, in large part, to immigration.

Some of the implications for organizational communication include the following:

• Increased emphasis will be placed on cultural diversity and intercultural communication. Organizations' training and education programs may have to give more attention to intercultural communication, as members, administrators, supervisors, and mentors will have to communicate with people from other national cultures or subcultures. Mandates from governmental agencies, such as the EEOC (Equal Employment Opportunities Commission) or affirmative action programs, may be beside the point as, inexorably, multicultural organizations in the United States and elsewhere become more diverse.

• Language will become a variable in organizational communication. Even as English becomes more widespread throughout the world and in many occupations, such as air travel, aerospace, and entertainment, organizations will become increasingly multilingual. In the United States particularly, as the figures regarding Hispanic populations indicate, organizational communicators will have to make decisions about whether and when to use Spanish as well as or in place of English. Language training may become a larger part of organizations' communication programs.

• Translation services and technologies may be of growing importance in the development of organizational communication systems. Not only will American organizations grow more internally diverse, but as they become truly multinational, communication will undoubtedly be carried out in many different languages.

In other words, linguistic and cultural differences may become a standard part of the decision-making process for organizational communicators. On the other hand, growing resentment of affirmative action programs among majority members in the United States could lead to increased bitterness and a brake on the move to "embrace diversity."

Concerns about Health and Disabilities

The fourth demographic trend that will impinge on organizational communication is concerns about health and disabilities. Like some of the other points raised so far, these are topics that have not in the past been considered relevant for organizational communication. The Americans with Disabilities Act (ADA) of 1990, however, added people with various sorts of disabilities to the list of protected classifications. Organizations had to begin to take cognizance of practices or policies that discriminated against people in these categories. At the same time, there was growing concern over drugs and drug abuse in large organizations, which led in some cases to policies of drug testing or screening.

Rather than seeing these conditions as obstacles, many organizations are beginning to realize that there is an advantage to be gained from these and other forms of diversity among their memberships. People bring many different kinds of skills and perspectives to their roles. In the increasingly complex environment in which organizations operate, it is to their advantage not to exclude certain people because of their age, sex, or ethnic origin, as we have seen, or because of a supposed physical handicap. One text points out, "In organizations, managers often speak of the need for different styles or approaches in solving problems. They recognize that there is more than one way to achieve a goal, but they then strive to create policies that encourage the same or similar ways to work."[9]

Implications of the changes involving health and disability issues include the following.

• Organizations will have to deal with controversies surrounding drug testing and screening. Some organizations have decided to avoid the problems of dealing with employees with long-term dependencies on certain drugs or alcohol by trying to exclude them from membership in the first place (drug screening of applicants or candidates). Others use drug testing as a way to discover members with problems so that they can be placed in support or treatment programs. As noted in the next section of this chapter, these matters also involve privacy issues.

• Organizations will be responsible for developing programs for support or treatment of people with various disabilities. The definition of disability is not limited to physical restrictions, such as those on sight, hearing, or mobility. People with injuries, progressive illnesses, and substance addictions may fall into this category as well.

Since 1987, Digital Equipment Corporation, one of the largest computer companies in the world, has administered a comprehensive program dealing with various aspects of AIDS and HIV infection. This program has both an educational function and a supportive one. The main thrust of the education program is to prevent misinformation and fear concerning working with people who may be HIV positive. Those who are so infected are encouraged by the company to work as long as they are reasonably able to meet performance standards, even if that requires some accommodation on the part of the firm. The supportive part of the program deals with help and counseling for those who have family members or friends who are infected. Issues related to living with chronic illnesses at home as well as in the workplace are thus discussed openly as part of corporate policy.[10]

• Organizations will need policies regarding communication involving people with physical disabilities. Although many organizations have been retrofitting their facilities to accommodate wheelchairs, visual impairments, and hearing or signing needs, few have considered the need to adapt communication practices. Training can help coworkers overcome the discomfort that they may experience when communicating with someone who is in a wheelchair or who is blind. Stereotypes about people with these and similar conditions can interfere with day-to-day communication interactions. Interestingly, the development of more computer-mediated interactions may serve to eliminate the physical cues that can trigger stereotypical responses.

• Organizations will need to respond to the "toxic" effects that they may have on members. In the latter part of this century, organizational change has meant downsizing or right-sizing, as we have seen. In addition, demands that members deal with increasingly diverse and potentially chaotic conditions can lead to increased stress, with effects on physical and mental well-being. Organizations may therefore begin to take a more active role in promoting programs for wellness, stress management, and the like.

• Multinational corporations and international organizations will face many health-related concerns. Throughout the text, we have observed that modern organizations tend to be involved in global operations. Improvements in transportation and communication allow organizations to operate with departments or units on other continents as easily as organizations used to set up branches on different cities or states. Organizational communicators must be aware of the health risks and situations in the different areas in which they conduct business. Drug-resistant malaria, for example, is a growing problem in parts of Africa and Latin America. Even in the United States, drug-resistant strains of tuberculosis have begun to appear, along with other infections that are increasingly resistant to antibiotics.

Review of the Communicators in Organizations

The people who constitute organizations and participate in organizational communication shape and imply the relevance of the various issues that make up the topics of that communication. Increased participation by women in organizations that in the past were male-dominated will shift attention to issues of child care, family life, and increased flexibility in definition of organizational roles and activities. Similarly, the aging of the workforce will raise issues related to refocusing of organizational values and motivators.

Increasing ethnic and linguistic diversity in domestic and especially in multinational organizations places more emphasis on training in intercultural communication. Language choice will become a more prominent issue than in the past, and issues and technologies for linguistic translation may become more prominent.

Finally, organizational communication may focus more on issues of health, safety, and disabilities than in the past. Organizations will need to cope with chronic illnesses and deal with responses to health changes and counseling more than before.

ISSUES OF INFORMATION CONTROL AND ACCESS

Information has some strange properties, especially if one begins to think of it as a commodity. For instance, unlike other commodities, when you share it with someone else, you do not give up any of it; it is not depleted with use, but it can be devalued. Observers of the modern scene like to say that culture has moved from the industrial age, ushered in by the Industrial Revolution at the end of the eighteenth century in England, into an information age. Others would qualify this view by adding that we have entered the age of electronic information, ushered in by the cathode-ray tube and the microchip. If industrial goods were the commodity of the industrial age, does it follow that information is the commodity of this new electronic age?

Control over information is thought to confer power. Access to information is considered to be essential for success in many kinds of organizations. For these reasons, modern organizations see acquiring and maintaining control over information as crucial. Still, it is not clear exactly what constitutes information in this new context. Information theorists define information in terms of reducing uncertainty, which can be calculated mathematically. In quantitative terms, any message that reduces by one-half any amount of uncertainty in a given matter is equal to one bit (binary digit) of information. Thus the information that you have been found guilty or innocent of murder by a jury (indicating which of two possibilities is selected) is quantitatively equal to the information that your friend prefers decaffeinated to regular coffee (also selecting from two alternatives). Both messages contain one bit of information.

Computer databases, CD-ROMs, and similar devices make it possible to store and retrieve information in quantities unimaginable in the past. As mentioned in Chapter 10, however, the problem is not so much quantity of information as it is quality. Vast amounts of data are stored simply because it is easy and cheap to do so. The generation of so much information means that the strain on human abilities lies in dealing with it, rather than in acquiring it.

Problems arise when organizations treat acquiring a quantity of information as equally important as or more important than determining the quality of information needed. Consider the economic measure often used for modern economies, the gross domestic product, or GDP, which has replaced the earlier measure GNP, or gross national product. These measures of economic performance go back to the 1930s, the time of the Great Depression, and were further refined during the Second World War as part of the efforts to mobilize the economy. Both the GNP and GDP are measures of economic *activity*, without concern for how one might value any individual activity. In that way, they are similar to the quantitative measure of information described above. The GDP counts any consumption involving the exchange of money. Thus, obese people contribute positively to the GDP when they buy food that they do not need, and then contribute again when they buy diet books or pills to undo the effects of that food. If one of these people needs a coronary bypass as a result of the consumption of too much fat, this adds even more to the plus side of the GDP.[11] If the GDP is taken as the only or the "most objective" measure of economic life, some important issues concerning the quality of life are obfuscated. Similarly, organizations must be careful about relying on measures of quantity when they really need to be concerned with issues of quality.

Neil Postman, communication theorist at New York University, in his critique of "technopoly," has argued that organizations are often paralyzed by an information glut.[12] Much new information technology, he claims, has as its primary function the accessing, managing, and storage of new information. What real-life problem is solved in this way? Only the need to access, manage, and store all the new information that is produced. But, Postman maintains, it is information for information's sake; it is not necessarily directed at the solution of any real problem. Information is thereby elevated to a "metaphysical status: information as both means and ends of human creativity."[13]

The kind of information that an organization collects and has access to serves to direct thinking along certain paths and not others. Information then drives the organization, instead of being used by the organization to solve problems. Because American policy makers have the GDP, for instance, they may think of solving economic problems in terms of stimulating cash consumption of goods of any kind, regardless of long-range consequences. Similarly, organizations may let the kind of information they have determine the range of alternatives considered in dealing with any problem, as we saw in regard to bounded rationality and satisficing in Chapter 11.

The ease with which certain kinds of information can be collected and stored can also raise concerns about the privacy and confidentiality of information on organiza-

Privacy will continue to be an important issue for organizational members.

tion members; reference to drug testing and screening was made previously. Record keeping in these areas can lead to fears of the "intrusive organization." Involvement of organizations in the medical and health conditions of their members could lead to the storing of personal data that may follow a person from one organization to another. Let's say that a person has sought information from an HIV support group set up by his or her organization. How will the information be handled? Should it be stored for the future protection of the organization or its members?

Consider the matter of violence in the workplace, which is of growing concern for many organizations. Courts have ruled that organizations can be held liable for hiring or retaining workers who injure others violently on the job. On the other hand, courts have also held that screening applicants or maintaining and passing on records indicating violence-prone behaviors or conditions can constitute invasion of privacy. You may recall that some courts have found organizations that maintained and passed on records of reasons for the dismissal of an employee to be guilty of slander.[14]

Organizations may thus be caught in a bind between the need to have information in order to protect all members, while at the same time not infringing on the privacy or other civil rights of individuals. An individual could fear that screening for HIV, for example, could damage his or her reputation as well as his or her working relations with coworkers. As organizations communicate about a wider range of potentially personal issues, as we saw in the first section of this chapter, they begin to run into dilemmas regarding the control over and access to that kind of information.

Increasing reliance on computer-mediated communication systems may only exacerbate some of these difficulties. Voice-mail systems are not always secure, nor is E-mail, nor are other electronic storage and media devices. Many people forget that cellular and personal communication telephones that rely on broadcast transmission are not nearly as secure as traditional phone lines. Hackers may gain access to the organization's records, sometimes with relative ease. Computer systems may allow for the processing and storage of vast amounts of data, but such data may be accessible in ways that were not anticipated. As noted earlier, many corporations and other organizations now maintain staffs of "Internet surfers" to keep track of the flow of information, some of it leaked, floating in cyberspace.[15]

Access to and control over vast amounts of information may lead complex organizations to see themselves as having a special role in deciding important public questions. The issue is taken up in the next section.

THE PUBLIC INTEREST AND ORGANIZATIONAL COMMUNICATION

In many ways, large, complex organizations deal with matters that affect the wider community or public interest. The section dealing with risk communication in Chapter 12 provides some good examples of the problems inherent in these matters. The reification of organizational identity, referred to at the very beginning of this book, leads to a feeling that individuals are not personally responsible for the actions of the organization as an entity.

Operations of an organization that affect public health or safety may thus tend to fall into the area of proprietary or secret information. In their well-known critique *Organizational America,* William G. Scott and David K. Hart refer to the personalization of the organization (thinking of it as a real person) providing a shield for those who really make the decisions: "To suggest that organizations 'do' anything masks these individuals from view and depersonalizes both the value and moral issues implicit in their conduct, thus relieving them of individual responsibility and public accountability."[16]

The original *Jaws* movie is based on a premise that is standard in movies of its kind. It's not the fear of sharks that is the issue, but rather the fear that organizations are keeping from us something that we ought to know. In the movie, the resort community's establishment, represented by police, tourist board, or town council, decided to keep the threat of the "great white" secret in order to avoid hurting the tourist business in the middle of the summer. A similar theme runs through movies like the older *Westworld,* about a futuristic amusement park gone haywire, or the more recent *Jurassic Park.* These movies touch on a widely held public fear that certain agencies or organizations are keeping something from us. Similarly, there is a fear that public health agencies or hospitals may hush up the outbreak of a dreaded disease or infection, that city governments may stifle news of crime in order to keep shoppers coming downtown, and so on.

Modern corpcrate-form organizations generally have access to up-to-date technology and technical expertise. This technology and expertise can easily lead to the argument that those in control of it have the best insight in determining public policy. The argument becomes one of saying that the general public lacks the knowledge or ability to understand the complex issues of the day. Therefore, decisions about these issues must necessarily be turned over to the experts, who are often found in organizations furthering a private rather than a public interest. Lobbyists thus become responsible for writing legislation in state legislatures and Congress because they are able to supply the technical knowledge and expertise lacking among legislative staffs.

Chapter 12, as we have noted, provides an explanation of the differences in the points of view of technical experts and the general public with regard to risk communication. The problem is not that the general public does not or cannot understand the technical issues involved, but rather that the public perspective can serve as a corrective to an administrative point of view represented by the experts. Recall that the members of the public are not concerned about the statistical probability of toxic emissions or explosions, but about issues of choice, trust, and participation in decisions concerning the location of risky operations.

On the other hand, organizations can play a role in public discourse through their internal communication activities as well as through public advocacy or issues management (see Chapter 12). The case of Digital Equipment and its development of an AIDS program, as described in the previous section, is a good example of an organization trying to take a responsible stand on a significant public issue. Of course, many corporations or organizations promote worthy causes through advocacy or public service advertising. The case of Digital represents an internal program rather than an externally directed one, however.

In a related vein, we have seen the role of and the risks to whistle-blowers in organizations, who alert the public or government agencies to the dangers of their own organization's operations. As we have noted, whistle-blowing is often a symptom of an internal communication problem, specifically the lack of open upward communication. Whistle-blowers thus come to represent what they conceive to be the public interest from within an organization when they perceive that the organization is acting against that interest in some way.

Finally, through their internal activities, organizations can shape, at least to some extent, members' perspectives regarding the nature of their society. People spend so much time in modern complex organizations, and the importance of these organizations for many people is so great, that what goes on in the internal communication of these organizations must have some effect in other spheres of members' lives. The next section takes up the issue of whether a society can effectively value democratic principles when organizations do not uphold similar principles.

DEMOCRACY AND THE MODERN ORGANIZATION

Although Americans pride themselves on living in a political democracy, they seldom expect that political ideal to be realized in their organizational or work settings. Members of one professional organization once answered in the following way when asked about shared decision making: "Yes, we practice shared decision making here. When the bosses make a decision, they share it with us." One source of American socialization as preparation for work organizations is school sports. Becoming part of the team, following the coach's orders without question, and sticking to one's role in the system are the values to be inculcated. Athletic teams are often not places for rugged individualists or for the practice of participatory democracy. Similarly, many people find that these same values are upheld in corporate-form organizations.

At the same time, this text has taken note of the movement in many organizations toward the development of self-managing teams, empowerment, and decentralization. These moves might suggest that organizational democracy is becoming a widespread idea. As noted earlier, however, these tendencies can be misleading in that a small group's self-monitoring can be more intrusive and less democratic than what obtains in more strictly hierarchical bureaucracies. Team members may so identify with the organizational values and commitments that they keep a closer watch on one another and allow less freedom of expression than would have been the case otherwise. Recall also that Gareth Morgan points out that the move to decentralized teams tends to dilute the collective power of larger groups, such as labor unions.[17] The individual teams themselves may be so small that they have little impact on the direction of overall policy of the organization, so that some exercise of democratic politics is lost through fragmentation of group interests. And, the "empowered" worker may find that she or he has "1½ or 2 jobs to do" as a result of reengineering, downsizing, or right-sizing.[18]

The introduction to this text describes the development of a prevalent type of organization referred to as the *corporate form*.[19] The idea here is that even if an organization is not actually a for-profit business, it may well mimic the form of a for-profit corporation. Religious organizations, schools, not-for-profit organizations, and even clubs have adopted the forms of corporate organization. In corporate-form organizations, decisions are made by a professional management group, which is often insulated from accountability to the organization's actual membership.

This kind of system may also be referred to as "managerial capitalism," or "managerialism." In higher education, managerialism is seen in the development of career tracks for professional administrators, separate from traditional faculty tracks. Thus one candidate for a deanship at a business school gave as his reason for applying for the job that it seemed the right career move at the time. In other words, the candidate saw the position as one in a sequence of positions in administration, rather than as a unique opportunity to provide educational leadership.

The growing role of corporate style organizations can be seen in the movement toward privatization in many spheres. In privatization, for-profit corporations, not just organizations with this form, actually take over some activities that had been seen as being in the public or governmental realm. Today, for example, there are more police working for private security firms than for public municipal forces. Charitable not-for-profit organizations turn over fund raising to professional fund-raising firms. Correctional institutions, some school districts, health care organizations, and even some schools have been privatized. The Olympic Games, proud showcase for amateurism, has increasingly become privatized in order to raise the funds necessary to put on the competitions.

Theorist Stanley Deetz refers to this ubiquity of the corporate-form organization, together with the move toward privatization, as the "corporate colonization" of most aspects of public and even private life.[20] Questions of public policy tend to be framed in terms of economics or technology, in which the expertise of ordinary citizens is seen as insufficient to allow them an active role in public debate. The corporate-form organizations, however, are presented as having the requisite technical expertise to make most of the important policy determinations. Within the organization itself, this privilege of expertise is extended to the members of upper management, whose special knowledge and perspective legitimates their ultimate decision-making prerogative. For Deetz and others, corporate colonization means that the range of decision making permitted ordinary citizens and organization members is restricted to an insignificant amount.

Of course, not all organizations are run as autocracies (rule by one person) or oligarchies (rule by a few). Workplace democracy is seen in certain settings and in certain organizations. Quality circles, self-managed teams, and alternative organizations may represent such settings.[21] W. L Gore & Associates has been held up as an example of a successful corporation run along more democratic lines.[22] Its most famous product, Gore-Tex™, is a kind of breathable fabric used in medical applications, parkas, ski gloves, running suits, and so on. This company is set up as a "lattice organization," which means that instead of there being a pyramidal hierarchy, the lines of communication and responsibility look like a lattice, connecting each position with all others, intended to represent unrestricted communication. Associates (rather than employees) are supposed to be free to move about within the organization, drawn to different projects depending on their interests. Leaders are to behave as sponsors, mentors, or coaches rather than as bosses.

As the company expands, however, the ideal of maintaining a fully democratic culture is threatened. Aristotle believed, after all, that democracy was most likely to survive only in a state small enough for the whole citizenry to meet together in one place.[23] When the organization or state becomes so large that most members are unknown to one another, impersonal means of control begin to appear. In a case-study investigation of workplace democracy in large co-ops in the Basque region of northern Spain, George Cheney noted the challenge of sheer size in attempts to maintain democratic participation in decision making.[24]

Democracy in an organization is largely a matter of communication, specifically a meaningful role in communication in the matter of making significant decisions in and for the organization. The extent to which decision making and communication within organizations are actually democratic has largely been of concern to scholars who take a critical perspective. Theorists such as Deetz and others look to the German philosopher of sociology, Jürgen Habermas, to provide a theoretical framework for the kind of communication most characteristic of democratic institutions.[25] Habermas formulated the notion of "systematically distorted communication" to refer to situations in which people were unable to participate openly and equally in the full discussion of issues affecting them. The reason for this disability is not that members are suppressed overtly, as in some obvious tyranny, but that they are somehow unaware of or unable to articulate their own best interests.

Communication within organizations can be distorted in situations in which some group within the organization is able to claim special status relative to other groups. Administrators thus may lay claim to special knowledge or objectivity, placing themselves above the fray of departmental politics, and thereby affording themselves more authority in discussions of organizational decisions. Other groups may accede to these claims of special status, thus contributing to the continuation of an unequal dialogue.

The outcome of this unequal dialogue is that decisions are taken not for the good of the organization or society as a whole, but for the benefit of some smaller group, typically the managerial class. To return to the terminology of the discussion on decision making, organizational decision making is based on bounded rationality. In the situation of systematically distorted communication, the bounds on rationality have been set in a particular way, one that favors and benefits one group at the expense of others and the organization as a whole.

This dilemma is one that many organizations seem to be struggling with at the end of this century. Many realize that increasing diversity and cross-cutting forces require organizations that can respond to this complexity quickly and in innovative ways. Karl Weick has repeatedly claimed that complexity in the environment must be met by complexity in the organization that would respond to it.

Decentralization, empowerment of individuals and small teams, and the move toward adhocracy and flexibility all represent methods for building complexity into organizations. These methods also imply greater participation in significant decision making being pushed further down into the membership, in other words, they imply a need for greater workplace democracy. Scholars of organizational communication should be especially interested in the communication climate and activities that respond to these needs and these times of increasing complexity.

SUMMARY

It is not possible to discuss, especially in depth, all of the many issues that confront students of organizational communication as they consider the role of organizations in contemporary life. The issues included in this chapter are suggestive rather than exhaustive. A premise of this text has been the idea that organizations are extremely important in the lives of most people. For that reason, public and social issues impinge on people as they work and communicate within organizations.

This chapter begins with an analysis of the changing face of organizational membership. Who makes up and communicates within our organiza-

tions determines the kinds of issues and topics brought up for discussion. We can no longer think of organizational members as basically interchangeable units. They are no longer mostly white males in the United States; this group is in fact already a statistical minority in comparison to women and racial minorities. Not only is organizational membership growing more diverse in terms of sex and ethnic composition in the United States and Western Europe, it is also growing older. The aging of the workforce can also shape the kinds of interests and topics relevant to organizational communication.

Ethnic, racial, and even linguistic diversity will increasingly affect organizations, especially global or multinational organizations. While English continues to spread around the globe as a standard language for much of business and entertainment, language selection may become an important matter for organizational communication. Certainly the need for training in intercultural communication will continue to grow.

Organizations will increasingly face important concerns regarding health, safety, and dealing with disabilities. Not only are these matters mandated by law in the United States and several other countries, but tapping into the experience, knowledge, and differing perspectives of different kinds of people may become increasingly good business in dealing with growing complexity.

Information processing and storage technologies present organizational communicators with problems concerning how to deal with vast amounts of data. A focus on quality of information when so much quantity is available may become more and more difficult. Organizational control over so many kinds of information may lead to further conflicts between organizational interest and a broader public interest. Organizations will find that they need to deal with public issues within the framework of existing organizational structures. Hence, programs such as AIDS awareness and support are being developed in some corporations.

Questions of quality of life necessarily concern quality of life within organizations, since, as Chapter 1 points out, so much of our lives is now spent in organizations. Can organizations ignore the democratic values of the larger society in decision making and other important forms of organizational communication? This question becomes increasingly relevant in the face of the movement toward empowerment of members, self-managed work teams, and similar trends.

EXERCISES AND QUESTIONS FOR DISCUSSION

1. Consider the list of suggested implications of the increased participation of women in work organizations. Discuss additions to this proposed list. Discuss the concerns that women bring to organizational life that may have been previously ignored or downplayed.

2. Although the population of North America and Western Europe is currently aging, on average, the opposite is happening in many parts of the Third World—in Asia, Africa, and Latin America. What will be the possible communication problems that could arise in organizations in which the age profile differs from region to region? How will multinational organizations accommodate the concerns of both older and younger workers?

3. To what extent can mentoring programs help to deal with issues concerning growing ethnic and linguistic diversity in modern organizations? What other methods can be suggested for creating a central organizational culture with a culturally heterogeneous organizational membership?

4. Should organizations place topics such as AIDS on their organizational communication agenda? To what extent can work organizations be responsible for or concerned about the physical health of members?

5. Discuss the differences between quantity and quality of information. Have you observed the effects of the information explosion? How can organizations determine the kinds of information they need for problem solving and decision making?

6. Should many of the important issues of the day be left to the technical experts? Why or why not? What are the social or political implications of our increased reliance on the experts to tell us what to do about public problems?

7. Is the democratic ideal really applicable to work organizations? Under what conditions do you feel that democracy is not workable in work settings? What are the limits on democratic participation in modern organizations today? Can or should these limits be overcome?

SOURCES FOR FURTHER STUDY

Alvesson, M. (1987). *Organization theory and technocractic consciousness.* Berlin: Walter de Gruyter.

Alvesson, M. (1993). Cultural-ideological modes of management control: A theory and a case study of a professional service company. In S. Deetz (Ed.), *Communication yearbook 16.* Newbury Park, Calif.: Sage, pp. 3–42.

Cheney, G. (1995). Democracy in the workplace: Theory and practice from the perspective of communication. *Journal of Applied Communication Research, 23,* 167–200.

Clegg, S. (1990). *Modern organizations.* London: Sage.

Clegg, S., and Dunkerley, D. (1980). *Organization, class and control.* London: Routledge and Kegan Paul.

Cobb, C., Halstead, T., and Rowe, J. (1995). If the GDP is up, why is America down? *Atlantic Monthly, 276,* 59–78.

Deetz, S. A. (1992). *Democracy in an age of corporate colonization.* Albany, N.Y.: State University of New York Press.

Deetz, S., and Mumby, D. K. (1990). Power, discourse, and the workplace: Reclaiming the critical tradition. In J. A. Anderson (Ed.), *Communication yearbook 13.* Newbury Park, Calif.: Sage, pp. 18–47.

Habermas, J. (1979). *Communication and the evolution of society.* Trans. T. McCarthy. Boston: Beacon Press.

Hale, N. (1990). *The older worker.* San Francisco: Jossey-Bass.

Held, D. (1980). *Introduction to critical theory: Horkheimer to Habermas.* Berkeley, Calif.: University of California Press.

Jamieson, D., and O'Mara, J. (1991). *Managing workforce 2000: Gaining the diversity advantage.* San Francisco: Jossey-Bass.

Johnson, W. B., and Packer, A. E. (Eds.), (1987). *Workforce 2000: Work and workers in the twenty-first century.* Indianapolis: Hudson Institute.

McDermott, J. (1991). *Corporate society: Class, property, and contemporary capitalism.* Boulder, Colo.: Westerview Press.

Larkin, T. J. (1986). Humanistic principles for organizational management. *Central States Speech Journal, 37,* 36–44.

Morgan, G. (1986). *Images of organization.* Newbury Park, Calif.: Sage.

Pacanowsky, M. (1988). Communication in the empowering organization. In J. A. Anderson (Ed.), *Communication yearbook 11.* Newbury Park, Calif.: Sage, pp. 356–79.

Postman, N. (1993). *Technopoly: The surrender of culture to technology.* New York: Vintage Books.

Scott, W. G., and Hart, D. K. (1979). *Organizational America.* Boston: Houghton Mifflin.

U.S. Department of Labor, R. B. Reich, Secretary. *Report on the American Workforce, 1994.* Washington, D.C.: U.S. Government Printing Office, pp. 5–6.

NOTES

1. *Wall Street Journal,* September 3, 1993, pp. B1, B2.
2. U.S. Department of Labor, R. B. Reich, Secretary, *Report on the American Workforce, 1994,* Washington, D.C.: U.S. Government Printing Office, pp. 5–6.
3. W. B. Johnson and A. E. Packer (Eds.), *Workforce 2000: Work and workers in the twenty-first century,* Indianapolis: Hudson Institute, Executive Summary, p. xiii.
4. D. Jamieson and J. O'Mara (1991), *Managing workforce 2000: Gaining the diversity advantage,* San Francisco: Jossey-Bass, p. 20.
5. *Report on the American Workforce, 1994,* p. 23.
6. N. Hale, (1990), *The older worker,* San Francisco: Jossey-Bass.
7. Jamieson and O'Mara, p. 75.
8. *Report on the American Workforce, 1994,* p. 25.
9. Jamieson and O'Mara, p. 3.
10. Jamieson and O'Mara, p. 95.
11. C. Cobb, T. Halstead, and J. Rowe (1995), If the GDP is up, why is America down? *Atlantic Monthly, 276,* 59–78.
12. N. Postman (1993), *Technopoly: The surrender of culture to technology,* New York: Vintage Books.

13. Postman, p. 61.

14. *Wall Street Journal,* November 26, 1993, p. B1.

15. *Wall Street Journal,* September 15, 1993, p. B1.

16. W. G. Scott and D. K. Hart (1979), *Organizational America,* Boston: Houghton Mifflin, p. 42.

17. G. Morgan (1986), *Images of organization,* Newbury Park, Calif: Sage.

18. G. Cheney (1995), Democracy in the workplace: Theory and practice from the perspective of communication, *Journal of Applied Communication Research, 23,* 167–200.

19. J. McDermott (1991), *Corporate society: Class, property, and contemporary capitalism,* Boulder, Colo.: Westerview Press.

20. S. A. Deetz (1992), *Democracy in an age of corporate colonization,* Albany, N.Y.: State University of New York Press.

21. Cheney.

22. M. Pacanowsky (1988), Communication in the empowering organization, in J. A. Anderson (Ed.), *Communication yearbook 11,* Newbury Park, Calif: Sage, pp. 356–79.

23. Aristotle, *Politics* VI.v.

24. Cheney, p. 174.

25. J. Habermas (1979), *Communication and the evolution of society,* Trans. T. McCarthy, Boston: Beacon Press.

Bibliography

Albrecht, T. L., and Hall, B. (1991). Relational and content differences between elite and outsiders in innovation networks. *Human Communication Research, 17,* 535–61.

Allen, M. W. (1992). Communication and organizational commitment: Perceived organizational support as a mediating factor. *Communication Quarterly, 40,* 357–67.

Allen, M. W., and Caillouet, R. H. (1994). Legitimation endeavors: Impression management strategies used by an organization in crisis. *Communication Monographs, 61,* 44–62.

Allen, M. W., Gotcher, J. M., and Seibert, J. H. (1993). A decade of organizational communication research: Journal articles 1981–1991. In S. Deetz, (Ed.), *Communication yearbook 16.* Newbury Park, Calif.: Sage, pp. 252–330.

Altman, I., and Taylor, D. (1973). *Social penetration: The development of interpersonal relationships.* New York: Holt, Rinehart & Winston.

Alvesson, M. (1987). *Organization theory and techocractic consciousness.* Berlin: Walter de Gruyter.

Alvesson, M. (1993). Cultural-ideological modes of management control: A theory and a case study of a professional service company. In S. Deetz, (Ed.), *Communication yearbook 16.* Newbury Park, Calif.: Sage, pp. 3–42.

Argyris, C. (1957). *Personality and organization.* New York: Harper & Brothers.

Argyris, C. (1962). *Interpersonal competence and organizational effectiveness.* Homewood, Ill.: Irwin.

Argyris, C. (1990). *Integrating the individual and the organization.* New Brunswick, N.J.: Transaction Publishers.

Bantz, C. R. (1983). Interpretivist approach. In L. L. Putnam and M. E. Pacanowsky (Eds.), *Communication and organizations: An interpretive approach.* Newbury Park, Calif.: Sage.

Bantz, C. R. (1993). Ethnographic analysis of organizational cultures. In S. L. Herndon and G. L. Kreps (Eds.), *Qualitative research: Applications in organizational communication.* Cresskill, N.J.: Hampton Press, pp. 107–20.

Barker, J. R., Melville, C. W., and Pacanowsky, M. E. (1993). Self-directed teams at Xel: Changes in communication practices during a program of cultural transformation. *Journal of Applied Communication Research, 21,* 297–312.

Barnard, C. (1938). *The functions of the executive.* Cambridge, Mass.: Harvard University Press.

Bass, B. M. (1990). *Bass & Stogdill's handbook of leadership.* New York: The Free Press.

Bazerman, M. H., and Lewicki, R. J. (Eds.) (1983). *Negotiating in organizations.* Beverly Hills, Calif.: Sage Publications.

Bennis, W., and Nanus, B. (1985). *Leaders: The strategies for taking charge.* New York: Harper & Row.

Berger, C. R. (1986). Uncertain outcome values in predicted relationships: Uncertainty reduction theory then and now. *Human Communication Research, 13,* 35.

Berger, Charles R., and Bradac, James J. (1982). *Language and social knowledge: Uncertainty in interpersonal relations.* London: Edward Arnold.

Berger, C. R., and Calabrese, R. J. (1975). Some explorations in initial reaction and beyond: Toward a developmental theory of interpersonal communication. *Human Communication Research, 1,* 99–112.

Bertalanffy, L. v. (1968). *General systems theory: Foundations, developments and applications.* New York: George Braziller.

Blake, R. R., and McCanse, A. A. (1991). *Leadership dilemmas—grid solutions.* Houston: Gulf Publishing.

Blake, R., and Mouton, J. S. (1964). *The managerial grid: Key orientations for achieving production through people.* Houston: Gulf Publishing.

Blake, R., and Mouton, J. S. (1968) *Corporate excellence through grid organizational development.* Houston: Gulf Publishing.

Blake, R. R., and Mouton, J. S. (1984). *Solving costly organizational conflict.* San Francisco: Jossey-Bass.

Blau, P. M. (1956). *Bureaucracy in modern society.* New York: Random House.

Blau, P. M. (1974). *On the nature of organizations.* New York: Wiley.

Bok, S. (1968). *Lying: Moral choices in public and private life.* New York: Pantheon.

Bormann, E. G. (1983). Symbolic convergence: Organizational communication and culture. In L. L. Putnam and M. E. Pacanowsky (Eds.), *Communication and organizations: An interpretive approach.* Newbury Park, Calif.: Sage.

Boyett, J. H., and Conn, H. P. (1991). *Workplace 2000: The revolution reshaping American business.* New York: Penguin.

Buller, D. B., and Aune, R. K. (1992). The effects of speech rate similarity on compliance: Application of communication accommodation theory. *Western Journal of Speech Communication, 56,* 36–53.

Bullis, C. (1991). Communication practices as unobtrusive control: An observational study. *Communication Studies, 42,* 254–71.

Bullis, C. (1993). Organizational socialization research: Enabling, constraining, and shifting perspectives. *Communication Monographs, 60,* 10–17.

Bullis, C., and Bach, B. W. (1989) Socialization turning points: An examination of organizational identification. *Western Journal of Speech Communication, 53,* 273–93.

Bullis, C., and Bach, B. W. (1991). An explication and test of communication network content and multiplexity as predictors of organizational iden-

tification. *Western Journal of Speech Communication, 55,* 180–97.

Burgoon, J. K., and Hale, J. L. (1984). The fundamental topoi of relational communication. *Communication Monographs, 51,* 193–214.

Burns, J. M. (1978). *Leadership.* New York: Harper & Row.

Burns, T., and Stalker, G. M. (1961). *The management of innovation.* London: Tavistock Publications.

Burrell, G., and Morgan, G. (1979) *Sociological paradigms and organizational analysis.* Ridgewood, N.J.: Forkner.

Burrell, N. A., Donohue, W. A., and Allen, M. (1990). The impact of disputants' expectations on mediation: Testing an interventionist model. *Human Communication Research, 17,* 104–39.

Canary, D. J., and Spitzberg, B. H. (1987). Appropriateness and effectiveness perceptions of conflict strategies. *Human Communication Research, 14,* 93–118.

Canary, D. J., and Spitzberg, B. H. (1989). A model of the perceived competence of conflict strategies. *Human Communication Research, 15,* 630–49.

Canary, D. J., and Spitzberg, B. H. (1990). Attribution biases and associations between conflict strategies and competence outcomes. *Communication Monographs, 57,* 139–50.

Carroll, G. R. (Ed.) (1988). *Ecological models of organizations.* Cambridge, Mass.: Ballinger.

Cheney, G. (1995). Democracy in the workplace: Theory and practice from the perspective of communication. *Journal of Applied Communication Research, 23,* 167–200.

Cheney, G., and McMillan, J. J. (1990). Organizational rhetoric and the practice of criticism. *Journal of Applied Communication Research, 18,* 93–114.

Cheney, G., and S. L. Vibbert (1987). Corporate discourse: Public relations and issue management. In F. M. Jablin, L. L. Putnam, K. H. Roberts, and L. W. Porter (Eds.), *Handbook of organizational communication: An interdisciplinary perspective.* Newbury Park, Calif.: Sage, p. 176.

Cherrington, D. J. (1989). *Organizational behavior.* Boston: Allyn & Bacon.

Chesebro, J. W., and Bonsall, D. G. (1989). *Computer-mediated communication: Human relationships in a computerized world*. Tuscaloosa, Ala.: University of Alabama Press.

Clair, R. P. (1993). The use of framing devices to sequester organizational narratives: Hegemony and harassment. *Communication Monographs 60*, 113–36.

Clampitt, P. (1991). *Communicating for organizational effectiveness*. Newbury Park, Calif.: Sage.

Clegg, S. (1990). *Modern organizations*. London: Sage.

Clegg, S., and Dunkerley, D. (1980). *Organization, class and control*. London: Routledge & Kegan Paul.

Cloven, D. H., and Roloff, M. E. (1991). Sense-making activities and interpersonal conflict: Communication cures for the mulling blues. *Western Journal of Speech Communication, 55*, 134–58.

Cobb, C., Halstead, T., and Rowe, J. (1995). If the GDP is up, why is America down? *Atlantic Monthly, 276*, 59–78.

Conrad, C. (1991). Communication in conflict: Style-strategy relationships. *Communication Monographs, 58*, 135–55.

Corman, S. R. (1990). A model of perceived communication in collective networks. *Human Communication Research, 16*, 582–602.

Cyert, R. M., and Marsh, J. G. (1963). *A behavioral theory of the firm*. Englewood Cliffs, N.J.: Prentice-Hall.

Dahl, R. A. (1957). The concept of power. *Behavioral Science, 2*, 201–15.

Dansereau, F., and Markham, S. E. (1987). Superior-subordinate communication: Multiple levels of analysis. In F. M. Jablin, L. L. Putnam, K. H. Roberts, and L. W. Porter (Eds.), *Handbook of organizational communication: An interdisciplinary perspective*. Beverly Hills, Calif.: Sage.

Deal, T., and Kennedy, A. A. (1982). *Corporate culture: The rites and rituals of corporate life*. Reading: Mass.: Addison-Wesley.

Deetz, S. (1982). Critical interpretive research in organizational communication. *Western Journal of Speech Communication, 46*, 131–49.

Deetz, S. (1988). Cultural studies: Studying meaning and action in organizations. In J. A. Anderson (Ed.), *Communication yearbook 11*, Newbury Park: Calif.: Sage, pp. 335–45.

Deetz, S. (1992). *Democracy in an age of corporate colonization*. Albany: N.Y.: State University of New York Press.

Deetz, S., and Mumby, D. K. (1990). Power, discourse, and the workplace: Reclaiming the critical tradition. In J. A. Anderson (Ed.), *Communication yearbook 13*. Newbury Park, Calif.: Sage, pp. 18–47.

DeTurck, M. A., and Miller, G. R. (1990). Training observers to detect spontaneous deception: Effects of gender. *Communication Reports, 4*, 81–89.

DeWine, S. (1988). The cultural perspective: New wave, old problems. In J. A. Anderson (Ed.), *Communication yearbook 11*. Newbury Park, Calif.: Sage, pp. 346–55.

DeWine, S. (1994). *The consultant's craft: Improving organizational communication*. New York: St. Martin's Press.

Dilenschneider, R. L. (1990). *Power and influence: Mastering the art of persuasion*. New York: Prentice-Hall.

Donohue, W. A., Weider-Hatfield, D., Hamilton, M., and Diez, M. E. (1985). Relational distance in managing conflict. *Human Communication Research, 11*, 387–405.

Drucker, P. F. (1974). *Management: Tasks, responsibilities, practices*. New York: Harper & Row.

Eblen, A. L. (1987). Communication, leadership, and organizational commitment. *Central States Speech Journal, 38*, 181–95.

Eisenberg, E. M., and Goodall, H. L., Jr. (1993). *Organizational communication: Balancing creativity and constraint*. New York: St. Martin's Press.

Etizioni, A. (1961). *A comparative analysis of complex organizations*. New York: The Free Press.

Fairhurst, G. T. (1993). The leader-member exchange patterns of women in industry: A discourse analysis. *Communication Monographs, 60*, 321–51.

Falcione, R. L., Sussman, L., and Herden, R. P. (1987). Communication climate in organizations. In F. M. Jablin, L. L. Putnam, K. H. Roberts, and L. W. Porter (Eds.), *Handbook of organizational communication: An interdisciplinary perspective*. Newbury Park, Calif.: Sage.

Farace, R. B., Monge, P. R., and Russell, H. M. (1977). *Communicating and organizing*. Madison, Wis.: WCB Brown & Benchmark.

Faules, D. F., and Drecksel, G. L. (1991). Organizational cultures reflected in a comparison of work justifications. *Communication Reports, 40,* 90–102.

Fayol, H. (1937). The administrative theory in the state. Trans. S. Greer. In L. Gulick and L. Urwick (Eds.), *Papers on the science of administration.* New York: Institute of Public Administration.

Feldman, S. P. (1990). Stories as cultural creativity: On the relation between symbolism and politics in organizational change. *Human Relations, 43,* 809–28.

Fiedler, F. (1967). *A theory of leadership effectiveness.* New York: McGraw-Hill.

Fisher, K. (1993). *Leading self-directed work teams.* New York: McGraw Hill.

Fisher, W. R. (1987). *Human communication as narration: Toward a philosophy of reason, value, and action.* Columbia, S.C.: University of South Carolina Press.

Folberg, J., and Taylor, A. (1984). *Mediation: A comprehensive guide to resolving conflicts without litigation.* San Francisco: Jossey-Bass.

Frost, P. J. (1987). Power, politics, and influence. In F. M. Jablin, L. L. Putnam, K. H. Roberts, and L. W. Porter (Eds.), *Handbook of organizational communication: An interdisciplinary perspective.* Newbury Park, Calif.: Sage.

Frost, P. J., Moore, L. F., Louis, M. R., Lundberg, C. C., and Martin, J. (Eds.) (1985). *Organizational context.* Beverly Hills, Calif.: Sage.

Frost, P. J., Moore, L. F., Louis, M. R., Lundberg, C. C., and Martin, J. (Eds.) (1991). *Reframing organizational culture.* Newbury Park, Calif.: Sage.

Fulk, J., and Steinfeld, C. (Eds.) (1990). *Organizations and communication technology.* Newbury Park, Calif.: Sage.

Goldhaber, G. M., Yates, M. P., Porter, D. T., and Lesniak, R. (1978). State of the art: Organizational communication: 1978. *Human Communication Research, 5,* 76–96.

Goodell, A. L. (1992). Organizational climate: Current thinking on an important issue. In K. L. Hutchinson (Ed.), *Readings in organizational communication.* Dubuque, Iowa: Wm. C. Brown.

Gudykunst, W. B. (1988). Uncertainty and anxiety. In Y. Y. Kim, and W. B. Gudykunst (Eds.), *Theories in intercultural communication.* Newbury Park, Calif.: Sage, pp. 123–56.

Gudykunst, W. B. (1989). Culture and development of interpersonal relationships. In J. A. Andersen (Ed.), *Communication yearbook 12.* Newbury Park, Calif.: Sage, pp. 315–54.

Gudykunst, W. B., Stewart, L. P., and Ting-Toomey, S. (Eds.) (1985). *Communication, culture, and organizational process.* Beverly Hills, Calif.: Sage.

Habermas, J. (1979). *Communication and the evolution of society.* Trans. T. McCarthy. Boston: Beacon Press.

Hackman, M. Z., and Johnson, C. E. (1991). *Leadership: A communication perspective.* Prospect Heights, Ill.: Waveland Press.

Hale, N. (1990). *The older worker.* San Francisco: Jossey-Bass.

Hall, E. T. (1976). *Beyond culture.* New York: Doubleday.

Hall, R. H. (1991). *Organizations: Structures, processes, and outcomes.* Englewood Cliffs, N.J.: Prentice-Hall.

Hamilton, S. (1987). *A communication audit handbook: Helping organizations communicate.* New York: Longman.

Hannan, M. T., and Freeman, J. (1989). *Organizational ecology.* Cambridge, Mass.: Harvard University Press.

Heath, R. L., and Nelson, R. A. (1985). Image and issue advertising: A corporate and public policy perspective. *Journal of Marketing, 49,* 58–68.

Heider, F. (1958). *The psychology of interpersonal relations.* New York: Wiley.

Held, D. (1980). *Introduction to critical theory: Horkheimer to Habermas.* Berkeley, Calif.: University of California Press.

Hersey, P., and Blanchard, K. (1982). *Management and organizational behavior.* Englewood Cliffs, N.J.: Prentice-Hall.

Herzberg, F. (1966). *Work and the nature of man.* Cleveland: World Publishing.

Hill, P. H., et al. (1979). *Making decisions: A multidisciplinary approach.* Reading, Mass.: Addison-Wesley.

Hirokawa, R. Y. (1988). Group communication and decision-making performance: A continued test of the functional perspective. *Human Communication Research 14,* 487–515.

Hofstede, G. (1980). *Culture's consequences.* Beverly Hills, Calif.: Sage.

Hofstede, G., Neuijen, B., Ohayv, D. D., and Sanders, G. (1990). Measuring organizational cultures: A qualitative and quantitative study across twenty cases. *Administrative Science Quarterly, 35,* 286.

Howard, L. A., and Geist, P. (1995). Ideological positioning in organizational change: The dialectic of control in a merging organization. *Communication Monographs, 62,* 110–31.

Hutchinson, K. L. (Ed.) (1992). *Readings in organizational communication.* Dubuque, Iowa: Wm. C. Brown.

Jablin, F. M. (1987). Formal organization structure. In F. M. Jablin, L. L. Putnam, K. H. Roberts, and L. W. Porter (Eds.), *Handbook of organizational communication: An interdisciplinary perspective.* Newbury Park, Calif.: Sage.

Jablin, F. M. (1987). Organizational entry, assimilation, and exit. In F. M. Jablin, L. L. Putnam, K. H. Roberts, and L. W. Porter (Eds.), *Handbook of organizational communication: An interdisciplinary perspective.* Beverly Hills, Calif.: Sage.

Jamieson, D., and O'Mara, J. (1991). *Managing workforce 2000: Gaining the diversity advantage.* San Francisco: Jossey-Bass.

Janis, I. L. (1972). *Victims of group think.* New York: Houghton Mifflin.

Janis, I. L. (1989). *Crucial decisions: Leadership in policymaking and crisis management.* New York: The Free Press.

Janis, I. L., and Mann, L. (1977). *Decision making: A psychological analysis of conflict, choice, and commitment.* New York: The Free Press.

Johnson, W. B., and Packer, A. E. (Eds.) (1987). *Workforce 2000: Work and workers in the twenty-first century.* Indianapolis: Hudson Institute.

Kahneman, D., Slovic, P., and Tversky, A. (Eds.) (1982). *Judgment under uncertainty: Heuristics and biases.* New York: Cambridge University Press.

Kanter, R. M. (1977). *Men and women of the corporation.* New York: Basic Books.

Kanter, R. M. (1975). Women and the structure of organizations: Explorations in theory and behavior. In M. Millman and R. M. Kanter (Eds.), *Another voice: Feminist perspectives on social life and social science.* Garden City, N.Y.: Anchor Books.

Katz, D., and Kahn, R. (1978). *The social psychology of organizations,* 2d ed. New York: Wiley.

Kelley, H. H. (1973). The process of causal attribution. *American Psychologist, 28,* 107–28.

Kiesler, S, Siegel, J., and McGuire, T. W. (1984). Social psychological aspects of computer-mediated communication. *American Psychologist, 39,* 1123–34.

Klimann, R. H., Saxton, M. J., and Serpa, R. (Eds.) (1985). *Gaining control of the corporate culture.* San Francisco: Jossey-Bass.

Knuf, J. (1993). "Ritual" in organizational culture theory: Some theoretical reflections and a plea for greater terminological rigor. In S. A. Deetz (Ed.), *Communication yearbook 16.* Newbury Park, Calif.: Sage, pp. 61–103.

Koontz, H. (1961). The management theory jungle. *The Academy of Management Journal, 1,* 174–88.

Kotter, J. P. (1985). *Power and influence.* New York: The Free Press.

Kram, K. E. (1988). *Mentoring at work.* Lanham, Md.: University Press of America.

Krone, K. J., Jablin, F. M., and Putnam, L. L. (1987). Communication theory and organizational communication: Multiple perspectives. In F. M. Jablin, L. L. Putnam, K. H. Roberts, and J. W. Porter (Eds.), *Handbook of organizational communication: An interdisciplinary perspective.* Newbury Park, Calif.: Sage. pp. 18–40.

Larkin, T. J. (1986). Humanistic principles for organizational management. *Central States Speech Journal, 37,* 36–44.

Lawler, E. E. (1992). *The ultimate advantage: Creating the high-involvement organization.* San Francisco: Jossey-Bass.

Lawrence, P. R., and Lorsch, J. W. (1967). *Organization and environment: Managing differentiation and integration.* Boston: Harvard University Press.

Leavitt, H. J. (1951). Some effects of certain communication patterns on group performance. *Journal of Abnormal and Social Psychology, 46,* 38–50.

Leavitt, H. J. (1986). *Corporate pathfinders.* Homewood, Ill.: Dow Jones-Irwin.

Levine, T. R., McCormack, S. A., and Avery, P. B. (1992). Sex differences in emotional reactions to discovered deception. *Communication Quarterly, 40,* 289–96.

Lewis, J., Jr. (1985). *Excellent organizations: How*

to develop and manage them using Theory Z. New York: J. L Wilkerson.

Likert, R. (1967). *The human organization.* New York: McGraw-Hill.

Lincoln, J. R., and Kalleberg, A. L. (1990). *Culture, control and commitment.* London: Cambridge University Press.

Lindlof, T. R. (1995). *Qualitative communication research methods.* Thousand Oaks, Calif.: Sage.

Litwin, G. H., and Stringer, R. A., Jr. (1968). *Motivation and organizational climate.* Boston: Harvard University Press.

Luhmann, N. (1992). Autopoesis: What is communication? *Communication Theory, 2,* 251–59.

Ma, R. (1992). The role of unofficial intermediaries in interpersonal conflicts in Chinese culture. *Communication Quarterly, 40,* 269–78.

MacCarthin, E. Z. (1989). Beyond employee publications: Making the personal connection. *Public Relations Journal,* July, p. 15.

MacCrimmon, K. R., and Taylor, R. N. (1983). Decision making and problem solving. In N. D. Dunnette (Ed.), *Handbook of organizational psychology.* New York: Wiley.

Manz, C. C., and Sims, H. P. (1993). *Business without bosses.* New York: Wiley.

March, J. G., and Simon, H. A. (1958). *Organizations.* New York: Wiley.

Marshall, R., and Tucker, M. (1992). *Thinking for a living.* New York: Basic Books.

Mayo, E. (1933). *The human problems of an industrial organization.* New York: Macmillan.

McDermott, J. (1991). *Corporate society: Class, property, and contemporary capitalism.* Boulder, Colo.: Westview Press.

Mead, G. H. (1943). *Mind, self, and society.* Ed. C. W. Morris. Chicago: University of Chicago Press.

Meyer, J. C. (1995). Tell me a story: Eliciting organizational values from narratives. *Communication Quarterly, 43,* 210–24.

Meyers, R. A., Brashers, D., Center, C., Beck, C., and Wert-Gray, S. (1992). A citation analysis of organizational communication research. *Southern Communication Journal, 57,* 241–46.

Miller, F. E., and Rogers, L. E. (1976). A relational approach to interpersonal communication. In G. R. Miller (Ed.), *Explorations in interpersonal communication.* Beverly Hills, Calif.: Sage.

Miller, G. R. (1990). Interpersonal communication. In G. L. Dahnke and G. W. Clatterbuck (Eds.), *Human communication: Theory and research.* Belmont, Calif.: Wadsworth, pp. 91–122.

Miller, G. R., and Sunnafrank, M. J. (1982). All is for one but one is not for all: A conceptual perspective of interpersonal communication. In F. E. X. Dance (Ed.), *Human communication theory.* New York: Harper & Row, pp. 220–42.

Millman, M., and Kanter, R. M. (1975). *Another voice: Feminist perspectives on social life and social science.* Garden City, N.Y.: Doubleday Anchor.

Mintzberg, H. (1973). *The nature of managerial work.* New York: HarperCollins.

Monge, P. R., and Eisenberg, E. M. (1987). Emergent communication networks. In F. M. Jablin, L. L. Putnam, K. H. Roberts, and L. W. Porter (Eds.), *Handbook of organizational communication: An interdisciplinary perspective.* Newbury Park, Calif.: Sage.

Moore, C. A. (1986). *The mediation process.* San Francisco: Jossey-Bass.

Morgan, B. S., and Schiemann, W. A. (1983). Why internal communication is failing. *Public Relations Journal,* March, pp. 15–17.

Morgan, G. (1986), *Images of organization.* Newbury Park, Calif.: Sage.

Morrill, C., and Thomas, C. K. (1992). Organizational conflict management as disputing process: The problem of social escalation. *Human Communication Research, 18,* 400–28.

Mortensen, C. D. (1991). Communication, conflict, and culture. *Communication Theory, 1,* 273–93.

Motley, M. T. (1990). On whether one can(not) not communicate: An examination via traditional communication postulates. *Western Journal of Speech Communication, 54,* 1–20.

Mumby, D. K. (1987). The political function of narrative in organizations. *Communication Monographs, 54,* 113–27.

Mumby, D. K. (1988). *Communication and power in organizations: Discourse, ideology and domination.* Norwood, N.J.: Ablex.

Nanus, B. (1992). *Visionary leadership: Creating a compelling sense of direction for your organization.* San Francisco: Jossey-Bass.

Neustadt, R. E. (1980). *Presidential power: The politics of leadership from FDR to Carter.* New York: Macmillan.

Newton, D. A., and Burgoon, J. K. (1990). The use and consequences of verbal influence strategies during interpersonal disagreements. *Human Communication Research, 16,* 477–518.

O'Keefe, B. J., and McCornack, S. A. (1987). Message design logic and message goal structure: Effects on perceptions of message quality in regulative communication situations. *Human Communication Research, 14,* 68–92.

O'Reilly, C. A. III, Chatman, J. and Caldwell, D. F. (1991). People and organizational culture: A profile comparison approach to assessing person-organization fit. *Academy of Management Journal, 34,* 487–516.

Pacanowsky, M. (1988). Communication in the empowering organization. In J. A. Anderson (Ed), *Communication yearbook 11.* Newbury Park, Calif.: Sage, pp. 356–79.

Pacanowsky, M. E., and O'Donnell-Trujillo, N. (1982). Communication and organizational culture. *Western Journal of Speech Communication, 46,* 115–30.

Pacanowsky, M. E., and O'Donnell-Trujillo, N. (1984). Organizational communication as cultural performance. *Communication Monographs, 50,* 126–47.

Papa, M. J., and Natalle, E. J. (1989). Gender, strategy selection, and discussion satisfaction in interpersonal conflict. *Western Journal of Speech Communication, 53,* 260–72.

Parks, M. R. (1977). Relational communication: Theory and research. *Human Communication Research, 3,* 372–81.

Pearce, W. B., and Cronen, V. E. (1982). *Communication, action and meaning: The creation of social realities.* New York: Holt, Rinehart & Winston.

Pelz, D. (1952). Influence: A key to effective leadership in the first line supervision. *Personnel, 29,* 209–17.

Perrow, C. (1972). *Complex organizations: A critical essay.* Glenview, Ill.: Scott, Foresman & Co.

Perrow, C.(1984). *Normal accidents: Living with high-risk technologies.* New York: Basic Books.

Peters, T. J., and Austin, N. (1985). *A passion for excellence: The leadership difference.* New York: Random House.

Peters, T. J., and Waterman, R. H., Jr. (1982). *In search of excellence: Lessons from America's best-run companies.* New York: Harper & Row.

Pettigrew, A. M. (1979). On studying organizational culture. *Administrative Science Quarterly, 24,* 570–81.

Pfeffer, J. (1981) *Power in organizations.* Marshfield, Mass.: Pitman.

Pfeffer, J. (1982). *Organizations and organization theory.* Boston: Pitman.

Pilotta, J. J., Widman, T., and Jasko, S. A. (1988). Meaning and action in the organizational setting: An interpretive approach. In J. A. Anderson (Ed.), *Communication yearbook 11.* Newbury Park, Calif.: Sage, pp. 310–34.

Poole, M. S. (1985). Communication and organizational climates: Review, critique, and a new perspective. In R. D. McPhee and P. K. Tompkins (Eds.), *Organizational communication: Traditional themes and new directions.* Beverly Hills, Calif.: Sage.

Porter, L. W., Crampon, J. W., and Smith, F. J. (1976). Organizational commitment and managerial turnover: A longitudinal study. *Organizational Behavior and Human Performance, 15,* 87–98.

Postman, N. (1993). *Technopoly: The surrender of culture to technology.* New York: Vintage Books.

Presthus, R. (1962). *The organizational society.* New York: Vintage.

Pugh, D. S., and Hickson, D. J. (Eds.) (1989). *Writers on organizations,* 4th ed. Newbury Park, Calif.: Sage.

Putnam, L. L. (1982). Paradigms for organizational communication research: An overview and synthesis. *Western Journal of Speech Communication, 46,* 192–206.

Putnam, L. L., and Pacanowsky, M. E. (Eds.) (1983). *Communication and organizations: An interpretive approach.* Newbury Park, Calif.: Sage.

Putnam, L. L., and Poole, M. S. (1987). Conflict and negotiation. In F. M.Jablin, L. L. Putnam, K. H. Roberts, and L. W. Porter (Eds.), *Handbook of organizational communication: An interdisciplinary perspective.* Beverly Hills, Calif.: Sage, pp. 549–95.

Query, J. L., Jr., and Kreps, G. L. (1993). Using the critical incident method to evaluate and enhance organizational effectiveness. In S. L. Herndon and G. L. Kreps (Eds.), *Qualitative research: Applications in organizational communication.* Cresskill, N.J.: Hampton Press, pp. 63–77.

Redding, C. (1972). *Communication within the organization: An interpretive review of theory and research.* New York: Industrial Communication Council.

Renz, M. A., and Greg, J. (1988). Flaws in the decision-making process: Assessment and acceptance of risk in the decision to launch Flight 51-L. *Central States Speech Journal, 39,* 67–75.

Roesner, J. (1990). Ways women lead. *Harvard Business Review* (November–December), pp. 119–25.

Roloff, M. E., and Campion, D. E. (1987). On alleviating and debilitating effects of accountability on bargaining: Authority and self-monitoring. *Communication Monographs, 54,* 145–64.

Salazar, A. J., Hirokawa, R. Y., Propp, K. M., Julian, K. M., and Leatham, G. B. (1994). In search of true cause: Examination of the effect of group potential and group interaction on decision performance. *Human Communication Research, 20,* 529–59.

Sass, J. S., and Canary, D. J. (1991). Organizational commitment and identification: An examination of conceptual and operational convergences. *Western Journal of Speech Communication, 55,* 275–93.

Saville-Troike, M. (1989). *The ethnography of communication: An introduction,* 2d ed. New York: Basil Blackwell.

Schall, M. (1983). A communication rules approach to organizational culture. *Administrative Science Quarterly, 28,* 557–81.

Schein, E. H. (1991). *Organizational culture and leadership.* San Francisco: Jossey-Bass.

Schneider, S. C., and Shrivastava, P. (1988). Basic assumptions themes in organizations. *Human relations, 41,* 493–515.

Scott, W. G., and Hart, D. K. (1979). *Organizational America.* Boston: Houghton Mifflin.

Scott, W. Richard. (1981). *Organizations: Rational, natural and open systems.* Englewood Cliffs, N.J.: Prentice-Hall.

Shannon, C. E., and Weaver, W. (1949). *The mathematical theory of communication.* Urbana, Ill.: University of Illinois Press.

Sheridan, J. E. (1992). Organizational culture and employee retention. *Academy of Management Journal, 35,* 1036–56.

Shimanoff, S. B. (1980). *Communication rules: Theory and research.* Beverly Hills, Calif.: Sage.

Simon, H. A. (1957). *Administrative behavior.* New York: The Free Press.

Smircich, L., and Calás, M. B. (1987). Organizational culture: A critical assessment. In F. M. Jablin, L. L. Putnam, K. H. Roberts, and L. W. Porter (Eds.), *Handbook of organizational communication: An interisciplinary perspective.* Newbury Park, Calif.: Sage.

Smith, Adam (1925). *An inquiry into the nature and causes of the wealth of nations, I.* London: Methuen & Co.

Smith, P. B., and Peterson, M. F. (1988). *Leadership, organizations and culture: An event management model.* London: Sage.

Stamp, Glen H., and Knapp, Mark L. (1990). The construct of intent in interpersonal communication, *Quarterly Journal of Speech, 76,* 282–99.

Stewart, J. (1991). A postmodern look at traditional communication postulates. *Western Journal of Speech Communication, 55,* 354–79.

Stinchcombe, A. L. (1990). *Information and organizations.* Berkeley, Calif.: University of California Press.

Sunnafrank, M. J. (1986). Predicting outcome value during initial interactions: A reformulation of uncertainty reduction theory. *Human Communication Research, 13,* 12.

Sypher, B. D., Applegate, J. L., and Sypher, H. E. (1985). Culture and communication in organizational contexts. In W. B. Gudykunst, L. P. Stewart, and S. Ting-Toomey (Eds.), *Communication, culture, and organizational processes.* Beverly Hills, Calif.: Sage, pp. 13–29.

Tagiuri, R., and G. H. Litwin (Eds.) (1968). *Organizational climate: Explorations of a concept.* Boston: Harvard University Press.

Tannen, D. (1994). *Talking from 9 to 5.* New York: William Morrow.

Taylor, F. W. (1911). *The principles of scientific management.* New York: Harper & Brothers.

Tichy, N. M., Tushman, M. L., and Fombrun, C. (1979). Social network analysis for organizations. *Academy of Management Review, 4,* 507–19.

Tomkins, P. K., Fisher, J. Y., Infante, D. A., and Tompkins, E. L. (1975). Kenneth Burke and the inherent characteristics of formal organizations: A field study. *Speech Monographs, 42,* 235–42.

Treadwell, D. F., and Harrison, T. M. (1994). Conceptualizing and assessing organizational image: Model images, commitment, and communication. *Communication Monographs, 61,* 63–85.

Trevino, L. K., Daft, R. L., and Lengel, R. H. (1990). Understanding managers' media choices: A symbolic interactionist perspective. In J. Fulk and C. Steinfield (Eds.), *Organizations and communication technology.* Newbury Park, Calif.: Sage.

Trice, H. M., and Beyer, J. M. (1993). *The cultures of work organizations.* Englewood Cliffs, N.J.: Prentice-Hall.

Turner, D. B. (1990). Intraorganizational bargaining: The effect of goal congruence and trust on negotiator strategy use. *Communication Studies, 41,* 54–76.

Tversky, A., and Kahneman, D. (1974). Judgment under uncertainty: Heuristics and bias. *Science, 185,* 1124–31.

Vance, V., Monge, P. R., and Russell, H. R. (1977). *Communicating and organizing.* Reading, Mass.: Addison-Wesley.

Waldron, V. R. (1991). Achieving communication goals in superior-subordinate relationships: The multi-functionality of upward maintenance tactics. *Communication Monographs, 58,* 291–92.

Waterman, R. H., Jr. (1990). *Adhocracy: The power to change.* New York: Norton.

Watzlawick, P., Beavin, J., and Jackson, D. (1967). *Pragmatics of human communication.* New York: Norton.

Weber, M. (1947). *The theory of social and economic organization.* Trans. A. M. Henderson and T. Parsons. New York: The Free Press.

Weeks, D., and Whimster, S. (1985). Contexted decision-making: A socio-organizational perspective. In G. Wright (Ed.), *Behavioral decision-making.* New York: Plenum Press.

Weick, K. E. (1976). Educational organizations as loosely coupled systems. *Administrative Science Quarterly, 21,* 1–16.

Weick, K. E. (1979). *The social psychology of organizing,* 2d ed. Reading: Mass.: Addison-Wesley.

Wert-Gray, S., Center, C., Brashers, D. E., and Meyers, R. A. (1991). Research topics and methodological orientation in organizational communication: A decade in review. *Communication Studies, 42,* 141–54.

Whaley, S., and Cheney, G. (1991). Review essay: Contemporary social theory and its implications for rhetorical and communication theory. *Quarterly Journal of Speech, 77,* 467–508.

Wilder, C. (1979). The Palo Alto Group: Difficulties and directions of the interactional view for human communication research. *Human Communication Research, 5,* 170–86.

Wiseman, R. L., and Shuter, R. (Eds.) (1994). *Communicating in multinational organizations.* Thousand Oaks, Calif.: Sage.

Witteman, H. (1988). Interpersonal problem-solving: Problem conceptualization and communication use. *Communication Monographs, 55,* 336–59.

Witteman, H. (1992). Analyzing interpersonal conflict: Nature of awareness, type of initiating event, situational perceptions, and management styles. *Western Journal of Speech Communication, 56,* 248–80.

Woodward, J. (1965). *Industrial organization: Theory and practice.* London: Oxford University Press.

Yukl, G. A. (1981). *Leadership in organizations.* Englewood Cliffs, N.J.: Prentice-Hall.

Zorn, T. E. (1991). Construct system development, transformational leadership and leadership messages. *Southern Communication Journal, 56,* 178–93.

Zorn, T. E., and Leichty, G. B. (1991). Leadership and identity: A reinterpretation of situational leadership theory. *Southern Communication Journal, 57,* 11–24.

Index